Caricaturing Culture in India

Caricaturing Culture in India is a highly original history of political cartoons in India. Drawing on the analysis of newspaper cartoons since the 1870s, archival research, and interviews with prominent Indian cartoonists, this ambitious study combines historical narrative with ethnographic testimony to give a pioneering account of the role that cartoons have played over time in political communication, public discourse, and the refraction of ideals central to the creation of the Indian postcolonial state. Maintaining that cartoons are more than illustrative representations of news, Ritu Gairola Khanduri uncovers the true potential of cartoons as a visual medium where memories jostle, history is imagined, and lines of empathy are demarcated. Placing the argument within a wider context, this thought-provoking book highlights the history and power of print media in debates on free speech and democratic processes around the world, revealing why cartoons still matter today.

Ritu Gairola Khanduri is a cultural anthropologist and historian of India. She is Assistant Professor of Cultural Anthropology at the University of Texas at Arlington. In addition to her research on media, she is currently completing a book on Gandhi and material culture.

Caricaturing Culture in India

Cartoons and History in the Modern World

Ritu Gairola Khanduri

CAMBRIDGE
UNIVERSITY PRESS

University Printing House, Cambridge CB2 8BS, United Kingdom

Cambridge University Press is part of the University of Cambridge.

It furthers the University's mission by disseminating knowledge in the pursuit of education, learning, and research at the highest international levels of excellence.

www.cambridge.org
Information on this title: www.cambridge.org/9781107043329

First published 2014

Printed in the United Kingdom by Clays, St Ives plc

A catalog record for this publication is available from the British Library

Library of Congress Cataloging in Publication data
Khanduri, Ritu Gairola, 1969–
Caricaturing culture in India : cartoons and history in the modern world / Ritu Gairola Khanduri.
    pages   cm
ISBN 978-1-107-04332-9 (hardback)
1. Indic wit and humor, Pictorial.   2. India – Politics and government – Caricatures and cartoons.   3. India – Social life and customs – Caricatures and cartoons.   I. Title.
NC1710.K46   2014
954.03–dc23

                                                              2014001811

ISBN 978-1-107-04332-9 Hardback

Contents

Illustrations

Acknowledgments

At the core of this book lies the generosity of all the cartoonists, who shared their stories and pointed me to the rich history of their art in India. I am most indebted to cartoonists Kutty (1921–2011), Samuel (1925–2012), and Bireshwar (1920–2007), who accompanied me in this long quest and sadly, are not here to see this book. For extended and deliberate interaction, I am particularly grateful to Suresh Sawant, R. K. Laxman and Mrs. Laxman, Mario Miranda, Subodh Kerkar, Vins, Ashok Dongre, Mr. and Mrs. Phadnis, Mr. Sarvade, Raobail, Jagjeet Rana, Dhodapkar, Kaak, Sushil Kalra, Shekhar Gurera, Sudhir Dar, Ajit Ninan, Sudhir Tailang, Pran, Govind Dixit, Mita Roy, Manjul, Irfan, Abhijit, Sanjay Mistry, Reboti Bhushan, Rajinder Puri, Unny, Kevy, BJ, Yesudasan, Toms, Satya N. Govind, Pawan, and Triambak Sharma. Several more interactions, too numerous to list, helped me to navigate the cartoon scene and have left their impression in the chapters that follow.

An unaccountable degree of gratitude is reserved for the incredible staff at the Nehru Memorial Museum and Library, the National Archives at New Delhi, the Lucknow State Archives, the University of Texas at Austin, the British Library, the cartoon archive at the University of Kent at Canterbury, the Library of Congress at DC, and the University of Texas-Arlington Inter-Library Service. Fieldwork and travel to various archives was sustained by generous fellowships from the Fulbright Foundation, the Social Science Research Council, and the Institute for Historical Research (University of London) Mellon Foundation. A timely Richard Carly Hunt Postdoctoral Fellowship from the Wenner-Gren Foundation allowed me to revise and complete the book manuscript. At the University of Texas-Arlington, my colleagues shared feedback and supported my professional growth in more ways than I expected – for this good fortune, I thank Christian Zlolniski, Kim van Noort, Amy Speier, Karl Petruso, Ben Agger, Desiree Henderson, Beth-Anne Shelton, Mark Cichock, and Chris Conway. Amy, Joci Ryan, Christian and graduate consultants at the UTA Writing Center posed questions and offered suggestions that have made this a better book.

Lucy Rhymer, Claire Wood, Sarah Payne, and Rima Devereaux at Cambridge University Press were a dream come true. I have tested the patience of this fine team of experts and thank them for their confidence in my book. Margaret Case offered much appreciated and vital input at the final stages of the manuscript's preparation.

Sarah Lamb, Mrinalini Sinha, Indrani Chatterjee, Laurie Graham, Gail Minault, Deepa Reddy, Lynn Kwiatkowski, Mithi Mukherjee, Donna Goldstein, Janice Leoshko, Kevin Dwyer, Lawrence Cohen, Purnima Mankekar and Lee Segal inspired ideas, provided helpful feedback, energized me through their writings, and on several occasions nudged me to take the next step. For this I am grateful.

My brothers Gaurav and Shaurav, and sisters Seema and Shalini and their families, my in-laws the late Drs. Sushila and Om Prakash Khanduri, and friends Charu Gauniyal and Sumita Shankar Garg provided a warm and welcoming home during my travels, allowing me to concentrate on my work.

At the University of Texas-Austin, James Brow, Gail Minault, and Kamran Ali shaped an earlier incarnation of this research in helpful ways. I am grateful to them and to Pauline Strong and Kathleen Stewart for always being available to read and comment on my work. Sandya, Nusrat, Nick, Chris, Keisha-Khan, and Jennifer provided friendship and much-needed helpful critique at important moments in my career.

Memories tend to evoke more memories, revealing surprising beginnings and connections. While engaging with cartoonists' stories about their past, my own stories about how and why I chose to research newspaper cartoons took me down several memory lanes. Neeladri Bhattacharya's fine mentoring and enthusiasm at the Jawaharlal Nehru University instigated this project, several years ago, when I wrote a seminar paper for his course in modern Indian history. I could hardly have anticipated Neeladri would be engrossed in NCERT cartoon debates as I finished writing this book! For thoughtful conversations, Ganga Dhabha chit-chat, and the short but lasting good times at the Jawaharlal Nehru University campus, I remember and thank Sumita, Prasanna, Anindita, Shikha, Chaitali, Archana, Ranjeeta, Chalapathy, and Niti.

My parents Usha and Krishna Gairola stood by me through thick and thin. Their trust and unconditional love is difficult for me to match. Pankaj has been a patient and supportive spouse. He took on more than his share of domestic chores and responsibilities while also offering liberal doses of love and affection. This book has grown with our daughter Vidula, who good humoredly tolerated my absences, accompanied me to India, showed what matters most, taught me a thing or two about patience and brought music into our life. Cissy and Lou lit up matters in unexpected ways by insisting on an evening walk and by purring for undivided attention.

Cartoonists and their families, libraries, archives, and presses have my sincere gratitude for permission to use their images. Versions of Chapters 1, 2, and 3 have appeared in *History and Anthropology*, *Visual Anthropology Review*, and *Visual Anthropology*.

I dedicate this book to GM – historian, teacher, and feminist extraordinaire.

Introduction: the empire of cartoons

In September 1993, a devastating earthquake rocked Latur, a district near Mumbai, India. To convey the unprecedented magnitude of this disaster, the mainstream newspaper the *Times of India* published editorials and photographs; in addition, their internationally famous staff cartoonist, R. K. Laxman, drew a cartoon depicting a human skull and a ravaged hut. A week later, the newspaper's "letters to the editor" column included an angry reader's note criticizing Laxman's insensitivity at caricaturing human misery. Almost a decade later, the Danish cartoon controversy took the world by surprise, as violent protests erupted in many places in reaction to cartoons depicting the Prophet Muhammad published in Copenhagen. As protests and debates began dotting the world map, the variability in people's sense of humor became a public litmus test used to draw a boundary dividing the secular from the religious, and freedom lovers from freedom haters. These moments that were not anticipated to provoke deliberation about what constituted "out-of-place"[1] cartoons and a sense of humor are at the heart of a question that has gripped me for the past fifteen years: why do cartoons matter in the modern world?

To answer this question, this book tracks nearly one hundred fifty years of cartooning in India. From the early nineteenth century on, cartoons proliferated in imperial Britain and in its colonies, proving to be persuasive representations that competed with photographs and films. The cultural traffic between the seat of empire and the colonies, and the circulation of images, had a lasting impact on India's print media, namely newspapers. Several cartoon albums from colonial times, available in various archival holdings, testify to the vibrant world of cartoons in India. Among these, Harishchandra Talcherkar's compilation of cartoons of the Viceroy Lord Curzon (1902) offers an early glimpse of caricatures and cartoons in colonial publications such as the *Hindi Punch, Bhimsen, Gadgadat, Bharat Mitra, Nagar Charcha, Bhut,* and *Gujarati Punch.* Closer to our own times, contemporary cartoonists have published editions of their own cartoons, yielding a number of booklets through which it is possible to sample the world of cartoons in India. Available in the popular

1

Wheeler bookstalls on railways stations and in local bookshops, and, when published by a mainstream press, such as Penguin, marketed more widely and available in libraries, these editions summarize decades of cartooning through hand-picked selections.[2] Although cartoons have long circulated as albums and edited collections, newspapers are their primary source in India and politics their dominant theme. This makes newspaper cartoons a critical form of political journalism and a special category of news. The bundling of caricature, prose, topical content, and a dash of humor makes the cartoon a medium of news with a character all its own. Seeing the visual as an uncertain representation of sociopolitical reality and harboring suspicions of its hidden meanings are most pronounced in the context of newspaper cartoons. This brings new insight into the immediacy of cartoons and their ability to configure empathy that redraws the lines of belonging. The history of these processes introduces a world of circulation, feelings and meaning-making preceding televison's "electronic empathy" (Hannerz 1996, p. 121).

A stunning daily circulation of 329,204,841 – the number of newspaper readers in India in 2010–11 – is perhaps the highest on the globe.[3] This represents an 8.23 percent rise in circulation from the previous year, which also signals a growth in India's vernacular newspapers.[4] For this growing readership, cartoons are a source of news that gives a view of the underside of politics. However, when further dissected, this statistic shows that as with the literate population in India, the newspaper readership is unevenly distributed by class, caste, and gender. Beginning in the 1850s, during India's colonial years, vernacular newspaper cartoons peeled back the layers of imperial duplicity, provoking humor and critique. With independence from British rule in 1947, India charted a democratic and secular path in which newspaper cartoons became critical modes of public communication and politics. Since then, cartoons have offered daily doses of humor by questioning India's developmental agenda, democratic governance, and secular credentials. Despite the popularity of such routine lampooning of grim realities, the anguished reader's letter in the *Times of India* after the 1993 earthquake suggested that certain topics, in uncertain times, were out of bounds for cartoons. Why? If cartoons satirized the asymmetries of power in colonial politics, then what role do – or should – they play in a democracy? If the play of caricature and witty captions can reveal what the prose of news might not dare, then must not cartoons always be celebrated by the disenfranchised? If satire, humor, and laughter have helped people cope with adversity, then how can cartoons hurt and whom do they hurt? What does it mean when those who refuse to laugh at some cartoons are dismissed as lacking a sense of humor and not being modern? When democracies prohibit the publication of certain cartoons, how does it make them different from colonial rulers? Why does a peripheral form such as the cartoon inform our knowledge of the world?

Organized in three parts, the book will take readers to colonial times, national times, and global times. Newspaper cartoons show how time intersects with places, so that the colonial, national, and global provide the conditions for their materialization. The reader will notice that as voices from archival texts, published interviews, and memoirs are interwoven with interviews and correspondence I conducted, the clustering of various vantage points also constructs a history. Single interviews are dated. Where my interactions included a series of conversations and correspondences, I have not included dates.

Affective registers of empire

Folios from eighteenth- and nineteenth-century British newspaper cartoons quickly yield a rich archive on representations of India. The deep roots in history should not be surprising. Beginning as a trading company in the seventeenth century, the British East India Company's gradual metamorphosis into a political power by the mid eighteenth century signaled an emerging colonial relationship that was formalized in 1877 with Queen Victoria's coronation as the Empress of India. This colonial arrangement lasted until 1947, when the subcontinent gained freedom and was simultaneously partitioned into India and Pakistan. These political transitions from trade to politics, resulting in India's growing prominence in imperial matters, were transmitted to the British public through a variety of images shaped by emerging visual technologies. Political cartoons remained a consistent medium for representing these overseas politics, even as painting, engraving, photography, and filming gained ground and promised the public new visual experiences. Thomas Rowlandson (1756–1827), James Gilray (1756–1815), and James Moffat (1775–1815) were among artist-cartoonists whose turgid engravings exposed the inelegance and ugliness of the imperial endeavor. Through color engraving and drooping speech bubbles, these cartoonists inverted claims of the empire's civilizational mission. These are not orientalist images; quite the contrary, they are views of the empire's violence, greed, lust, and bigotry. The art historian Ernst H. Gombrich famously noted the core technique of caricature: "the cartoonist can mythologize the world of politics by physiognomizing it" (Gombrich 1963, p. 291). Emotion and feelings were central to this physiognomy. If art strived to represent the essence of the subject, then the cartoonist was similar to the artist: "The caricaturist has a corresponding aim. He does not seek the perfect form but the perfect deformity, thus penetrating through the mere outward appearance to the inner being in all its littleness or ugliness" (Gombrich and Kris 1938).[5]

It would not be a stretch to observe this process and technique at work in the cartoons of Rowlandson, Gilray, and Moffat, who delighted in emphasizing deformity to articulate the unethical politics central to empire. Such inglorious cartoons drew a stark contrast to *Punch*'s gentler cartoons that began publication in 1841. Indeed, critics have noted this distinction as a refinement in the art of British cartooning. The shift in the form of caricature from the grotesque to a palatable likeness and various visual tropes made cartoons increasingly lean toward the category of "art." John Doyle (1797–1868), or HB as he was popularly known, was a painter and cartoonist who deftly embodied this new cartooning aesthetic. Doyle built an enviable reputation as an artist, and his son Richard Doyle gave *Punch* its signature cover and was a celebrated cartoonist.[6]

Colonial cartoons weave a fascinating tale about a critique of colonial politics, shifting aesthetics, and the ways in which colonial impressions configured British cartoonists' visual vocabulary. *Punch* regularly pictured imperial politics and, in particular, caricatured colonial India.[7] The lion, tiger, sepoys, and Colonia offer visual tropes signaling how cartoons employ gender, animals, and objects to formulate the human experience of colonial politics. This is not simply a process of anthropomorphizing. Instead, through caricature, the *Punch* cartoons categorize human experience and produce colonial affect. It is possible to approximate some of this affective production when attending to readings of *Punch* cartoons. This is particularly true in the case of John Tenniel's famous Cawnpore cartoons (and his introduction of "animal types"). During the embattled months of the 1857 Sepoy Mutiny, also termed the first battle of Indian independence, Tenniel drew several cartoons that represented the unrest. These often-reproduced *Punch* cartoons from 1857 and their critical assessment exemplify some of the contours of this critique. In a column titled "Punch on India," the British newspaper the *Free Press* noted on September 16, 1857:

The last number of *Punch* presents us with a wonderful cartoon. Justice, in a Greek peplum, accompanied by British soldiers, mangling Hindu bodies, and with the features of revenge. In the distance there is a row of guns with Sepoys about to be blown from them. In the rear, disconsolate women and children of Hindus. The title of it is Justice. Leaving to the imagination of the reader to fill in the words "of English CHRISTIANS IN THE YEAR 1857." Was the drawing designed to horrify Britons with the sight of themselves, or to brand upon them their new demon.[8]

The *New York Daily Times*, too, published an assessment of Tenniel's famous cartoon, "The British Lion's Vengeance on the Bengal Tiger" (see Figure I.1), explaining:

THE BRITISH LION'S VENGEANCE ON THE BENGAL TIGER.

I.1 John Tenniel, "The British Lion's Vengeance on the Bengal Tiger." *Punch*. August 22, 1857. London. Courtesy of the Punch Archive.

Tenniel's India cartoons in general "suddenly brought about an increase in circulation that year" (Layard 1907, p. 156). This success assured *Punch* proprietors of the demand for colonial content.

A recent number of *Punch* has a large picture, in which the state of feeling in England towards India is forcibly represented by a fierce lion springing upon a Bengal tiger, which is crouching upon a woman and her infant child. The lion is England, the tiger is rebel India, and the woman and child the Anglo-Indian subjects who have been sacrificed by the cruel sepoys. The temper of the British nation has been thoroughly aroused, and sooner or later a terrible retribution will be visited upon the heads of the rebel Indians who have shown a disposition to glut their revenge for a century of oppression and misgovernment ... The roar of the British lion will soon strike terror into the heart of the Bengal tiger. (September 9, 1857)

The significance and attention Tenniel's Cawnpore cartoons garnered cannot be overstated. The cartoons were featured in Spielmann's illustrated *History of the Punch* (1895), which aimed to narrate almost half a century of *Punch* years:

Once this fine drawing is seen, of the royal beast springing on its snarling foe, whose victims lie mangled under its paw, it can never be forgotten. It is a double spread cartoon splendidly wrought by the artist at the suggestion of Shirley Brooks; and while it responded and gave expression to the feelings of revenge which agitated England at the awful events that had passed at the time of the Indian Mutiny, and served as a banner when they had raised a cry of vengeance, it alarmed the authorities, who feared that they would thereby be forced on the road which policy and the gentler dictates of civilisation forbade. (Spielmann 1895)

These readings of *Punch* cartoons persuasively suggest that cartoons evoked sense and sentiment: terror, horror, and fear constitute the vocabulary for translating a visual form. Thus, how cartoons were read offers insightful cues to the affective register of the imperial experience.

The other side of these readings of colonial representations is the British cartoonists' incorporation and imagination of colonial tropes that had an enduring impact in the empire and colony. About 1832, John Doyle published a cartoon called "Serpent Charmers" that caricatured domestic politics related to the British constitution by drawing upon the image of snake charmers blowing a pipe and controlling the entranced cobra as it emerges from its round covered box (McLean n.d.). This image became an enduring trope to represent not only colonial Indian politics but also politics at home, in Britain, and was repeatedly used by popular British cartoonists David Low, Emmwood (John Musgrave-Wood), and Nicholas Garland, among others.[9] In the decades thereafter, the bed of nails became another trope that was a quick reference to India and was also included in the cartoonists' toolbox.[10] These two tropes – the snake charmer and bed of nails – continue to be evoked in current cartoons, testifying to their enduring presence in the Western imagination.

For many years, *Punch* charmed the world of cartoons, and in this world the representation of imperial culture was shaped by racial discourses of the time; these representations were also considered important for influencing the business of humor among potential "native" subscribers in the colony, especially India.[11]

British cartoons found their way into India and most colonies through readers and library subscriptions, and they were copied and appropriated by colonial cartoonists. In this regard, the *Punch* archives have proved to be a rich source for the reconstruction of imperial discourses. Appropriations of *Punch* cartoons in colonial and vernacular newspapers (Mahood 1973 and Mitter 1994) and the multiple indigenous versions of *Punch* that thrived in several colonies have offered considerable scope for debating the impact of British cultural forms and print media (Harder and Mittler 2013). The history of newspaper cartoons in India, then, offers a remarkable vantage point for observing the multi-directional flow of images, imagination, and people. Adopting this vantage point makes it possible to get away from a Eurocentric narrative of modern cultural forms that analyzes the colony as solely a point of reception of modern forms. This tenuous link between empire and colony and our understanding of how images are produced, perceived, and circulated, transcending the borders of time and place, is nicely evoked when opening an authoritative contemporary dictionary of modern British cartoonists (see Mark Bryant 1991). Here it might surprise readers to see that the history of modern British cartoonists, listed in alphabetical order, begins with the Indian cartoonist Abu (Abu Abraham), who I discuss in Chapter 7.

The lateral history and collateral anthropology of the present study keeps in mind Bernard Cohn's cautionary note that the goal of historical anthropology is not merely to fill a gap (1996, p. 21). For even as they fill a gap, cartoons provide moments to know the world and to see India. For example, in a parallel experience of seeing and knowing, I urge readers to take a few steps back in time to the French anthropologist Claude Lévi-Strauss's visit to India, when he got his first glimpse of an English university ambience at the University of Dacca, then in East Bengal. From those postwar years and that sighting, Lévi-Strauss continued to perceive Oxford as part of India (Lévi-Strauss 1961, p. 36). Such perceptions form the "sensory keyboard" that seem to fuse places and times, imparting knowledge and belief that last a lifetime. Cartoons and caricatures reinforce this aspect of the visual sense; through the play of exaggeration and likeness, they simulate places and times and stimulate people's political knowledge.

This book turns away from an evaluation of primarily iconographic elements to their reception, situating discussions around cartoons, showing that a deeper understanding of cartoons involves a form of knowing, so that they become a source of knowledge. In doing so, this book claims new terms of engagement with visual texts as history and ethnography; it also becomes part of a tradition in which to claim cartoons as knowledge is a ploy. Taking a cue from Peter van der Veer's observations that far from being inert and replete with answers to all our questions, a historical archive is alive and needs to be located (2002, p. 176), the research for this book constructs an archive that includes a variety of cultural texts and interviews. In so doing, the book shows that a peripheral visual, the newspaper cartoon, is generative of public debates that demand exacting answers about modern politics. The debates that cartoons generated in colonial and postcolonial times become vital sources for illuminating the interconnections among discourses of liberalism, representation, development, citizenship, and religion. The various versions of *Punch* and discussions of their cartoons exemplify the enduring impact of a format that entwined politics, caricature, and humor; examining these advances insight into cartoons as a cultural text that historically offered a space for deliberation, for opposition, and for returning the empire's gaze. To give another example: When cartoon-based newspapers commenced publication in nineteenth-century India, speculation arose about the effect on those who were unschooled in the appreciation of caricature. The concern found its way into the pages of *Chitravali*s – slim "caricature albums" with assorted cartoons. Baijnath Kedia's *Vyang Chitravali* ("satirical album") from Calcutta, Sukhdeva Roy's *Vyang Chitravali* from Allahabad, and Shiva Narayan Mishra's *Svang Chitravali* ("mimicry album") from Kanpur circulated in various parts of India in the 1930s.[12] The caricatures of Indian society and politics rendered reality in a new form (see Figures I.2 and I.3). They evoked alternative ways of thinking about social reformation through topics such as untouchability, education, religious practices, attitudes toward women, and hygiene. Unlike Talcherkar's large album of cartoons that gave a view of various cartoon-based publications in India (1902), these small albums contained signed Hindi cartoons of T. K. Mitra, D. N. Bannerjee, D. N. Verma, H. Bagchi, and Binoy, giving a glimpse of a generation of cartoonists who were occupied in various artistic activities such as painting and advertising. These artists also contributed to the vernacular *Punch* newspapers, and mentored India's upcoming professional newspaper cartoonists such as Bireshwar (Bireshwar Prasad), whose life story I narrate in Chapter 4. The notion of cartoonist-as-artist is significant in India and, as I show in Chapter 7, a source of debate about technique and practice. This brings cartoons to the realm of art, thus situating it uniquely on the border between news and art.

Although much has been written about new media technologies and political imagination, less is known about the history and growing influence of older media forms such as newspaper cartoons. By taking cartoons in India seriously, by tracing the professionalization of cartooning, by looking through the eyes of readers, cartoonists, and activists who are busy interpreting the world of cartoons, this book offers a route to understanding the social life of images. It explores the things we say about deeply held political convictions when we see the newspaper cartoon. It was precisely through such engagement as a newspaper reader that I became interested in cartoon talk: things people say or record when they see a cartoon.

We are not dinosaurs!

I find it difficult to pinpoint when and how anthropology and history intertwined as research for this book began; each time I settle on a defining moment, another leaps to take precedence. Because cartoons have occupied me for nearly two decades, readers will see more than one point of intersection; one of these intersections is my meeting with cartoonist *Singh, in New Delhi, in the winter of 2003.[13] "Oh, so are we dinosaurs now?" said an astonished Mr. Singh, a prominent cartoonist in Delhi,

I.2 M. Verma, "Uncle Tom-Touchy and Untouchable Child." *Svang Chitravali: Caricature Album*. n.d. (*c*. 1929). Kanpur.

after I introduced myself as an anthropologist. Mr. Singh's astonishment, rather than mine, reversed the order of surprise that ethnography tends to register as part of fieldwork. Embarrassed, I struggled to rephrase my research project: "No, Mr. Singh, that would be archaeology, which is another sub-discipline of anthropology; but I am a cultural anthropologist writing ethnography, a book. I study Indian culture." "Absolutely inadequate and unconvincing," I quietly berated myself.

Although I had experienced this confusion of sub-disciplines several times in the United States, I was not prepared for the new way this question would resonate during my fieldwork; here I expected no confusion. But the dinosaur perfectly conveyed the perceived difference – a cultural gap anthropology has long created, only to triumphantly bridge it ethnographically and empathetically for a Western audience. As a disciplined study that strives to produce a cultural relativist perspective, anthropology operates with a notion of time that is quite different from the historian's. Anthropologists evoke the "ethnographic present" – a signal for readers that ethnographic narratives are rooted in the recent past. Such movement between the unfamiliar and familiar, and between time zones through long-term observation, description, and analysis has long generated many dinosaurs and cultures.[14]

But audiences for anthropological writing have since broadened to include scholars, the mythical "general educated reader," and in the case of this book, the cartoonists themselves. This readership, then, provides one condition for ethnographic writing. Another comes with the conduct of fieldwork. The history and life stories cartoonists were aware of offered "new conditions of ethnographic production" (Clifford 1986, p. 117). When conducting fieldwork, even though I did not see any cartoonist open a version of the "Raponda-Walker compendium" that James Clifford offered as an example of the circuit of data – text to text, rather than oral to text – that intervenes in contemporary interviews, and thereby in ethnographic writing, it is apparent in my own field experience. When I

Caption for I.2 (cont.)

Uncle Tom-Touchy: "A sorcerer's shadow too is polluting. If you ever again touch the temple's steps, I will eat you raw. Lowly, sweeper, sorcerer . . ."

Cartoons on the practice of untouchability highlighted the inhumanity in its logic. By showing the priest's reprimand of a mere child and "touching" him by holding him aloft, the cartoonist points to the incredulity of Hindu social thinking. The man with the broom, perhaps the child's father, gapes in disbelief at the priest who touches and reprimands in the name of untouchability.

The Sangathan.

सङ्गठन ।

I.3 M. Verma. *Svang Chitravali. c.* 1929. Kanpur. This cartoon on the Shuddhi (purification) and Sangathan (organization) movements of the 1920s re-imagines the organic trope of the Hindu *varna*. Each arm holds a material artifact to denote the varna tradition: scriptures (Brahmin), broom ("Untouchable"), purse (Vaishya), and sword (Rajput). The feet and footwear, or its absence, complement the varna-marks held by Madan Mohan Malviya, the architect of Sangathan. The fusion of the multiple arms and legs reorders the traditional hierarchy of the varna classification, rendering all ranks equal. Led by the Arya Samaj and the Hindu Mahasabha this movement sought to reclaim marginalized Hindu communities in the context of nationalist and communal politics. As the party symbol of the Aam Aadmi Party (AAP), the broom has recently resurfaced in the contemporary Indian imagination to denounce corruption and reform politics.

explained to Mr. Singh that the history of Indian cartooning was the crux of my research, the conversation began to flow. If with anthropology I was exoticizing Indian cartoons, digging up their archaeological remains, rendering them prehistoric, then the history I was researching was contemporary and alive. It signaled that cartoons were not just something of the past but were of the present, with a past. Mr. Singh's comment reminded me that disciplinary distinction is a reality that matters to people we turn to, in order to collect stories – it is not just an academic debate for contesting methodological territories.[15] After this fumble, I decided that it was better to describe my research as a history of Indian cartooning; indeed it is, and one from an anthropological perspective: it attends to cartoons through meanings people made about them in the past and continue to make in the present.

For anthropologists and historians, cartooning in India presents a venue for observing the construction of norms and exclusionary practices. Its peripheral status as art and news notwithstanding, cartooning creates an aesthetic border to distinguish non-cartoons, that is, those without artistic merit. This duality in extending and retracting the border between cartooning and art provides insight into the comparative nature of history, ethnography, and fiction; it offers a foil for disturbing a border among these competing forms of representing social reality. Like the cartoonists who magically present facts and history through the action (but not fiction) of caricature, historians and anthropologists caricature culture to produce archival and ethnographic facts. During our meeting at his home in New Delhi, in 2003, cartoonist Sushil Kalra, an art college graduate, narrated his dilemma about confirming his identity. With his many talents, he was an artist, a cartoonist, and a writer. If all his peers made a claim on him, he said, he would be torn to pieces.[16] To surmount this demand, in the company of artists, he claimed the identity of writer. The playwright, artist, and cartoonist Manjula (Manjula Padmanabhan) echoes this reluctance to be pinned down. Manjula asks why writing and drawing should be seen as an either–or option (2004).[17] These perspectives on identity are useful for thinking about the claims demanded concerning academic selves and writing. Over the years, the similarity between anthropologists and cartoonists in India struck a deep chord in me, supplying the title for my book, *Caricaturing Culture in India*.

Forms of knowledge

Across the disciplines there is much ambivalence about the use of images for understanding sociohistorical processes. In one view, art historians

and historians previously critiqued the "physiognomic fallacy" of images
(Gombrich and Kris 1938, Ginzburg 1992). This fallacy surfaces because
images are interpreted to reflect analysis gleaned from other archival
sources. Images, particularly cartoons, therefore tend to be situated as a
supplement to both social experience and to theories of culture. In this
framework, the cartoon is neither a form of knowledge nor expected to
produce knowledge. In this book, I present newspaper cartoons as a form
of knowledge, making a critical contribution to both political knowledge
and theory.

Cartoonists convey complex issues through succinct inky strokes and
easily reach a broad audience. Their brevity, acuity, and fascination with
the slippery slope of life in India were an ideal model when writing my
book.[18] But readers' comments nudged me to also read between the
seductive lines of caricature, and to think about the cartoon's interpretative dilemmas and sensory effects, and the meanings people make.
Situated at the intersection of history and anthropology, this book will
demonstrate the newspaper cartoon to be both a form and a source of
political knowledge. In his trilogy discussing the state of Indian politics
in the mid to late 1970s, around the years of the notorious Emergency
(1975–7) when democratic governance in India was stalled, anthropologist G. S. Ghurye used newspapers for his fieldnotes. Ghurye's goal was
"interrogative" rather than an "interpretive approach to the facts revealed
in the daily newspapers" (1978, pp. vii–viii). Laxman's cartoons were
among the news items he discussed, though he did not reproduce them
in his books. For Ghurye, "the cartoonist saw deeper and put up the true
import more correctly" (p. 41). This acknowledgment of both newspapers
and cartoons as ethnographic fieldnotes has revitalized in recent years.
Although they have long constituted important historical source and, as
colonial archives show, cartoons were engaged for situating culture, such
analysis was not circumscribed as an anthropological endeavor. When
cartoons from pulp pamphlets, ritually circulated during the boisterous
festival of Holi during his fieldwork in Banaras, caught anthropologist
Lawrence Cohen's attention, it laid bare an unexplored text of same-sex
cartoons that were highly political (1995). The primary audience for these
choti "line" cartoons, young and petty bourgeois middle-aged Hindu men,
enjoy these representations of obscenities between men (1995, p. 405).
With these *gupt* (secret and sexual) cartoons, which Cohen terms "political
pornography" (p. 408), Holi is a site that historicizes "shifting sexualized
politics" (p. 405). This alternate lens brings new orientation to Holi – a
festival that allows for social transgressions and has invited analysis of
its sexual violence against women. However, within the context of the
choti "line" cartoons, the festival marks the production and circulation of

an informal sexual humor that reveals much about politics, sexuality, and modernity. In a contrast to Cohen's hermeneutic reading, K. N. Sahay's elaboration on the characters, types, and symbolism of newspaper cartoons (1998) attempted to situate it anthropologically within a structural framework. Primarily analyzing Moni Chakravarti's cartoons in the *Ranchi Express*, Sahay cast cartoons as a part of the "mechanism," which enabled a social structure to "exist and persist" (1998, p. viii). In this framework, Moni's cartoons were both a social mirror and a source of change through their impact on society. However, a dissection of the cartoon's symbolic categories and its "decoding" tells little about the relationship between cartoons and the maintenance of social continuity and change, which is the core anthropological claim of Sahay's project.

Given Benedict Anderson's influential anthropological framework linking newspaper cartoons and the imagination of modern nation states (1978, 1983), and aforementioned studies of cartoons in India, there is a surprising paucity of research on cartoons by anthropologists. Historians and literary theorists have been quick to acknowledge cartoons as an archival source. Literature from history (Coupe 1967; Brummett 2000, Douglas 2002 and Hung 1994) cultural studies (Terdiman 1985), and art history (Wechsler 1982, Guha-Thakurta 1992 and Mitter 1994) highlight cartoons as a visual source that reflects discourse and counter-discourse. This overlooks the cultural context of production and the meanings people construct when seeing cartoons, the perspective anthropology fosters. Anthropologists really first noticed cartoons after the Danish cartoons controversy in 2005, partially addressing this gap (Asad 2009, Keane 2009 and Mahmood 2009). Recent linguistic analysis of non-verbal representations of politics has also brought new attention to cartoons as integral to public culture. In anthropological analyses, the cartoon's iconography discloses its links with other media, for example political appropriation of a television cartoon in postsocialist Georgia (Manning 2007) and the traditional political oratory, *Kabary*, in Madagascar (Jackson 2008). In Brazil, through parody, cartoons can operate as a "white space" that racializes indigenous politicians such as Mario Juruna (Graham 2011) or alternately, foster a "community of imagination" to counter state power (Schwarcz 2013). Overall, in these studies, cartoons were where the "action is" (Lewinson 2003).[19]

Cartoons offer additional vantage points for dwelling on the relationship and the ambiguity of visual texts, a central theme in the anthropological discussion of colonial photographs. Cartoons also bring a new visual practice within the ambit of visual anthropology – a sub-field of anthropology that connects visual and media studies across disciplines. Building on the notions of the photographs' "evidential power" (Barthes 1984, p. 106) and the "cultural entanglement of objects" that transform the category and meaning of things beyond those of its producer (Thomas 1991, p. 125), Elizabeth Edwards points to the ambiguity of photographs, arguing that "in many ways a photograph denies history" (1994, p. 3). Rooted in the news of the day and topical events, newspaper photographs and cartoons with their captions certainly complicate the relationship between evidential power, cultural entanglement, and history. Newspapers renew the use of photographs as history, creating new genres of truth that compete with prose. Shaving off some of the ambiguity, they in fact affirm history. But unlike newspaper photographs, cartoons are easily appropriated, translated, rescripted, and reproduced.[20] Simply put, cartoons are easily copied. The ability to copy and republish cartoons renders them provocative archives. Emphasizing the reception of cartoons and the practice of cartooning reveals that "copying" was a key signifier for proximity and distance from modernity.

Visual anthropology and India

Anthropology has a long history of engagement with photographs and films that marked the birth of the sub-discipline of visual anthropology. Since its earlier phase, with Gregory Bateson's and Margaret Mead's photograph-based research on Bali (1942), the visual has moved away from being a technique for scientific recording toward representation. This sentiment and methodological shift played out in India at two agenda-setting international seminars in 1978 and 1987, which sought to revitalize visual anthropology in India. Leading to the publication of a new journal, *Visual Anthropology Bulletin* (1979), the 1978 conference resolved, among other issues, to highlight India's "multicultural viewpoints" in order to overcome the assumption of "a single culture." It also aspired to a "new type of humanistic orientation" toward "cross-cultural studies and documentation" (Sahay 1993, pp. 12–13). Although the overarching assumption of visual anthropology was the realm of film, interestingly this conference enlarged the sub-discipline's mandate to include "fiction films" that were "realistic and come close to life" (Sahay 1993, p. 111). Perceived as having fallen behind in the global arena in the late 1950s and early 1960s,[21] the 1987 seminar sought to revitalize visual anthropology in India by emphasizing the use of the camera, the art of film-making and the growing presence of television in India's social fabric. Within this framework, visual anthropology would make a timely intervention in representing "little/folk" traditions, peripheral communities, and broadly picture "human expressions" between the "simple" and the heartland while noting "local, regional, national and international orbits"

(Roy and Jhala 1992, p. 20). The timeliness received some attention: visual anthropology would represent minority communities, and have a "soothing role to play in assuring minorities about their status within the nation" (Roy and Jhala 1992, p. 22). This time also marked the growth of television and an opportunity for visual anthropologists to mediate the representation of non-mainstream and dominant cultures. The urgency to harness media as integral to a responsible anthropology coincided with its institutionalization as part of India's democratic ambitions. In both events, the visual remained ethnographically significant as a cultural text, which was later exemplified in John and Malcom Collier's equation of the camera's data as the ethnographer's tool.

Contrasting ethnographic photographs with the anthropologist's notes, John and Malcolm Collier advanced the use of the camera as an "extension of our senses" and a more accurate tool for observation (Collier and Collier 1996, p. 7). The discussion on the camera as a tool of recording data and representing struck at two cherished modes of eliciting the "insider" knowledge: talking with "natives" and the anthropologist's notes. A significant parallel impetus for ethnographic films of India came from institutions in independent India such as the Film Divison instituted in 1948, regional state Departments of Information, Publicity, or Public Relations, and the Anthropological Survey of India in 1954. These internal initiatives were complemented by a demand for films to support pedagogical purposes in US universities that had begun to offer courses on South Asia (Sahay 1993, pp. 7–8). Since the 1990s, with the growing interest in emergent media practices and materials, this sub-discipline acknowledges a broad spectrum of visual experiences as a focus for ethnographic study. This primacy of the visual invited interdisciplinary intersection with media studies and visual culture.[22] Beginning with Sara Dickey's ethnography of Tamil cinema (1993), which I will discuss in a following section with other significant contributions to visual anthropology, reception and the meanings people make when viewing visual texts returned as key to ethnography. Karin Barber has noted that "in anthropology it is more common to follow Bakhtin's lead and treat all types of utterances (which in Bakhtin's terminology included written texts) as being generated in accordance with recognized, shared conventions and thus as constituting genres" (2007, p. 32). My emphasis on talk about cartoons and how it is written into reviews, biography, art discourses, and petitions, links the verbal, the visual, and the written rather than opposing them. As a contribution to visual anthropology, my book is at the border of history, anthropology, and art history.

I take newspaper cartoons as a point of entry for thinking about how a seemingly peripheral visual form that is at the border of news and art provides remarkable insight into key political themes: modernity and liberalism. In so doing I build on ethnographic studies of India's visual culture that prompted introspection of deeply held ideas about the place of images in history and anthropology. This circuit of images, history, and anthropology is significant for the study of cartoons because it captures three intersecting moments: media circulates to generate interpretative communities across territorial borders, making everyone a critic; new archival spaces and sources challenge "History of the academic variety," making everyone archivists (Burton 2003, p. 139); and "culture," now a debated term in anthropology, is widely embraced as the logic for a range of politics, making everyone an ethnographer. Furthermore, global and postcolonial cultural processes cannot be studied without acknowledging "colonial formations of modernity."[23] In this history and anthropology, a multitude of visual forms of representations have played a significant role. These aspects make ethnographic studies of India's visual culture significant beyond South Asia and they offer a framework for acknowledging distinct ways in which the visual impinges on everyday life and whereby individuals and collectives engage with cultural politics.

Still photography reached Indian shores in 1840, soon after it developed in Europe, and Christopher Pinney's ethnography of Nagda photographic studios brings attention to the history and practice of this form of visual culture. Emphasizing the local history of photography in India, Pinney's work provides a context for thinking about the relationship between media – in his case, photography and painting. The relationship of cartoons with art came up in my conversations with cartoonists. Some of their concerns germinated from the fact that several of them were art school graduates. But even those who were not had a perspective on the necessity of draughtmanship as a technique for cartooning. In the creation of a new visual culture, photography, Pinney contends, was not "the eruption of some unchanged Indian psyche." Instead, photographs were "highly complex, 'modern' attempts to formulate visual identities under specific historical and political conditions" (1997, p. 96). Such queries resonate in this book when discussing "Indian" cartoons and whether cartoons have a linguistic rather than a national and regional identity.

In a discussion of another form of visual media, asserting the links among politics, gender, and soap operas, Purnima Mankekar's ethnography of television viewing in New Delhi focuses on lower middle-class women's experience, interpretation, and negotiation of nationalist discourses. The production of "nationalist affect" (1999, p. 17) and women's agency by simultaneously engaging them emotionally and allowing them to critique hegemonic state discourses highlights their multiple subjectivities rather than any contradiction. Mankekar thus situates television as a site of both resistance and suppression. Similar strategic oppositional readings of newspaper cartoons are central to understanding their generative role in producing public intellectuals and critics who mediated among interpretative communities in colonial and contemporary India. I use "intellectuals" here to encompass individuals from a spectrum of persuasions that participate in the "creation, circulation, and contestation of national culture" (Boyer and Lomnitz 2005, p. 107).

Dickey's trailblazing ethnography of Tamil cinema in Madurai and its audience presented viewers' personal readings, together with the resolution of discrepancy between representation and lived reality and the role of fan clubs in obviating collective action, specifically organized around class. Although "viewers actively evaluate what they see on screen," Dickey holds that "escape and reality are intimately connected" (1993, p. 141). As a precursor to the question of what people do with images, the critique and public action triggered by readers of newspaper cartoons provide an interesting contrast to Tamil cinema. Hindi-Urdu cinema – widely known as Bollywood – the focus of Tejaswini Ganti's ethnography, offers a narrative of "gentrification" and globalization that strengthened the film industry, making it the most dominant media in the country. Ties to diasporic markets and neoliberalism are key to Bollywood's success (2012).

The tempo and social life of visual culture shift with time, gaining new form, meanings, and significance. When once journalists such as the well-known Joseph Lelyveld and other correspondents opened their India reports in the *New York Times* describing cartoons in the *Times of India*, the *Hindu*, and on roadside billboards, now cartoons receives less notice in the Western media as a form to access political insight into India.[24] The *New York Times* pages from the 1950s, 60s, and 70s frequently published cartoons by Shankar (Keshav Shankar Pillai), Laxman, Kutty (Puthukkody Kottuthody Sankaran Kutty Nair), Thanu (N. Thanu), Bireshwar, and Samuel (Thomas Samuel), who all had ties to the *Shankar's Weekly* and are central to the story this book tells.[25] Their cartoons were published to represent an insider perspective on India's political scene, as well as world politics, involving China and the USA, for example. In other words, these cartoons were not just a venue to glean local perspective; instead they were seen side by side with cartoons on topical interest, such as China, made by prominent British cartoonists, including Herblock (Herbert Block) and several others.[26] This rubbing of shoulders in the *New York Times* pages is reminiscent of the practice of early-twentieth-century British news digest *Review of Reviews* that sought cartoons from around the globe, including the *Hindi Punch* (1854) from

India, to contrast political perspectives. This eclipse of Indian cartoons in the *New York Times* indicates changes within India as much as its place as foreign news key to US interests. Newspaper cartoons have transformed in the last decade. The front-page three-column cartoon has reduced in size, appearing in the newspaper "as a bonsai" (Unny 2006, pp. 83–4). They paved the way for a larger number of the smaller "pocket cartoons" – one-column cartoons. This transformation in format paralleled the increasing number of "local" and vernacular editions that major newspapers publish simultaneously. However, this does not signal that cartoons are diminishing in India. Instead, they are an example of cultural forms that thrive in contemporary global times by circumventing the West. The "stamp-sizing" of cartoons, to use Unny's term (2006, p. 84), at a time when India's economic engagement is on a global scale, also marks a proliferation of cartoons in unprecedent quantities – both the number of cartoons and of cartoonists. When I began my fieldwork for this book, Kutty's personal directory was the foundational building block, leading to other cartoonists. I built a chain of contacts – a slow but sure process. Cartoonists Kaak's (Harish Chandra Shukla's) website "Kaakdrishti" and Shekhar Gurera's blog were already active when I visited them in 2003. With the recent transition to online newspapers and digital copies of print called e-paper, news and cartoons circulate more widely. For cartoonists the web interface has given rise to a new space for archiving their work and maintaining digital albums. Now the Internet hosts a large number of websites such as Telugucartoon.com, archives and blogs of Indian cartoonists such as Unny (E. P. Unny), Manjul (Manjul Sharma), and Shreyas Navare, and Twitter broadcasts, providing a more accessible route for building a network.[27] The Indian Institute of Cartoonists in Bangalore, India, for example, also maintains a gallery and a website, with a directory of cartoonists. Although the reach of the Internet in India should not be overstated, such digital imprint and its free access offer a new visibility to cartoonists, increasing their readership base beyond their newspaper subscribers.

With its close tie to a commodity – the newspaper, and its role as the publication's signature, newspaper cartoons in India have a kinship with images in advertisements. William Mazzarella draws attention to this fascinating realm of visual production as a site for ethnographic study of media, globalization, and the construction of a national identity (2003). Laxman's public persona as the *Times of India*'s brand and more recently the appropriation of his cartoon character as the brand ambassador for an airline (Chapter 6), yields a perspective on the commodification and imagination of a "common man." In contrast, the profusion of local cartoon characters in the local editions of newspapers that comports well with local news and humor tells another story of commodification and globalization.

Collectively, ethnographic studies of visual culture in India have provided the opportunity to proceed beyond reception studies and know what people do with visual texts. In the process these studies contribute to the rich literature on art, popular prints, films, and comic books.

The politics of seeing and sensing

Even as ethnographic studies of media and, more broadly, visual experience in India are gaining ground, anthropologists and literary critics detect an "ocularcentric bias" in social science's pictorial turn (Fabian 1983, Stoller 1989). These scholars critique privileging vision because it is a form of imperial knowledge and power. Another direction this in-house critique has taken is to point out that even though anthropologists have incorporated images, especially photographs, in their ethnographic writing, for a long time they conveyed little about the place of these images for intellectual production and representation of ethnographic evidence (Ruby 2000).[28] My ethnography of newspaper cartoons offers a counterpoint to these critiques: cartoons usher in a visuality that is tied to a sensory experience of modernity. Cartoons in India are elusive – seen as art, they quickly remind us that they are news; emphasize their ephemerality, and they will demonstrate how they shape public memory and feelings of the past; insist cartoons are about a message, and they will make you laugh, cry, or be angry. In India, the many identities that the newspaper cartoon occupies open them to public deliberation about meaning. Among readers – including fans, activists vigilant about public representations, and brand managers – the multiple discourses on cartooning lead to debate: Is this news? Is this art? Is this humor acceptable? Is this history? Why is this nostalgic? Thus cartoons are not just about seeing but also about a politics of seeing and emotion. In this direction, I analyze the cartoon to show the "bundling of senses" (Keane 2005) for understanding multiple modernities. For example, in their comments in guest books at cartoon exhibitions, fans consistently recorded nostalgia, an ineffable loss, and anxiety about the Indian nation's future. These emotions were accompanied by a marvel at the cartoonist's acuity and the cartoon's clarity in recording the past. In emphasizing the politics of emotion as integral to the visuality cartoons foster, I extend the argument for a visual anthropology that integrates the senses, emotions, and media.[29] Although assertions of modernity as a visual age (Levin 1993), the emphasis on bourgeois society's technologies of seeing (Lowe 1982), and the colonial return of the empire's gaze are now considered "not of much heuristic value" and as "generating more images" (Erlmann 2004), I hold that newspaper cartoons bring a new orientation to the significance of the visual. Senses other than the visual are crucial for the ethnographer's participation and observation during fieldwork, but the role of visual media in shaping people's experience is beyond debate.[30]

That was true even before the Danish cartoon controversy took hold of the global stage in 2005.

This controversy captured processes of circulation and interpretative differences that are of interest to anthropology, and was instrumental in bringing newspaper cartoons to anthropologists' attention. My own interest in newspaper cartoons has followed this trajectory from history to anthropology and historical anthropology. These disciplinary orientations and mergers have reconstituted my understanding of cartoons as a form of knowledge. I first studied the *Hindu Punch* (Hindi, 1925) cartoons and the colonial distrust of specific representations for my M.Phil. thesis in history. When I began studies in the United States, as an ethnographic project, newspaper cartoons seemed tantalizing and formidable. Since colonial archives record cartoons in surveillance reports, and colonial newspapers offer a rich display of political critique, I was curious about how this visual form was doing in postcolonial India. Growing up on Laxman's cartoons in the *Times of India*, cartoons were for me front-page news. My ambition to be a cartoonist and not becoming one made me wonder how things might have been different. That I could not recall names of women political cartoonists, other than Maya Kamath (1951–2001), made me wonder about the connection between gender and professional political cartooning. The production of newspaper cartoons does not lend itself to participant observation. Cartoonists would often tell me about the long hours thinking and reading before settling on their cartoons for the day. Readers glance at cartoons over breakfast and tea, while travelling to work, and as part of their daily routine. I did not find fan clubs that could offer an ethnographic site for discussing cartoons. In fact, I realized that an ethnography of newspaper cartoons could not be anchored in place, demanding a rethinking of my fieldwork site. The absence of a "field" did not mean I had to abandon my study; instead this realization pushed me to explore other spaces where newspaper cartoons are talked about. Thus my fieldwork was conducted between texts and persons – in archives and holdings of press reports, which in turn took me to individual cartoonists and activists. These individuals returned me to archives and to scan more published reports. This circuit of texts and persons took me to many places. It led me to situate my ethnography as cartoon talk that offers insight into the refusal of laughter as a form of politics and a modern sensibility.

Tactical modernity

When the Danish cartoon controversy was widely reported and debated in 2005, my project acquired an unexpected global sense of timely knowledge and urgency. The series of events surrounding the Danish cartoons, which I discuss in Chapter 9, led to a widespread acknowledgment of the significance of newspaper cartoons. Since the episode conjoined Islam and cartoons, India, a place with the third highest Muslim population on the globe, had answers to offer. This book shows how, historically, colonial and contemporary debates about cartoons in India have preempted discussion about how representation and meaning play out uniquely in newspaper cartoons. With respect to the Danish cartoon controversy, my book allows for a deeper understanding of cartoon controversies by pointing to their longer history and specific politics, and shows that the issue is not one of Western tolerance and appreciation of cartoons' humor as against its denial in the name of Islam. Instead, the issue is the place of a visual form in the articulation of humor as a modern sensibility. This I term a "tactical modernity." De Certeau's concept of "tactic" as an everyday practice in which "propitious moments" are seized serves well to situate this display of rational debate and appropriation of cartoons as the articulation of a tactical modernity.[31] Casting modernity as tactical allows a closer look at when, how, and which claims are made in the name of modernity. This is important when aesthetics and taste are deployed to signal mentalities and identities. In this framework, modernity is not necessarily elsewhere and bears agency when artists and cultural interlocutors such as editors, cartoonists, and activists claim a better understanding of modernity than their Western counterparts and seek its repatriation.

Cultural practices have been particularly useful for thinking through the construction of modernity as a disposition about the past and the present. Distinguishing between "hard" and "soft" cultural forms, Arjun Appadurai's analysis of cricket in contemporary India as a unique example of the indigenization of a hard cultural form serves as a fruitful starting point for situating cartoons in India.[32] Cartoons certainly nurtured a new disposition to politics and humor – a quality of hard cultural forms. But at the same time, cartoons also were malleable in new contexts – a quality of soft cultural forms. Casting indigenization as a "product of collective and spectacular experiments with modernity, and not necessarily of the subsurface affinity of new cultural forms with existing patterns in the cultural repertoire" would mean that to understand the popularity of vernacular *Punch*es it is not sufficient to evoke colonial traditions of satire and their kinship with the British *Punch* (Appadurai 1996, p. 90).

Scholars note that the idea of the classical in performance arts did not exist prior to the twentieth century (Bakhle 2005, Peterson and Soneji 2008). Dance forms such as Bharatnatyam (O' Shea 2007), music styles such as Hindustani music (Bakhle 2005) and Karnatik music (Weidman 2006) were "reinvented for nationalist purposes" (Peterson and Soneji 2008, p. 3) and thrived at the juncture of claims of tradition and modernity. Such reinventions signal regional, class, and caste-based identity politics, and the continuation of these inventions in contemporary India when stakeholders participate in the construction of "tradition" continues the modernity project. The link between region and style is striking in these artistic forms. This emerged in my research in the form of two questions that evoked cartoon style in relation to the nation and language: Is there an "Indian" cartooning? Can there be a distinct Hindi cartooning? In contrast to the "indigenous" dance and music forms, cultural imports such as the English language, the novel, oil painting, and cricket have also been at the center of distinct nationalist articulations of modernity but confronted the charge of cultural colonization. Posed as a question: did the "native" adoption of Western cultural forms and aesthetics signal colonial conquest? Often compared as inferior copies of their Western counterparts, practitioners of these new arts were caught in a bind. Such evaluations were aplenty for cartoons by "native" cartoonists in colonial India. For example, the Anglo-Indian *Hindi Punch* cartoons. A close examination of the social life of these cultural imports in the colony extends the discussion in new fruitful directions that reveal new beginnings, embedded cultural politics, and forms of agency. For example, the institutionalization of English in India preceded its incorporation in the curriculum in Britain (Gauri Viswanathan 1995). Shefali Chandra has shown how the English language was "rendered an Indian language" (2012, p. 27) primarily through deliberation of its "power to change the parameters of Indian culture" (2012, p. 6). In the context of the popularity of the British novel in colonial India, Priya Joshi highlights the readers' "consumption through selection," and their intervention through interpretations and translations (2002, p. 29). Joshi makes the important point that this colonial taste in reading was documented and cultivated by leading publishers such as Macmillan and Company, and was instrumental in their publishing initiatives and business decisions.[33] The history of cartooning in India engages with these possibilities of agency in a distinct manner, emphasizing a tactical modernity that does not have to opt between either creating a tradition or indigenizing a Western form. To appreciate this distinction, three points are noteworthy. First, unlike aforementioned cultural practices, cartooning was not institutionalized and was therefore outside the ambit of comparable patronage and canonization. Even now, although animation has gained institutional presence, cartooning has not. Yet, cartoonists engage in debates about technique, style, and artistic merits that present an alternate genealogy for the discussion of visual representation. Second, the British *Punch* archive demonstrates the proprietors' eagerness to tap India as a market and accordingly shape the iconography of the colony in its cartoons. However, when *Punch* sought to carve a market in India, the region had several vernacular versions already in circulation. Talcherkar's evocation of the "bright pages of *Punch*" as a model and the "cartoonist's craft" as one among many gifts of the British – "Aryan kinsmen," returning to the "land of Hind" – preempted critique and fenced a defensive space for broadcasting Indian cartoonists and their caricatures of colonial politics. Offense could not be taken, for these cartoons were examples of "the manner in which the Aryan brother is beginning to make use" of the imperial gift.[34] This "use" was not an abuse. Talcherkar unequivocally claimed cartoons as forms that "silently instill wisdom, hit foibles and, on the whole, elevate character."[35] To buttress his own authority, and in line with the idea of the knowing subject, Talcherkar claimed a long history of the "oriental mind's" exposure to the language of symbols and hence the "allure" of caricature and cartoons for it. Claiming to be kin and imitators allowed native editors to puncture British official reading of impropriety in the vernacular cartoons.

The making of professional cartoonists, which I discuss through the lives of Kutty and Bireshwar, as well as several discussions of the place of copying in order to learn and acquire a unique signature or to claim parity with a Western sense of humor, bring forth a new perspective on mimicry. For example, when I asked Kutty why some of his cartoons had a note, "with apologies," he informed me that when cartoonists draw inspiration from a published cartoon, they include this footnote and name the cartoonist: "'Idea is sacred, drawing is free' was the attitude. You could copy a drawing without any acknowledgment or apology – but in the case of ideas you had to acknowledge. 'With apologies' was meant for the idea. Over the years some ideas became clichés. They no longer needed an 'apology.'" Such citations of acknowledgment of idea and composition give these cartoons a history and new meaning. Third, claiming lateral histories for cartooning illuminates a plot about visuality – ways of showing and seeing that can "provincialize Europe" (Chakrabarty 2000). This makes cartoons a site for "a global narrative of intersecting histories" (Sinha 2007) of the link between modernity and visual representation. For historian Mrinalini Sinha, this framework allows for "*both* the demonstration of generic European concepts as partial or parochial, and their simultaneous remaking as potentially universal."[36] By attending to its representations and construction of "visual subjects" (Mirzoeff 2006, p. 54), the rhetoric of native cartooning in colonial times, and the making of the professional cartoonist, and by recording interpretative dilemmas, it is possible to concur with the creative agency in the adoption and reproduction of visual practices and in the plurality of visuality without necessarily siting its history only in the shadow of the empire and capital.[37] This allows staging newspaper cartoons in India as a form of visual culture that is "the product of the collision, intersection and interaction of Visuality 1 and Visuality 2, between capital's picturing of the world and that which cannot be commodified or disciplined" (Mirzoeff 2006, p. 66).

As a conceptual lens, modernism presents cultural manifestations that experience a new kind of subject. Approaching this experience broadly allows, as Marshal Berman shows, for a "creative interplay" and "conditions for dialogue among the past, the present and the future" (Berman 1988, p. 5). The debates about a cartoon's meaning and the petitions it may generate urge us to recognize the many ways in which people can be modern. This means that the differences in experiencing modernity are not a cultural clash that can be presumed to fit easy distinctions of Western and non-Western, developed and developing, and secular and religious. Indian cartoons have long illuminated these processes at work, and the Danish cartoon controversy showed how these dynamics unfold on a global stage. Those who studied this controversy noted that the *Jylland Posten*'s culture editor Flemming Rose overlooked the fact that "courts in Denmark have treated artistic representation with less leniency than the written or spoken word" (Klausen 2009, p. 19). This distinction is reversed in India. As I discuss in Chapter 8, the quasi-judicial Press Council of India (PCI) holds that cartoons are a special category of news that demands a more liberal attitude than prose. Expectations from newspaper readers thus place the history and practice of Indian cartooning at the center for thinking about a dilemma that surfaces almost every day and in most parts of the world: the connection between political cartoons, humor, and liberal attitudes.

Since cartoons are among the earliest examples of images that traveled across time and place, the historical linkage between cartoons and news illuminates the making of modern politics. With their capacity to succinctly show and tell, cartoons were published, republished, and copied in newspapers and journals. Intellectuals in the nineteenth and twentieth centuries frequently referenced cartoons in their writings and speeches. This should not surprise, since they were closely associated with journalism as political activity. Karl Marx, Friedrich Engels, and Mahatma Gandhi referenced cartoons to emphasize their perspective on imperial politics and the world around them. Cartoons supplemented the ineffable; quite simply, they mattered in a literate world. Cartoons tempted, informed, and humored through a visual vocabulary that required literacy and knowledge of a universe of symbols. Those who had these cultural skills did not necessarily interpret the cartoons alike. And although it is misleading to assume that what appeared in the newspapers had an immediate attraction for nonliterates, nevertheless, the cartoons' visual aspect rendered them available for interpretation even to those who could not read the newspaper.[38]

As images that join thought with laughter or the refusal to laugh, newspaper cartoons offer much insight into humor. In earlier works on humor, the anthropological project was framed to ask whether humor is universal. This question, which also surfaced in colonial times, was evoked to distinguish the colonized 'natives' in their 'lack' of humor. This made humor one of the marks of colonial modernity, to represent the other and to claim similarity (I discuss this in Chapter 1). In the chapters that follow, the anthropological approach emphasizes local discourse as a significant context for understanding the humor of newspaper cartoons. Following this direction of analysis, anthropologists have attended to the social role of joking relationships and, drawing upon Gluckman (1954), the agency of laughter within transgressive and permissible cultural contexts of rituals. Within this framework, recent ethnography has turned attention to laughter as a form of resistance and a "coping mechanism" of the everyday "carnivalesque" (Goldstein 2003), and the public arena of theater (Seizer 2005). This also implies that, rather than elaborating on structural transformation, ethnographers now observe and acknowledge the private performance of resistance as a "weapon of the weak" (Scott 1985). Within distressing conditions of poverty and violence, laughter that is "out of place" has also invited consideration as a "coping mechanism" (Goldstein 2003) and to view "serious social conditions" (Downe 1999) in everyday experience. Attention to how humor is used and created in this everyday context combines a cultural framing of humor with its creative production and deployment.[39] Angelique Haugerud's study of the satirical activist group Billionaires' "empathic humor" (2012, p. 155), positions this lens on public critique of the wealthy in the USA. In all these studies, the anthropologists' astonishment at alienating laughter is made familiar for readers by casting it as a provisional restructuring of a culture's power dynamics, and by situating it as a specific cultural performance. By looking at refusals to laugh, rather at than my own sense of alienation, this book draws attention to modern politics in order to understand the uncertainity of humor and its place in the public sphere. This limits the broad brush of culture's explanatory role, suggesting a more nuanced approach to people's experience. For a contemporary example, debates between activists, protesting at a newspaper cartoon, and newspaper editors at the PCI, exact a dialogue on taste and politics that lead to uneasy and "politically incorrect" submissions by the editors. This chain of movement from visual to word, and from laughter to debate, triggered by the cartoon, skillfully maneuvers a critique of bourgeois cultural capital: through rational debate, minority activists expose bourgeois visuality, "good taste," and liberal humor as a form of dominance (Khanduri 2009a). These positions on cartoons and humor not only emerge as a result of specific social identity but serve as a platform to assert and articulate identities.

The cartoon's visual vocabulary is anchored in caricature and particular cultural and historical contexts, making it difficult to interpret when seen by an audience from another place or from another time. It is crucial to acknowledge here that my lack of alienation with the humor sensibility of the offending cartoons, although shaped by my cultural insider status, was not seamless. On several occasions when I struggled to understand the cartoon, its topicality demonstrated that newspaper cartoons are local to both space and time. My familiarity and interpretative skills were also limited to Hindi and English cartoons. But when interpretative challenges emerge among readers of the same place and of the same time, then it compels a closer look at how people from the same cultural and historical moment interpret cartoons differently. The particular contexts for understanding how a visual and humor aesthetic works constitute the heterogeneity of cultural experience (Chatterjee 2008). A close attention to how people explain their refusal to laugh – for it is refusal that is always held accountable – evokes analysis that theorists and anthropologists often register as part of their intellectual contribution. For example, in contemporary India, petitions against offensive cartoons make connections between visuality and humor, demonstrate competing notions of democratic culture, and qualify what it means to be modern in India. Defining modernity involves a consideration of how individuals conceptualize political subjectivity and rights in relation to the colonial and postcolonial state. Integral to this identity is the ability to acquire the skills and taste for cultural forms that enable the pursuit of the modern. And part of this self-identity is to be prepared to be critical of the politics of one's own subordination. It can be conceptualized as a consciousness that is already aware of the limits of the core ideals of political freedom, and is ever willing to claim freedom as a tactical move. Modernity, then, is always an unfinished task that leaves deep traces in the cultural landscape.

Approaching the newspaper cartoon as a form that connects humor and politics offers a critical vantage point for theorizing modernity. In these debates about representation in cartoons, the evocation of competing models of modernity points to the dynamic that renders modern sensibility, such as the appreciation of political cartoons, contingent and not simply cultural. I perceive these articulations of modern sensibility as subaltern tactics to negotiate the meaning of liberal politics and democracy. This tactical modernity provides the basis of my engagement with existing scholarship whose focus has centered on the multiplicity and the coevalness of modernity (Appadurai 1996, Escobar 1995, Ivy 1995, Rofel 1999). In the context of India's history of inequitable caste and gender rights, modernity is contentious: it is a sign that recognizes that democratic rights belong to all citizens of the nation state, but it is also a sign that questions a definition of liberalism that is distinctly bourgeois, permitting illiberal conduct in peripheral public spaces such as the newspaper cartoon.[40] This allowance complicates democracy's permissive and prohibitive behaviors. In India, questioning newspaper cartoons' humor for its illiberal attitudes serves new public criteria for defining its democracy. This opens up inquiries into democracy, which, as Julia Paley contends for anthropology, is not about making precise definitions, instead it is about "variations associated with the term democracy" and "the way democracy has been conceptualized in public discourse" (Paley 2008, p. 5).

Newspaper cartoons generate counter-hegemonic interpretative discourses, which I conceptualize as the small voice of visuality (here I am drawing upon Kamala Visweswaran's "Small Speeches" (1996)). There are no specialized critics to dissect cartoons' authentic meanings; this makes everyone a critic. The public emotions and critique that cartoons stir tell a lot about its unique mode: cartoons reveal the politics of seeing. A fine-combed history demonstrates the political convincingly in relation to colonial photographs; newspaper cartoons amplify and intensify this fact. Newspaper cartoons are significant because their inherent ambiguity withstands scrutiny as historical and anthropological texts. Establishing this long history of cartoon analysis from the people's perspective, this book makes larger claims about the place of cartoons in the world – it holds that in the "media-saturated" world, cartoons grip our attention because they cluster seeing with a sensory experience to generate laughter, hurt, and political thought.

Although I conclude this book with a chapter on this controversy, in India cartoons continue to demonstrate that its multiple publics produce cultural politics that confront Indian democracy and its promise of an equitable society. Bringing together newspaper cartoons and cartoon talk within the same analytical framework, I take a cue from the historian Antoinette Burton's questioning of vision and voice as tropes for the recuperation of marginalized subjects as history (2000, pp. 21–2). Burton's nuanced analysis of these tropes referencing women's history is equally applicable to all peripheral histories. Following this cautionary note, my project in this book is not about recovery and rescue. Instead, in showing how utterances about cartoons shaped the visual landscape in intricate ways, I demonstrate a way in which visuality can be "imagined and reconsolidated in new historical forms" (p. 22).

Cartoon talk

Through interactions, interviews, and intensive research in individual and institutional collections, I assembled an ethnographic archive of cartoon talk, creating it jointly with cartoonists, readers, fans, and activists. Cartoon talk took different forms – for example, through interviews I initiated it, in guest books it was already recorded, and in petitions the cartoon was verbalized and transcribed. Furthermore, I constructed talk as dialogue. For example, the history of the Common Man character emerged by converging published interviews and interviews I conducted. Talk often took a circuitous route, encompassing transformation from one form of talk to another – from visual to transcript, from visual to verbal to transcripts, and from visual to verbal and back to the visual. This process forged "links between different knowledges" (Haraway 1988, p. 39). Cartoon talk from the perspective of the cartoonists, readers and fans, activists, critics, archives, and brand managers provides "situated knowledges" about this in-between visual form. It offers a peek into interpretative processes in both individual and collective registers. But the different spaces and forms of cartoon talk – life stories of senior cartoonists, personal archives, institutional archives, guest books, exhibitions, interviews with junior cartoonists and amateurs, newspaper reviews, and blogs – made this talk multi-sited. It allowed me to consistently think through my fieldwork as ethnography on the move, for there was no field in which to reside in this ethnography. Much of the talk recorded here was also invoked by events, even as talk, at times, produces events. This "event + dialogue" format, to draw upon Kevin Dwyer's reflection on fieldwork, shows a "complex process of adjustment and readjustment" (1979, p. 217). Writing this book took me to a community bonded by their connection with newspaper cartoons – a community existing in moments and fragments. These engagements offer an unexplored theoretical space between history and ethnography.

As a source for history and ethnography, "talk" urges a reconsideration of the constituents and methods of ethnography. In their analysis of television programs, cultural theorists have recognized that, during and after viewing, viewers engage in television talk, interpreting televisual texts to socialize and introspect about their own everyday life (Abu-Lughod 2004, Bausinger 1984, Fiske 1987, Gillespie 1995, and Mankekar 1999). This turn to talk as interpretation is significant for anthropologists who study media, as it adds to their toolkit of participant observation (Jackson 2008 and Khanduri 2009a) and reconfigures their research method in the face of a critique of "visual root metaphors of knowledge" (Fabian 2001, p. 2). This emphasis on talk and listening comes with the reminder that talk is accompanied by refusals and silences, which too should be theorized (Visweswaran 1994).[41] Cartoon talk complicates the place of talk as it has been previously understood and approached – it involves listening and reading public inscriptions and transcripts of talk. Gandhi's cartoon talk, which I discuss in Chapters 2 and 3, is a fine example of how it operates both as oppositional – the small voice of visuality – and as hegemonic.

The link between visual and talk to discern visuality – the politics of seeing – and for its historical and ethnographic potential has surfaced in a couple of ways that merit discussion here. Colonial photographs have invited considerable scholarly attention; much of this scholarship has provided fascinating insight into the role of photographs as ethnographic representations that were produced by anthropology and in turn reproduced anthropology. Photographs are interesting, historian Geraldine Forbes holds, "not only because they can be read for stories of rebellion but because they invite 'telling,' a process that allows for continual renewal of the act of rebellion" (2007, p. 82). These perspectives make it an analytically useful horizon for gauging cartoons' generativity in the past and present. Elaborating on the "raw history" and "historical potential" of photographs, Elizabeth Edwards has drawn attention to the "visual sovereignty" that allows not just the production of photographs but also the opportunity to interpret and "give 'voice' to images and through them to insert the human voice" (2001, p. 235).[42] The cartoons I discuss, for example, in the context of Gandhi's interpretations situate this visual sovereignty coevally with ethnographic potential. Debates and alternate interpretations of cartoons scratch the surface of the myth of solidarity to disclose frictions in imperial and national ideologies. Simultaneously, these verbal translations seek to construct mythical publics and counterpublics – interpretative communities bound by a visual experience. The evocation of cartoon "taste," as a pedagogical move, surfaced in Gandhi's cartoon reviews (Chapter 3) and in the Press Council of India's arbitration of complaints against cartoons (Chapter 8). Cartoon talk thus provides a telling context for showing that the "idea of a public is a cultural form" (Warner 2002). A taste for cartoons was a cultural form of knowledge that could mark an "outsider" and "insider." As I show in Chapter 2, Gandhi suffered culture shock not as a colonial subject in England and in South Africa but as a colonial subject in India. Furthermore, in South Africa, Gandhi deployed cartoons to interpret colonial politics for his newspaper readers and facilitate their access to a form of knowledge. This complicates the heuristic deployment of the "insider" and "outsider" status; it is also a reminder that not place but practices shaped by cultural politics play a powerful role in experiencing belonging and alienation.

Gender politics

Gender politics interweaves all the chapters in this book and is discussed in depth in Chapter 6. If cartoons brought politics home through the material artifacts of public media – newspapers and cartoon albums called *Chitravali* – then, in their representations and gender reversals, cartoons choreographed politics as domestic scenes. Gender politics were central to modernity (Chatterjee 1993, Chakrabarty 1993, Sinha 1995, Burton 1999, Sinha 2007). Domestic space as well as "scientific" training of women through curricular offerings such as Home Science and the establishment of the Lady Irwin College in 1932 demonstrate the engendering of private and public space as part of the colonial project (Hancock 1999). Anti-colonial critique took on many hues, ranging from a critique of British policies to a critical assessment of Indian culture and contemporary society. In these cartoons, domestic space, gender reversal, and maternal and matrimonial sentiments provided the emotional cues for figuring out politics, which was otherwise played out in the male public space. This curious insertion of public politics as domestic practices was not just a humorous ploy. Instead it shows the domestic as a powerful mode for imagining public politics, and its continuation as a visual technique in postcolonial cartoons, for example by Kamath, invite attention to these "reversible worlds." "All symbolic inversions," according to Barbara Babcock, "define a culture's lineaments at the same time as they question the usefulness and the absoluteness of this ordering" (1978, p. 29). Attending to gender as analytical category in cartoons reveals that, in writing about the past (writing history by women), "historiography may be feminist without being exclusively women's history" (Sangari and Vaid 1989, p. 2). For colonial and contemporary India, recognizing that gender intercepts understanding of all social issues can be further illuminating when it is clustered with religion. Social bodies animating the cartoons in colonial India were imagined embodying gender and religious identities, so that a woman's caricature was also calculated either as Hindu or Muslim. To represent meant to picture these marks of the social self, generating a "visual subject" (see Figure I.4).

In this book, gender surfaces not only as a mode of representation of the empire and colony for attracting colonial readers of cartoons, as a business sense, and for articulating a "common" experience, but also as a

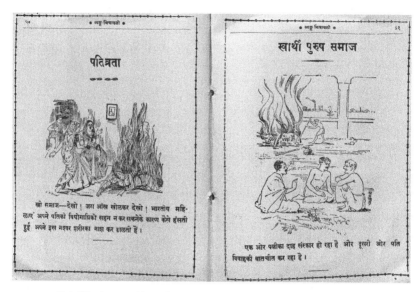

I.4 "Pativrata (the chaste wife) and 'the selfish male community.'"
Vyang Chitravali. 1930. Calcutta.

"The chaste wife." Hindi caption (left): Women's community: Just open
your eyes and see! Unable to bear the bereavement of their husband's
demise, see how cheerfully Indian women destroy their mortal bodies.

"The selfish male community" (right): On the one hand his deceased
wife's last rites are underway and, on the other, the husband discusses
plans of marriage.

The two scenes followed a popular format for special critique by
contrasting behavior between men and women in contemporary India.
While celebratory of women's selfless and self destructive love, this
scene evokes the practice of sati in which women were cremated with
their deceased husband. This cartoon can also be read as exhorting
women to open their eyes and measure if their husbands were worthy
of their love and chastity. The cremation and clothing situated this
gendered social milieu in Hindu terms.

position of interpretation. Gender makes itself visible in cartoon talk
about how to represent and interpret. The *Punch* proprietors' discussion
of representing "Colonia" as a graceful dancing partner for marketing
the humor magazine in India; the *Vyang Chitravali* editor Baijnath
Kedia's reassuring note about cartoons in his publication being safe for
women and children, the Congress activist and leader Rajkumari Amrit
Kaur's complaint to Gandhi about cartoonist Shankar's representation
of Lady Irwin graduates as women with pouted lips and lipstick;

cartoonist Kamath's representation of everyday politics through the social place of women in Indian society; cartoonist Mita's (Mita Roy) struggle to author a specific "common woman" character that was denied by her editor; and, in the precincts of the PCI, scholar-activist Kalpana Kannabiran's petition against the objectification of women that cartoons tend to normalize in the name of humor – these moments discussed in the book illustrate not only how cartoons make gender visible but how this visibility opens a special window of opportunity to track the articulation of modern liberal politics.

Gender shapes interactions in the social formalities that are accorded and expected in meetings and conversations. I consulted many cartoonists – probably more than a hundred. This list includes retired, senior, junior, and amateur cartoonists, some of whom are now well established. Of these, I only corresponded with some in letters and email, for I could not meet them in India. My fieldwork did not involve sharing and seeing cartoons that circulate informally, unlike the world of *gupt* (secret and sexual) cartoons that Lawrence Cohen was privy to in Banaras (1995). Several years ago, among a handful of women, I shared the amateur cartooning and graphic art circuit of the annual youth festival in New Delhi, Yuva Mahotsav, with some of India's current popular cartoonists, such as Shekhar Gurera and Jagjeet Rana. Although I did not meet them there or know them then, when talking to them about their becoming cartoonists, I realized during this research that we might have crossed paths in the well-known site for this annual event, the Sapru House grounds. These amateur circuits are important because cartooning is not an institutionalized practice in India. I met few women cartoonists there or anywhere, an indicator that the profession of political cartooning in India is gendered and built around a strong network of mentors.[43] The paucity of women political cartoonists is not unique to India; scholars have noted so for the USA too (Gilmartin and Brunn 1998). The intersecting concerns pivotal to gender politics are persuasively illustrated by Urvashi Butalia's analysis of Manjula's cartoons. Manjula is internationally very well known but she had faced challenges placing her cartoons. For Butalia, Manjula's gender and the absence of "hard" politics in her cartoons explains Manjula's experience.[44] However, Manjula might not readily embrace gender identity, which complicates Butalia's analysis. In her column "Life Lines," Manjula wrote (2003):

The other day, a friend asked me why my name wasn't on the list of invitees to the festival of women's literature scheduled to start this month. I said it's because, for some years now, I have been avoiding events which require body-type affiliation. I no longer consciously think of myself as a woman, so it seems to me a bit ridiculous to be included amongst others for whom being a woman is the main focus of their lives and work.

In contrast, cartoonist Kamath deployed her experiences at home, at times featuring her two children in her cartoon strip, *Geetha*.[45] These divergent approaches to gender, both as representation and identity, complicate the narrative of gender politics.

Teachable moments: textbooks, Klan cartoons, and campus news

When cartoons from the past resurface in the present as pedagogical material in school textbooks, and provoke debate, it is a reminder of the unexpected ways in which the present reconfigures the past. In 2012, the Indian Parliament was embroiled in a discusson of unprecedented intensity over a cartoon that depicted India's first prime minister, Jawaharlal Nehru, with a whip ready to strike, following Dr. Bhimrao Ambedkar, who also holds a whip and is seated on a snail. The snail depicted the Indian constitution and, as the Chairman of the Constitution, Ambedkar is known as its architect. In the background the Indian public is shown laughing at the scene. What were they laughing at? Were they laughing because they saw Nehru whip the snail behind Ambedkar's back to hasten its pace? Or was the scene funny because they saw Nehru about to whip Ambedkar unknown to him? That conclusion is for the reader to reach. This cartoon was made by Shankar and originally published in *Shankar's Weekly* on August 28, 1949. In a bid to stimulate critical thinking and student interest, in 2006 political cartoons were introduced in social science textbooks for various grade levels issued by the National Council of Educational Research and Training (NCERT), the division of the central government that produces school textbooks. The decision was an outcome of the revised National Curriculum Framework (National Council of Educational Research and Training 2005) deliberated among the board of prominent academic advisors to whom NCERT allocates responsibility for shaping the content of its textbooks.[46] For the social sciences, the NCF guidelines held:

A paradigm shift is recommended, proposing the study of the social sciences from the perspective of marginalised groups. Gender justice and a sensitivity toward issues related to SC and ST [Scheduled Castes and Scheduled Tribes] communities and minority sensibilities must inform all sectors of the social sciences. Civics should be recast as political science, and the significance of history as a shaping influence on the child's conception of the past and civic identity should be recognised. (p. xi)

With reference to the use of cartoons, the introductory note in the ninth grade political science textbook explained to teachers:

You would notice lots of cartoons and pictures in this book. This brings visual relief and some fun. But these images are meant to do more. These are parts of the teaching and learning process. . .Please do stop at each cartoon or visual and get the students involved in reading the message. If you can please select some cartoons from your regional languages and use them. (National Council of Educational Research and Training 2006, p. viii)

In the textbook, cartoon-based exercises stage the cartoon in relation to the topic in hand and then pose a question. For example, "How many images on the wall do you recognize? Do many common people feel the way the common man in this cartoon does?" (see Figure I.5).

Paradoxically, for critics, the inclusion of the Ambedkar cartoon exemplified exactly the opposite of what the NCF intended. The cartoon was deemed offensive to Dalits and to their prominent leader Ambedkar. Member of Parliament Thol. Thirumavalavan contended that the cartoon was insulting to both Nehru and Ambedkar. Several political parties voiced their protest. President Pranab Mukherjee, who was then the finance minister, opined that the cartoon was "totally wrong." Bahujan Samaj Party leader Mayawati, a prominent Dalit leader, sought criminal action against the erring officials overseeing the textbook's contents.[47]

Curiously, the cartoon was apparently not noticed by offended individuals and groups until 2012, six years after its publication in 2006. A popular collection of Shankar's cartoons titled, *Don't Spare Me Shankar* (Pillai 2002), includes this cartoon (see p. 22) and others featuring Ambedkar. For example, in the cartoon "Hit Hard, Hit Well," Nehru is a pugilist with "punch bags" that is, Ambedkar and other political peers, who have been hit hard and well (see p. 80). The "whipping the snail" imagery also resurfaced in a cartoon titled "Indian Derby" in 1954 that commented on the slow progress by the coterie of ministers. It depicts Nehru's prominent cabinet ministers, such as Maulala Azad, Amrit Kaur, Jagjivan Ram, and Lal Bahadur Shastri, among others, each aloft a snail, whipping and goading their mounts to move.[48] According to the *Hindu*, a prominent English-language newspaper, the Ambedkar cartoon was first raised as an objectionable issue by Ramdas Athavale, a politician of the Republican Party of India. In protest at a conference, Athavale burned the page with the cartoon, which was contained in the chapter "Constitution, Why and How" of the political science textbook.[49] After the issue rocked the Parliament, the human resource development minister Kapil Sibal, representing the government, tendered an apology, and banned and

2.4 BROADER MEANINGS OF DEMOCRACY

This famous cartoon by R K Laxman comments on the celebrations of the fifty years of independence. How many images on the wall do you recognize? Do many common people feel the way the common man in this cartoon does?

read the cartoon

In this chapter we have considered the meaning of democracy in a limited and descriptive sense. We have understood democracy as a form of government. This way of defining democracy helps us to identify a clear set of minimal features that a democracy must have. The most common form that democracy takes in our times is that of a representative democracy. You have already read about this in the previous classes. In the countries we call democracy, all the people do not rule. A majority is allowed to take decisions on behalf of all the people. Even the majority does not rule directly. The majority of people rule through their elected representatives. This become necessary because:

- Modern democracies involve such a large number of people that it is physically impossible for them to sit together and take a collective decision.
- Even if they could, the citizen does not have the time, the desire or the skills to take part in all the decisions.

This gives us a clear but minimal understanding of democracy. This clarity helps us to distinguish democracies from non-democracies. But it does not allow us to distinguish between a democracy and a good democracy. It does not

I.5 "Broader Meanings of Democracy." National Council of Educational Research and Training (NCERT). 2012 (2006). New Delhi. Courtesy of NCERT.

With its use as a pedagogical exercise to comprehend Indian democracy and its political system, newspaper cartoons gain a longer shelf life in public cultural memory. This exercise in the social science textbook issued for the grade IX curriculum encourages students to "read" the cartoon, thus presenting it as a text for interpreting "broader meanings." The chapter, "What is democracy? Why democracy?" and the accompanying sidebar prompt students to "recognize" the caricatures while also asking them to reflect on R. K. Laxman's "Common Man" as a representation of the "Common People."

removed the cartoon, along with several others that were also deemed offensive. Professors Yogendra Yadav and Suhas Palshikar resigned from their positions on the advisory board. As commentary on the cartoons continued, it shifted from the representation of Ambedkar and Dalits to the negative image students had developed about Indian politicians and the democratic process by seeing these cartoons in their textbooks. The NCERT cartoons were held responsible for poisoning children's minds and for maligning the entire breed of politicians. Removing the cartoons would not, according to the politican Laloo Yadav, "clear" the minds of the children – the damage had been done and it said much about how Laloo Yadav believed images had a lasting imprint on the mind. The politician Sharad Yadav commented about the need for maturity to comprehend political cartoons: "Such cartoons need mature minds to understand. The minds of the youngsters who are being taught are not."[50] Such apprehensions about understanding cartoons, as I showed earlier in the colonial context of cartoon-generated knowledge for women and children, presumes a suitable subject that can correctly interpret political cartoons. That "correct" interpretation is already in place but without any discussion of what that might be. In the face of competing interpretations by "mature" minds, for example in the cases adjudicated by the PCI, Sharad Yadav's comment would find little agreement.

It is a rare event to witness politicians of all stripes in India articulate their understanding of the place of cartoons in shaping knowledge. It was even rarer, and a show of collective threat that overcame ideological positions, for politicans to resolutely unite on the cartoon issue. The Ambedkar cartoon controversy sparked a pitched battle between academics and politicians over interpretative politics involved in seeing, reading, and teaching with newspaper cartoons. The academics themselves were divided, rousing debate between the Jawaharlal Nehru University historian Neeladri Bhattacharya and the Columbia University philosopher Akeel Bilgrami.[51] Since the political science textbook included cartoons by a long list of cartoonists, many with national honors, including Shankar and Laxman, the politicians did not necessarily single out any one in particular for condemnation. Although politicians in India frequently inaugurate cartoon exhibitions, pen complimentary prefaces to cartoon books, and celebrate cartoonists, their sense of humor dwindled when cartoons were situated as source for thought, knowledge, and pedagogy.

Lest there be an assumption that debates about cartoons are few and far between, it is helpful to note that cartoons may seem to be more important on their surface in India than they may seem to be in places such as the United States, where they have a longer history. If we put our ear to the ground, however, some of the ways in which cartoons impact social life is palpable and at home in the United States. Look around youthful US college campuses and their newspapers. As I began writing this book, the *Eastern Echo*, the campus newspaper of Eastern Michigan University, tendered an apology for a cartoon showing two romantic Ku Klux Klan members ruminating about the first time they met, near a tree with a noose (September 28, 2010). The seemingly uneasy juxtaposition of the history of US race relations and the sentiment of romance, of symbolic hate and love, is the central puzzle animating this cartoon. To read between the cartoons' image and words is to engage in cultural politics. With most newspapers fronting an electronic version and a forum for public comments, such politics manifest in real time, energizing the cartoon and extending its lifespan beyond a day. Judging from the news surrounding this cartoon's offense and the animated online comments following its publication, opinions varied about the nature of the offense. Doubts were cast over whether there indeed was intent to offend or to provide humor. As the discussion unfolded, online posters claimed a bewildering array of opinions. For one graduate student, Laura, this "overreaction to a cartoon" was a "teachable moment." The campus newspaper editor's measured explanations barely cleared the air. Words failed, and feelings hurt. So when reaction is seen as an overreaction, what does it teach about interpretation? As I bring this book's conclusion to a close, my attention is drawn to a controversy about a cartoon in the *Daily Texan*, the campus newspaper of my alma mater, the University of Texas (March 27, 2012). Caricaturing the recent killing of the unarmed black teenager Trayvon Martin in Florida, the cartoon referred to the victim as a "colored boy," creating a stir. Peacemakers stepped in, the vice president for diversity and community management intervened, urging respect and civility, apologies were issued, and the cartoonist was removed from her position. The ensuing online discussion points out that the cartoon was not meant to be racist; to the contrary, it sought to question the senseless killing, yet, somehow it quickly came to be criticized as the "colored-boy" cartoon. But what answer can the vice president for diversity and community management offer to an online comment by Laurence: "in modern use, the term 'colored' is offensive, why does the National Association for the Advancement of Colored People (NAACP) use the term?"[52] Once again, the "modern" paradox brings good questions for which we seldom have good answers.[53]

As alternate ways of seeing, these episodes about cartoons and contemporary debates about its meanings shed light on the nature of political conflict in shared media spaces. The focus on India will illuminate why newspaper cartoons generate political debates in most parts of the world, provoking readers to question the limits of their modernity and their senses of humor. In showing that cartooning is a sacred art of a secular democracy, this book claims that a deeper understanding of newspaper cartoons and its history will prepare us to be sensitive to the nature of political issues of media and representation. Collectively, the chapters show an entwined story of the past and the present, of the empire and the colony, of India and its global connections, and of a humor sensibility and modern visual politics.

Chapters

Part travelogue that moves between places, continents, and more than a century of cartoons, and part biography of cartoonists, *Caricaturing Culture in India* tells a historical anthropological story of cartoons. Such history and ethnography of cartooning must of necessity be partial. With its twenty-two officially recognized languages, India's linguistic diversity ensures that no single narrative can convey all its regional particulars. Following a chronological order from colonial to contemporary times in India, I have assumed varying vantage points in presenting this story about stories of cartooning. Each chapter is a vantage point, a beginning, that takes back and forth the story of cartoons in India and in modern times.

The first part, "Colonial times," sets the stage, centering on newspaper cartoons as a form and source of political knowledge. With vernacular newspaper editors in India, and Gandhi in his role as an editor in South Africa and later as a politician in colonial India, these colonial times witness the making of public intellectuals in an era of newspaper culture, and the rise of India's most influential cartoonist, Shankar Pillai. Chapter 1 delves into the lateral history of the British humor magazine, *Punch* (1841), in colonial India and the embryonic stage of India's cartooning story. The publication of the *Hindi Punch* in 1854, the *Oudh Punch* in 1877, and thereafter the *Hindu Punch* in 1925, and several others published by local editors, marked the beginning of vernacular comic newspapers in India. Modeled after *Punch*, these "comic papers" satirized colonial politics, caricatured British and Indian politicians through gender reversal, and recast the British Mr. Punch in several indigenous avatars, while also ushering in cartoons as a new form of news.[54] The second chapter develops the theme of cartoons and of satyagraha (truth force) to show the connections between modes of anti-colonial political thought in the context of Gandhi in South Africa and India. Gandhi's analysis of cartoons offers a unique insight into the unspooling of their hidden meaning. Early in his journalistic activity in South Africa, while editing the *Indian Opinion* and bruised by his experience of racial discrimination, Gandhi sought to educate his readers about the political meanings of cartoons in British newspapers. Later, when Gandhi became the icon of India's nationalist struggle, he kept watch on the popular cartoonist Shankar's sharp caricatures and his depiction of the Muslim leader, Muhammad Ali Jinnah, as discussed in Chapter 3. Despite Gandhi's admonishment, Shankar went on to become a nationally known cartoonist. This juxtaposition of a political and visual vocabulary gave the first glimpse of the emerging sensitive links among politics, media, and the representations of Hindus and Muslims.

"National times" are the frame of Part II and its four chapters. In Chapter 4, I interweave archival research and my interviews and correspondence with the two cartoonists: Kutty (1921–2011) and Bireshwar (1920–2007), to build their life stories, the role of their gurus, and the making of a new profession in the Hindi, English, and Bengali press. India's diverse linguistic map accorded preference and prestige to cartoonists in the English press, thereby creating a hierarchy in the profession. Kutty's and Bireshwar's life stories also convey the impact of pioneering cartoonist Shankar's mentoring and the national influence of India's first cartoon-based magazine, *Shankar's Weekly* (1947–75). Shankar's biting cartoons inspired a generation of professional cartoonists, and *Shankar's Weekly* launched two generations of Indian cartoonists.

Chapter 5 focuses on how cartoonists learn by looking at cartoons. Conversations with amateur cartoonists and many other professional cartoonists bring to the fore the role of observing and learning. In this landscape, cartoonist Laxman is the guru of all. As the cartoonist most emulated in India, few conversations are complete without a reference to his cynical humor, his work, and his life.

The Common Woman and Man characters, the pocket cartoon, and the developmental agendas they lampoon, share the focus of Chapter 6. This chapter asks why and how the Common Man and pocket cartoon became ubiquitous in India. The gendered caricature of the person-on-the-street is a unique characteristic of Indian cartooning. Most prominent cartoonists have their own stylized version of this public spokesman. With India's independence in 1947, cartoonists turned their attention to representing the new Indian citizen in a free country. Embracing a clarion call of the first prime minister, Jawaharlal Nehru – "unity in diversity" – the Common Man displaced all social differences among Indian citizens. Almost always a man, this character appeared in the pocket cartoon, a popular single-column format. Conversations with Samuel, the "father" of Indian pocket cartoons, and Mita, the first woman political cartoonist in India, and a reading of Kamath's pocket cartoons, give a peek into the politics of gender, language, and cartooning. These pocket cartoons in English and Indian languages called attention to the nation and its people's common problems, thereby creating a sense of unity of purpose and simultaneously producing a linguistic hierarchy.

If linguistic politics fostered a hierarchy among cartoonists, then drawing style further complicated a cartoonist's place. Chapter 7 engages with the cartoon as art. This aesthetic category introduces debate and norms about cartoons' creative labor and its purpose, generating divisions in the world of Indian cartooning. Abu's cartoons, the art school degrees of several cartoonists, and the emergent practice of exhibiting cartoons renewed discussion about the cartoonist as artist. These analyses of cartoons offer a previously unexplored vantage point and insight into the production of a discourse on art and ask: Are cartoonists fine artists?

"Global times," the theme of Part III, situates a bureaucratic site – the PCI – and a controversy, the Danish cartoon episode as it unfolded in India, in a web of interconnected global discussions about ethical representations. Chapter 8 discusses two petitions lodged in the PCI against cartoons that debate class, gender, and caste inequities in India. The cartoons and petitions discussed in this chapter reveal that, for representatives of minority communities, the quasi-judicial PCI is an important space for staking claims over the meaning of offensive cartoons and debating the unfinished project of secular democratic politics. Since its inception, the PCI has become a model for the press in South Asia, and it has extended its reach to include the Internet, where several newspapers are freely available as e-newspapers.

Chapter 9 looks at the Danish cartoon controversy in India. The debate around the Danish cartoons that began simmering in Amsterdam in 2005 until its worldwide reverberations the next year offers a painful glimpse of the repercussions of dismissing cartoons as mere representations and laughing matter. The United States, Egypt, and India prohibited the republication of the Danish cartoons. This proscription generated unexpected convergence among modern politics of different stripes. But India offers an alternate context for thinking about portrayals of humor in relation to deities. Darshan (the experience of seeing a divine image) is central to Hindu religiosity, but paradoxically from a Western point of view, caricaturing Hindu gods and goddesses is an established tradition in India. The Hindu pantheon has long provided cartoonists with a pool of images to caricature politicians. Although evoked as a cultural clash, the Danish cartoon controversy did not open India's communal wounds. This remarkable moment of India's modernity felt by the people, has gone unnoticed by those who study images.

The Conclusion reconnects the long history of Indian cartooning as a series of deliberations about who constitutes the liberal subject. The answer has varied over time, and is key to understanding the experience of modernity and democratic politics. This chapter wonders if in global times cartoons are a dying language. The British cartoonist Nicholas Garland, who has created several India cartoons, is skeptical of the future of caricaturing cultural difference in global times. R. K. Laxman, now retired, on the other hand predicts no dearth of political miscalculations and a bright future for cartoonists in India.

Part I

Colonial times

1   Upstart *Punch*es: Why is impertinence always in the vernacular?

Kolkata-based cartoonist Chandi Lahiri showed me his periodicals collection to point out that, in the decades following its publications in 1854, the pioneering Anglo-Gujarati *Hindi Punch*, reached British shores and its cartoons returned to readers in colonial and contemporary India through their republication in W. T. Stead's monthly periodical *Review of Reviews* (see Figure 1.1).

In the words of popular Hindi cartoonist Kaak, these vernacular *Punch*es, and the *Hindu Punch* which he remembered his father used to subscribe to in the village, were "newsy" and not literary (see Figure 1.2).[1] Detailing the role of the press in the development of Urdu literature, historian Muhammad Sadiq notes that *Oudh Punch*'s humor was "excessively topical and common place" and "its prose was seldom of a high order, being too self-conscious, clever and slangy to be entirely agreeable" (1995, p. 616). Historian Mushirul Hasan differs from Sadiq, claiming instead that *Oudh Punch* was "notable for dignity, geniality or satire and good taste" (2007, p. 11). These assessments made me wonder about the vernacular cartoon newspapers – were they literature or news and how did they shape cartooning in India?[2] Lahiri's and Kaak's knowledge of vernacular *Punch*es was not echoed in my conversations with other senior cartoonists, however. Those conversations and a review of accounts of the press in India draw attention rather to the centrality of the British *Punch* in shaping cartooning in India. The popular cartoonist R. K. Laxman's reminiscences of his early encounter with cartoons and *Punch*, for example, echo the narrative of cartooning I heard in several accounts during my fieldwork in India.[3] In their conversations with me, Kutty (1921–2011) and Bireshwar (1922–2007), both contemporaries of Laxman, and my interlocutors in the world of Indian cartooning, acknowledged the influence of *Punch* in the formative years of their professional lives. In the "cultural memory" (Sturken 1997) of this generation of professional cartoonists, *Punch* was entrenched as a significant point to frame the history of cartooning in India. Through their "life stories," the cartoonists participated in the retelling of this history both as actors and as narrators (Trouillot 1995).[4]

45

1.1 Cartoonist Chandi Lahiri at his home in Kolkata, showing me *Hindi Punch* cartoons in his collection of the *Review of Reviews*, March 3, 2003. Photograph by the author.
Lahiri called himself the "fastest cartoonist in India."

The cartoonists' narratives, like those of existing scant histories that build on institutional archives, give little or no attention to the impact of the numerous vernacular *Punch* versions that began publication in India in the 1850s. *Punch* and not the vernacular publications have become the vanishing point for narratives of Indian cartooning.

Why do the vernacular *Punch*es recede from public memory? A part of the answer rests in the context when memory is evoked. Another part is in memory's resetting of history. If memory and history are "different kinds of knowledge-making" (Ortner 2003, p. 7), then what narrative of cartooning in India do these produce? And if "facts and interpretation are mutually constitutive" (White 1978), then how does attention to the vernacular *Punch*es interrupt the existing narrative of cartooning in India? To rethink this particular narrative about colonial India, a major theme of this chapter is to capture perspectives and events that convey an alternative plot. Building on the gap between memory/history and archive, this alternative story of cartooning in India is less a story of rescue, of forgotten texts, than it is about vernacular impertinence. Orienting the

1.2 Popular Hindi cartoonist Kaak Sahib at his home in Ghaziabad, November 17, 2003. Photograph by the author.

Kaak recalled seeing the vernacular *Punch* cartoons and considered the publication "newsy." A professional engineer for twenty years, Kaak (crow) switched to political cartooning to become a leading Hindi cartoonist. His "Kaakdrishti" (Kaak's vision) is one of the earliest cartoon websites in India. Kaak also experimented with a cartoon journal that closed down in 1975 with the declaration of Emergency (1975–7) in India.

British *Punch* in relation to colonial India, and tracking "copying" the quality of British humor and cartoons as a key signifier for colonial proximity and distance from modernity, entwines two plots. I emphasize the epistemological significance of this rupture of colonial hegemony by situating these two plots – that is, the failed market for *Punch* in India, and the small voice of visuality of the *Agra Akhbar* editor – as "critical events" (Das 1998).[5]

The divergent evaluations of the Anglo-Gujarati *Hindi Punch* cartoons' draughtsmanship and humor told much about the reviewers and the politics of humor. If the vernacular *Punch*es were so unremarkable, as some British editors claimed, then why was the colonial state intent on weekly reports of their contents? The "native" proprietors used their publications to analyze the cartoons of the popular vernacular *Punch*es in order to talk back and expose the duality in the colonial authorities' liberal sense of humor. The editor of the popular Urdu newspaper *Agra Akhbar*, for example, conceded that the vernacular *Punch* cartoonists in colonial India had indeed learned the art of cartooning from *Punch*. This acknowledgment came in the form of a small question: in their offensive taste and humor, were the vernacular cartoons "imitators or inventors" of impertinence? In the pages of the *Agra Akhbar*, this puzzle was followed by a condemnation of the British sense of caricature and humor and was contrasted with a more refined sensibility of the colonial cartoons. Through this appraisal, the *Agra Akhbar* turned British taste on its head. Not only had the vernacular *Punch*es learned cartooning from *Punch*, they had achieved a higher moral standard. Such turbulent assessments echo the impact of the vernacular in colonial times. Elsewhere, for example, social farces in mid-nineteenth-century Bengal juxtaposed "'high' morality through a 'low' language" paving a path for "the farce audience to reclaim respectability for its literature and culture" (Ghosh 2008, p. 189).

My evocation of an unfamiliar plot about cartooning in India is an attempt to offer a "gaze that returns" to "provincialize Europe" (Chakrabarty 2000). This tale unfolded in different parts of the empire, and it resonates to convey a history of aspects of colonial interaction that engage the narrative of the derivative nature of nationalism and colonial modernity (Chatterjee 1986; Nandy 1995). Here I examine archival sources about India in *Punch* and its vernacular versions in India, and the archives of the North West Provinces and Central Provinces, to show an alternative history of *Punch* and cartoons in colonial India. Cartoon talk, in the archival context of a question posed by a vernacular newspaper editor, made a claim on adjudicating the universal from the perspective of "native" humor, which even as it mimicked the British tutors, was hoisted as having a finer understanding of the norms of caricature.

Remember *Punch*: "Tenniel with Eastern flavoring"

A cartoon-based weekly, *Punch* began publication in London in 1841. "*Punch* has made a strong impression upon the public ... It was considered a wonder in current literature. Nothing so pretentious in form and material had ever been published at so low a price. It was quoted much by the press, and excited proportionate interest in society" – so mused the founding editor of *Punch*, Mark Lemon (Lemon 1870, pp. 28–9). His reflections set the stage to grasp the economics and popularity of a rib-tickling visual form that was not just about laughter. *Punch* was widely quoted, it was current, cheap, and it was literature.

In 1857, nearly two decades after it began publication, *Punch* cartoonist John Tenniel's stunning two-page cartoon, "The British Lion's Vengeance on the Bengal Tiger" (see Figure I.1) caught the public imagination. It is a widely reproduced cartoon that conveyed the empire's political troubles during a widespread soldiers' uprising. The various allusions to this uprising as a mutiny, war of independence, and rebellion convey the various stances taken by scholars on the nature of this movement. Cartoonists and popular imagination at the time encased this moment of unrest in fears of "native" incivility and threat to British women and children residing in the colony, imparting a sinister moral tone. Among Tenniel's Mutiny series, which triggered analyses among contemporary writers, reviewers, and cartoon watchers, this cartoon notably encrypted the violence of a landmark event in India's colonial history. It became the text for understanding the uprising and what it meant for the imperial future. Tenniel's India cartoons in general "suddenly brought about an increase in circulation that year" (Layard 1907, p. 156). This success assured *Punch* proprietors of the demand for colonial content.

These images of overseas violence for consumption "at home" will scarcely surprise media watchers today.[6] The press played a critical role in shaping public debate on empire in Britain's late nineteenth and early twentieth centuries (Kaul 2003, p. 6). However, cartoons had a lasting impact by interweaving representation and emotion to forge knowledge. In 1857 and for several years afterwards, Tenniel's cartoons mediated the sensation and spectacle of unbridled violence. Readers embraced Tenniel's cartoons as chronicles of the past. The slippage between event and cartoon for knowing the past shapes much of the way cartoons are routinely remembered, even today, as historical sources with a political perspective. Tenniel's cartoons facilitated a template for imagining mental states and the violence in 1857. Nicholas Dirks's observation that the Mutiny was a watershed in colonial logistics – it made ethnography the key to knowledge about natives in India (2001, p. 43) – resonates with the impact of cartoons of these times. In fact, the confluence of the Mutiny and cartoons marks a modern moment of cartoonists being perceived as intellectuals, shaping public opinion. In later years, artists outnumbered writers on *Punch*'s payroll, pointing to the increasing tilt toward graphic content that included both sketches and cartoons (Appelbaum 1981, p. xx).

At the pinnacle of *Punch*'s popularity in Britain in the 1870s, a flock of vernacular versions gained popular ground at the turn of the century. Alluding to the *Delhi Sketch Book* (1850) and the *Indian Punch* (1859),

Charles Dickens offers one of the earliest commentaries on *Punch* versions in India in his journal *All the Year Round* (1862). Presuming an absence of "Asiatic" temperament for comedy and instead, a "contemptuous" laughter among the "natives," in the essay, Dickens delights in holding up cartoons as a mirror to discern cultural difference and the pitiful paradoxes of colonial life. Additionally, the "incongruence" of the Indian landscape made *Punch*-style publications "out of place" in India and the sole logic of their presence was the British readership among administrators and subalterns. In the essay, Dickens elaborates that India's colonial context transformed the moments and imagery of humor in the English-language versions of *Punch*, providing remarkable contemporary insight into the imperial context as a new way of seeing and perceiving cartoons and representation. These *Punch* versions, however, were also the text through which Dickens and others analyzed the colonial difference through the senses of humor. Revisiting themes of native indolence and scenes that captured the Indian experience, in such analysis, humor appeared as a sensibility that marked the British and the *Punch*-style publications, and as a creative act by the British and for the British in India, one that produced humor at the expense of natives. In the pages of the *Delhi Sketch Book*, this humor provided "a nearer view of military and official life than any other periodical." In these pages, London streets, servants, and youth – recurring themes in the British *Punch*, gave way to "mess and club gossip, with a dash of the drawing-room and the field."[7] The "new subject of satire and food for fun" included the governor-general and the commander-in-chief. "Such profanity" was to be expected, according to Dickens, because the *Delhi Sketch Book* was created and consumed by the military and civil "subaltern mind":[8]

Punch in India. The idea seems unpromising. A professed jest must surely be out of place among people who have but little turn for comedy. The Asiatic temperament is solemn, and finds no enjoyment in fun for its own sake. A Bengalee or a Hindustanee can laugh at what is ridiculous; but his laughter is contemptuous, and it may be malignant ... Look too at the incongruity of the thing. Fancy Punch among Palm-trees and palaces all domes and minarets, and going about in a palanquin. Fancy him deep in the silent jungle or out on the arid plain. Fancy him scorched by a burning sun whenever abroad, and bored by inane enjoyments whenever at home – with hookahs and sickly scent, dancers of monotonous motion, fiddlers of soulless music. Fancy him – but there is no need to fancy anything of the kind. Not for the Indolent Asiatic does Punch disport himself in India, but for the Active European.[9]

The social imaginary of Tenniel's cartoons was followed almost fifty years later by sketches of images experienced by *Punch* cartoonist (Leonard) Raven-Hill during his visit to India, timed to coincide with the great Delhi durbar on January 1, 1903 – an immense event that marked the coronation of King Edward VII as emperor of India. Organized by Lord Curzon, the viceroy of India, this durbar was awaited with much anticipation and attracted several visitors from Britain, particularly journalists, photographers, and artists. Raven-Hill was thus a suitable representative for a leading cartoon magazine. Peppered with "native" terms – *ekka*, *bhishti*, and *tonga* to name a few – Raven-Hill's commentaries on his India visit, published in the *Pall Mall Magazine*, were ethnographic in description and temper. He detailed the physical and mental deportment of the natives he saw: "fat and complacent natives" and "Babus who walked meekly hand in hand." Trekking through Punjab, Bhutan, Bombay, and the breadth of the subcontinent led him to note that there were various native "races," including some Caucasian types: "tall, hook-nosed fierce-looking men from Cabool and Peshawar with high conical caps, with thick waistcoats or yellow fur lined jackets over long shirts and baggy trousers."[10] But at the time Raven-Hill was touring India, Bernard Partridge's cartoons in *Punch* presented a visual trope that would persist for many years: an intricate, ornate, and dusky feminine India.

By the first decade of 1900, *Punch* proprietors and chroniclers were also well aware that *Punch*'s popularity inspired "unblushing imitation," in India as elsewhere.[11] The constitutive nature of the empire and the colony was also shaped by the *Punch* proprietors' desire for a market in colonial India. Although the colonies were referred to as a cluster of markets, it was embodied specifically in terms of a particular market that the proprietors thought would potentially yield the most enthusiasm and profit – India. The *Punch* proprietors thus imagined a visual content that would appeal to a readership in colonial India: "Partners" was one such composition. This image marks a strategic intertwining of business and visual representation.[12] The representation of imperial politics and of India was no longer simply an ethnographic project for British consumption. India now had to be seen through different eyes to embrace and court the Indian readership. Thus the story of *Punch* and the empire moves beyond the mapping of its cartoons as representations and a site of discourse of racial ideology (Wechsler 1982). In fact, it is a moment at which the colonial market and the native as potential consumer interrupted the connections among racial discourse, imagination, and caricature to become "counter-discourse" (Terdiman 1985). But despite their sustained efforts, the proprietors of the London-based humor magazine *Punch* failed to establish a market for their publication in colonial India.[13] *Punch*'s failure to carve a niche for itself was a contrast to the tremendous success of the *Punch*-style vernacular newspapers, which, following the publication of the Urdu *Oudh Punch* in 1877, saw cartoons becoming integral to newspaper culture in colonial India. Writing a history of British cartoonists, in which *Punch* has a prominent part, the famous cartoonist David Low noted that "Punch had inspired emulation overseas" (1942, p. 41) and listed the *Hindu Punch* among other titles, observing that its cartoons were "suggestive of Tenniel with Eastern flavoring."[14]

Cartoons in *Punch* and the vernacular *Punch*es often poked fun at "natives" in their attempts at copying British cultural practices. For example, the *Indian Charivari*, an English-language comic newspaper published in colonial India, in successive frames carefully dissected the Babu's "progress" into a failed copy of the modern British subject.[15] Caricaturing the Babu's morality, his loyalty and acquisition of British sartorial taste, the full-page panel cast sophistication and progress as a cultural inheritance that the Babu did not own. In turn the *Hindu Punch* ridiculed the accouterments of modernity embodied by foreign-returned Saheb Babu – a cigar, trousers and a jacket, a hat, a pet dog, and a white wife on his arm.[16] Although such representations flourished in newspaper cartoons, the ability of the cultural form itself to be copied – the making of cartoons, and the ability of the natives to appreciate humor was hotly debated in colonial years. The indigenous proprietors' insistence on being imitators of *Punch* added a new dimension for understanding the place of cultural forms such as the cartoon, which was neither absolutely "hard" nor "soft" (Appadurai 1996). Appropriating Punch, whether in the newspaper's title or its cartoon style, implied a kinship that tested colonial officials' tools for critiquing a persuasive copy: It was a close call.

Vernacular *Punch*es

Essays, dialogue, and cartoons in local "comic papers" modeled after the British *Punch*, along with newspapers and periodicals became the site for consolidating the boundaries of middle-class norms.[17] The emergence of the public sphere and the formation of the middle class around the 1870s coincide with the beginning of *Oudh Punch*, followed by several other *Punch* titles. Circulation figures indicate that these and other "comic papers" were as popular as papers based on written text. With the profusion of *Punch* titles, the late nineteenth century marks the acknowledgment of satire and a new kind of visual literacy – political cartoons as a medium of communication and form of political engagement.[18] While Mr. Punch appeared in his various incarnations speaking Hindi, Urdu, Punjabi, Gujarati, and English in colonial comic papers, he was also a stock character who appeared in literary devices such as skits and dialogues published in the periodicals.[19] The hunchbacked, hook-nosed Mr. Punch was the leitmotif of the vernacular *Punch* versions (see Figure 1.3). Some

CARTOONS FROM THE " HINDI PUNOH."–1904·

A HAPPY NEW YEAR.
(A hearty exchange of the Parsee New Year Greetings between the two Grand Old Men of India.)

[*Hindi Punch, Sept , 1904.*]

1.3 "Happy New Year." *Hindi Punch.* September, 1904. *Cartoons from the "Hindi Punch" 1904.* Bombay.

"A hearty exchange of the Parsee New Year greetings between the two Grand Old Men of India" – Mr. Punch and Dadabhai Naoroji, an economist and Congress politician, who espoused a moderate brand of nationalism through civic participation. By now Mr. Punch is "of India."

The *Hindi Punch* annual albums published reviews of its work from newspapers and magazines in India and overseas. This 1904 album included a notice from the *Punch*'s March 2 issue that refered to the "Brahmin Punchoba" as its "Indian cousin."

Punch stereotypes that had a consistent presence and symbolized the British Empire – John Bull and Britannia – were also absorbed by the Indian journals in their depictions of the colonizing British. The image of Britannia was also incorporated and reconstituted by Indian *Punch* versions to depict Bharat Mata (Mother India). These various *Punch* versions and their wide distribution subsisted on a well-developed postal distribution network. Subscriptions meant that copies of the newspapers were delivered at home or in the office and had the potential of being misdelivered. Subscribers complained that their copies were often stolen. Such complaints were not unfounded. A correspondent of the *Oudh Punch* writing from Lahore in 1879 spoke of the men of the postal department at Lahore as *dakaits* (dacoits) and plunderers, and complained that they appropriated copies of the *Oudh Punch* for their own use and did not deliver them to the addressees.[20]

Even though the vernacular *Punch*es were linked to the celebrated British *Punch* and, in turn, to the European tradition of Pulcinella of the *commedia dell' arte* (which in Britain was the popular puppet show *Punch and Judy*), they also evoked traditions familiar to the emerging middle-class constituency in India. The historian Vasudha Dalmia recognizes in these dual lineages the embodied license both to clown and critique and to assert authority. The Punch character was, among other things, a fusion of the *vidushaka* (clown and commentator) traditions of Sanskrit drama, and also a play on the term *(sar)panch*, the title of the judicial head of an Indian village (Dalmia 2001). But there was something more going on in adopting *Punch* in newspaper titles as well. Both officials of the colonial state and newspaper proprietors were cognizant that using the British *Punch* as a template for humor aesthetics offered a particularly effective challenge to British claims of liberal governance. The *Punch* versions in India thus need to be cast not merely as a derivative form of a colonial modernity but also as a tactical and tactile sensibility for subverting colonial politics.

In its politics, the vernacular press in colonial India in the late nineteenth century could be broadly divided between supporters and critics of the British Empire. It was further distinguished by language. Language determined the regional reach of the newspapers, but Hindi and Urdu papers attracted a mix of readers and were not restricted to a communal readership based on religion. By 1890, in the North West Provinces and United Provinces of colonial India there were intense rivalries among the various *Punch* versions and other vernacular newspapers. The emergence and popularity of political cartoons in vernacular newspapers in colonial India created new anxieties about control for the colonial state. Although Britain had a long tradition of newspaper cartoons, and in the 1870s *Punch* was at the pinnacle of its popularity in Britain, for the colonial state comic papers were particularly contentious because political cartoons and caricature blurred the distinction between factual reporting and the clever play of meanings. This posed a challenge to the interpretation of local news and editorial content. In order to be effective in their control, the state found itself engaging in a heightened mode of surveillance of comic newspapers, but unable to respond to questions about cartoons and humor. Even as vernacular cartoons were dismissed as nonsensical, they were ironically also deemed worthy of surveillance. Did the nonsensical plant the seeds for disloyalty, or was it perhaps disloyalty that was nurturing the nonsensical? Why was the nonsensical popular? These questions required answers that only an insider translator could provide, and so the state undertook surveillance by hiring English-educated colonial subjects as translators and surveyors of the vernacular press.

Lists in the colonial records indicate the local profusion of *Punch* versions. By 1910, a number of *Punch* titles in Hindi were published in the North West Provinces and Oudh.[21] In the midst of many rivals, the *Oudh Punch* had a circulation of 300 copies, comparable to Munshi Nawal Kishore's popular daily edition of the *Oudh Akhbar*, although the circulation figures were highly unstable from year to year.[22] The *Oudh Punch* and *Oudh Akhbar*, both Urdu newspapers, belonged to different political factions, and this aspect of their relation to the colonial state led to intense rivalry.[23] A weekly from Lucknow, the *Oudh Punch* was also distributed to libraries in various universities, such as Allahabad University.

Outside of the North West Provinces, the surveillance records include brief notes on comic newspapers in Gujarat which included the *Gujarati Punch*, *Gup Shup*, and the *Hindi Punch*. Their circulation figures for 1910 far exceed those of the Urdu *Punch*es listed above.[24] Earlier I noted Dickens's commentary on the Anglo-Punch-style publications *Delhi Sketch Book* and the *Indian Punch* as both text and context for asserting a colonial difference in the senses of humor. The wide distribution of the *Hindi Punch* review copies garnered considerable interest in the press; its annual numbers were widely reviewed, providing a glimpse of the critical language of difference by assessing cartooning skill and humor sensibility in the vernacular *Punch* versions in India. This connection between the visual, racial, and cultural has been persuasively tracked by Partha Mitter (1992) in relation to a long history of colonial interpretation of Indian architecture and art. Preempting some of the arguments elaborated in Edward Said's *Orientalism*, Mitter details the production of knowledge about India through an interpretive framework based on Western aesthetic principles. In this history of visual engagement, according to Mitter, "Indian art could at last be said to have arrived" in 1910 with the art historian E. B. Havell's insistence on art as part of the Indian philosophical, religious, and mythological milieu and on "artistic intention" (270). The cartoon reviews and the issues of representation, style, skill, and humor seem to be unfolding alongside this re-evaluation of Indian art and with a different set of interlocutors, namely newspaper editors and within the framework of mimicry.

Shrewd spectator and Western eyes: reviewing the *Hindi Punch*

The reviews of the *Hindi Punch* offer another vantage point for observing the construction of colonial distinctions through cartoons and humor. In a pioneering analysis of cartoons in colonial India, Partha Mitter noted that in 1881, a few years after its publication, Archibald Constable referenced *Oudh Punch* cartoons to counter the notion of a lack of "native" sense of humor.[25] Showcasing both peer praise and criticism, these reviews published in the newspapers and republished in the Annual *Hindi Punch* numbers, broadly showed that assessments by "native" editors were warmer and encouraging while British editors, such as of the *Times of India*, were distant and biting. Interspersed in these analyses of vernacular *Punch*es in relation to *Punch* were ruminations on cartoons as "amusement and instruction."[26] Although the *Hindi Punch* received notice in the British *Review of Reviews*, and in the Indian press, it should not be surmised that the publication was widely circulated outside the Bombay Presidency. The *Hindi Punch* cartoons may have successfully reached W. T. Stead's *Review of Reviews* and attracted his attention because it was a bilingual, Anglo-Gujarati publication, and due to editor Barjorjee Nowrosjee's enterprise in sending review copies of his annual cartoon albums to press editors in India and abroad. The bilingual aspect also gave the newspaper a "provincial stamp" and restricted circulation in India.[27] Reviewing *Hindi Punch* provided editors with an opportunity to situate it against a larger canvas of the world of Indian cartoon-based newspapers. From the *Indian People*, published in Allahabad, readers learn that around 1909 very few newspapers "indulge in cartoons." Yet, the report continues, the cartoon's unique form of critique is "the very best method of pointing out the shortcoming of any individual or a constitution, and it is the only method in which the individual towards whom the finger is pointed is not likely to take umbrage."[28] The *Indian People* editor seems to be Nowrosjee's fan for he heaps praise, adding that the *Hindi Punch* was the "only high class humor paper in the whole of India," could "hold on its own with the London *Punch*," and "rouse the envy of many an eminent cartoonist in the west."[29] Complementing this assessment, the *Oriental Review* gave a snapshot of the history of humor in India, comparing it to the West. In this view, the *Hindi Punch* exemplified the "progress of civilization" and demonstrated that "our humor also is becoming more delicate and less boisterous." Although not directly responding to Dickens, but certainly touching on the theme of native humor that he described in his long 1862 essay, "Punch in India," the *Oriental Review* was convinced that although the "Indian people are said not to have a great stock of "the saving sense of humor," such claims were "falsified by many ancient works which have in them a distinct gleam of humor." This brief history of Indian humor gave it a past and the ability to transform – to become delicate and therefore, "civilized" like *Punch*.[30] In these favorable reviews, the *Hindi Punch* cartoonist had "caught the highest phase of humor – the laughter that is ever near to tears" and the influence of such humor was "cast on the side of purity and progress in social life and sobriety and dignity in politics."[31]

Sharply contradicting the accolades showered by friendly peers, the *Times of India* projected the *Hindi Punch* as far removed from British norms and senses of cartooning. In this perspective, the *Hindi Punch* cartoons were "merely an illustration to a political moral." They did not adhere to the British cartooning practices of "Master" *Punch* cartoonists, such as Sir Carruthers Gould, John Tenniel, Bernard Partridge, Edward Sambourne, John Leech, Charles Keene, and Leonard Raven-Hill. That is, the *Hindi Punch* cartoonist neither prioritized "drawing" nor "fun." Furthermore, the scathing review noted the cartoonist's "lamentably weak" draughtsmanship, which was concealed by overloading "unnecessary detail" and the inability to evoke likeness. The final nail in this coffin was the proclamation that the "Indian cartoon" has "neither wit nor humor." Offering some consolation, the *Times of India* review acknowledged that the *Hindi Punch* cartoonist had "political insight," and unlike Carruthers Gould, was not spiteful. Nevertheless, this was not adequate to stake claim of being a "Punch artist." Thus, to "western eyes," which the *Times of India* had, the *Hindi Punch* was no *Punch* but it was comparable to the "smaller western papers."[32]

The *Hindi Punch* albums were designed as a record of the social and political history for the year. W. T. Stead's fascination with cartoons as news was predicated on their accessibility – important to the format of the *Review of Reviews*, which was designed as a news digest for the busy professional (Khanduri 2007). And even while there was interest in tapping colonial news, for Stead, these cartoons as well as others from the world provided a glimpse and knowledge of how others, especially the colonies, perceived the British Empire. This emphasis on cartoons as political knowledge was not unique to Stead. The published reviews of the *Hindi Punch* cartoons also convey the conviction that these graphic satires were not just about refreshing the "dryness" of life but valued as a source of news, sociopolitical knowledge, and for "sly hints" to tackle the "social problems of the day."[33] The *Hindu* editor, for example, considered the *Hindi Punch*, a valuable "study of contemporary political and social history."[34] The *Bombay Gazette* praised the *Hindi Punch* cartoons as presenting a "true exponent of reasoning Indian opinion."[35] The *Madras Mail* welcomed the *Hindi Punch* cartoonist for taking the view of the "shrewd spectator rather than the partisan."[36] The *Praja Bandhu* went a step beyond these perspectives on cartoons as knowledge and contended that the *Hindi Punch* cartoons appealed "more powerfully than written articles covering many pages."[37] Thus, for some observers, newspaper cartoons did not merely compete with prose, but exceeded it.

Nonsense or liberty?

For the colonial government, the profusion and popularity of the comic newspapers, particularly in the vernacular, transformed satire into something dangerous and therefore worthy of surveillance. Since the vernacular press considered itself and was in effect an unofficial spokesman of the public, its movements and fluctuations were registered in detail, as the weekly *Selections from the Vernacular Newspapers* made for the perusal of government officials amply testify. The selector and translator of these press items became an important intermediary between the press and the government (see Dalmia 2001, pp. 230–2). In the North West Provinces, Priya Das, MA, was the government reporter, and he prepared fortnightly reports of the vernacular press for these years. Although Hindi and Urdu were not communalized to denote Hindu and Muslim identities, caste factions marked the politics and rivalry of the vernacular newspapers. In his records, Das notes that "the *Oudh Punch* obviously rails at the proprietor of the *Oudh Akhbar* and the first article was critical of 'Banias.'" Das adds:

The *Oudh Punch* is at enmity with the *Oudh Akhbar*; therefore neither of them loses an opportunity to have a fling at the other. The *Oudh Punch* is more explicit and outspoken in its attacks upon its contemporary. It usually calls the *Oudh Akhbar* the *Banian Akhbar* in contempt. In its issue of the 26th March it censures the proprietor of the *Oudh Akhbar* as being of "those men who are in the habit of extorting money from native chiefs, and to whom His Excellency the Viceroy and Governor General of India referred in his speech at the legislative council at the time of the passing the Vernacular Press Act."[38]

Das's notes on vernacular newspapers not only suggest the rivalries that shaped their politics but also the convergence of caste categories as crucial for signifying publications. Caste is interpreted in current scholarship as a "modern phenomenon" that emerged with the colonial encounter (Dirks 2001). The comment on the *Oudh Akhbar* proprietor exemplifies the processes through which caste categories came to be seen as embodying certain characteristics. Bania as a discreditable social category came to embody the "habit of extorting money."

The colonial state's anxiety about the potential danger from vernacular satire was also triggered by the ambivalent space of cartoons, in which liberalism marked by a tolerance for political satire was articulated through the nonsensical. Such nonsense, exemplified by vernacular cartoons and modeled after *Punch*, taunted liberal ideals. As a response to this popular visual "nonsense," supporters of the colonial state felt compelled to distinguish between liberty and irresponsible critique and dismissed the colonial *Punch*es as "upstart *Punch*es." In 1890, the *Lytton Gazette* complained that "some of our contemporaries were under the impression that the liberty of the Press meant nothing more than the practice of abusing the government and the Native Chiefs. Some vernacular newspapers specially the upstart *Punch*es depended for their success upon writing nonsense" (*Selections*, 1878, p. 307). Such dismissal of colonial cartoons was also part of a strategy to consistently harp on the incompleteness and impossibility of colonial modernity and its accompanying liberalism. Assertions of colonial failure in the realm of political cartoons and journalism were critical for the logic of imperial presence and surveillance. The colonial officials cast the success of these nonsensical newspapers as a social lacuna in which colonial subjects grossly misunderstood liberalism. Not only the colonial state administrators, but also their loyal editors and scribes, reported on nonsensical newspapers. The *Lytton Gazette*, an example of the loyal faction of the press in colonial India, was among newspapers which deemed the satirical modes of journalistic writing, particularly in the vernacular, nonsensical and problematic. For this loyal faction of the press, the *Punch* versions in particular had mistaken the norms of journalistic propriety; rather than exercising their "liberty" judiciously, the vernacular newspapers were misinterpreting liberty as the freedom to criticize the colonial state. For example, the *Lytton Gazette* cited the *Rewari Punch* from Gurgaon as among the newspapers "that needs to be watched":

This paper was formerly well conducted but its tone has changed for the worse. It made an offensive attack on the viceroy in 1903 and used to criticize the affairs of native states in a very objectionable manner. It contains religious news and often personal attacks in which real names are not given. It occasionally published seditious extracts from other papers. The comic supplement was political in nature. (*Selections*, 1910)

Lytton Gazette's observations about the upstart vernacular *Punch*es also registered the colonial state's frustration and surprise at the popularity of the nonsensical. This elision of the nonsensical and abuse of liberty (disloyalty) opened up several questions about the relationship of politics and satire.

Facetious writing and picking holes

In his notes on the Urdu newspaper *Oudh Punch*, Das identified select articles which he mostly described as "facetious writing," thereby affirming for officials what the English newspaper *Lytton Gazette* had remarked for the vernacular press. Das gave particular attention to comic newspapers, noting their circulation and details of the editors and proprietors, and often included comments on the political tone of each newspaper. For the *Oudh Punch*, he also noted some cartoons, simply describing but not interpreting them. Thus details about the social world of the "comic papers," as well as their intense rivalries, are available now as records of surveillance.

As part of the state's surveillance for 1910, Das tracked not only the newspaper contents and circulation numbers but also the social background, family genealogy, professional links, castes, and politics of various editors and proprietors of the *Punch* newspapers. Das also noted the age of all proprietors, who usually doubled as editors. Thus the colonial reports contain a mix of details: for example, that Sheikh Sajjad Hussain of the *Oudh Punch* was the son of Mansur Ali, a deputy collector in the Nizam's dominions, and Mahmud-ul-Hasan Sheikh of the *Rafiq Punch* was from a family with landed property. Das also noted that Saiyid Zahur Ahmad of the *Sar Punch* was twenty-five years old, and for a year was a professor of Arabic and Persian at St. Andrew's College at Gorakhpur. He had thereafter worked in the *Punch Bahadur* Press in Bombay for a year and started his own publication on September 27, 1909. The *Punch Bahadur* was an Urdu comic weekly published in Bombay with a circulation of 1,500 copies in 1910. It was edited and owned by Muhammad Abdul Hamid Azimullaakhan, who was then forty-four years old and a native of Delhi.

Das's fine-combed review revealed a quarrel between the *Panjab Punch* of Lahore and the *Suhel-i-Hind* of Meerut: "They pick holes in each other's writings, and abuse each other." The satirical newspapers in the region were competing with each other as well as with non-satirical popular newspapers like the *Oudh Akhbar*. Such competition was fraught with bitter rivalries. The proprietors of the *Oudh Punch*, for example, were engaged in a long-standing dispute with Munshi Nawal Kishore Sharma, the proprietor of the leading Urdu newspaper, *Oudh Akhbar*. The *Oudh Punch* of September 17, 1910 noted:

Some ill conditioned fellow has spread a rumour to the effect that the Lieutenant Governor of the North-Western Provinces is so displeased with the *Oudh Punch* that His Honour has called for a list of its subscribers in order to exhibit his anger towards them. We think it necessary to state for the satisfaction of our subscribers that no such list has been demanded from us. We ask the ass by whom this rumour was propagated how His Honour can legally do this, or how it is possible for His Honour to chastise those of the subscribers who live in native States, and other provinces outside the limits of his jurisdiction. Even if it be granted that His Honour is not favourably disposed toward the *Oudh Punch*, yet he is a man of high rank and culture, has a grave disposition, and perhaps also has wit. The conduct of the man who has propagated such a false rumour is foolish and ungrateful and is that of an enemy in the guise of a sycophant. In a stroke, the editor of the *Oudh Punch* not only criticized propagators of such vile rumors against its paper but also made a clear connection between rank, culture, and wit, which it supposed the "esteemed" lieutenant governor possessed.

As the colonial state confronted its anxieties about satire in journalism by intensifying the surveillance of vernacular newspapers, such surveillance also led to the proscription of some vernacular cartoons. While on the one hand proscription closed the space for political critique, on the other it opened a space to critique colonial liberalism.

Bull dog or British officer?

Criticism of the "upstart *Punch*es" and their supposed misunderstanding of journalistic ethics was countered by the vernacular press. This counter-criticism in defense of the *Punch*es was leveled at the loyal factions that included both English and vernacular newspapers. Among those defending the vernacular *Punch*es was the *Agra Akhbar*, an Urdu weekly. The *Agra Akhbar* published a long article criticizing the conduct of those members of the vernacular press (like the Urdu *Oudh Akhbar*), "who abuse the whole body of native editors in order to ingratiate themselves with the government." For the *Agra Akhbar*, the politics of such vernacular newspapers was suspect. Further, the colonial government and the loyal faction of the press's criticism leveled against the *Punch*es (like the Urdu *Oudh Punch*) was misdirected and contradictory to the liberal ideals upheld for the press both in the colony and in Britain.

The *Agra Akhbar* expressed surprise at the colonial government's displeasure at some of the vernacular newspapers' satire and chipped away at the image of imperial liberalism. *Agra Akhbar* explicated its position through a particular caricature that was published in a Bengali *Punch* in Calcutta and reversed charges about dubious journalistic practices of its faction, by charging the colonial state and its loyal faction in the press with misunderstanding the true nature of liberalism. By implying a better understanding of true liberalism, the *Agra Akhbar* was making a radical claim for (re)defining liberalism:

Hundreds of articles like those condemned by the government in vernacular newspapers are published every day in English papers both here and in England. Our native journalists learnt this excellent style of writing from the civilized nation. But as the vernacular languages are impure, the thoughts and sentiment of English journalists when expressed in the vernacular languages lose their purity and become impure and mischievous. The truth is that we are condemned for writing what we had learnt from our tutors. The correspondent of the *Oudh Akhbar* has at times written articles in condemnation of the Urdu comic paper (the *Oudh Punch*). But we will speak here of a cartoon of an English paper which will serve to purify or enlighten his mind. During the administration of a redoubtable high European officer of a fiery temper an English *Punch* was started at Calcutta to explain the object and scope of the speeches of that officer. In one number of the *Punch* there appeared the picture of a bulldog. The picture looked at from the front, appeared to be that of a dog, but when it was looked at from the side, the head of the dog appeared to resemble that of the officer in question. The letterpress of the cartoon was – "I fear this only barks but has not the power to bite." The whole English community, resident in India, praised the cartoon, and perhaps the whole community of Calcutta were jubilant over the cartoon for several months. Has any Urdu or Bengali *Punch*, we ask ever published such an indecent and impudent cartoon? Has any Urdu paper ever been guilty of such impertinence? If an Urdu *Punch*, in imitation of the above cartoon, publishes a picture placing the head of a fool on the body of an ass, will the writer of the Urdu *Punch* be considered as the inventor or imitator of this kind of impertinence? Thousands of articles, like the extracts from the writings from the vernacular newspapers laid before the legislative council, have already been published in the English papers of India and England ... In these circumstances it would have been proper to chastise the tutor and not to punish and reprove the innocent pupil." (*Agra Akhbar*, May 21, 1910, in *Selections*, pp. 463–7)

Visual tricks: impertinence or imitation?

In rallying support for the cartoons of the *Oudh Punch*, the *Agra Akhbar* asked important questions around the seemingly deceptive liberalism of the colonial government and its contradictory set of standards for the colony. But even more than disrupting this charade of the colonial government, the *Agra Akhbar* raised two issues that complicated its critique. First, the *Agra Akhbar* denounced as "indecent" and "impudent" the particular cartoon, which had in fact received wide appreciation from British quarters. Thus the *Agra Akhbar* set its own higher standard for a moral aesthetic that would disallow such caricatures. An underlying observation of the *Agra Akhbar* was that the thought of such base cartoons hardly emanated from vernaculars; it was, in fact, a product of colonial tutelage.

Second, it questioned whether the Indian vernacular writer and cartoonist who had come into being only by imbibing journalistic and cartooning skills from the British should be seen as an "inventor" or "imitator." If the colonial journalist and cartoonist were imitators, then would it not be a contradiction to penalize them for producing something they had learned from their British tutors? Thus penalizing the vernacular press implied they were inventors crafting their own cartoons and journalism.[39] Having identified this quandary, the *Agra Akhbar* laid claim to the British lineage for vernacular writing and cartooning in colonial India, laying open the contradiction inherent in the censorious colonial government, which could laugh at the cartoon in English but not when it was reproduced in the vernacular. Why, the *Agra Akhbar* questioned, was impertinence always in the vernacular? Why was it that English cartoons when translated to the vernacular became "impure" and "mischievous"? The cartoon and caricature of a bulldog that tricked the eye were perhaps deemed clever and therefore lauded by the English readers but, claimed the *Agra Akhbar* in a tactical move, the vernacular press did not play such visual tricks that demeaned individuals, and if it did, chastisement and not applause would greet them.

With their objection to an Urdu *Punch* cartoon and their constant surveillance, the British were confronted with the paradox of going against their conventions of liberal principles, which accommodated political humor. The colonial "native" proprietors candidly acknowledged the British *Punch* as their model for the vernacular versions. This acknowledgment of "borrowing" and "learning" the visual vocabulary of *Punch* posed a challenge to the colonial state's logic of surveillance and proscription of cartoons. If the British metropolis could celebrate *Punch*, then surely the officials would be equally tolerant of *Punch*-style graphic satire in the colonies. After all, the civilizing mission was tied to native inculcation of modern habits.

Given the absence of a cultural memory of vernacular *Punch*es, colonial records and archives offer an opportunity to access some aspects of the discussion around colonial cartoons. The small voice of visuality of the *Agra Akhbar* editor is a generative and propitious moment that brings into sharp focus native recognition of the imperial ploy that distinguishes between "imitator" and "inventor" in order to sustain the fiction of Western liberalism. The native editors asked colonial authorities if vernacular cartoonists, particularly those charged with impertinence, were "imitators" or "inventors"? In response to their own question, the vernacular editors claimed they were imitators. This acknowledgment of being imitators is a productive moment for understanding the derivative nature of colonial politics, and of postcolonial memory. Furthermore, as sites of rational debate the marginal space of vernacular cartoons where native editors claimed authority for interpreting and practicing liberal discourse made mimicry a tactical modernity.

The vernacular *Punch*es, and their retrieval as a moment of disbelief in colonial liberalism, complicates the place of memory as a space for subaltern recalling. Stoler and Strassler's critique of the "hydraulic model" in postcolonial contexts signals caution about romanticizing subaltern memory as an alternate narrative and therefore as resistance (2000, p. 7). In the context of India, feminist historians have justly sought to recover and highlight women's memory and biography as knowledge of the past (Chakravarti 1998; Minault 1998; Burton 2003; Forbes 2005). The relationship between memory and archive is tenuous; what the cartoonists I met remember and told me, and what I read in the archive, are entwined in the politics of representation, as well as in the politics of authors who tickle the presumed border between memory and archive. Marjorie Shostak's dilemma confronted me when facing both memory and archive: "I didn't know what to make of it. It seemed too strange to be a lie ... What was clear however was that Nisa believed the story as she told it" (Shostak 2001, p. 29).

When evoked in relation to the nation state, colonial memory can be hegemonic remembering.[40] Building on the commentary in the pages of the *Agra Akhbar* and the ambivalence of colonial experience (Bhabha 1984), memory about the aesthetic sensibility of cartooning as derivative (and therefore mimicry) can be framed as a tactical modernity to claim resemblance and retain the potential for menace.

"Bhayankar drishya! Napunsak darshak": terrifying scene! impotent spectators

"I have a file that that you should see." When I was reading colonial surveillance notes for the vernacular press, the Lucknow State Archive librarian's suggestion immediately interested me. It contained some proscribed cartoons from 1931. As I took a closer look at the faded cartoons, I recognized the stylized signature in Hindi on the left corner – "Kedar." The two pages were a composite of smaller cartoons. They reminded me of the *Hindu Punch* cartoons I had seen in New Delhi's Nehru Memorial Museum and Library Archive.

"Bhayankar drishya! Napunsak darshak" was a scene unfolding in a railway station. While alighting from the train, a woman in a sari is mishandled by a man in hat, black coat, white pants, and black shoes.

He is probably the stationmaster. The medley of onlookers, all men, is differentiated through their dress. They include various clothing styles – the English hat, the boat cap, the Muslim cap, pants, dhoti; one man was smoking a cigar, and others were holding long walking sticks. Dress was identity. These were men from the city, the village; they were Western and traditional. The railway station, a public space and transitory point, was the scene for terror and impotence. The terror was in the manner Hindu women were treated and touched. Impotence lay in the act of witnessing and not intervening to protest.

Visualizing colonial subjects, the cartoon suggested that all Indian men – Western, traditional, Hindu, and Muslim – were impotent. New public spaces such as the railway station, where Hindu women came into contact with strangers, mainly men, then, became a scene that captured a moment of masculine degeneration and feminine/Hindu danger. Such space was also a pretext for men such as the stationmaster to trespass expected social norms of respectable distance. The threshold of this impropriety was captured tellingly in the woman's movement alighting from compartment number 3 that has just arrived at the station – one hand gripping the handlebar, the other nudging away the stationmaster; the passenger has one foot on the train and the other almost set on the platform. Black coats, striped coats, white hats with a ribbon, boat caps and the cap with a fez, the passenger's white sari and black blouse, the details on the train and the plume of smoke from its steam engine – the play of shapes, black and white, fine and bold lines to stage the scene – were carefully contrasted and constructed for the reader, who viewed both the scene of terror and the onlookers viewing the scene.

The spectator, witnessing, and seeing are a significant part of cartoonist Kedar's plot. If, on seeing, the cartoon readers were not provoked, then they too would be among the spectators, impotent witnesses. The message for intervention called to all readers, and the underlying presumption was that they were obviously male. The cartoon's inclusion among proscribed materials tells that it attracted the attention of more than the expected audience. Although the cartoon was in Hindi, surveillance through interpreters extended the colonial state's reach.

Tactical, tactile, and stratified liberalism

The ambivalence of satire cast it as a particularly problematic genre of journalism and invited condemnation of the vernacular *Punch*es as "upstart." Situated at a gray boundary between satire and truth, the cartoons trod an uneasy line between form and deformity through the use of caricature.[41] "The truth is that we are condemned for writing what we had learnt from our tutors," wrote the editor of the *Agra Akhbar*. With this far-reaching observation he struck at the logic of colonial rule's liberal standard. The cartoon's visual ambiguity generated a forceful critique in the form of an important editorial question for colonial administrators: Why was it that the colonial state recognized a risk of impertinence in the vernacular? Such concerns with the empire's conspiratorial tendencies unfolded in another direction, too – the perceived adverse impact of cartoons on women and children. The native editor's question could be turned around: Why was it that the native editors recognized a risk of impertinence in women and children?

Baijnath Kedia's *Vyang Chitraval*, a cartoon album published in Hindi from Calcutta and priced Rs. 2, was among publications that contained an assortment of cartoons. Containing seventy-nine cartoons, this first volume dealt with modern times – graduate education, Gandhian politics, and Hindu–Muslim relationships. The preface preempted and soothed the male reader's nervousness about cartoons and whether the book was worth the expense, and assured the reader that the cartoon book could be safely handed to children and women as a pedagogical text that would make them think without stress:

Children, the old, youth, women, and men – thereby everyone's attention is drawn very quickly to pictures. This is the reason that when explaining any subject with the help of pictures, the extent of the impact it has on the mind on all ordinary persons, such is not possible through blank definitions, writings, or books.

With the help of pictures [illustrations] people with very little effort acquire knowledge of a very large amount of things, but along with it they also get entertained. And when there are cartoons then what more is there to ask? With those illustrations there is even more entertainment and their impact is deeper. Because on seeing the peculiarities or deformities of the satirical illustrations people double up with laughter and in this way their mind is relieved of the weight of exercising its self. Thereafter when their attention goes to the emotion then those thoughts are deeply imprinted on their mind.

It is with these thoughts in mind we resolved to publish a cartoon album. Fortunately some satirical drawings published in the weekly "Vijay" were also present with us. Then we arranged for some more illustrations and mustered the courage to present them to the readers in this form. Certainly it is the reader's job to judge the extent to which the issue has been entertaining and educational; nevertheless, we can at least say that in this book we have attempted to give religious, social and political satirical illustrations, numerous subjects and have also given attention to the issue of ornate aspects. Our thought is that this book will work for the readers/patrons as a stationary bioscope, from which their entertainment will continue and along [with it] many useful things will be known.

Apart from this the biggest thing is that this book can be given without any hesitation even in the hands of children and women. Our belief is that they will benefit from this book. (Kedia 1930, Preface)

The reassuring note on cartoons as safe reading materials also points to the fact that women were among readers solicited for this genre. An advertisement in the *Hindu Punch* for its special Congress issue shows a winged woman aloft, dropping copies of the issue to the readers below. The readers, both women and men, shown receiving and reading the publications are marked Hindu through their dress and turbans – not surprising since *Hindu Punch* advocated a Hindu politics.[42] Like speech, which conveys the nuances of language, written words about the cartoon – a novelty for colonial India – presented an emerging vocabulary for talking to readers about an unusual form. The social problems the cartoons satirized – such as university education and Hindu conventions of "untouchability" – were tied to other modern practices and things, and the social reform aspect of the *Vyang Chitravali* could not be dissociated from politics. Laughter was a way of thinking about these social issues and modern selves in the quest of self-education. Parenthetically including women and children as the constituency that needed caution in being introduced to novel cultural forms reinforced the position of adult males as responsible, rational social subjects in the family unit – they would make the call about subscribing to comic newspapers and cartoon books at home. Such infantilizing of women gendered the imagined liberal subject and resulted in native editors mirroring the colonial state's anxiety about vernacular impertinence.

Although in relation to the colonial state vernacular print media were indeed marginal, they can be seen as elite attempts to establish authority through local idioms of humor (Pollock 1995). As a form that disclosed tactical, tactile, and stratified liberalism, critiquing British dualism, vernacular *Punch*es and cartoons in India set the stage for an important form of subversion. They were the early shoots of a long future growth in India of political cartoons and humor, demanding inclusive liberal values. With these cartoons begins a history of uneasy questions about the logic of liberal governance, which, in the colonial context of a racialized and gendered power differential, infused political cartoons with a surplus of meanings. To track some of the ways in which cartoons somersaulted and accumulated this surplus, Gandhi's experiments with cartoons in colonial South Africa and India are strikingly eye-opening.

2   Gandhi and the satyagraha of cartoons: cultivating a taste

Cultivating a liking for British newspapers, London 1888

"My mother's love always haunted me," wrote Gandhi of his time in London. "At night tears would stream down my cheeks" (1993, pp. 44–5). Disoriented by the new cultural milieu and the limitations of his vegetarian diet, and during mealtimes too overcome by shyness to ask his host for more helpings to satisfy his appetite, Gandhi was eighteen, hungry, and homesick in London. It was 1888, and he was in London's Union College to study law. He "continually had to be on guard"; he learned from his mentors not to touch other people's things and not to address people as "sir," as was customary in India, because in England, only servants and subordinates used the term. Trying to fit in, Gandhi "cultivated a liking" for newspapers, and regularly spent an hour glancing over the *Daily News*, the *Daily Telegraph*, and the *Pall Mall Gazette* (p. 47). During that same year, 1888, there was much happening in the world of British cartoons. The popular Francis Carruthers Gould became the first newspaper staff cartoonist, contributing a topical cartoon to the *Pall Mall Gazette*, and Bernard Partridge's *Punch* cartoons were being widely celebrated.

In London, reading newspapers became part of Gandhi's training in British etiquette under the tutelage of one of his contacts, Sergeant Shukla. These years saw a profusion of illustrated journals in England, and although photographs were yet to become a part of news, Gandhi must have seen several cartoons. This exposure may have shaped his enduring interest in their interpretative politics. Other aspects would have played a role too, including Gandhi's acute sensitivity to cultural forms and practices as sources of knowledge and power.

After completing his law studies and prior to his departure to India, Gandhi lacked the confidence to emulate his role model, the England-trained luminary and lawyer Sir Pherozeshah Mehta, who had the ability to "roar like a lion" in court. A mentor to Indian students, Frederick Pincutt, recommended that Gandhi finesse his professional skills by

68

polishing his knowledge of Indian history and human nature. He recommended Sir John W. Kaye's and Colonel George B. Malleson's six-volume study of the 1857 Mutiny in India (1889) to supplement Gandhi's lack of history, and Johann Casper Lavater's book on physiognomy (1878) to inform him about human nature. Gandhi read Lavater's *Physiognomy* in London, and the books on the Mutiny he read later, in South Africa.

Physiognomy was extremely popular in England. Since its German publication in 1770 and subsequent translations in French and English, the essays had appeared in various forms – summaries, pirated copies, abridged versions, parodies, imitations, and serial volumes (Graham 1961). The book's interest lay in Lavater's exposition of the relationship between physical features and inner traits, allowing a textual reading of human nature based on people's looks, such as the shape of lips, nose, forehead, and brows. The book's translation of the physical into mental and emotional disposition was illustrated with rich engravings by famous artists such as William Blake. The visual imagination of the link between inner and outer made *Physiognomy* particularly useful for attorneys and cartoonists – professionals, who in glimpses and strokes, size up human character. Those with greater knowledge of biology, zoology, anatomy, physiology, and anthropology may have found the book lacking scientific merit, but it "at least acknowledged these fields and made some pretense at employing their information and methodology" (Graham 1961, pp. 562–3). Lavater's book did not move Gandhi, however, who found it "scarcely interesting" (1993, p. 82). In those pages, Gandhi would have seen the illustrations, and he read the description of Shakespeare's physiognomy. On Shakespeare's appearance, Lavater exclaimed: "Where is the outline that can portray genius? Yet who does not read, in this outline, imperfect as it is, from pure physiognomical sensation, the clear, the capacious, the rapid mind, all conceiving, all embracing, that, with equal swiftness and facility, imagines, creates, produces?" (Lavater 1878, p. 34). Nevertheless, after reading this, Gandhi wrote that he "did not acquire the knack of finding out the Shakespeares walking up and down the streets of London" (p. 82). He remained tentative about his skill in oration and law, but with a law degree from London, Gandhi left Britain to begin his practice in India.

Culture shock and bitter poison, India 1891

Gandhi's homesickness in London was followed by distressing culture shock on his return to India. After a disappointing stint in Bombay's legal circle, Gandhi moved to Rajkot, in Gujarat, where his brother also worked performing legal documentation. The "poisonous atmosphere" there would give Gandhi a bitter taste of colonial power. After moving there,

Gandhi received an uncomfortable request. His brother was in the grip of an official inquiry led by a British officer of Gandhi's acquaintance from his days in England. Although Gandhi hesitated to intervene on ethical grounds, upon his brother's insistence that "only influence worked here," he decided to meet the officer and put in a word on his brother's behalf. Gandhi's brother swayed him by assuring that things worked differently in India: "You do not know Kathiawad. And have yet to know the world" (Gandhi 1993, p. 98). At the appointed meeting, Gandhi soon realized, indeed, that Kathiawad was different from England – but not in the way his brother had assured him. Midway through their meeting, the officer refused to entertain further conversation. Gandhi's plea to be heard prompted the Sahib to command his peon to oust Gandhi from the room. Although later Gandhi consoled himself about the impropriety of seeking the meeting, he was shocked by the Sahib's impatience and the inordinate extent of his power. The follow-up plan to petition against the Sahib's rude behavior also proved futile. Consulted for advice, Sir Pherozeshah Mehta, a prominent lawyer visiting Rajkot at the time, returned a cautionary message for Gandhi: "Such things are the common experience of many vakils and barristers. He is still fresh from England and hot-blooded. He does not know British officers . . . Tell him he has yet to know life" (Gandhi 1993, p. 99).

This advice was "bitter poison," swallowed begrudgingly by the twenty-one-year-old Gandhi. Now he found himself again in a world about which he was unsure. "I had heard what a British officer was like, but up to now had never been face to face with one" Gandhi wrote (1993, p. 97). It seems that his years in England (1888–91), had made him a stranger to colonial authority in his own country. It was telling that the Sahib had been acquainted with Gandhi, albeit briefly, while on leave in England. But now when face to face with Gandhi in Kathiawad, his role was an "officer on duty" in India. Gandhi was a colonial subject, and he felt it at every moment in Rajkot.

Disillusioned with the lack of professional ethics, witnessing the exercise of power, Gandhi's recollections of these years were replete with disappointment and depression. If his time in Rajkot taught young Gandhi about colonial arrogance, then in South Africa, which he first visited in 1893 on legal business, he learned that gestures, dress, and words could construct and dent colonial authority.

The coolie-barrister: an unwelcome visitor in South Africa, 1893

"I took my seat in a first class compartment and the train started. At Germiston the guard came to examine the tickets. He was angry to find me there and signaled to me with his finger to go to the third class. I showed him my first class ticket. 'That doesn't matter,' said he, 'remove to the third class.'" But Gandhi remained where he was. The lone white passenger in the compartment objected to the guard's directive. "If you want to travel with a coolie, what do I care?" Disgusted, the guard went his way, leaving Gandhi and the white passenger to their journey (Gandhi 1993, p. 117). A small victory. On other occasions, after several attempts with a valid ticket, Gandhi finally secured a place in the first-class cabin. Emotionally bruised, angry, fearful, humiliated, and assaulted by white railway officials during such train journeys, Gandhi – the British-educated barrister from India visiting South Africa – learned that here he was a "sami" (drawn from a common Tamil suffix, Swami) and a "coolie" (a porter). Samis and coolies could not travel in the first-class compartments or even check into hotels. This social ostracizing illuminated for Gandhi that place and time could easily reverse social status. Hindus practiced "untouchability" in India, relegating "low-caste" individuals as social pariahs. But here in South Africa, all Indians were "untouchables" and called coolies, the Hindustani term for a porter transformed into a slur.

In South Africa and before that in London and in India, Gandhi's encounter with power embedded in colonialism's cultural politics made him attentive to the significance of dress, gesture, newspapers, cartoons, and ordinary details of everyday life. In South Africa, Gandhi was quick to record the immense potential of language to paralyze power, albeit momentarily:

"*Sami*" is a Tamil suffix occurring after many Tamil names, and it is nothing else than the Samskrit *Swami*, meaning master. Whenever, therefore, an Indian resented being addressed as a "*sami*" and had enough wit in him, he would try to return the compliment in this wise: "You may call me *sami*, but you forget that *sami* means a master. I am not your master!" Some Englishman would wince at this, while others would get angry, swear at the Indian and, if there was a chance, would even belabor him; for "*sami*" to him was nothing better than a term of contempt. (Gandhi 1993, p. 107)

If, in appropriating Indian vocabulary, whites in South Africa produced new social categories and offensive terms, then asserting native knowledge to correct this misuse of terms vexed power and prompted chuckles.

The *girmit* on turbans

Not all Indians in South Africa were the same, nor had they traveled so far away from India for the same purpose. The majority, Gandhi noted, were "ignorant pauper agriculturalists," and a few were educated merchants.[1] Historian Uma Mesthrie notes two phases of Indian immigration and their shifting professional profile. The first came in 1860 as laborers. By 1905, forty-five years after their arrival in South Africa, some of the descendants of indentured laborers constituted the "nucleus of the Indian petty bourgeoisie." The second phase in 1865 included primarily Gujarati traders and some Christian Indians from India and Mauritius who were teachers, interpreters, catechists, and traders (1997, pp. 99–100). A few days in Natal, observing Indians, revealed to Gandhi that religion and class shaped the experience of colonial power: "One was that of Musalman merchants, who could call themselves 'Arabs.' The Hindu clerks were neither here nor there, unless they cast in their lot with the 'Arabs.' The Parsi clerks would call themselves Persians. These three classes had some social relations with one another. But by far the largest class was that composed of Tamil, Telugu and North Indian indentured and freed laborers."[2]

Indentured laborers or Girmitiyas worked under harsh conditions. If they chose to leave their employers – masters – without notice, then they would endure criminal proceedings and be imprisoned. Indentured labor resembled slavery in that the laborer was treated as property. The relationship also resonated with the practice of untouchability. South Africa was, for Gandhi, a prism for viewing the ways in which familiar forms of hierarchy, segregation, and difference from various social worlds gained new meaning and were reinforced in novel ways. Indians invited particular attention because after serving the five-year term of indentured labor, they were free to settle down in South Africa. They seized this freedom and opportunity to cultivate cane and other produce, while living frugally. Their enterprise and thrift resulted in prosperity, success, and unwelcome competition for their white neighbors. Brown colonized people received welcome only as long as they were visible as indentured laborers.

As Gandhi settled into Natal, a visit to the Durban court quickly set him on track with the region's demographics and turban politics. Appearing in connection with his patron Sheth Abdullah's case, Gandhi experienced the complex social messages surrounding headgear. Contrary to the magistrate's expectation and court rule, Gandhi refused to remove his turban, and walked out of the meeting. The brief episode provided a teaching moment for Sheth Abdullah, and he told Gandhi of the cultural *girmit* (pidgin for "agreement") on headgear: Muslims, if wearing their Islamic dress, could don the turban in court, but all other Indians had to remove theirs. Indentured laborers and any "Indian stranger" in the presence of a European had to remove headgear, whether it was a cap, scarf, or turban.

The rule to remove the turban in court appropriated Indian cultural practices (across region and faith), creating an ensemble of gestures for the performance of colonial subjugation. These practices circumscribing sentiments of honor and dishonor were enforced within institutional spaces such as British courts, in the presences of white officials, and in the conduct of official matters. However, imposing the general remove-the-turban rule when it comprised part of Muslim dress, the British presumed, would ruffle religious sensitivities. Indian cultural norms of honor and respect provided the British with traditions for evoking their own exalted social status, but they remained cautious about encroaching on the perceived religious domain. For Gandhi and others from the Indian milieu of turbans, to remove one was a sign of dishonor but it also came to be imbued with colonial politics and its sense of order.

An obvious solution would be to begin wearing a British hat, but Sheth Abdullah dissuaded Gandhi from that option. He informed Gandhi that among the indentured Indian laborers in South Africa there were three categories: Hindus, Muslims (Musalmans, as Gandhi referred to them, following Hindustani vocabulary), and Christians. Of these groups, Christians were numerous at the time, converted descendants of indentured Indians. They wore English dress and primarily worked as waiters in hotels. Thus an Indian wearing a hat was presumed to be a waiter. So there was every chance that Gandhi, a "coolie-barrister," would be mistaken for a waiter. Sheth Abdullah embellished his advice with some more angles for consideration – the turban looked nice on Gandhi, and would show solidarity with others who continued to wear it as part of their cultural identity. This sealed the matter, and Gandhi wrote a letter on this subject to the local newspaper. Gandhi's letter to a newspaper in favor of the turban quickly attracted supporters and critics.

The politics of name calling and dress set the stage for the observant Gandhi to tap into colonial forms of authority in daily routines. For Gandhi, such knowledge was important for understanding the mentality of the colonizer and inventing practices for subverting authority. Gandhi's moments of angst and despair, leading to reflection, coincided with the observation of social norms that he had to learn as an outsider in South Africa. This attention to gesture and dress is striking, given contemporary anthropology's marginal attention to this matter (Tarlo 1996, p. 4).[3] Along with Sheth Abdullah, Gandhi shared awareness about how the British were symbolically exercising power and creating new codes of authority and submission. Such gestures of submission that related the colonizer and the colonized also marked the relationship between Indians of varying status in South Africa. The coolie barrister soon built a reputation as an advocate for expatriate Indians.

"I had put in scarcely three or four months' practice, and the Congress was still in its infancy, when a Tamil man in tattered clothes, head-gear in hand, two front teeth broken and his mouth bleeding stood before me trembling and weeping. He had been heavily belaboured by his master."[4]

When he faced Gandhi, Balasundaram held his headscarf in his hand. Embarrassed at this momentary equation with colonial authority, Gandhi asked Balasundaram to wear his scarf, which he donned with some hesitation: "I could perceive the pleasure on his face."[5] As Gandhi's short stay gradually lengthened, he founded the Natal Indian Congress, and his interactions extended to the indentured community. With Gandhi's intervention, Balasundaram was re-employed with another European – Indians could not employ indentured labor, and his old master was convicted.

Balasundaram's case reverberated across Natal and reached the shores of Madras, from where a large number of laborers had migrated. It was not the violence that made news, but that someone sought justice and received it was unheard of among the indentured laborers. With these aspirations of mobilizing Indians in South Africa and of attuning them to decode the everyday nature of colonial authority, Gandhi began editing a weekly paper, *Indian Opinion*. He reproduced and reviewed British cartoons to expose their political meanings, developing arguments about satyagraha (truth force), Western civilization, and the "mind of the whites." A core concept of Gandhi's politics of non-violence, satyagraha was a technique, a law, and an ethic. Illustrating the logic of satyagraha, Gandhi noted,

Strength does not come from physical capacity. It comes from an indomitable will. An average Zulu is any way more than a match for an average Englishman in bodily capacity. But he flees from an English boy, because he fears the boy's revolver or those who will use it for him. He fears death and is nerveless in spite of his burly figure.[6]

As a form of "non-cooperation" and "civil resistance" which Gandhi saw as new names of the "ancient law of self sacrifice," satyagraha also entailed the "law of suffering." Crediting the sages from ancient India, who "discovered the law of non-violence," as "greater geniuses than Newton," Gandhi also saw satyagraha as "conscious suffering" (Mukherjee 1993, p. 99).

Gandhi's brief professional visit to South Africa unexpectedly turned into a twenty-one-year stay, during which he galvanized the Indian public against colonial discrimination. These long years in South Africa saw the crystallization of Gandhi's concept of non-violence and satyagraha (truth force), and the important role of journalism in the Mahatma's politics and life. Journalism became an inextricable part of Gandhi's politics and mass communication. Eleven years after his arrival, in 1904, he saw the publication of *Indian Opinion*, a multilingual weekly newspaper for Indians in South Africa; this was the first of three newspapers Gandhi edited during his lifetime: *Indian Opinion* (1903–14) in South Africa, *Young India* (1919–32) and *Harijan* (1933–48), both in Ahmedabad.

Gandhi's train journeys in South Africa in relation to the case he was negotiating showed another side of apartheid politics in British South Africa. Not all whites agreed with the official degradation of "colored" people. Among those dissenters were some of the English newspaper cartoonists, on whose drawings Gandhi soon kept a close eye. With aspirations of mobilizing Indians in South Africa and attuning them to decode the everyday nature of colonial authority, Gandhi reproduced and reviewed British cartoons in *Indian Opinion*. His reviews exposed political meanings in the "comic drawings" and developed arguments about satyagraha, Western civilization, and the "mind of the whites."[7] If vocabulary and dress embodied visible forms of power, then newspaper cartoons offered Gandhi another interpretative strategy: these images concealed a truth that only the initiated could collectively comprehend. To decode the political message and make it available to Indians would require an integrative communication – cartoon talk.[8]

Cartoons as journalism: *Indian Opinion* (1903?–14)

Gandhi's analysis and interpretation of cartoons came as part of his political effort to generate a newspaper-literate readership. Developing the habit for newspapers required literacy, by which news, photographs, editorials, and cartoons could compose the everyday fare of modern life. *Indian Opinion* started publication in 1903, steered by the efforts of M. H. Nazar, a secretary of the Indian Natal Congress; Madanjit Viyavaharik, the owner of the International Printing Press; and Gandhi. By the second year *Indian Opinion* had 887 subscribers, and over its entire fifty-eight years of publication its subscribers averaged about 2,000 (Mesthrie 2003).

Indian Opinion's text appeared in English, Hindi, Gujarati, and Tamil. Primarily concerned with the condition of indentured labor in South Africa, this multilingual publication marked a moment in the collective "black protest press" that since 1900 addressed separate "African, Coloured and Indian audiences" (Switzer 1997, p. 1). At this time, Gandhi was convinced that colonial discrimination was counter to British ideals of justice and equality, embodied in Queen Victoria's 1858 proclamation of equality for all British subjects.[9] Thus *Indian Opinion* was conceptualized to further true imperial values while being the voice of the colonial subjects.[10] The gradual introduction to and appreciation of cartoons among *Indian Opinion*'s readers was routed both through the English cartoons that Gandhi frequently reproduced and translated from among several South African newspapers and through the Anglo-Gujarati newspaper published in Ahmedabad in colonial India, the *Hindi Punch*.[11] Gandhi's interest in newspaper cartoons coincided with his early period of political activism, when he was also developing the language and concept of satyagraha. In 1907, in a note to his readers, Gandhi invited their contributions for carving out a language for patriotism:

To respect our own language, speak it well and use it in as few foreign words as possible – this is also part of patriotism. We have been using some English terms just as they are, since we cannot find exact Gujarati equivalents for them. Some of these terms are given below, which we place before our readers. We shall publish in this journal the name of the person who supplies Gujarati equivalents for them which may be found acceptable ... We hope that our readers will take the trouble of suggesting suitable equivalents not for the sake of the prize but out of patriotism. The following are the terms in question: Passive Resistance; Passive Resister; Cartoon; Civil Disobedience. There are other words too, but we shall think of them some other time. It should be noted that we do not want translations of these English terms, but terms with equivalent connotations. There will be no objection if the words are derived from Sanskrit or Urdu.[12]

Along with concepts that were soon to develop and to shape his political tactics in colonial India (passive resistance, passive resister, and civil disobedience), the term "cartoon" made an early appearance in the political vocabulary that Gandhi formulated with the help of his readers.[13] Readers were not merely consuming news; they were participating as newsmakers, shaping vocabulary and engaging in a pedagogical process. An early example of a translation of "cartoon" in Gujarati was "comic drawings which carry some meaning." With this initial list of words, Gandhi took a step toward situating "cartoons" as a part of the necessary vocabulary for resistance.

Gandhi's direction that these Gujarati, Sanskrit, and Urdu terms were not to be a mere translation of the English terms but rather meaningful equivalents, revealed his search for a patriotic language with roots in India and not derived from the empire. Translation would be an implant – an imitation. Equivalent words would assert identity and be identifiable to those who spoke the language. Gandhi's call for forging a distinct vocabulary is a startling revelation for those attempting to interpret imperialism. Presenting patriotism as resistance, Gandhi pressed readers to develop a critique of imperialism in a language other than the language of the empire. In mobilizing indentured laborers – immigrants to South Africa – Gandhi did not set them up as an "imagined community" via the emotion of nationalism. Rather, Gandhi used language and patriotism to critique imperialism: the love of language as love of one's motherland served as a platform for demanding immigrant rights for respect and equity. Gandhi saw the persistent denial of these rights and the absence of a vernacular political vocabulary among Indian immigrants as the lifeline of the empire. Gandhi's interpretation of selective cartoons unfolded a fascinating tale of his politics, undermining the bulwark of imperialism with the visual tools of the cartoon.

Seeing is feeling: a glimpse of the "divine light of satyagraha"

To convey the political sense of these cartoons, linguistic translation in itself was inadequate; Gandhi incorporated lengthy interpretations and when possible, reproduced the cartoon, such as "The March of Civilisation." Gandhi's exhortations to feel the cartoon and to allow it to touch one's heart linked the eye to the heart, and the sense of sight to emotions and feelings. Gandhi's directions on how to understand the cartoons correctly by deriving emotion and a sense of their components introduced the readers of *Indian Opinion* to the idea that the making and reading of the cartoon was a political act, deserving of their attention.

An English journal called *The New Age* has published a cartoon on this subject, which we reproduce in this issue [see Figure 2.1]. It shows an army on the march. Behind, there is a grotesque figure, that of a general. On the body of this terrible form are hanging a gun emitting smoke in every direction and swords dripping with blood, and on its head a cannon. There is the drawing of a skull on a badge hanging on one side. On the arm, moreover, there is a cross. (This cross is the emblem of a batch which looks after the wounded.) In the mouth, held in the teeth, there is a dagger dripping with blood. On the shoulder is seen a belt studded with live cartridges. The drawing is entitled "March of Civilisation". No one who reads this description of the cartoon can help becoming grave. On reflection, we cannot help feeling that Western Civilization is as cruel as, perhaps more cruel than, the terrible expression on the face of the man in the cartoon. The sight which fills one with the utmost indignation is that of the cross in the midst of weapons dripping with blood. Here the hypocrisy of the new civilization reaches its climax. In former times, too, there used to be bloody wars, but they were free from the hypocrisy of modern civilization. While drawing our readers' attention to this cartoon, we want to give them at the same time a glimpse of the divine light of satyagraha. On the one side look at the picture of civilization drawn above, a civilization grown so terrible as a wolf through its hunger for wealth and its greedy pursuit of worldly pleasures. On the other, look at the figure of a satyagrahi who, out of his loyalty to truth, to his nature as a spiritual being and out of a desire to obey God's command, submits to the suffering inflicted by wicked men with fortitude in his breast, with a smile on his face and without a single tear in his eyes. Of the two pictures, towards which will the reader feel attracted? We are sure it is the vision of the satyagrahi which will touch the heart of mankind, and the effect will grow deeper as his sufferings increase. Is there anyone who, looking at this cartoon alone does not feel in his heart that satyagraha is the only way in which mankind can attain freedom and strength?[14]

Although the satyagrahi was not pictured in this cartoon, he could be imagined as a foil against the cruel, greedy, and pleasure-seeking West.

No. 14—Vol. 8.   SATURDAY, APRIL 2ND, 1910.   Registered as a Newspaper
PRICE THREEPENCE

"The March of Civilisation"

Reproduced by kind permission of *The New Age* (London).

2.1 "The March of Civilisation." *Indian Opinion*. April 2, 1910. Natal, South Africa.

The promise of the future lay in truth, spirituality, and formidable suffering. Posing the reader a question and then answering it, Gandhi skillfully steered to a conclusion glorifying the satyagrahi's strength as the true embodiment of power. This detailed Gujarati narrative became a brief moral comment in the English section of the same issue of *Indian Opinion*:

Our thanks are due to the editor of the *New Age* for permission he has given us to reproduce the excellent cartoon which appears on the front page of this issue. The picture tells its own tale. Here we see modern civilization groaning under the weight of armaments. This may appear exaggerated to many of our readers, because it represents only the evil and none of the good in modern Civilization. But to those who realise what a curse and a burden modern armaments are, and how the spirit of selfishness, miscalled patriotism pervades the nations of Europe, the picture will not appear overdrawn. In any case there is no denying the fact that the march of modern civilization proceeds along the lines of brute force rather than those of soul force or love. (*Indian Opinion*, April 2, 1910, p. 113)

In the English text, Gandhi's brief commentary was prefaced by the observation: "The picture tells its own tale." The Gujarati text pitted satyagraha against modern civilization, and Eastern against Western. Such a confrontation of ideas was not discernible in Gandhi's English text, which simply criticized one aspect of modern civilization, its violent armament. The Gujarati language of the explanation provided a safety net, ensuring Gandhi's interpretation did not leak beyond the ambit of the desired readership. The English translation was a ploy to hoodwink censors and others monitoring natives and immigrants in South Africa.

As the editor of *Indian Opinion* and the subject of British cartoons, Gandhi was both the observant critic and the object of analysis. He conveyed to his readers that cartoonists projected satyagraha's force as an armament that punctured imperial plans. With this role of translator and interpreter, Gandhi arbitrated the cartoons' meaning, projecting both his own strength and satyagraha as a formidable oppositional soul force. Along with this self-presentation, Gandhi urged his readers to see the cartoons as a peep into "the mind of Whites." Thus through translation

---

Caption for 2.1 (cont.)

Gandhi reproduced John P. Cambell's cartoon from the *New Age* literary supplement (January 6, 1910, London), micmicking its front-page cartoon format. Gandhi noted about the cartoon: "The picture tells its own tale," and incorporated a lengthy explanation to his readers. Since August 1908, several issues of the *New Age*, a weekly socialist magazine, featured a large front-page cartoon, which were also sold as postcards.

and interpretation, English cartoons became an available cultural and political text for immigrant Indian readers to surreptitiously encroach upon the imperial mind:

The government is betraying more signs of weakness everyday on the question of the new law. Even the Whites see this. Two amusing cartoons (comic drawings which carry some meaning) are published in the *Rand Daily* and the *Sunday Times*. One of them shows General Smuts firing a pistol of the new law at the Indians. The Indian says: "Do your worst. We shall never submit to the law." General Smuts then explains: "don't say so pal. My blooming gun is out of order." In the other cartoon General Smuts and some government officers want to cut off the heads of the Indian leaders with spears. But the horses are all together exhausted with the effort, and the riders themselves have become breathless; and still the heads of the leaders are intact. Both these cartoons reveal the state of mind of the Whites. The editor of the paper is trying to secure the two cartoons for the readers of *Indian Opinion*; hence I don't write more about them.[15]

Editorial efforts to secure the two "comic drawings" were successful. The *Indian Opinion* devoted a full page to each cartoon. "The desperado and the resister" and "Removing the heads" were published with captions in Gujarati. In these readings of cartoons, Gandhi repeatedly redefined true strength and equated it with satyagraha, rather than the empire, which was an example of "force."[16] "Both these cartoons reveal the state of mind of the Whites," wrote Gandhi. Such interpretations and explanations were at other times formulated as a question and answer. In his discussion under the headline "Mr. Gandhi's Dream and Thorns of Passive Resistance," the question-and-answer format directed readers to see how questions deconstructed the visual text and revealed imperial force, the strength of satyagraha and colonial mentality:

The *Sunday Times* has been giving much publicity to our struggle. It pokes a little fun at the law and at Mr. Smuts under the title, "Mr. Gandhi's Dream". One of the figures in the cartoons is Mr. Smuts. Leaning his head upon his hands, with the elbows resting on the table he is musing:

> "Registration" is a great bother;
> And "Resistance" greater than that;
> The old C.B worries me a lot,
> And Gandhi drives me mad.

This is what Smuts is muttering to himself. "C.B" refers to the Prime minister of England, M. Campbell-Bannerman. In the second cartoon, Mr Gandhi is shown with armour on. It is covered all over with pointed nails. There's a notice above the picture, "Do not touch me". And it is signed below, "yours passively Gandhi". What is being suggested is this: Why does he sign himself "yours passively" when touching any part of his body would give sharp pricks? The point is that when the law is pricked with the thorns of passive resistance, it loses all its force.[17]

By now, Gandhi was also aware of cartoons in the Indian press, namely, the Anglo-Gujarati *Hindi Punch* published in Ahmedabad. The *Indian Opinion*'s readers' appreciation of cartoons was facilitated both through the English cartoons and through the *Hindi Punch*.[18]

Remembering the tickle: Smuts, Hitler, and the prose of caricature

Although Gandhi published his detailed cartoon interpretations in Gujarati, leaving a brief note for the part in English, he also introduced references to cartoons in his public talks. When Gandhi referenced cartoons in this way, he strategically picked examples that he had already shared with his *Indian Opinion* readers. For example, he evoked the "Steam-Roller" cartoon (see Figure 2.2) in his public talk against indentured labor in the first meeting of the Transvaal Closer Union Society in Johannesburg in August 1908:

2.2 "The Steam-Roller and the Elephant." *Indian Opinion*. January 11, 1908.

A local application of the old riddle of the "irresistible force" and the "immovable body," this is a reproduction of AWLL – Arthur Wynell Lloyd's cartoon from the *Sunday Times*, South Africa. Gandhi is the mahout astride the elephant, labeled "Indian Community," which is saying "Stop that ticklin Jan." "Jan" referred to the South African Jan Smuts, the colonial secretary, who opposed Gandhi and steers the steam-roller.

The better policy would be to stop indentured labour entirely; and three years should be the period fixed ... This kind of labour has not done any good whatsoever to the Indians who have emigrated under those conditions to Natal, or to the Colonies themselves ... If the Colony persists in that policy, I should admire General Smuts or anyone else using the steamroller (Laughter) and compelling Natal to stop indentured immigration.[19]

Mentioning the title of the cartoon generated familiarity, context, and laughter among the community of readers. Laughter is social glue. This collective recollection of particular cartoons and sharing the experience of reading the cartoon, of knowing it, and of having laughed at it, transforms a personal and private reading moment into a collective public moment. This communal laughter based on collective remembering of the cartoon is an important moment to recognize the developing role of the cartoon in public space. Joining in laughter establishes a sense of belonging and affinity. When people laugh together, their collective sense of humor marks and forges a kinship. Perhaps some in the audience remembered seeing the cartoon and its sequel in the *Sunday Times*; others may have seen the long explanatory text in the *Indian Opinion*:

Though the editor of the *Sunday Times* writes against Indians, their cartoonist is doing a great service to the cause. He has portrayed the Indian community as an elephant, with its feet firmly planted on the ground. Mr. Smuts is forcing him with a steam-roller from the rear. The elephant remarks: "Stop your tickling, Jan!" The point of the cartoon is that the steam-roller has been unable to budge the elephant. In the event, the cartoon has only served to publicize our cause widely and has occasioned some merriment at General Smuts' expense.[20]

The cartoon was followed by a sequel:

The paper has now published a sequel showing the wrecked steam-roller, and General Smuts, lying on the ground amid the ruins of his chair, miserable, looking unhappily at the elephant. He is wearing a convict's cap. The elephant seems pleased with himself as he surveys the wreckage and, with his trunk raised to General Smuts, inquires, "everybody happy?" Mr. Gandhi, as mahout, had his digits extended fan-wise at the extremity of his nose, as much as to ask General Smuts, "So you have had a taste of digit-impressions?"

Underneath the cartoon is the caption: "Picture of Colonial Secretary Receiving Mr. Gandhi's digit-impressions."[21] The issue at hand was the long-brewing Asiatic Law Amendment Ordinance, which sought to monitor and limit Indian immigration to South Africa. The Ordinance required all Asians above the age of eight to register and submit their finger and thumb impressions. A three-pound tax was imposed on free indentured laborers to discourage their stay in South Africa and hasten their return to India (Mesthrie 1997). *Indian Opinion* and Gandhi organized opposition to this discriminatory decision, thus heralding a stand-off between Gandhi and Smuts, which is portrayed in the cartoons.

In "The Steam-Roller and the Elephant," the uninitiated reader learns that the elephant in the cartoon is the Indian community and the unnamed caricature is meant to be Jan Smuts. By the early twentieth century, the political cartoon was a prominent part of the English press and had developed a visual vocabulary that included symbols and caricatures, but this could be alien to a public that did not share the symbolic and cultural milieu of the English cartoonist. By drawing attention to English cartoons that visualized politics of Indian interest in South Africa, Gandhi prompted his readers' attention to the imagery of the cartoon and its political content. The cartoon thus was firmly situated as a political and cultural text that, though alien to the outsider's eye, could be comprehended correctly through a process of learning. In his analysis of this cartoon, Gandhi alerted the reader to the nuances: "Though the editor of the *Sunday Times* writes against Indians, their cartoonist is doing a great service to the cause." A close look at the signature reveals A. W. L. L. – the cartoonist was Arthur Wynell Lloyd (1883–1967). Born in Britain, Lloyd was twenty-two when he came to South Africa in 1905; he began his career with the *Rand Daily Mail* and moved on to several other newspapers. Lloyd returned to Britain and became a *Punch* cartoonist.[22] Gandhi informed his readers that despite the antagonistic stance of the *Sunday Times* to Indian interests, the newspaper's cartoonist ruptured this stance and opened a gap to protest and to present the truth. Thus the *Sunday Times*'s ideology and its cartoon's counter-ideology coexisted precisely because, if read with care, the cartoon exposed the truth. These cartoons revealed the divided state of mind of the imperialistic whites. Gandhi's praise for Lloyd's politics and cartoons was on the mark. In his *Punch* cartoons Lloyd depicted imperial politics, South Africa, and India. For example in 1913 his cartoon of an alarmed caged tiger – Indians in South Africa who were imposed a poll tax – shows the Viceroy as a zookeeper, reprimanding General Botha of South Africa (see Figure 2.3).[23] In another cartoon in 1931, Lloyd caricatured a seated Winston Churchill with a turban: "The autocrat for all the Indias."[24] In Lloyd's *Punch* cartoons, the elephant continued to represent India and was complemented by the tiger with its stripes spelling "India."

The Indian population in South Africa was not a cohesive group. Language, social identities, and class separated them into smaller units of collective experience. These divisions among the colonized were not unique to South Africa. Oral and visual culture has time and again challenged a consolidation of the colonial experience. For example, in the context of Kenya and Mau Mau, John Lonsdale has shown "Behind the surface solidarities of war, myths of Mau Mau were more disputed than has been

Viceroy of India (to General Botha) " I 'M SURE YOU ONLY MEANT TO
HAVE A LITTLE HARMLESS FUN WITH HIS TAIL, BUT WHAT 'S FUN TO YOU
MAY BE VERY ANNOYING TO THE REST OF THE TIGER."

2.3 Arthur Wynell Lloyd's (AWLL) cartoon on the British Empire and
Indians in South Africa. *Punch*. December 3, 1913. London. Courtesy of
the Punch Archive.

At the earlier stage of his career, Lloyd's cartoons on Gandhi and
Indians in South Africa were published in South Africa and
reproduced and analyzed in the *Indian Opinion*.

thought, with Africans as divided as whites" (Lonsdale 1990, p. 395). The racialized divides during Gandhi's South Africa years leave their imprint in contemporary times among those who read and speak English. Thomas Blom Hansen notes, "A racial–cultural separation of readership and audiences persists between papers seen as 'white' (e.g., *Sunday Times*, *Mail and Guardian*, *Cape Times*) and such African newspapers as the *Sowetan* or Indian newspapers as the *Post*" (Hansen 2005, p. 300). Gandhi experienced the challenge of a divided audience in other ways, too. The logistics of translation and lack of finances hampered the publication of *Indian Opinion*. Gandhi wrote the Gujarati texts of the *Indian Opinion*, but he was not skilled in Hindi and Tamil and depended on translators (Mesthrie 1997).

Not trivial matters

The power and politically creative force of satyagraha were mediated to the *Indian Opinion* readers through the interpretative politics associated with the cartoon. This was in line with other aspects of life that Gandhi politicized after his return to India: *khadi*, fasting, and vegetarianism.

In most instances when he referenced a cartoon, Gandhi also reproduced it in the *Indian Opinion*. Gandhi walked the reader through each component of the cartoon. These explanations and Gandhi's reactions to the cartoons embodied the earliest reviews of cartoons in the context of Indian politics, urging the public to read, feel, and respond to the cartoon and make political choices. As in his use of the "March of Civilisation," the notes accompanying the cartoons appeared solely in the Gujarati section of the *Indian Opinion* and did not appear in the English section.[25] In this selective publication of his interpretation, Gandhi prudently took a measured step against potential charges of sedition. Just as with the South African newspapers that addressed their specific audience, the vernacular languages in *Indian Opinion* disclosed meaning only to the selective newspaper-reading publics. Thus even though the newspaper was available publicly, it was not equally meaningful to all, thereby escaping notice of the watchful eyes of the colonial government.

Through symbols and imagery, the cartoon calls to particular members of the public while screening out others. Such screening occurs not because of a lack of material access but because of the lack of cultural capital required to interpret the politics of symbols and caricature. Gandhi struck at the root of this disjuncture, and his exegesis of the cartoons signaled his recognition of the lack of cultural capital, thus political capital, among the expatriate Indian readers of *Indian Opinion*.

The hegemonic transcripts of the English cartoon could be mobilized and materialized only through its circulation in the public domain: by its

publication in the newspaper. Through his notes on the English cartoons –
the public, yet "hidden transcript" of the whites – Gandhi urged his
readers to notice, read between the drawings, and actively interpret
along the lines he suggested.[26] To be alert and interpret the cartoon – a
visual expression, circulated in the public sphere – would lead the Indian
readers to know the hidden and private minds of the whites. Public yet
hidden, these transcripts/cartoons were also in fact "public secrets" shared
by the English readers of South African newspapers. It was a secret
Gandhi knew, and that his selective exposition in Gujarati (and not in
the English section of *Indian Opinion*) further fueled; the secret was now
covertly shared among a public not meant to share the knowledge.
Through one cartoon after another, Gandhi revealed the secrets and the
mind of the whites. But for this sort of access, it remained imperative that
the Indian public read newspapers and become active interpreters of
symbols in the public sphere. It might seem a paradox that although he
was dismissive of Lavater's *Physiognomy* and the assumption of scientific
correlation between appearance and character, as editor of the *Indian
Opinion* in South Africa, Gandhi unraveled the representations in newspaper cartoons to reveal the British mind. More precisely, Gandhi saw
cartoons as a form of journalism that was not only a humorous take on
daily news, but transcripts that could be closely studied to reveal the
political mind – the "minds of whites." This intimate connection between
the visual and political thought grew from Gandhi's sensitivity to everyday
practices and the exercise of power. Much like an anthropologist coming
to terms with his or her first days of fieldwork, Gandhi was observant and
conscious of his own discomfort. His cartoon reviews marked him as a
partial insider to British culture.

Representing the cartoons and his own caricatures that he culled from
the British newspapers, Gandhi scratched the surface of the myth of white
solidarity to disclose frictions in imperial ideology. Simultaneously with
his verbal forays in the multilingual *Indian Opinion*, Gandhi sought to bind
readers with a shared visual experience, thereby constructing a mythical
counter-public. In this colonial milieu, the English cartoons and their
iconography circulated among the British in South Africa as coded transcripts of political humor, which Gandhi intercepted. It is of considerable
interest that in these cartoons, Gandhi was frequently caricatured, thus
the cartoon analysis in the pages of *Indian Opinion* gave Gandhi an opportunity to represent his self.[27] Such avenues for the presentation of his
self were few and far between. On most occasions during his lifetime in
India, Gandhi was a spectator of his own image appropriated in bazaar
prints, advertisements, and cartoons, retelling political events.[28] The world
of newspaper cartoons provided Gandhi, the arbitrator of meanings, with a

visual arena for subordinating and exercising power.[29] After discovering their power during his stay in South Africa, Gandhi continued to be aware of their usefulness in Britain and in India.

Low creates Windhi

Gandhi's 1931 visit to Britain marked his only visit since his student days in 1888. He was now a Congress nationalist participating in the second Round Table Conference about India's dominion status. Gandhi was popular among London's poor, and pictures abound of him mingling in their midst. Actor Charles Chaplin and cartoonist David Low were among several luminaries he met in London. David Low, the world-famous cartoonist from New Zealand, who had immigrated to Britain, created several cartoons on the British Empire and world politics. In the 1920s and 1930s, India figured frequently in Low's cartoons, and Gandhi was prominent. Gandhi was among Low's "most pleasant subjects."[30] For Low, "dark types" were easier to caricature and he had a "professional leaning towards dark people" because they had "more strongly defined keypoints" than the "fair types." In these cartoons, the skullcap gave way to the charkha (spinning wheel), and a petite, scantily robed Gandhi. English newspapers frequently reproduced Low's cartoons in India, and Low played a formative role in inspiring a generation of Indian cartoonists to picture Gandhi with a goat.[31]

Low's 1931 meeting with Gandhi was memorable; in his autobiography he devotes a few pages to the several minutes he spent meeting Gandhi, first in London's House of Commons and later in Gandhi's Knightsbridge flat, his abode during the London visit. Gandhi was evidently a voluble talker, and it was difficult to get him to subside when answering questions. His son, a round-faced youth, and disciple, Miss Madeleine Slade (Mirabehn) stood on one side modestly, speechless:

> He received me with loud laughter as though I were a very funny friend of the family. He was waving the evening paper about with a cartoon of mine on the meeting of Gandhi and Windhi (my name-play for Winston). Mouth a wide gap with three teeth on each side lower jaw. On this encouragement I invited myself around to his abode to see him more privately.

Low wanted to meet Gandhi not to scoop news but to "get the flavor of the human being." He planned to ask Gandhi a few questions; Low knew the answers, but thought it a good ploy to keep Gandhi busy while he observed and made caricatures (Low 1957, pp. 220–1).[32]

At the meeting in the Knightsbridge flat, Low was ushered in by Gandhi Junior, the "round-faced" Devdas, and Low found Gandhi squatted on the floor, spinning yarn. He was encircled by friends sitting on chairs. Here Low had a more intimate look at Gandhi, the subject of his numerous cartoons: "little brown head with short grey hair peeping elfishly out of copious home-spun blanket – large hands and feet – skin warm and pleasant to touch – all very welcoming." Gandhi gave detailed answers to Low's questions, glorifying agricultural India and sounding alarmed at the deplorable state of the industrial USA. Even workers in South Africa fared better than their counterparts in the USA, he said. Hearing this anticipated assessment of industrialization's gloomy prognosis, while caricaturing Gandhi, Low sensed something fresh in the conversation: "eye to eye, his face close to mine, breathing a perfume of goat's-milk over me as he talked animatedly" (Low 1957, p. 222). Low was reduced to silence when Gandhi "deplored the dearth of cartoonists" in India and proposed that "the well-known appreciation of satire possessed by Indians might make it a congenial place" for Low to spend some time. Did Gandhi know that Low was still recovering from an unforeseen burst of protest against his cartoon in Calcutta? Difficult to tell. The parting shot was "Mr. G's": "Do you also want to interview my go-o-oat Mr. Lo-o-o-ow?" (p. 223).

"You are now immortalized, Mahatmaji"

By 1931, colonial politics in India gripped the empire's imagination, while the empire's grip on the colony was beginning to slip. Low noted that "the [British] people had grown a conscience about India by the nineteen-thirties" and "old imperialism was wearing out" (Low 1957, p. 223).

Gandhi was now Mahatma – the Great Soul. Letters exchanged with his political associates show he kept an eye on the newspaper cartoon and read the British *Punch*.[33] Since his days in South Africa, he had been acutely aware that he caught the imagination of the cartoonist. Gandhi's personality and politics seduced the media, and he was a brand to reckon with, and much more: magazines, cigarettes, saris, autographs – the magic of Gandhi's touch through his image and his writing was formidable (Khanduri 2012b). In South Africa, Gandhi had been a fixture in cartoons about immigrant politics – he was depicted in various guises, as a mahout, in Western clothing, and as a "passive resister" in a sherwani with a cap and umbrella, among others.

Although colonial officials dismissed satyagraha as passive resistance, the cartoons showed otherwise. In Britain and in India, caricatures of Gandhi symbolized a peculiar nationalist politics that *Punch* found irresistible (see Figure 2.4). Such representations continued to be seen as an insight into the British mind and encouraged Indians to subscribe to

THE ELUSIVE MAHATMA.

SHE ONLY SAID, "MY LIFE IS DREARY;
  HE COMETH NOT," SHE SAID;
SHE SAID, "I AM A-WEARY, A-WEARY;
IF I WERE NOT A PERFECT LADY
    I'D LIKE TO SMACK HIS HEAD."—*With apologies to* TENNYSON.

2.4 Leonard Raven-Hill, "The Elusive Mahatma." *Punch.* August 26, 1931. London. Courtesy of the Punch Archive.
   Jawaharlal Nehru was taken by this cartoon of Gandhi in *Punch.*

Punch. Gandhi's protégé Jawaharlal Nehru's subscription to the *Punch* and other English newspapers began in 1931, after seeing a "lovely" Gandhi cartoon.[34] The cartoon, entitled "The Elusive Mahatma," depicted Britannia waiting and a portrait of Gandhi on an easel next to her. For Nehru this cartoon and *Punch* was a source "to read" what the British said about "Bapu" – his affectionate and deferential address of Gandhi. Perhaps a couple of months earlier that year, Nehru might have also seen David Low's "The Elusive Mr. Gandhi" cartoon in the *Evening Standard*.[35] Nehru's interest in *Punch* seems to have been recent and might have swayed favorably with its cartoons on Gandhi. When he referenced it in his *Autobiography* (1936), which was written between 1934 and 1936 during his imprisonment, Nehru listed *Punch* in India among illustrated reading material that was part of the routine of the British official class's "intellectual and cultural torpor": "After a day in office, dealing with ever rotating and never-ending files, he will have some exercise and then go to his club to mix with his kind, drink whisky and read *Punch* and the illustrated weeklies from England."[36] These evocations of *Punch* – as a source of political knowledge and as exemplifying the reading materials of dull official lifestyle – is revealing of how a cultural text can be imagined as shaping colonial life.

Gandhi's cartoons had an afterlife that tells much about the visual imprint of history. In a new twist to Gandhi's interpretation of the South African cartoons, almost two decades after their publication in South Africa, Indian cartoonists appropriated some of these cartoons, such as "The Steam-Roller and the Elephant" (1908) and "The Snake Charmer" (1908) to depict colonial politics in India, giving them new meaning and context (see Figure 2.5). These republications and appropriations in India gave a new lease on life to these cartoons, which circulated among a new audience that purchased and appreciated "caricature albums" – *Chitravali* – and in a new language, Hindi. Reproduced in Shiv Narayan Mishra's edited cartoon album, *Svang Chitravali* (n. d., *c*. 1929), the cartoons on South African colonial politics now represented bureaucracy and the Indian public. The "Steam-Roller and the Elephant" cartoon was titled "India and Bureaucracy" and the caption below in Hindi explained that it depicted the Indian public and the bureaucracy's administrative cycle. The steam-roller represents the bureaucracy, General Smuts becomes the generic face of colonial rule in India and the elephant remains the "Indian community" but now located in India. The bureaucratic cycle can be read as a critique of bureaucracy that was the locus of the nexus of colonial rule sustained by a retinue of civil servants. The mahout on the elephant, labeled "Gandhi," has a new speech balloon encouraging the elephant, "well done!" The elephant's speech balloon

India & Bureaucracy.

भारतीय जनता और नौकरशाही का शासन-चक्र ।

2.5 Shiv Narayan Mishra, "India and Bureaucracy." *Svang Chitravali: Caricature Album.* n.d. (*c.* 1929). Kanpur. Hindi caption: "The Indian public and the cycle of bureaucratic rule." Gandhi's speech bubble: "Shabaash" (Well done). The elephant is Janata (the people), and the steam-roller is the bureaucracy.

The South African colonial secretary, General Jan Smuts reappeared as the British driver. The "Steam-Roller" cartoon was revised to depict the link between colonial rule and bureaucracy. The cartoon also becomes bilingual and the text in Hindi gave new meaning to Arthur Wynell Lloyd's cartoon.

from the South African cartoon is also reproduced though it is difficult to imagine what to make of "stop your tickling, Jan." Despite the passage of time, a new context, and his own changed comportment, Gandhi's caricature in the Steam-Roller cartoon remained communicable and recognizable. Such durability and circulation of cartoons to represent the colonial experience in different parts of the empire extended the life span of cartoons and caricatures from a day to decades. It also meant that Gandhi caricatures from his younger days in South Africa, from his mature political years in India, and from his London visit, crafted by cartoonists in Britain, South Africa, and India, comingled in the public imagination. These many Gandhi caricatures certainly made representation elusive in more than one way.[37]

As interpreter and arbitrator of meanings, Gandhi too played a part in this revitalization of his old cartoons. Nearly three decades after its first appearance, in June 1940, Gandhi once again evoked the Steam-Roller cartoon (Figure 2.2). In his newspaper *Harijan*, Gandhi contrasted Hitler's politics with satyagraha, explaining:

> Whatever Hitler may ultimately prove to be, we know what Hitlerism has come to mean. It means naked truth, ruthless force reduced to an exact science and worked with scientific precision. In its effect it becomes almost irresistible.
>
> In the early days of satyagraha when it was still known as passive resistance, the *Star* of Johannesburg, stirred by the sight of a handful of Indians, wholly unarmed and incapable of organized violence even if they wished it, pitting themselves against an overwhelmingly armed Government, had a cartoon in which the latter was depicted as a steam-roller representing irresistible force, and passive resistance was depicted as an elephant unmoved and comfortably planting himself on his seat. This was marked as immovable force. The cartoonist had a true insight into the duel between the irresistible and the immovable forces. It was then a stalemate. The sequel we know. What was depicted and appeared to be irresistible was successfully resisted by the immovable force of satyagraha – call it suffering without retaliation.
>
> What became true then can be equally true now. Hitlerism will never be defeated by counter-Hitlerism.[38]

Gandhi's abiding interest in the public role and politics of cartoons continued throughout his political activity in colonial India.[39] If "in adopting the vocabulary of civil disobedience, Western commentators dramatized the challenge and disorder of Gandhi's way" (Scalmer 2011, p. 84), the cartoons presented another perspective on that disorder – humor at the expense of the British.

3   "Dear Shankar . . . your ridicule should never bite"

Long and frequent imprisonment as a consequence of political activity against the British provided Jawaharlal Nehru with uninterrupted time to read and write, and see cartoons. For Nehru, *Punch* and cartoons were more than news and perspective – they were a way of "direct touch" with loved ones, particularly when separated by imprisonment. Such sentiments were in Nehru's mind when, during imprisonment in 1932 he had a "brain wave" to send *Punch* directly by post to his sisters Nan (Vijaya Lakshmi Pandit) and Betty (Krishna Nehru), who were also imprisoned but in another city, in Lucknow.[1] Nehru's letters from prison to his daughter Indira (who later followed in her father's footsteps and became India's prime minister, Indira Gandhi) frequently noted his delight at receiving books of cartoons, such as *Lancaster: More Pocket Cartoons*. "I liked the two books of cartoons," Nehru wrote to his daughter and in turn sent her newspaper cuttings of India's most popular cartoonist, Shankar Pillai (1902–89).[2] Shankar was the staff cartoonist of the *Hindustan Times*, a nationalist English-language newspaper edited by Gandhi's son Devdas. In the 1930s, at the helm of the nationalist movement, Gandhi continued to watch newspaper cartoons; now his gaze and that of his fellow Congress workers followed Shankar's cartoons. With the increasing tempo of nationalist politics in India, newspaper cartoons invited interpretation not just about the British mind, but also about competing Indian political minds. They also generated sentiments of pleasure and hurt that place representation in the tricky terrain of emotion. To pinpoint the emotion of the cartoons involved meaning-making that insisted upon articulating subjective experience as a social reality of colonial politics, and pinpointed the position of women and Muslims in the liberal agenda of a "gestating nation-state" (Sinha 2000, p. 626).

From 2002 until 2008, I had several conversations with Shankar's protégé, Kutty. In the course of these, Shankar's work and his times, and the making of professional cartooning, came to life before me.

Shankar in the words of Kutty

"Shankar was a great caricaturist," Kutty told me.

KUTTY: He knew painting too. Nobody in India has surpassed him in the field
of cartoons and caricatures. I have seen great cartoons by the greatest of the
cartoonists of the world. I consider Shankar the greatest among his contemporaries in the world. It is practically impossible for me to enumerate the
great cartoons he drew. I am not saying this simply because he was my guru.
His drawing skill, humor, and political insight were unique. No Indian
cartoonist has ever come up to his standard. He had a special gift by which,
by looking at the front view of a face he could correctly guess the profile view
of that person!

Shankar had a very good system for drawing caricatures. He used to meet
all politicians and other dignitaries too. He had a very good Leica camera.
He took portraits of people from different angles. He took at least three
portraits of each person – front view, left profile, and right profile. They
were pasted on cardboards. These cards were then arranged in alphabetical
order. Foreign faces were collected from other sources. For several years
it was my job to keep those photo files intact. When he was drawing, it
was my job to get the photos he needed and whenever he needed them
[see Figure 3.1].

Before he became a full-time cartoonist, Shankar was a secretary with
Walchand Hirachand Company, which was the Scindia Steam Irrigation
Company in Mumbai. He used to draw cartoons on the side and send them to
the *Indian Daily Mail*. Pothan Joseph, one of the greatest Indian editors,
would tell Shankar how to draw the cartoons. When Joseph joined the
Hindustan Times, he persuaded Shankar to come to Delhi to join his newspaper. That was 1933.

When Shankar started cartooning, his drawing was very poor. His trip to
England and the intense training for one year he took in the Slade School
of Art (UK) did enormous good to him. He was getting his salary in England
and sent some cartoons from there by ship! Shankar went to England at his
own expense and initiative, *Hindustan Times* did not send him. Before Low,
there were cartoonists Will Dyson (he was Australian) and Sydney George
Strube in London. Their cartoons might have inspired Shankar.
Surprisingly, Shankar never talked of those things with anybody. I was too
respectful to ask him, too. He returned an accomplished draftsman and
artist. He came back to the *Hindustan Times* and his improved drawing gave
his cartoons a greater appeal. His humor and grasp of politics made
his cartoons very popular.

You must see his cartoons from 1940, until he resigned in 1945 or perhaps
it was 1946. In 1954 when I met Low in London, he inquired of me about
Shankar. Low said, "I hear he is a big man now." When he resigned, Gandhi
asked Shankar, "Did *Hindustan Times* make you famous or did you make
Hindustan Times famous?" Shankar did not say anything. But it was true that
he made *Hindustan Times* famous.

3.1 Famous Indian political cartoonist K. Shankar Pillai, working in his studio, December 31, 1942. New Delhi. Photograph by William Vandivert/Time Life Pictures/Getty Images.

Photo files maintained by his protégé, Kutty, were important for caricaturing politicians and other leading personalities.

Feminist suspicions: biblical verse, lipstick, and the modern citizen

In 1937, Congress activist Rajkumari Amrit Kaur (1889–1964) wrote a letter to Gandhi complaining and sharing her doubts about a cartoon. Amrit Kaur was from the Kapurthala royal family and a Christian. She was among several political followers with whom Gandhi had a special

3.2 Shankar, "Lords' Prayer." *Hindustan Times*, March 22, 1937. New Delhi. "In a speech in the Assembly during the debate on the Finance Bill, Mr. Sri Parakasa said that the Finance Member was the God of capitalism and imperialism." Figures on left are labeled J. C. Nixon, J. B. Grigg, and J. B. Taylor. Prayer: "To the glory of our Lord J. C., for the love of Grigg and the fellowship of Holy Taylor – Amen."

Congress politician and Gandhi's confidant, Raj Kumari Amrit Kaur, took umbrage at Shankar's depiction of the Trinity and sensed mischief in this cartoon. This cartoon figured in their correspondence with each other where they deliberated its meaning and intent.

relationship, positioning them as his daughters and sisters. The historian Judith Brown notes the endearing quality of these relationships in their correspondence with Gandhi: "He called her 'idiot,' and she addressed him as 'tyrant'" (Brown 1994, p. 287). For sixteen years, Amrit Kaur served as Gandhi's secretary, giving her access to discussions of all sorts.

The cartoon she complained about was no ordinary one; it caught her attention and Gandhi's interest in large part because Shankar drew it (see Figure 3.2). Shankar's cartoons in the *Hindustan Times* were both part of and marked the ethos of an emerging nation. Amrit Kaur was "agitated enough" to discuss the issue with Devdas Gandhi, the managing editor of the newspaper. The cartoon caricatured the Congress luminary Sri Prakasa's speech in the Legislative Assembly debate on the Finance Bill that revisited the issue of an income tax to boost the state's revenue during the interwar years. The finance member James Grigg led this bill, and the cartoon showed Sri Prakasa praying to Grigg ("the God of capitalism and imperialism"), J. C. Nixon, and J. B. Taylor (governor of the Reserve Bank of India) as members of the "Trinity."

Amrit Kaur's letter about Shankar's offensive cartoon, like so many others, would receive Gandhi's prompt reply. Addressing her as "My dear rebel," Gandhi's cautious response to Amrit Kaur suggested that it was not possible to interpret a cartoon's definite meaning; at the very least, the process of interpretation was complex: was interpretation in the cartoon or in the mind of the reader? Could its meaning unravel solely on the basis of feelings? The gaps among image, mind, and feeling were confounding:

Still on the train. I wrote yesterday but forgot to tell you that when I saw the cartoon I felt what you felt. The joke was quite innocent. Only a suspicious mind could find a sinister purpose behind the cartoon. But the suspicion is there and has to be taken account of. Therefore you were wholly right in drawing Devdas's attention to the cartoon.[3]

On the one hand, Gandhi found the cartoon "innocent" and cast the responsibility of "sinister" interpretation on a "suspicious mind." Yet, on seeing the cartoon, Gandhi "felt" what Amrit Kaur also felt. The ambiguity that Gandhi raised subtly critiqued Amrit Kaur's reading, yet Gandhi acknowledged her interpretation at the level of feelings. Was Amrit Kaur's mind suspicious? For Gandhi, the agreeable cartoon had to pass the test of propriety at the level of feelings. Since the cartoon was already published, clearly the editor, Devdas Gandhi, had not found it wanting in propriety. However, once open to a wider public, cartoons evoke interpretations unanticipated by the editor and the cartoonist. Putting himself in that position – of a reader – Gandhi revisited the question in another letter to Amrit Kaur, expressing his curiosity about another cartoon: "What answer did you get, if any, from Devdas about the cartoon in which a Biblical verse was caricatured?"[4] The query about the biblical cartoon will need to rest here, for archives do not always provide the luxury and security of complete answers.

This was not the last of Amrit Kaur's conflicts with Shankar's cartoons, however. In 1938, as president of the All India Women's Congress, Amrit Kaur also held the honorary position of chair of the prestigious Lady Irwin College for women in Delhi. Shankar was invited to the convocation and was inspired to draw a cartoon: "Thinking of opening a Lipstick Service Station at Connaught Place." Offended, and taking matters to her senior colleague and fellow nationalist Sarojini Naidu (1879–1949) without much success, Amrit Kaur forwarded her grievance to Gandhi.[5] Such disagreements between Amrit Kaur and Sarojini Naidu mark a critical moment to dwell on gender politics that did not coalesce around a shared ideal of liberal perspective. Naidu's reputation as a poet and politician gave her a "complex feminism" (Alexander 1985) and a "double consciousness of England as the place of her literary language and initial literary aspirations and India as the place of her national belonging" (Reddy 2010, p. 573). This "cosmopolitan nationalism" (Reddy 2010) emerged also from Naidu's claim to belong to India and not merely to Bengal, her birth place, or to the Madras Presidency, her regional identity, or Hyderabad, her place of affiliation through marriage and residence. Her linguistic use of Urdu and not Bengali (Alexander 1985, p. 68), and keenness to bridge Hindus and Muslims further positioned her as a distinct colonial subject. But Naidu's cosmopolitanism and her advocacy of the rights of women to be equal political participants did not accommodate Kaur's objections to gender representations. Indeed, Naidu distanced herself from the term "feminist," preferring to situate herself as a "mere woman" (Forbes 2005, p. 145). Asking both Kaur and Shankar to present themselves before him, Gandhi heard the charge and the defense. Shankar described the scene: "They all had blindly applied lipstick across their mouth, without caring what their complexion was – whether black, white, pink, yellow, brown – they all had applied a dark lipstick. Shankar was irritated at the graduates; Amrit Kaur felt the same way about Shankar. 'You are acquitted, Shankar,' Gandhi ruled after another look at the cartoon, and laughed" (Shankar 1984, pp. 166–7). I cannot imagine Amrit Kaur was swayed by Gandhi's judgment and his laughter but, disappointed by Naidu and Gandhi, she had no choice but to withdraw.

Lipstick continued to irritate Shankar. When he began his own weekly in 1948, it prominently featured a socialite couple portrayed as donkeys with human bodies, Bada Saab and Memsaab (Big Sir and Madam). Memsab had full lips with dark lipstick. Browsing the range of Shankar's cartoons, I saw that lipstick symbolized both empty lip service and the distorted aesthetic of city women, who misunderstood modernity and feminist activism (see Figures 3.3 and 3.4). In these cartoons, educated women – the gendered youth of modern India – were a new threshold of how education can lead young women astray and create "superior women," who were out of touch with social reality and instead, by consuming commodities such as lipstick, high-heeled shoes, bags, and fashionable saris, painted an inglorious picture of the nation. Such alarm echoed colonial cartoons in the *Vyang Chitravali* (1930, discussed in the Introduction and Chapter 1) that questioned education's role in the

REAP THE WHIRLWIND!   August 1, 1948

"If you go out in that superior mentality of doing good to
others, it is far better that you remain at home, because
there is not much use in the world today for the superior lady"
— Nehru on role of Indian women.

3.3 Shankar, "Reap the Whirlwind!" *Shankar's Weekly*. August 1, 1948.
New Delhi. Courtesy of the Children's Book Trust.

Pouted lips, high heels, short hair, and lipstick symbolized empty lip
service and the skewed aesthetic of elite women, who misunderstood
modernity and feminist activism. Lipstick was Shankar's primary
signifier for lip service and numerous cartoons depicted women's
misunderstanding of modern India in postcolonial times. The woman
on the right side busy touching up her lips with a compact in hand,
reinforced the reader's attention to painted lips, rendering elite women's
speech dubious and pretentious. The home and the world spatially
demarcated arenas of significance for the new nation, according them
new roles in public and private spheres. "Superior ladies" and "superior
mentality" were recommended to "remain at home."

productive modernization of male youth.[6] In addition to the shift in
gender, these postcolonial cartoons assume a new role for the educated
subject – with their education, women incurred a "debt" that had to be
repaid with the performance of social service. Shankar's socialite stereotype is a recurring imagery in his cartoons featuring women activists'
skewed feminist practices. Such portrayals, even if they represented recognizable types, countered Amrit Kaur's commitment to empower women in
India by educating and training them for a professional and public life.

Those who had received superior education owed a debt to society or the community as a whole and they must repay it in the form of selfless service to the people, said Nehru addressing the students of a women's college in Delhi.

3.4 Shankar, "Bridging the Gulf." *Shankar's Weekly*. March 27, 1949. New Delhi. Courtesy of the Children's Book Trust.

Continuing the theme of women's role in India, Shankar modeled elite socialites living on a cloud and "real" women grounded on earth. For Nehru, "superior education," need not lead to "superior ladies" but was a social debt that was to be repaid by "selfless service to the people." It is noteworthy that women's education became the context for discerning the role of women in independent India. Short hair, pants, cigarettes, high heels, and lipstick signified "superior ladies," who were a contrast to the laboring and "traditional" women marked by long hair, covered head and bare feet. In Shankar's cartoons, class was pictured through social capital in the form of modern accouterments and the comportment of women's bodies.

Amrit Kaur's long association with Gandhi gave her an influential platform, but it was her brand of feminist nationalism and activism that earned her worldwide attention. Along with Sarojini Naidu and Vijaylakshmi Pandit (Nehru's sister) and many others, she is celebrated among the influential women leaders in the Indian National Congress who obtained a place in governing independent India. In 1948, Amrit Kaur went on to become free India's first health minister. The nucleus of her politics was the emergent "liberal Indian feminism" that arose in the wake of US journalist Katherine Mayo's controversial book, *Mother India* (1927).

The book critiqued Indian nationalism and claims of a glorious Hindu on the basis of its duality in the treatment of women. It argued that the nationalists glorified women through the discourse of "Mother India" but not in day-to-day treatment, wherein women succumbed to social mores related to child marriage and premature maternity.

While nationalists such as Gandhi could not but acknowledge the stark reality of Mayo's book, the British were hesitant to encroach on what they believed were cultural issues, outside the political domain. This demarcation of the cultural and political had shaped colonial administrative thought since the 1857 uprising, and was being challenged by liberal feminism. The passage of the Sarda Bill, which increased the marriageable age of girls to fourteen and of boys to sixteen, was supported by Indian women's organizations. Historian Mrinalini Sinha demonstrated how it brought into focus questions about women's status as equal citizens, giving pause to both the nationalists and the colonial state: "The discursive figure of the modern Indian woman, once the signifier of national cultural difference, was now rearticulated in the discourse of liberal feminism as the model for the citizen of a new nation-state" (Sinha 2000, p. 626). Amrit Kaur was among agents of India's feminist nationalism who modeled a modern liberal citizen, a new type of subject in the nationalist movement. She forcefully argued for Indian women's equal citizenship, coming from a rubric of rights and duties but ensconced in the liberal agenda of a "gestating nation-state" (Sinha 2000. p. 626).

Amrit Kaur's interpretation of Shankar's cartoons subject it to the rigor of a modern liberal eye that would brook no caricature of religion and gender in the name of another modern sensibility – political humor at the cost of marginalized subjects. Indeed, within the new context of citizenship, such cartoons were nagging reminders of the checkered past of India's emergent liberalism. Gandhi's ambivalence on the biblical verse cartoon marks how religion tested the limits of liberal sensibility. When caricaturing the Lady Irwin College graduates and their fashion trends, however, Gandhi agreed with Shankar and did not find much worthy of protest. But Amrit Kaur did. However, her challenge to the subtle ways in which prejudice toward minority religion and women gets cozy with modern liberal principles that insist on the equality of all citizens was not successful. After independence, when Amrit Kaur joined Jawaharlal Nehru's cabinet as health minister, she was part of the pantheon Shankar lampooned in *Shankar's Weekly*. In his cartoons, Shankar frequently deployed reversal, portraying Nehru as a matron, and at other times the entire bevy of politicians, including Nehru, were shown as children. As the leading woman politican in the cabinet, Amrit Kaur is conspicuous as the figure draped in a white sari with the *pallu* (edge of the sari) covering her head. At other times Amrit Kaur was a little girl with a frock and shoes and a *Jamadarin* (sweeperess).[7]

These disputes and resolutions about Shankar's cartoons were peripheral moments in the main course of events, anecdotally recorded in memoirs and in letters. This marginality notwithstanding, the divergent sense of humor disrupted, divided, antagonized, and created alliances among followers, who were otherwise united in their acceptance of Gandhi and the Congress.

Good art but bad taste: Jinnah and the Muslim League

In 1939, Gandhi sent Shankar a postcard while traveling by train from Wardha, criticizing a recent cartoon and offering him advice on the ethics of cartooning. For the week of September 28, when Gandhi wrote the postcard, Shankar had drawn two cartoons on Muhammad Ali Jinnah, so it is difficult to detect which cartoon Gandhi had in mind in his complaint (see Figure 3.5). His judgment of the cartoon's good art, factual inaccuracy, and bad taste delineated three layers for a critical reading:

Your cartoon on Mr. Jinnah was in bad taste and contrary to fact. You fulfill merely the first test of a cartoonist. Your cartoons are good as works of art. But if they do not speak accurately and cannot joke without offending you will not rise high in your profession. Your study of events should show that you have an accurate knowledge of them. Above all you should never be vulgar. Your ridicule should never bite.[8]

When Shankar received the postcard critical of his cartoon, much had transpired in the subcontinent and between Gandhi and Jinnah. Nationalist politics became complicated, veering toward a two-nation ideology for an independent India and Pakistan. Gandhi and Jinnah became iconic leaders of the anti-British crusade in India, representing in the public imagination irreducible differences between Hindus and Muslims. Jinnah defined the "vital principle" of Pakistan in five words: "The Muslims are a nation."[9] But both leaders defined religious identity as culture with history, thus reinscribing nation and belonging as a cultural and historical issue. "You must remember that Islam is not merely a religious doctrine but a realistic and practical code of conduct," Jinnah continued. "I am thinking in terms of life ... of everything important in life. I am thinking in terms of our history, our heroes, our art, our architecture, our music, our laws, our jurisprudence." In all these matters, including names, clothes, food, and treatment of women, Jinnah saw a fundamental difference and antagonism between Hindus and Muslims: "We are different beings ... We eat the cow, the Hindus worship it. A lot of Englishmen imagine that this worship is

"I WILL BE DROWNED"

The resolution passed by the Working Committee of the Muslim League states: "So far the special powers of the Governors have remained dormant and obsolete and the Governors have failed to protect the rights of the Muslims."

3.5 Shankar, "I Will Be Drowned." *Hindustan Times*. September 20, 1939. New Delhi. Courtesy of the *Hindustan Times*. The resolution passed by the Working Committee of the Muslim League states: "So far, the special powers of the governors have remained dormant and obsolete and the governors have failed to protect the rights of the Muslims."

Gandhi was critical of Shankar's visual liberties with his cartoons on Jinnah, prompting an advisory postcard on the importance of maintaining accuracy and good taste in cartoons.

merely a picturesque convention, an historical survival. It is nothing of the sort."

"Mr. Gandhi," as Jinnah chose to address the Mahatma, made several overtures to deflect this difference. Addressing "Brother Jinnah," Gandhi wrote him in Gujarati with an Urdu translation: "Don't regard me as the enemy of Islam or of any Muslims of this country."[10] Jinnah saw clearly that the claim of a united India was a British mythic creation that Gandhi, too, preached. Well-positioned spokesmen in the West and a powerful organization of the Hindu press, capitalists, and industrialists normalized the fiction, "Congress is India." This appealing slogan easily fabricated a popular picture of nationalists inching toward independence, slowed

down by separatist forces such as the Muslim League. It effortlessly
marked Jinnah and Pakistan as illiberal, reactionary, and sinister.[11]

To certify their politics in relation to the imagined futures of India
and Pakistan, newspapers were increasingly demarcated as Hindu and
Muslim. In this braid of nation, religion, and media, the newspaper cartoon
was a particularly generative space for churning conversations about
offenses given and taken, and the aesthetics of visual representations. For
all the differences that came to mark publicly the Congress and the
Muslim League, these two shared an immense faith in the force of the
English-language newspaper and the political cartoon. While the newspaper provided a mass medium for politics, cartoons rendered the divergent ideologies in a free play and friendly fire of caricature and humor.
M. A. Hassan Ispahani, a businessman and strong supporter of Jinnah
and the Muslim League, ran the *Star of India*, a Bengali newspaper from
Calcutta. He was also instrumental in establishing the League's newspaper *Dawn* as a Delhi-based daily rival of the *Hindustan Times*. The *Star
of India* and *Dawn* flourished under the editorship of Pothan Joseph, well
known for nurturing two cartoonists: Shankar Pillai and Enver Ahmed
(1909–92), and bringing cartoons to the front page of Indian newspapers. The Congress and the Muslim League kept a close eye on cartoons,
which frequently provoked correspondence and consultation like the
following from Ispahani:

> My dear Mr. Jinnah,
>
> I am enclosing a cartoon in the *Jugantar* dated 7th October, 1943.
> The *Jugantar* is the Bengali edition of the *Amrita Bazar Patrika* owned
> by the same concern. It shows to what depths of degradation politics
> in Bengal can go. The cartoonist actually makes fun of his gods and
> goddesses.
>
> With kind regards to Miss Jinnah and yourself,
>
> Very sincerely yours,
> HASSAN

Ispahani's letter to Jinnah was written in the midst of massive relief efforts
during the Bengal Famine, which saw unprecedented starvation and a severe
outbreak of cholera, leading to hundreds of thousands of deaths. The
reference to the cartoon gives pause. It certainly did to Jinnah, who did not
read Bengali and could not understand the cartoon: "Many thanks for your
letter of the 18th of October along with the enclosed cartoon in *Jugantar*, but
I am afraid, my Bengalee is not so good as to follow this unless you explain it
to me. However, I have kept it and would like to know what it means." What

Jinnah learned from Hassan is difficult to discern, for the latter replied that he would "explain the cartoon when we meet" (Ispahani 1967, pp. 89–91).

Let there be dawn

The cartoon rivalry between the *Hindustan Times* and *Dawn* became more than friendly fire between the Congress and Muslim League. Posting cartoon cuttings of their rival newspapers as evidence of impropriety, letters between leaders of these turbulent times give one pause to think about the place of cartoons in political representation. These matters of offense between officials and nationalist leaders were included amid discussion of the unimaginable violence and brutality that were engulfing a subcontinent in the throes of a territorial partition. Cartoons mattered in such violent times.

If Shankar and the *Hindustan Times* stayed busy caricaturing the League, then *Dawn* ensured equal frostbite for Nehru's Congress. "Will you please see the cartoon in *Dawn* of 1 January? This is particularly offensive," wrote Nehru in 1947 to the Congress stalwart Sardar Patel, drawing attention to Jinnah's newspaper.[12] Following cartoons was important; it provided a field for impropriety in which offense could be taken, registered, and administered – all in the name of good humor. Even Lord Wavell, the governor general and viceroy of India (1943–7), chimed in, cautioning Patel about the *Hindustan Times*'s cartoons:

The *Hindustan Times* of 15 March, both in its cartoon and in the report from the Punjab, seems to me to contain matter which is actionable under the Press Ordinance. I realize the depth of feeling that has been aroused by these communal disturbances, but I think you should look into the question whether or not action should be taken against the *Hindustan Times*.[13]

Patel agreed that the cartoon was "open to objection" but questioned whether it fell within the purview of the ordinance, since it did not incite communal hatred:

It would be impossible to establish that the cartoon has this effect. It is no doubt a vulgar or mischievous cartoon, but if you have been reading the *Dawn*, you would find that even worse things have been appearing there; I enclose a cartoon which appeared some time ago. I am sure this cartoon does not suffer by comparison with the one to which you refer.

Due to the communal bloodshed that soon became a nightmare for the two new nations, the press was legally bound not to publish reports that would incite violence. But these letters, like other correspondence by political players of the time, betray an ambiguity about the effects of cartoons. Do they incite violence or merely embody a breach of propriety in which vulgarity and friendly mischief were inseparable?

Whereas cartoons fell into a gray area, prose could ignite passions. In a letter to Wavell a week later, Sardar Patel enclosed a letter from the president of the Singh Sabha in Gujarkhan that the *Hindustan Times* refused to publish, fearing it would incite violence: "I thought that the description given there would be of interest to you. It may be an exaggerated picture, but it could not be wholly untrue."[14] The Singh Sabha president had noted in his letter of March 19, 1947, to the *Hindustan Times*:

Muslims launched a campaign of general slaughter and arson of Sikh life and property in the districts of Campbellpore Rawalpindi and Chakwal subdivision of Jhelum . . . To save their honor and religion hundreds of women jumped into wells and committed suicide. Hundreds of Sikhs and Hindus have been burnt and butchered although they valiantly defended themselves against heavy odds. Sikhs are the chief target.

The letter detailed people being burned alive, and affairs had "surpassed all inhuman atrocities." Emphasizing their refusal to publish this letter as an example of the editors' prudence, Patel's note to Wavell tells much about attitudes toward newspaper cartoons and prose, and the representation of reality. The Singh Sabha president's letter and plea for help in the Gujarkhan area rampage was easily deemed unpublishable because it seemed only remotely plausible, and certainly an exaggeration. (More than half a century later, however, on hindsight, that description carries a ring of possibility.) Ironically, the inherent exaggeration of caricature allowed it to remain permissible as news, unlike prose, which, using representational conventions of a witness's report about horrific violence, could be dismissed as exaggeration. The boundaries of permissible and prohibited representations tumbled in those macabre times when two nations were formed, confusing human possibilities and impossibilities.[15]

Fans and foes

Shankar's cartoons were published under multiple gazes – of the colonial state and of nationalist leaders like Gandhi and Amrit Kaur, whose nationalism converged from different vantage points. Gandhi's cartoon columns in his newspaper *Indian Opinion*, his disagreement with Amrit Kaur's complaint, and later his rebuke of Shankar all point to a pedagogical process of establishing norms for producing and interpreting cartoons. These interpretative foreclosures were not unlike that engaged in by the colonial state. But in the midst of these disapproving nods, Shankar could boast of a clutch of fans among colonial officials.

Sir Stafford Cripps, of the visiting three-member British Cabinet Mission that in 1946 mediated the last steps between the Congress and the Muslim League, wrote that

the best [cartoon] was where I was depicted as hiding myself underneath a bench and overhearing the confidential talks that were proceeding between [Maulana] Azad and others. I liked this cartoon so much that I made Lord Wavell [India's viceroy at the time] write for the original and obtained it. I am taking it with me. (Iyengar 2001, pp. 123–4)

Such compliments from a high British official could only further complicate public judgment on taste, politics, and Shankar's humor. Shankar presented Cripps with a bound volume of fourteen original "Cripps Cartoons." Lord Wavell, too, wrote Shankar a letter praising his cartoon "All is well that ends well." He received almost a hundred cartoons by Shankar (Lyon 1952, p. 24). In his lifetime, Shankar was candid about the official notice. While he was instrumental in caricaturing the human face of colonial villainy, Shankar voiced a desire to be unknown as their creator: "I get appreciations almost every week I think, but I want to remain unseen, if not unknown" (Iyengar 2001, p. 127). Since his cartoons were signed and part of a prominent newspaper, such obscurity could hardly be expected. Shankar's cartoons became desirable and collectible for British officials, unprecedented for an Indian cartoonist. They also ushered in the idea of the "original" to the Indian cartooning scene. This dual quality – collectibility and the original – signaled an emerging value system that brought cartoons a step closer to being considered a transcript of history and a work of art.

Soon conflict between Shankar and his editor Devdas Gandhi became public knowledge and caught Gandhi's attention. In a letter to Shankar, Gandhi noted his awareness of a lingering "jar" between his son Devdas and Shankar. Shankar's protégé, cartoonist Kutty, informed me that Shankar resigned from the *Hindustan Times* because he was consistently being pulled up by Devdas Gandhi for caricaturing the Congress stalwart Rajagopalachari, who coincidentally was Devdas's father-in-law. Another version of Shankar's departure was noted by the veteran journalist Prem Shankar Jha. Writing the history of *Hindustan Times*, Jha noted the newspaper rivalries and a "change of culture" initiated by Durga Das (1900–74), the manager of the *Hindustan Times*, which sparked Shankar's departure.[16] The various circumstances surrounding Shankar's resignation from the *Hindustan Times* suggest that by 1947, the press in India began to experience the strains of political affiliations made more complex by the interweaving of kinship among the industry, press barons, and politicians. In India, industrialists owned and financed the press, an unsurprising fact, since industrialists financed the Indian nationalist movement. This confluence of interests – political, industrial, and journalistic – marked the "culture" of each leading newspaper and shaped the movement of editors and cartoonists from one newspaper to the other.

The *Times of India* could not steal Shankar, neither could the *Hindustan Times* retain him. It is telling that Shankar resigned from the *Hindustan Times* a year before India's independence. Ahmed from Jinnah's *Dawn* took Shankar's place on Durga Das's staff. This coup of considerable proportion generated much excitement, as it brought Shankar's rival and Jinnah's arch-cartoonist to a Congress newspaper.[17]

The Partition decision and independence years saw Ahmed mercilessly caricature his former boss, the Muslim League leader Jinnah. In a cartoon titled "Separation, Not Liquidation" (see Figure 3.6), Ahmed not only evoked a mercantile imagery of the nations as a trade but also gave Nehru and India a history, making Pakistan the errant partner breaking away to set up his own business. Pakistan was about Jinnah. These notions of the Partition and Jinnah were humorously represented in the *Hindustan Times* – and this continues to inform popular understanding of India and Pakistan.

Ahmed's political potpourri in Kutty's words

As I prepared to track Shankar's cartoons, I wanted to know more about Shankar's rival, Envar Ahmed. Who better to ask than Kutty? He told me the story of Ahmed's life.

In 1930, a few years after Kutty was born, Envar Ahmed was a chemist in a sugar factory in Lucknow. When due to the depression the factory closed down, Ahmed, then 23, secured a position with the English newspaper in Lucknow, *Pioneer*. His job was to canvas for advertisements. When few advertisers showed interest, he was confronted with an unexpected proposition from his editor Desmond Young: "Why don't you become a cartoonist?" Ahmed could only reply, "I don't know how." "I'll tell you how" assured Young, and Ahmed's first cartoon appeared in *Pioneer* in 1933 (Shankar and Narula 1974, p. 89). At the time, Shankar was already an established cartoonist. Kutty went on with his memory of events:

Ahmed was a Muslim and later became a Christian after his marriage to a lady of British extraction (it is of no importance for our story, of course). He started life as a police officer in the United Provinces service. His schooling was Anglo-Indian, so that he was the so-called Westernized Indian of those days who knew very little of Indian culture or traditions. He was a very good artist. The Britisher, Mr. Desmond Young, editor of the *Pioneer*, noticed him and persuaded him to try cartoons and took him into the *Pioneer* of Lucknow. *Pioneer* was a British-owned

SEPARATION, NOT LIQUIDATION

"The June 3 Plan means the end of India as a nation."—Mr. Bhopatkar, President, All-India Hindu Mahasabha.

—June 25, 1947.

3.6 Ahmed, "Separation, Not Liquidation." *Hindustan Times*. June 25, 1947. New Delhi. Source: *Ahmed's Political Pot-Pourri*.

Nehru in his jacket, kurta, churidar, and Gandhi cap coolly stands at the door of a store called India – "The oldest firm in the East." Nehru matter-of-factly calms the sobbing Hindu Mahasabha president, "Dry those tears, friend. This shop is still the same even if my partner has decided to open his own firm." In the corner of the cartoon frame, Jinnah with rolled-up sleeves is perched atop a ladder, setting up his store's board, "Pakistan Stores, General Merchants. Proprietor M. A. Jinnah." A notice informs the reader and passersby: "Just opening. Entirely new venture. Goods expected any minute." Ahmed's hire in the *Hindustan Times*, drawing him away from Jinnah's newspaper, *Dawn*, was considered a coup.

paper. They wanted Ahmed to draw anti-Congress cartoons and he did it well from their point of view. His cartoons had very little Indianness. Later in 1943 or so, *Dawn*, Jinnah's newspaper, which was the mouthpiece of the Muslim League, published from Delhi, offered him the cartoonist's job. He was keen to migrate to Delhi. In *Dawn* he was really happy. He went on drawing anti-Congress cartoons. I am highlighting this anti-Congress aspect with a reason which we will soon come to. He regularly used to draw the Congress leaders as prostitutes and Gandhi as the madam.

Devdas Gandhi, the editor of the *Hindustan Times*, wanted to get rid of Shankar as the cartoonist for *Hindustan Times*. His advisor Durga Das evolved a plan. They declared *Hindustan Times* needed two cartoonists. They offered Ahmed a huge salary and every prerequisite he demanded, and Ahmed joined the *Hindustan Times*. The man who had been drawing such vulgar cartoons about Gandhi was embraced by the son of Gandhi! Shankar had no other alternative but to resign. Ahmed, of course, could not take Shankar's place of prominence. I wish you could see some of his *Dawn* cartoons. As you know, when Pakistan was born, *Dawn* shifted to Karachi.

The following year, on January 30, 1948, at a daily prayer meeting in Delhi's Birla House, Gandhi was assassinated. The same year, on September 11, Jinnah too died. By then, Shankar was busy with his new magazine, *Shankar's Weekly*, which would play a major role in providing a platform to aspiring cartoonists.

Shankar's Weekly (1948–75)

"You must see *Shankar's Weekly*." Kutty's parting words steered me to the home of India's longest running cartoon-based magazine – the Children's Book Trust (CBT). CBT stands in New Delhi's busy center for newspaper offices. The building is shared by other offices, and I remember visiting this place as a child; it housed the famous Dolls Museum, which now looked dusty, and in need of a makeover. For many of my generation, Shankar's name is familiar because of the annual Shankar's art competition that attracted hundreds of school-going children to Modern School's green grounds. But *Shankar's Weekly* marks a confluence of events of independent India. Its inauguration coincided with India's first year of independence. "For a few months [after leaving the *Hindustan Times*] he vegetated until his friends from far and near encouraged him to develop his idea of running a cartoonist weekly like the *Punch* now called *Shankar's Weekly*," the well-known journalist and India's first press information officer, A. S. Iyengar, recalled in his autobiography (Iyengar 2001, p. 122).

To aid my visit to CBT, Alka, Shankar's daughter-in-law, promised to help me find my way around the leather-bound collection of *Shankar's Weekly* issues and Shankar's drawings. She has also produced a biography of Shankar for children, published by CBT. "You can learn all about Shankar from that book," Alka assured me. Ravi, Alka's husband, has a prominent office on the premises, although he appeared a bit reticent, and, in fact, nobody in the family had much to say about Shankar. Ravi informed me of his plans to laminate all the drawings. The musty room where Shankar worked has a chest and big wooden reclining chair with a cover on it. "Shankar Sahib used to sit here. He worked in this room," said Narendraji, the office assistant. I imagined Kutty visiting this place and the many cartoonists who found a platform for their work in *Shankar's Weekly*.

Over the days, as I browsed among the cartoons and several drawings for Shankar's later project, a children's magazine, Ravi showed me a postcard wrapped carefully in a plastic envelope. It was Gandhi's 1939 postcard to Shankar advising him to be careful and considerate in his cartoons of Jinnah.

If these *Shankar's Weekly* issues could talk, what would they say? I turned the pages and admired the cartoons, film reviews, and articles. Thousands of cartoons and so many names! *Shankar's Weekly* was a national platform for aspiring cartoonists in various part of India until the magazine folded in 1975. This was effectively a compendium of cartoonists and caricature styles. The signatures below the cartoons included those of R. K. Laxman, Thackeray, Kevy, Rajinder Puri, Bireshwar, Reboti Bhushan, Chackalethu John Yesudasan, and of course Kutty, among many other prominent cartoonists. It was indeed a marvel that a magazine became a convergence point for so many regional artists. *Shankar's Weekly* also invited readers to contribute cartoons and designated a space for them. Blending in readers as cartoonists complicated the notion of a clear demarcation of producers and consumers. It placed cartooning as a public art, not just because it was meant for the public but because it was also of the public. Such contributions from readers might have also given Shankar a feel for talent, something akin to *American Idol* and other national talent-scouting that is the rage on television these days. In fact, several cartoonists have evoked Shankar as the "father of Indian cartooning." At the new Indian Institute for Cartooning in Bangalore, a photograph of Shankar hangs gracefully overlooking all who enter the institute's office. Yesudasan, a nationally fêted cartoonist based in Ernakulum, Kerala, has a caricature of Nehru by Shankar under a glass cover on his desk.

"Don't spare me, Shankar": feeling the nation

Contrary to Gandhi's stern rebuke in 1939, years later independent India's first Prime Minister, Jawaharlal Nehru, quipped, "Don't spare me, Shankar." Nehru's encouragement of Shankar and his cartoon weekly embodies a national lore repeatedly evoked through his famous remark.[18] Nehru took Shankar with him on his visit to the USSR in 1955, marking his elevated stature in Nehru's India (Figure 3.7). It also conveyed the place of cartoons in a new nation's media.

3.7 Jawaharlal Nehru receiving some books and badges from the Dean of Moscow University, USSR. 1955. Cartoonist Shankar (on the far right in a dark suit, tie and spectacles) with Prime Minister Nehru's entourage and Nehru's daughter, Indira Gandhi, in Moscow. Courtesy of the Nehru Memorial Museum and Library.

Such visits marked Shankar's elevated stature in Nehru's India and signaled the importance of his cartoon magazine, *Shankar's Weekly*.

To get a deeper sense of how the public responded to Shankar's cartoons, I read several exhibition guest books in the Shankar family holdings. Browsing through the pages from Shankar's 1989 traveling exhibition in major states such as Gujarat, Karnataka, Kerala, New Delhi, Tamil Nadu, and Uttar Pradesh gives a sense of what the visitors saw. The comments convey the experience of seeing cartoons, offering a peek into the inscription of perception in a public space. In their comments, visitors insisted on Shankar's accurate representation of the past: Shankar's cartoons were real, they were truth and history. Comments reveal a broad spread of the readership and national reach of Shankar's cartoons. Facing the guest book at a recent Japan Foundation exhibition in New Delhi, I realized I was flipping pages before composing my own comment. Such browsing sets the tone, an invitation to join an ongoing conversation – peeking into other comments and writing one's own. But who was I writing for? And what destiny awaits these books when the exhibition concluded?

The guest books from Shankar's exhibit began to speak, and the conversation became clearer with each page I turned. This was not just a catalogue of a general public and prominent personalities, taking turns writing. Sometimes brief, at other times offering lengthy analysis, these comments repeatedly evoked history and nostalgia. Sense and sentiment leapt from these pages. Seeing, feeling, and writing in turn, fans, visitors, friends, peers, and political observers gave a glimpse of perspectives. They were an ephemeral community, archived for posterity in nine volumes. Turning pages, pausing to read. Feeling the pleasure and loss. Thinking about the visitors. Where were they now? I imagined these comments as a long conversation.

Chetna aur chintan: alertness and thought in guest books

G. L. BHATNAGAR: I came across the *Shankar's Weekly* magazine and till its closure I have read all his weeklies. I do not foresee such a genius of the stature of Cartoonist Shri Shankar Pillai. Late Pandit Nehru was amused by Shankar's sketches and took them lightly, but now it is impossible for a cartoonist to say things against the high-ups. (New Delhi)

B. L. PARIMOO: If Nehru was great, Shankar was equally great because he could clearly steer into Nehru's mind. (New Delhi)

A. K. VINOD: He did it. But he has a lot of acquaintance with Nehru, which helped him to watch him carefully. Maybe this is the case with many other cartoonists. Anyway, his approach is elegant and fantastic. (Kerala).

A. SUBRAMANIAM: Shankar must have truly loved the object of his caricature. It shows in every picture. (Tamil Nadu)

HEMANG PATEL: I think Shankar was praising Nehru all the time. I find no criticism about his government's policy or any of his decisions. However, excellent. (Gujarat)

DR. DESAI: Good exhibition, but not a complete one. Because by this Nehru is figured out only as a politician. But first he was also a philosopher and progressive thinker of any situation. Second, in this exhibition there is only praise and not a single fault of him. (Gujarat)

DR. DUMRA: After seeing the cartoons my impression of Nehru has changed toward respecting him a bit more. But Shankar has not shown us his other side except political. (Gujarat)

VIPIN JAIN: *Shankar ke kartoon ki nazar se Nehruji ko padhna, dekhan ek yaadgaar anubhav hai* (To read and see Nehruji from Shankar's perspective is a memorable experience). (Uttar Pradesh)

JAYASRI LALITHA: The exhibition could as well be called modern Indian history through Shankar's cartoons. (New Delhi)

K. LALIT: A historical nostalgia. As if going through the events after independence. An epoch-making event in the capital. (New Delhi)

V. JANAKIRAMAN: Revived nostalgic memories of the "originals" seen in the *Weekly*. (Tamil Nadu)

M.S. PRASAD: For two hours I became younger by thirty years. (Karnataka)

RAJESH BHAN: Past our era. Not quite understood by the youth. (Gujarat)

MRS. SODHI AND FAMILY: They show how democratic our country is. (New Delhi)

V. THIYAGARAJAN: How intellectual Shankar is! No problem is solved even now itself. These are all immortal. (Tamil Nadu)

PROFESSOR GOPAL: The present-day politicians and administration should study the cartoons carefully and draw inferences. (Karnataka)

SAKKIR HUSSAIN: All the cartoons show that Shankar is the "King" of Indian cartoonists. (Kerala)

YESHUDRA BHARDWAJ: This has been my first visit to a gallery exhibiting cartoons – Shankar was stupendous indeed in every creation of his. (Gujarat)

That Nehru figured prominently in the guest book comments is not surprising; independent India's first Prime Minister was Shankar's muse. Their camaraderie and the cartoons stirred exhibition visitors such as S. K. Poshi from Orissa to reflect on the cartoons as something more – an emotional bond: "A true friend can only draw such cartoons about his beloved and best friend." For T. C. Rao of New Delhi, the exhibition was not about cartoons but about "the bond that existed between Shankar and Nehru."

These cartoons embodied a history lesson in images; they were about Shankar, Nehru, and a more elusive intangible something – nostalgia: "The exhibition made me relive those days in fifties and sixties when we grew up along with Nehru's ambitions and his flashes and fame ... Brings back nostalgic memories of old times."[19] Visitors frequently noted their experience seeing this pictorial history. They got "a feel of the past": touching, spellbinding, memorable, nostalgic. Nostalgia seemed a strange sentiment to encounter in these guest books. Barely four decades since India's independence, what had been lost? *Shankar ke vyang chitra se guzarna ek yug se guzarna hai* (to traverse through Shankar's cartoons is to traverse an era): Arvind's comment in a guest book from Shankar's cartoon exhibition in New Delhi's Rabindra Bhavan gallery is among several hundred recorded in nine volumes. Dr. Akavoor Narayan, a Shankar fan, whom I visited to speak with and to see his collection of *Viswaroopam*, was among the visitors who recorded their tributes in the guest book: "It was for me a nostalgic journey through those times." Reboti Bhushan's comment in the Delhi guest book caught my eye: "Quite nostalgic." Reboti Bhushan, whose work I had seen in *Shankar's Weekly*, would tell me in a later interview that Shankar had declared him the best animal caricaturist in India. What the visitors wrote told as much about themselves as about Shankar, Nehru, and India: their nostalgia for the lost vision of a modern nation. Until his death in 1964, Nehru was Chacha (Uncle) to India's young citizens; in seeing these cartoons, many of the visitors may have briefly returned to their adolescent years. Several comments expressed a yearning for a past that disappeared too soon and their satisfaction in reliving history through the cartoons.

Ravi Jain of New Delhi had seen the cartoons when they were originally published in *Shankar's Weekly*. But "to see them together was fascinating," he wrote. A part of this fascination was due to the nostalgic interweaving of the biography of the self with that of the post-independence nation, evoked by the memory of having seen these cartoons. T. V. K. Warrier wrote, "I used to see Shankar's cartoons week after week in late forties, fifties and early sixties. I could identify each and every leader in these cartoons with whom Panditji had been caricatured. But I could not laugh aloud ..." Warrier's comment trails away, making it difficult to decipher accurately. It seemed he could not laugh aloud again when he saw those cartoons in the exhibition. Something stole that laughter.

These visual cues not only represented a factual, historical past but also triggered imagination of impossible futures. The possible future was not promising. Nostalgia here was a sense of loss not just of the past but of what could have been. It was about disappearance and also the disappointment of an appearance that was a no-show – an "ambivalent longing."[20] The visitors' longing for the Shankar-Nehru era was an "exhaustion of cultural resources and creativity" of their time (Huyysen 1986, p. 162). The visitors' nostalgia surfacing in Shankar's cartoon exhibition placed the modern nation as the center of desire. "What a farsightedness in the cartoons! We are where we were almost decades ago. But we don't have a Panditji among us to save us from the rot."[21] The farsighted cartoons from decades ago, it seems, were prophetic: Shankar showed the readers that they were building an elusive modern nation.[22]

If nostalgia was about elusive desire, then nostalgia, too, could elude. Those of another generation, for whom the political moment in the cartoons was passé, were distant and indifferent to Nehru and Shankar. For some visitors this yearning was a puzzle and the cartoons strange. Language had a part to play: "All the pictures are good but their meaning in Kannada will be useful for people's knowledge": Rajakeerth's note reminded me that Shankar's cartoons and the exhibition addressed a public who knew English. The barrier of language was apparent to me in other ways too: several comments were in Tamil and Kannada, which I could not read. Time, too, was insurmountable in the attempt to commiserate with the prevailing nostalgia. "We wish we could relate to the cartoons. We are not aware of the political happenings during Nehru's era": Kavita, Geetanjali and baby Anupama (1+ years) were strangers to this time from the past. Living in the nearby Sangli Apartments, they may have been curious about the busy exhibition and stopped by to see, but they were certainly not *Shankar's Weekly* readers. Such visitors were doubly inconvenienced. The exhibition did not have background material to contextualize the cartoons. Each guest brought his or her own background to make sense of the exhibition, prompting a frustrated Rajeev Ashish to register a suggestion: "A short life sketch of Shankar and his career was absolutely necessary." But the past holds emotions other than wistful desires.

Contrary to nostalgia, some visitors were critical of the past Nehru and Shankar embodied. Among them, C. T. Vairavan had a lesson for visitors after him to consider:[23]

Some are born great like Swami Vivekananda and some become great (by their own efforts) like Mahatma Gandhi. But there are some on whom greatness is thrust upon, like Nehru.

So it is not a wonder Shankar too like any other cartoonist of his times joined in glorifying (the so-called great) Nehru.

Nehru had the tactics to ask Shankar not to spare him, as he knew well the common human mind's tendency to do just the opposite of what is being asked to do. If Nehru asked Shankar to spare himself, Shankar would not have spared him (Nehru) and would have criticized Nehru badly for all his commissions and omissions. But as Nehru asked him cleverly not to spare him (from criticism), naturally Shankar tended to spare him, and so one could hardly see any harsh criticism of Nehru in all these cartoons. None of these cartoons bring out boldly the Himalayan blunders and vested interests of Nehru. All cartoons depict Nehru as superstar megastar of India. Present-day politicians too, if they are portrayed like this, would only praise the cartoonist and they too would ask him not to spare him (like this). Because they are all high glorifications of an ordinary human mortal, portraying him as a superhuman, while he is only an ordinary human, having the chance of fortune smiling on him.

India has produced really great men like Gandhiji, Rajaji, Sardar Patel, and Nethaji Subash Bose, but pathetically power has gone in to the hands of an ordinary politician like Nehru and his family till date, so that Nehru seems to be a really great man – while in fact NEHRU meant only as follows: National-Exploitation-Horrible-Ruthless-Unimaginable – which would be understood by the whole nation tomorrow after the exit of Nehru dynasty rule. Which is as sure as the sun rising in the East tomorrow. Thank you.

Vairavan doubted Shankar lived up to the cartoonist's mantle, and as an observant reader, commenting in the guest book, he spared neither Shankar nor Nehru. Such review of what Nehru really meant sharpened because, by the time of this cartoon exhibition in 1989, almost two decades since his death, Nehru's daughter and grandsons dominated the political scene, charting a dynastic rule in a democratic polity. This presumptive dynasty frowned upon leadership contests and was part of a process that cartoonist Rajinder Puri has noted was Nehru's and the Congress party's "convoluted view of democracy" (1971, p. 23). Nehru's daughter Indira Gandhi (1917–84) held the post as India's Prime Minister for several years until her assassination. During her lifetime, her son Sanjay Gandhi (1946–80) was an influential Congress leader and heir until his fatal helicopter crash. Indira Gandhi was succeeded by her son Rajiv Gandhi (1944–91), a reluctant political debutant, who enjoyed electoral victories and, like his mother, was assassinated while in office. Vairavan's critique of Nehru emanated from Shankar's cartoons that showed him in a positive light, and is indicative of oppositional readings in the context of a press that was adulatory of Nehru. "With independence," cartoonist Chandi noted, "the big press formed with Nehru a mutual admiration society" (Lahiri

1994). It was Puri, then a young cartoonist with the *Hindustan Times*, who broke tradition and was "perhaps the first cartoonist to have attacked Nehru, sometimes irreverently, sometimes angrily in the national press of India (1971, p. 159).

These years were marked by the scrutiny of India's press and the maintenance records of newspaper production and circulation, which were undertaken by the Registrar of Newspapers in India. Cartoons too figured in this calibration because they were perceived as "increasing in popularity." In 1956, 28 percent of daily newspapers report carrying cartoons.[24] In 1964 the Annual Report noted cartoons' increasing popularity: "Cartoons are becoming more and more popular as a form of political and social satire on topical subjects. Strip cartoons also are proving a powerful attraction for the readers. All the big papers intimated that they publish cartoons more or less regularly. 'Hindustan Times' and 'Times of India' (Bombay) had engaged staff cartoonists."[25] That year, daily newspapers employed 45 cartoonists.[26] By 1967, the number rose to 50.[27] In 1965, 24 big, 72 medium, and 45 small papers published cartoons. Although the numbers reflected the response returned from only 383 newspapers, the Report indicated that, on average, big newspapers published most cartoons, followed by medium and small papers. The 20 big papers together employed 14 cartoonists, the maximum for any one newspaper being two. Medium papers reported employing 25 cartoonists, and small papers 18.[28] Among these numbers the prominent cartoonists Kutty and Bireshwar stood tall. Their life stories convey a nuanced understanding of the making of cartoonists that statistics cannot capture.

Part II

National times

4   Becoming a cartoonist: Mr. Kutty and Bireshwarji

"Seeing these cartoons is like meeting an old friend," Kutty wrote as he pored over his cartoons. We would frequently email each other, and I tracked Kutty's old cartoons beginning from the 1940s, sending him copies and scans. These cartoons became narrative cues, reviving memory and creating new memories. There were occasions when Kutty would deny he drew a particular cartoon, and I too could not be sure since Kutty changed his signatures until he became an established cartoonist and settled for "KUTTY." But when he saw the cartoon, Kutty would recant and scold himself for a failing memory. One such moment was Kutty's first cartoon in the *National Herald* in 1941 – it marked an important step in Kutty's career, but until he saw the cartoon, he would not easily believe me:

KUTTY: Yes, Yes, Yes! This cartoon is mine! I can't believe it. I landed in New Delhi on January 3 and here is my cartoon appearing in the *National Herald* on fifteenth! (That is why I wrote to you before seeing it that probably it could have been somebody else's cartoon.) One side is Jinnah. On the other side are Sarvarkar and Dr. Moonjee of the Hindu Maha Sabha. Jinnah was the most Anglicized man of that generation. He could be recognized only in that dress. The three-piece suit was as much the trademark of Jinnah as the waistcoat was that of Nehru or the long walking stick of Gandhiji. Additionally this was a way of emphasizing that Jinnah was a stooge of the British.

Telling the story of cartooning through individual lives is to traverse the space between ethnography and biography. Such "ethnographic biography," as Michael Herzfeld lucidly called it, "allows us to move along a trajectory of life that has bisected many histories" (Herzfeld 1997, p.1). In their succinct history of the biography as an anthropological mode of writing, Lewis L. Langness and Gelya Frank have pointed to the impulses that led to biography among anthropologists.[1] Drawing on their work, I would like to emphasize particular dimensions of this history of the uses of biography as it relates to understanding culture. The biographical can be situated as emerging from a new mode toward eliciting the 'insider's perspective' (Radin 1999); as an outcome of a psychiatric methodology

121

that focused on the individual and personality as the locus of cultural effects (Du Bois 1944); and finally as a method for exploring the relation between individual and structure and therefore cultural change (Kennedy and Fahim 1977). This schema for historicizing biography in anthropology was further nuanced by feminists who, in the decade around the publication of *Writing Culture*, proposed a feminist ethnography in which the auto/biographical was among a mix of genres that converged the creative and critical.[2] The biographical mode as a feminist methodology has also been situated against discourse, as "history" (Chakravarti 1998) and to also constitute an archive for a counter-history in which discourse and reality are "interdependent" rather than in "opposing domains" (Burton 2003, p. 5). Although Antoinette Burton made this claim for women's narratives of home told as colonial subjects at the intersection of home and history, and related to both imperialist and nationalist projects, this framework for a counter-history of modernity resonates well with the life stories of cartoonists. As colonial and postcolonial subjects, Kutty's and Bireshwar's narratives, caricaturing everyday political life, rest at the inter-section of representation and history. As a daily ritual of visualizing the key political event of the day, the newspaper cartoon intervened in the prose of news, to render reality in a snap. As a particular type of talk, the biographical narrative is also a strategic style for articulating "a different voice" (Gilligan 1993, p. xiii) that is relational.[3] For Carol Gilligan, speaking and listening are relational (p. xvi) and, indeed, I elicited this narrative of cartooning by listening and picking on comments and remarks that made a deeper impression on me. This auto/biographical narrative constitutes a different voice because the cartoon's in-between form situates its practitioners uniquely within and without the discourse and history of modernity. Becoming a cartoonist is about acquiring legitimacy as an image-maker, who resides among journalists, artists, and humorists.

"Life is what happens to you, when you are busy making other plans," Kutty, a voracious reader of biographies, repeatedly quoted. Becoming a cartoonist was one of those happenings. To adapt Kutty's favorite saying, ethnography is what happens when you are busy making other fieldwork plans. My chance meetings with Kutty and Bireshwar quickly opened new possibilities to learn about their cartooning years. The two cartoonists were contemporaries, both well connected with Shankar and *Shankar's Weekly*, and they also both spent a part of their career in Kolkata and Lucknow. This intersecting world of the two cartoonists yielded contrasting life stories about becoming a cartoonist. For several years, I corresponded with Kutty and Bireshwar, apprising them of my research and engaging them with the story I was crafting. Although Kutty had a successful career in several English-language newspapers, his enduring impact was as a Bengali-language newspaper cartoonist. This struck me as odd, because Kutty was from the southern state of Kerala, where Malayalam is spoken, and he did not know Bengali. Furthermore, given the prestige associated with the English press, I wondered why, after a stellar foundation as Shankar's protégé, Kutty would secure a future in a regional-language newspaper in West Bengal. Bireshwar moved from a Hindi-language newspaper to an English-language newspaper with a national standing, charting a predictable upward mobility in the complex world of Indian linguistic politics and its press.

India's linguistic culture partially overlaps with its twenty-eight states and seven union territories. The Indian constitution initially recognized fourteen languages, according them a national status. That number has grown to twenty-two. The linguistic expertise demanded by this sheer number of languages humbles any attempt at writing a history of the Indian press. Due to the number of Indian cartoonists and their diverse linguistic and regional contexts, it would be impossible to envision a definitive history of Indian cartooning. Such acknowledgment of partial histories is not a postmodern conceit; in India it is a reality. However, a history can be told as experiential knowledge touched by personal memory. My field notes were a part of this emerging historiography and not "mere recording of data."[4] Such modes of knowing can be absorbed as history and ethnography, and at this boundary between genres and disciplines, I engaged with cartoonists.

Kutty (1921–2011)

Retired and living in Madison, Wisconsin, with his wife Gouri and their daughter Maya and her family, Kutty was actively in touch with his peers through email and letters. He wrote me on December 16, 2002:

Dear Ms. Ritu,

You seem to have already done a lot of research. Your reference to *Viswaroopam* astonished me! I can go on supplying you facts about cartoons and cartooning as and when I remember them. Your list of questions will keep me busy for quite some time. I will need some time to recall all the things I used to know.

After going through your list of subjects I am to cover, I feel it may be better if you could meet me and record the information you need. I feel there is a great deal of information I may be able to give you. I had an occasion to go deep into this subject, but unfortunately I do not have any records. Talking about it may revive my memory.

So, I believe it may be better if you can come down to Madison. Do you have any contact here? How can you organize the visit? We will be happy if you can join us for Xmas. Along with the festivities we can manage to do some worthwhile work afterwards. I leave it to you. Let me know how you can manage it.

I never knew Bharathi did cartoons! My God. I would like to see some of his cartoons. Really, you are doing a great service to cartoon history. Give me some time to ponder over the history of Indian cartooning. I shall certainly love to help you along. I wish you all success and pledge whatever little contribution I can make to your great project.

With regards,
Kutty

Kutty and Bireshwar, in fact, constantly reminded me about their advancing age and told me to hurry before it was too late. "I must be the oldest Indian cartoonist alive today, you should hurry up and ask me all I know," said Kutty. Bireshwar cautioned me, "I am waiting for death. I am now facing hazards of old age and becoming weak day by day." With this urgency in tow, after our initial meeting, we continued five years of correspondence while I traveled to various archives in India and Britain, and met with other cartoonists.

Cat sannyasi: the world's first cartoon

To be an anthropologist, to walk into people's lives and talk, was initially torturous for me. For the next several years, I would frequently find myself in such discomfort, for I met most cartoonists at their homes. Soon, the cartoonists' and their families' kindness and patient conversations helped me to overcome my reticence. But the guilt at my self-interest and at being at the receiving end of knowledge about Indian cartooning and generous hospitality weighed heavily.

It was Christmas and I was in Madison to meet Kutty. I was shy about disturbing his family at this usual time for reunions and intimate celebration. This time, I decided to spend the day in my extended-stay hotel and visit the Kutty household after Christmas.

Their cozy home had a pleasant wintry view through the living room. Strings of small green, pink, and yellow bulbs adorned the window frame and arch in the large room. A big Christmas tree grabbed my attention as I entered the expansive room. Framed cartoons of Maya's portly husband Tony and a signed cartoon by the Pulitzer Prize-winning cartoonist Bill

Mauldin hung on the wall. "He is like Ganesh, isn't he?" Kutty smiled affectionately at his son-in-law's caricature. Maya's warm welcome soothed my nerves.

Kutty had several typed notes to show me, a book to present, and many anecdotes to share. We both knew that it would take several months to recount what Kutty had to say about his nearly six-decade cartooning career. It was with this sense of a beginning that I sat across from Kutty on a large brown sofa and started to piece together our email exchange (see Figure 4.1).

"No, no," interjected Kutty, adjusting his gold-rimmed wrist watch; he set another beginning for our conversation. Raising his right hand and forefinger, pointing back to a time long ago, "but to begin with, Indians have a habit of claiming they discovered everything."

Computers, they say, were there during the time of the *Ramayana* and *Mahabharata*. Even aeroplane. The oldest cartoon I have seen was in a temple in south India.

4.1 Cartoonist Kutty at his home, December 26, 2002. Madison, Wisconsin, USA. Photograph by the author.
   "Indians have a habit of claiming they discovered everything. Computers, they say were there during the time of the *Ramayana* and *Mahabharata*. Even aeroplane. The oldest cartoon I have seen was in a temple in south India. I don't remember the name, you will have to research and find out."

I don't remember the name, you will have to research and find out. The old cat became a sannyasi in order to catch the mice. Cat sannyasi is a famous *Panchatantra* story. The cat's face resembled the Maharaja, who ordered the temple to be constructed. The sculptor wanted to make the point that, in his old age, the cruel Maharaja was absolving himself of his sins by building a temple. This is 3,000 years old. This is the first cartoon!

In the next five years, Kutty's emails and letters took me to the past he lived and experienced.

Mad drawings

KUTTY: Truth, when it gets old, has the tendency to look like fiction. I was born in Ottapalam on September 4, 1921. At that time a revolt of the Muslim community, who are called the Mapillas, against the British was going on. This revolt was confined to an area near Ottapalam in the state now called Kerala. Many people died. Many refugees from the affected areas moved away and some came to our town for protection. My father, being a prominent man of the area, had to extend his hospitality to several of them. My birth at that time added to the already prevalent confusion.

Early in my life my mother died. I grew up in a joint Hindu *maumakka-thayam* (matrilineal) family. Survival then was not difficult, basic food was there. But for luxuries one had to strive hard; I had to work harder since I had no mother to care for me. I found I could draw. My older sister, she was a teacher in a convent in Malabar. She was a good artist and mastered watercolors; she made her own New Year cards and Christmas cards for the nuns. When she visited home, she brought paints and colors. My sister encouraged me, even though my father dissuaded me from that art. Poor man, he could see no financial future in that field. He was convinced drawing was a waste of time. Somehow God maneuvered me into acquiring the rudimentary abilities to draw, especially caricatures. I realized I had the ability to make people laugh. I exploited this God-given gift and was coasting along comfortably. I used to make caricatures of my friends and teachers, sometimes with painful results. I had a general idea of what was politically happening around me. I was fascinated by the freedom struggle. I followed British politics, too. My history teacher at school encouraged me in that I knew Lloyd George, Ramsay McDonald, Baldwin, and Churchill of Britain. I knew Gandhi, Nehru, Patel, Jinnah, and other leaders too. In those days, textile mills used to market their products such as the cotton dhoti with color pictures of national leaders stamped on them. I copied those pictures and painted them. In those days only pictures of gods and goddesses were available in the market.

When my sister visited, to please her I would draw birds and trees, but the rest of the time I drew political leaders. I used to show my drawings only to my friends, never to my drawing teacher. You see, in those days we had peculiar drawing teachers. Those fellows who were unable to get any job could get a diploma to teach art in small schools by just learning how to make rectangles and quadrilaterals. We had such a teacher. He would not allow me to go beyond his scope of drawing. If I drew a horse, he would say, "No, this is not a horse. Draw it like I have drawn."

In my childhood, no cartoons or comic strips were available. Cartoons were not part of Indian weeklies or monthlies or daily newspapers of those days. I used to see these distorted pictures in the old British newspapers that were imported to India for using as packing materials. You know the *raddi walla* [scrap dealer who recycles newspapers] in India. Just the same, the British dumped their old newspapers such as the *Daily Mail* in India; it was a big business in those days. Every store used to pack groceries in these papers. These pictures caught my fancy, and I would bring home cuttings of these cartoons and copy (the same thing had happened to some others also who came into the field). When I was about ten years old or so I came across *My Magazine*, which was a humorous magazine modeled on *Punch*. Of course, I had at the time not even heard about *Punch*. Another competitor of *My Magazine* was *The Merry Magazine*, also from Madras. Mali [a cartoonist][5] used to draw in one of the two. One had to read English magazines to be considered prestigious then. Since I did not know Tamil I had to be content with *My Magazine* and *Merry Magazine*. I do not remember the names of any of those Tamil cartoonists. These were some of the influences I had.

These magazines did not come to my house. Our neighbors, who were lawyers and doctors, had these magazines, which also used to come to our teachers' room in my school. The newspaper boy and I were of the same age, so when delivering magazines he would let me take a peep at them. Later, some Indian newspapers started reproducing current and topical cartoons from British papers. The *Madras Mail* used to reproduce cartoons by the British cartoonist Wyndham Robinson. In addition to these, the Madras-based Sunday paper the *Sunday Observer* used to reproduce many other British cartoonists. Gradually, I too tried to fashion some pictures modeled on the cartoons in the papers – just for amusing my friends. I never even imagined cartooning could be a profession or even that one could earn any money from these mad drawings.

I drew cartoons in my college magazine in Madras Christian College that was edited by the well-known humorist Professor Mannikoth Ramunni Nair, whose pen name was Sanjayan. He had a big library and a big bundle of *Punch*, which he got regularly. That was a treasure house for me. I was young then and thought I knew enough about cartoons. Later when he started the magazine *Viswaroopam*, his cartoonist M. Bhaskar was briefly sick and I worked for the magazine in Calicut. I got paid for this, about twenty or thirty rupees. I got intrigued by this. I brought presents for everyone at home and became a local hero.

I kept my contact with *Punch* throughout my life until the magazine closed down. I even subscribed to *Punch* for a few years when I was in Delhi. M. Bhaskar was a graduate of the Madras Art School; he was a great draughtsman. His cartoons were the first I saw drawn by a Malayalee which had drawings as they should be. I would say Vasu Pillai and David Low were my first teachers of cartooning. Vasu used to draw like Low; after meeting Vasu I decided I too wanted to draw like Low. Low did not draw any anti-India cartoons but we were interested in his anti-Mussolini and anti-Hitler cartoons. However, my first response was to Low's drawing, not his subject. Low's drawing fascinated me: black and white. Just black blocks of drawing on white. In the case of Vasu too, I liked his drawing; the subject matter – Indian politics – was known to me but not the drawing. Low's cartoon appeared once a week but Vasu's I could see every day. Vasu was my inspiration, until I met Shankar.

Cold Delhi, 1941

KUTTY: By sheer luck I got the chance to become the understudy of the great cartoonist Shankar at Delhi. He gave me thorough training for a few months and sent me to Lucknow to join the National Herald as staff cartoonist. This paper was started by businessmen friends of Jawaharlal Nehru. Nehru had asked Shankar to train a cartoonist for his paper.

Mr. V. P. Menon was the highest Malayalee official in Delhi. He hailed from Ottapalam, my home town. He was related to my father. Mr. Menon used to visit his old mother almost every year. Every time he came to the village he was surrounded by fathers bringing their sons to him. The highest ambition in those days was to get a clerical job. In 1940 when he came, my father took me to him to request for a job for me in Delhi. Menon was a very pleasant-mannered man. Even though he was a very important officer, he did not put on any airs. Whether he could give me any job or not, he did not want to displease my father. He asked my father, "Does he know shorthand and typewriting? When he gets a very good speed in both and a diploma then let me know." In those days, typewriting and shorthand were two accomplishments absolutely necessary for any aspirant to a clerical job. I said I was studying those subjects at Ottapalam. Mr. Menon advised my father to send me to Calicut to a recognized institute to acquire a diploma in these subjects. I butted in and said, "Calicut will suit me. I have some professional connection." "What connection?" asked Mr. Menon. "I draw cartoons for a magazine." That information seemed to electrify him: "What! You are drawing cartoons?" Actually I just wanted to escape from that interview with Mr. Menon. But my reference to the magazine intrigued him.

From then on he forgot my father and started talking to me direct. Mr. Menon was extremely happy that I was a budding cartoonist. He could not contain his excitement. He asked me whether I had any samples of my work. I had not carried any with me. I had not even imagined that Mr. Menon would be interested in my mad drawings. Mr. Menon told me that as soon as he went back to Delhi he would send me a book of cartoons drawn by a cartoonist named Shankar. I had no idea who Shankar was. Even though he was a famous cartoonist, his cartoons never appeared in papers in south India; I had not seen any of his cartoons. Mr. Menon asked me to go through that book and draw some new cartoons and send them on to him in Delhi. He wanted me to send some cuttings of my work in Viswaroopam, before he left for Delhi. I did not believe anything could come out of this meeting. Anyway, I sent through a brother of Mr. Menon some of my cuttings from Viswaroopam. I thought, and I believe my father suspected too, that Mr. Menon had cleverly got rid of us. I forgot all about this encounter.

A few weeks later, I got a registered parcel. It was a book of Shankar's cartoons, which Mr. Menon had promised to send me! From then on things looked rosier to me. I was all the time thinking of current politics. I managed to draw twelve or thirteen new cartoons and sent the whole lot to Mr. Menon. A couple of weeks after I had posted the cartoons to Mr. Menon, I received a letter from him. It was history repeating itself (a similar letter from my professor Sanjayan had pushed me into the cartoon arena). Mr. Menon asked me to come to Delhi as early as possible. Mr. Menon showed Shankar my work and requested him to take me on as his understudy. Mr. Menon was such an important man in Delhi, Shankar agreed to Mr. Menon's suggestion. There was the hand of providence in this development too. It so happened that a few months earlier Pandit Nehru had asked Shankar to provide a cartoonist for Nehru's daily English newspaper, *National Herald*, which his friends had financed and started from Lucknow as the Congress party's official paper. Shankar was close to Nehru and had been trying to get a cartoonist for that paper. None was available in Delhi. By luck I was chosen. My appearance at this particular time was a lucky turn of events for Shankar, too. He examined my work. He was sure he could do something with me. He asked Mr. Menon to arrange to bring me to Delhi.

My father must have reasoned that if Mr. V. P. Menon thought this was good for me it must be OK. But most others thought I was making a mistake. Their advice was that, since I was so close to Mr. Menon, I must try to get a clerical job in the central government, which was the ambition of most young men those days. That sort of job assured one a pension in old age. When I realized that, as a cartoonist, without doing much work I could not only make good money but also make a name too, I decided to stick to this profession. "Life is what happens to you while you are making other plans"– I have no idea who said that, but I fully agree with that statement. God had decided that I was to be a cartoonist. All of my friends, relatives, and well-wishers were happy for me. At least I was going to see Delhi. Since it was January, Delhi was very cold. Shankar advised me to be prepared with a woolen suit and a minimum of woolen things to fight the cold of Delhi. He told me other woolen things could be bought in Delhi. My sister gave me all the money needed for the woolen suits, the rail fare, and the money to stay in Delhi for some time. All my friends were there to see me off to Delhi. What touched me most was that the headmaster of my high school was one of my well-wishers who came to see me off. He blessed me. The railway fare for a third-class ticket to Delhi from Ottapalam was twenty-five rupees. In Delhi I was to stay in the South Indian Boarding House in Connaught Place.

Shankar, my guru

KUTTY: Very soon, I started working with Shankar, and whatever cartoon he approved, I started sending to the *National Herald* in Lucknow. From then on, I became Shankar's devotee until he died. My relationship with Shankar was just like the traditional *guru shishya parampara* of old times:[6] I became a part of his household. He took me almost everywhere he went. He entrusted all sorts of work to me; I was his shadow, literally. When people met me the first question used to be, "How is Shankar?" All the politicians and journalists treated me as a godson of Shankar. I was loyal to him like an Alsatian dog. Many people believed my cartoon ideas were actually his! Once one cabinet minister phoned Shankar and congratulated him on a cartoon of mine!

When I started my apprenticeship with Shankar, every morning I would go to his office. I would sit near him and draw ten or twelve ideas. He would pick two or three and then I would draw and show him. He would say, "No, not like this." Sometimes he would get very angry. My ideas were good, but I was poor in anatomy and technical things. Until his death, Shankar would keep telling me, "Improve your drawing. Improve your drawing."

"It is better to be the head of an ass than the tail of an elephant"

KUTTY: I joined the *Hindustan Standard*, the English paper of the *Ananda Bazar Patrika* group, in 1951. The first general election after the new Constitution was adopted was in 1952. Beginning with that election, every election found my cartoons and parts of them being used on the walls of buildings, not only in Calcutta but all over Bengal. In every nook and corner of the state my cartoons could be seen on the walls. All parties did it! Nothing could be done about it. They never bothered to get my permission. Bengal political parties not only copied my cartoons, they dissected and cut them, like their fish, and threw away portions they did not like!

In 1975, I switched over to the Bengali paper *Ananda Bazar Patrika*. By that time I had perfected my visual type of cartoon drawing – the least written matter in a cartoon. Within months I became a household name even among the so-called lower classes of people in Bengal [see Figure 4.2]. The Bengalis of all walks of life cannot live without fish, sweets, and *Ananda Bazar Patrika*. I became a celebrity. I knew it because I used to visit Calcutta once a year or so. After I became a Bengali cartoonist everybody [in Delhi] forgot me. I did not mind it. I enjoyed full freedom where I was. I followed Shankar's advice. He once told me, "It is better to be the head of an ass rather than the tail of an elephant." But I never lived in Calcutta. All my working life, from 1946 to 1997, I lived and worked from New Delhi. My cartoons about Bengal regularly appeared in Calcutta. I lived in Calcutta only after I completely retired from cartooning, from October 1988 to March 2001.

Kutty's comment on being the "head of an ass" conveyed Shankar's advice that it was preferable to be a leading cartoonist in a regional news-paper rather than occupy a peripheral role in a mainstream national news-paper. The puzzle about Kutty's switch from English to Bengali newspapers was solved. Shankar's career advice, along with Kutty's per-fection of the "visual-type" cartoon, allowed easy translation and familiar-ity for Bengali readers. Kutty's long-distance association also gave him insight into the Bengali psyche and love for their language. Such notions of culture and personality shape the everyday understanding of difference in India:

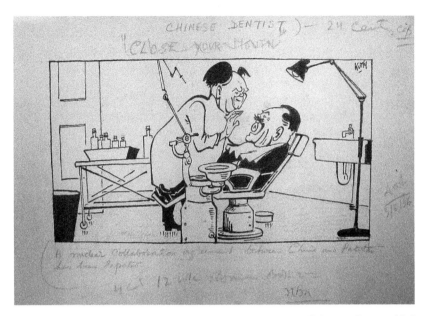

4.2 Kutty, "Chinese Dentist." August 3, 1966. Calcutta. Pen and ink artwork. Courtesy of *Ananda Bazar Patrika*. "A nuclear collaboration agreement between China and Pakistan has been reported."

Initially entitled "Close your Mouth," an editorial pen made the change. Kutty made the big four-column cartoon for the *Ananda Bazar Patrika*, a leading Bengali newspaper. The cartoon would be translated from English to Bengali.

KUTTY: The Bengalis are a very hypersensitive and temperamental people. Since I was staying in Delhi I was safe. If I had been living in Calcutta those days, some reader in a momentary rage could have hurt me physically, objecting to some cartoon. Angry letters used to come to me addressed to my office in Delhi. Later, when I retired and decided to stay in Calcutta since we had some close relatives there, I was amazed to find I was worshiped by the people. All doors opened for me. In several public occasions, people declared they were proud to have me live in Calcutta. They would have been doubly happy if I knew their language too! They love their language so much that they will excuse you anything if you, a non-Bengali, can speak Bengali.

When I visited Kolkata, I met several talented cartoonists. The *Ananda Bazar Patrika* library had a collection of Kutty's original cartoons, which they allowed me to browse and photograph. As I went over the yellowing sheets of pencil drawings, captions, sticky newspaper cuttings, and blue pencil marks, I continued to wonder at Kutty's seemingly odd career – there was no dearth of talent in Kolkata, yet an outsider, Kutty, became the pulse of the city's cartooning scene. That such matters were sensitive came to my attention through a well-known Bengali cartoonist's son, who advised that I not mention Kutty when interviewing his *Baba* (father). Kutty's large drawing sheets were replete with imagery from the cartoonist and illustrator John Tenniel's *Alice in Wonderland* and he seemed to be fond of using the imagery of the boiled egg placed on the cup. In these drawings lay the answer to the question that occupied me for a long time: What made Kutty popular in West Bengal? I also got a clue from Kutty's explanation of Victor Weisz's (Vicky, 1913–66) success in Britain. Belonging to a generation that looked up to David Low, Vicky established himself as a leading cartoonist and was associated with Britain's prominent newspapers, the *News Chronicle*, the *Daily Mirror*, the *Evening Standard* and the *New Statesman*.[7] Vicky's talent was obvious to those who recruited him, but so was his unfamiliarity with English and more importantly, British manners – a vital knowledge for cartooning. To remedy and retain Vicky, Gerald Barry, the editor of the *News Chronicle*, began "a patient process of conditioning."[8]

Like Vicky, who was Berlin-born and of Hungarian-Jewish descent, Kutty was an outsider to his readers:

KUTTY: Vicky was a Hungarian, who migrated to England. He did not know English. He became one of the greatest cartoonists in Britain. When asked how he managed this miracle, he said, "If a cartoonist in England knows the nursery rhymes and *Alice in Wonderland*, he can have ideas for cartoons for a lifetime." I know how right he was. You can see how much influence Alice had on me in my cartoons. *Panchatantra* stories were always useful, because most of the stories appeared in Aesop's fables too, and so were known to the English readers too.

John Tenniel's *Alice in Wonderland* drawings were Vicky's favorite[9] and brought together Vicky and Kutty. Among his Bengali readers, their familiarity with English literature assured language was no barrier for Kutty and his "visual type of cartoons."

Like his guru, Shankar, Kutty traveled abroad; he went to the USA, France, and Britain as part of a cultural exchange program. These travels, involving meeting Low and ascertaining techniques and cartooning practices, were a professional pilgrimage. Recalling details of this interaction gave a seal of authority, as it did for Kutty who worried he was erring in repeating his cartoons but was reassured when he met Low: "When I asked Low about this, he said it cannot be helped. The fact that public memory is short is the only consolation, he told me. He said every creative artist has this problem."

Apart from foreign travels, American and British magazines also provided a window into Western cartoons, for not all cartoonists had the opportunity to be sponsored for foreign travels. In fact, such sponsorship was the privilege of English-language newspaper cartoonists, who were also well connected politically and based in the nation's capital, New Delhi, or in the Mumbai metropolis. This traffic, both literal and literary, could indicate the global south's eagerness to know the West, as well as signal modernity's temporal lag in most of the world – always catching up with the West. But this synergy can be read in another way: if early anthropology shared a fuzzy boundary with imperial urges to know the darker world, then such eagerness to know the other had its counterparts in Indian cartoonists. Kutty joked with me that in his professionally active years, he had seen more of the USA than the "average American."

Bireshwarji (1921–2007)

Kutty started his career with the *National Herald*, and Bireshwar concluded his with the same newspaper. The two cartoonists were my companions through letters and emails during most of my research time. I would frequently send them old cartoons I could not figure out and pose questions about gaps in my findings. Both cartoonists have now passed away.

Bireshwar's career began in the world of Hindi newspapers. His career trajectory from Hindi to the English-language press marked an obvious progression. After gaining experience in the Hindi-language newspaper in Benaras, Bireshwar established himself as the staff cartoonist of the Lucknow-based English-language *National Herald*, which had recruited Kutty in 1941. Bireshwar and I corresponded through letters, and though our conversations in Lucknow were in Hindi, our letters were in English. I would enclose a self-addressed stamped envelope each time I sent a letter. However, Bireshwar would send me his letter either in an aerogram or a recycled envelope by unfolding and reversing an old envelope. For more than a decade before his death in 2007, Bireshwar led a retired life in Lucknow surrounded by his son's family, and he was busy with *satsang* (in good company, remembering God).[10]

Cartoonist Bireshwar's home was near the railway station. Lucknow's sweltering summer heat made it difficult to do much during the daytime, so Bireshwar's family asked me to visit in the evening. It was a good time also because Bireshwar would have taken his nap and rested. As is customary, I took a box of *mithai* – Indian sweets – when I visited. My husband's parents lived in Lucknow, and my father-in-law had insisted on accompanying me to Bireshwar's home. Bireshwar's daughter-in-law greeted us and invited us in. I was introduced to her and then to Bireshwar as a *bahu* – daughter-in-law – with a husband in the USA and a young child, who traveled with me. *Bhabhi*, meaning brother's wife, was how I addressed her; it gave us a comfortable social position and a mode of address. Though I don't remember Bhabhi addressing me by my name, she could have, since she had a higher status due to her age. Bhabhi handed me a sleek and small air horn to speak through. Bireshwar was eighty-two years old and his hearing had become impaired over the years. I had not spoken to any one through an air horn, and my mind began racing as to how I could hold a conversation. Bireshwar slowly walked into the living room. He wore a full-sleeved white shirt, spectacles, and a knee-length folded dhoti. "Namaste," I said, folding my hands and bowing in greeting. Bireshwar raised his hand in acknowledgment, gesturing me to stay seated. Bhabhi was there to make sure we were all comfortable. She spoke to Bireshwar through the air horn, demonstrating how to use it.

There was no need for me to say another word that evening. "You should first ask him where he was born," commanded my father-in-law, a retired professor of anatomy. Bhabhi promptly broadcast the question to Bireshwar.

BIRESHWAR: I was born in Kashi [Banaras, also referred to as Varanasi] and am from the middle class, the only son and child of my parents. My father was a postal employee in the Head Post Office of Banaras. My father and Bua [father's sister] came from a village near Chunar [Mirzapur in Uttar Pradesh]. Actually my father lived with my *bua* and *phupha* [father's sister's husband]. Phuphaji was his guardian after the death of my grandfather. He fixed my father in service of the Post Office and married him off also. My father and mother lived with them. My mother died very young and my *bua* adopted me and raised me, as she had no children. My father remarried but had no more children. I was very weak, because I didn't drink my mother's milk. I was zero in studies. Later I changed schools and improved in studies.

Some minutes through the conversation, Bhabhi got tea and the sweets: "You shouldn't have worried about the sweets, treat this as your own house. Pitaji [father] has 'sugar' [colloquial for diabetes] and will not eat sweets, so go ahead and help yourself to more." The evening passed with me transcribing and eating sweets while my father-in-law asked and Bireshwar answered all the questions. "No Luck Now," I told myself, would be a good caption, as I scribbled the scene before me. There was nothing more for me to say that evening; this was not going the way I wished. I began wondering how I could delicately tell my well-meaning father-in-law that next time I wanted to visit Bireshwar on my own.

Guruji Kedarji: "If you want to learn to beg, then learn art"

The next day I conspired with Balakramji, the family driver. Although I knew Bireshwar took an afternoon nap, I announced to my father-in-law that he would still meet with me. My little lie was timed to make a polite get-away because I knew my father-in-law would not forego his afternoon nap. Balakram and I waited near Bireshwar's house until evening. When we entered, a framed black-and-white photograph high up on the living room wall caught my attention. It was a photograph of Kedarji, Bireshwar's guru, who taught him all about drawing and art. Each year, Bireshwar celebrated Guru Purnima, a day allotted to acknowledge and honor the teacher. When he saw me gazing at the photograph, Bireshwar began telling me about his guru as follows.

BIRESHWAR: My guru was Kedarnath Sharma. Kedarji was a famous artist of Banaras and I am his student. How I met Kedarji is interesting. After passing the matriculation with drawing as my optional subject, I decided to learn fine arts with the inspiration of my drawing teacher in school. I didn't study after high school. I didn't have money to enroll in Lucknow College of Art [this was the leading art college in the region]. So I learnt from *guru shishya parampara* and started teaching art in a school. The *guru shishya* tradition in art was common practice those days. Art schools and the *guru shishya* tradition were quite different. In school they take fees and teach. There are many students in a class and the teacher cannot pay attention properly to a crowd. Whereas in *guru shishya* tradition the students are very few and they are devoted to Guru. Guru teaches with love and affection. He does not charge any fees for his teachings.

In 1936, I first went to Kedarji to learn drawing, and thereafter went to him daily for four years. Fortunately, I was introduced to one student of Kedarji named Prem Shankar. I requested him to introduce me to Kedarji. Prem Shankar agreed, and in July 1936 he took me to Kedarji. I touched Kedarji's feet and requested him to adopt me as his student and teach me fine arts. He smiled and asked me, "What will you do by learning drawing and painting? If you want to learn to beg, then learn art." I was stumped by his comment. He told me to think for three days about a career in art, after which he asked me what I had decided. I told him "I've decided to learn from you." This is how I reached him. Later by my devotion to him and art I became his favorite student. I would show him my works, which were life sketches, and he would point out mistakes [see Figure 4.3]. He used to be happy with my effort. I remember his comment about begging. Till the end he regarded me well.

There was no hard-and-fast rule in his teaching. Generally, I used to go to him around 1 p.m. and work for three or four hours. I did model drawing in watercolor. He used to suggest color mixing, light and shade, and corrected mistakes if any. Then he asked me to copy some pictures in a magazine. He corrected mistakes. There were landscapes also. In 1938, I got a job of drawing teacher in a middle school. Then I could not be regular. I went to him on holidays and showed him my sketching, paintings done from life. Later, I got a job of drawing teacher in a better school and the same routine continued. I also met one artist, T. K. Mitra, and he was a friend of Kedarji.

I do not know the birth date of my Guruji Sri Kedarnath Sharma. He was born in Varanasi in a respectable Brahmin family. In Allahabad there was an

4.3 Cartoonist Bireshwar showing me his sketch book from the 1940s in
Lucknow, May 31, 2004. Photograph by the author.
    Part of Bireshwar's training in art involved drawing everyday life, such
as the cooking scene here.

Indian press and there was a foreigner from whom Kedarji learnt art. He learnt
drawing of commercial arts from a German artist employed in the famous
Indian Press of Allahabad. He worked with him for some time in Allahabad.
After that, he learnt as he drew; then he did commercial art, that is, labels for
medicines, book covers [for Hindi-speaking people]. He returned to Varanasi
and started commercial art drawing on the basis of "earn as you draw." He did
not join any art school. Kedarji did bazaar work – illustrations. No, he did not
paint film posters. Kedarji's only profession was commercial art drawing and
that was his source of income. Actually he did not paint signboards himself. We
his students painted under his guidance. Kedarji did a variety of illustration
work like the covers of books, stories in Hindi magazines, various types of
advertisements such as for tobacco companies, and so on. He had some
humor, and he developed a character called Mandook. This character's body
was human but its face resembled a frog. This was a strip and he published it in
newspapers. He had his own sense of humor, and at times he illustrated
humorous articles in magazines with a cartoon touch and style. He used to
make cartoons. He was not employed in any service [monthly paid job].
    Kedarji was a free bird, but though he had monetary hardships and
had many students, he never took anything from his students. He had ten or

twelve students and durries used to be laid on the floor for us. From 1936 till 1943, I learnt from Kedarji. He guided me. Kedarji never took money from his students. Mostly we copied photographs and line works from the *Illustrated Weekly* and he would point out the mistakes. My *guru bhai* [Rama Kant] Kanthale also worked in the *Herald*. *Guru bhai* means student of the same guru. Kanthale and I were students of Kedarji. Kanthaleji was second and I was fourth in the line. Sri Rama Kant Kanthaleji was a senior student of Kedarji. He was a Maharashtrian Brahmin of Benaras and was of very simple nature. He was doing watercolor paintings and had developed a good command of it. Besides this, he was doing commercial works like design of book covers and so on, and he earned money out of it. Kedarji was very affectionate toward him.

Kanthaleji did both commercial art and fine art. He earned good money. As *guru bhai* I had great regard for him. At times he guided me in fine arts, like Guruji Kedarji, and wanted his students to pick up some line in fine arts as a career. As a well-wisher, he once tried to establish me in block-making in a workshop, but I was fed up after a short time and gave it up.

I was curious about who Kedarji's guru was. Bireshwar had an inkling that a German lithographer taught Kedarji cartooning. Over the next year, through several letters exchanged with Bireshwar's old friend in Allahabad, Vilasji, I learned that Kedarji's guru was the German lithograph artist Louis Jomar.

From teacher to cartoonist

BIRESHWAR: I have worked with three editors, Vidya Bhaskar of *Aj*, in Banaras, Yash Raj Chaudhry of the *Hindustan Standard* in Calcutta, and M. C. of the *National Herald*, in Lucknow. *Aj* was Babu Shiv Prasad Gupta's paper from Gyan Mandal. Gyan Mandal Limited published *Aj*, Hindi books of great writers like Premchand and Sampurnanand, and special magazines. It was a very rich company. Babu Shiv Prasad Gupta's secretary was Anapurnand, younger brother of Sampurnand. Ana was fond of humor; he was given the responsibility of the paper. I was distantly related to him. He came to me and asked "What are you doing? . . . Join us as a cartoonist." I felt strange – *dhuk dhuk*, nervous. I was a drawing teacher in a school. In 1942, the government closed the school, and in 1943 the school began again. He said, "Not to worry, I'll give you ideas and you could draw." He told me, "Leave the teaching job; I'll give you more money." I used to earn twenty-three rupees, he gave me fifty. But I was nervous about working for a paper and kept procrastinating. Then he gave me an ultimatum. My wife told me, "What are you thinking? Join, and you'll get more pay," so I resigned from the job at school. I joined *Aj* in 1943. When I joined I was scared, and then as my cartoons got published I felt better. Though my wife was not very educated, she was wise and practical. She pushed me at the turning points of my life.

It was important for me to study the works of other cartoonists – their ideas and technique. I used to see how cartoonists dealt with the same political subject. *Punch* was available in Lucknow; sometimes I bought it and still have some copies. The British *Punch* was read by those who kept informed of cartoons of that time. During my career as a cartoonist I did not get any opportunity to visit foreign countries and so did not meet any foreign cartoonist. In foreign countries, David Low Sahib was there. Low used brush [to draw with]. During World War II, Low made many good cartoons. Indian cartoonists were emerging at that time and copied his technique. Shiv Sena's Bal Thackeray made cartoons exactly in the technique of Low – cent percent [100 percent] strokes, the same strokes as R. K. Laxman does and to some extent Ahmed also. Shankar Sahib was also influenced by Low; he had gone to Low to learn cartooning and had a lot of influence on Indian cartooning. Shankar was a modern cartoonist.

At that time there was also Vicky from Poland. Vicky had his own style with pen and ink; Vicky's cartoons came in the *New Statesman* and *Daily Mirror*. The weekly *New Statesman* came to our *National Herald* office. I used to study his work. What I liked was that he had developed his own style of work in pen and ink; he had very good drawing and ideas and I used to study them. Also he has his own sense of humor entirely different from other foreign cartoonists. Vicky's technique had impressed me much. But his biggest complaint was that British people never accepted him, he committed suicide in remorse. I started a feature, "Aj Ki Duniya" ("The World Today"), inspired by the weekly feature of Shankar, "March of Time," in the *Hindustan Times*.

When I was working on *Aj* and the *National Herald*, many newspapers came to the office, mostly in exchange. So it was very easy for me to study the cartoons appearing in them. Some weekly magazines like *Blitz* carried cartoons. The magazines *Thought, Eastern Economist*, and foreign magazines came to the *Herald* office in exchange, and I would browse through them.[11]

Editor M. C. [Chalapati Rao] had introduced me to Nehru twice when he visited the *Herald* office. M. C. used to introduce me to leaders who visited him, like Krishna Menon, Rafi Ahmed Kidwai, Mrs. Vijay Lakshmi Pandit, and many others from Delhi. Political leaders used to come here. When I got a chance, I used to go and meet them and study their face and use a pencil to catch what was special on the face of those big Congress leaders. I used to utilize the study for cartoons later. As needed, I used to have a large newspaper photographs collection. I didn't make any crooked face, so people recognized the face. So life drawing, newspaper photographs, other newspaper cartoons and my observation of how Shankar did the drawing – all this went into my observation for caricatures and cartoons. For foreign press photographs I used to pick and keep the ones I liked. I used to study how Shankar Sahib, David Low, and Vicky made caricatures. I learnt caricature from a book titled *The Art of Caricature* by Len Doust of Britain. The character of a man is hidden in his lips and the expression of his eyes. One has to observe the eye expression of a black marketeer [person engaging in the gray economy], the lip expression of a corrupt officer. The vigilance officers are the best observers of faces. They can trace out a culprit by facial expressions. Drama, theater, film, and so on have nothing to do with caricature art. Cartoon figures have to be part of caricature, bringing out the characteristics of the politicians.

Artistic forms are closer to cartoon. The cartoon is of course a picture. In
terms of expression, the emotion comes close to satire and humor (not anger
and sorrow).

Bireshwar was emphatic in denying any connection with other art forms,
such as drama and theatre, in caricaturing the human experience. He did
not evoke aesthetic theories of Bhav and Rasa from Indian traditions and
history. Bireshwar's reference to Vicky reconnected me to Kutty.
Cartoonists in India learned of Vicky's cartoons through foreign newspapers to which their offices subscribed. But there was a special connection that brought Vicky closer to India's cartoonists and readers than most
of his contemporaries. Cartoonists are remembered for their characters
and the staying power of their iconic images. Vicky's contribution in this
area was Supermac – a caricature of the British Prime Minister Harold
Macmillan as Superman. A stark contrast to this juxtaposition of politics
and a comic-book superhero was his heavy and despairing portrayal of the
human condition during a famine in India. This book of nine drawings
(1944) with an introduction by the well-known author Mulk Raj Anand
was a Reuters news item in the *Hindustan Times* – Indian Famine in
Cartoons: "The drawings are full of grim irony and recall the drawings of
Picasso and Grosz."[12] For Anand, the scenes were "a shock to civilized
intelligence." This genre of grim irony would become Vicky's signature; he
would produce it as part of his advocacy against poverty and violence.
These drawings came to be known as his "Oxfam style." Vicky supported
Oxfam (the Oxford Committee for Famine Relief) and this commitment
materialized in his contributions to the charity and in his drawings. Vicky
visited India in 1953, stopping in Delhi and Bombay and returning to
England with sketches of everyday life and street scenes.[13]

When I returned to Austin, I obtained a used copy of Doust's book,
which Bireshwar had mentioned. Indeed, Doust informs readers in
his manual, published in 1932, "There is no humor in bitterness or
cruelty" (1936, p. 5). Doust illustrated features of the face and analyzed
the draftsmanship of *Punch* and leading British cartoonists such as
W. M. Thackeray, Phil May, Percy Fearon Poy, and Strube. Through
Doust's book, Bireshwar might have learned not just the techniques of
caricature and to differentiate styles of British practitioners but also how
to critically assess the "action, the muscles, the creases in the clothes, the
poses of the figures" (1936, p. 8). Doust's principles complemented
Guru Kedarji's "learn to draw before you attempt to caricature." I was
amazed at Bireshwar's recollection of Doust's instructions after all
these decades. The world of Kedarji, Doust, and Bireshwar began to
appear before me – these were circuits of mentoring and pedagogy that

brought together two worlds in Banaras, where Bireshwar spent his earlier years learning the art of cartooning.

The conversations in Lucknow continued over letters while I was in both India and the USA. These letters were punctuated by visits to the archives and my increasing awareness of Bireshwar's work.

Switching newspapers

BIRESHWAR: Sri Vidya Bhaskar was the editor of *Aj* those days. He was a Tamil but had a good command of Hindi and wrote good editorials. He had good knowledge of cartoons and gave me ideas. He felt the necessity of cartoons in Hindi newspapers. He was a great admirer of cartoonists Shankar and Vasu. From 1943 to 1947 I worked on *Aj*. The income from the salary was adequate enough to meet my expenses and so I did not do any side work. I was appointed in 1943 on the salary of 50 rupees per month and was give increments yearly. The last salary I drew in 1947 was 175 rupees. Those were cheaper days and things were available in abundance. So, no problems. We were very happy in every walk of life. Gone are those days.

RITU: Bireshwarji, did you have any favorite themes?

BIRESHWAR: My favorite theme was imperialism wherever it existed and to attack the mischief around the world. *Rangbhed neeti* [apartheid] in South Africa was also my theme. Imperialism and racism in South Africa were crushing people of slave countries. So cartoonists had to attack imperialism and racism (see Figure 4.4).

RITU: Why did you leave *Aj*?

BIRESHWAR: I left *Aj* due to two reasons: There was change in the management of *Aj* in 1945 and the group of editors to which I belonged left the paper. Morally, I also had to resign and before leaving *Aj* I had to search for a job. The editor of the *Leader* newspaper visited the *Aj* office on one Sunday and saw originals of my cartoons. He was impressed by my drawing and commented that my work was very suitable for an English newspaper. Next day I went to the office and heard his comments from the editorial staff. This encouraged me to join an English newspaper. In search of a service, I went to Calcutta and met the editors of English newspapers. All of them appreciated my work but could not appoint me. Last of all, I went to the office of the *Hindustan Standard*. The managing director, Suresh Majumdar, appointed me as staff cartoonist and offered me a salary of 250 rupees per month and a free room to live in. At that time, *Aj* was paying me 175 rupees per month. So considering better prospects, I resigned from *Aj* and shifted to Calcutta.

Moving from Banaras to Calcutta was not easy. Geographically, the places are far apart and I wondered why Bireshwar thought of going to Calcutta and not some other place. I did not get any answer to that question.

BIRESHWAR: I started drawing cartoons for the *Hindustan Standard* around Christmas in December 1945 as freelancer and continued till February 1946.

4.4 Bireshwar, "Black Unrest," ink and pencil. Original artwork *National Herald*. n.d. (*c.* 1978–9). Lucknow.

This cartoon of South African apartheid politics during B. J. Vorster's presidency is an example of a visual cartoon celebrated by several senior cartoonists. The visual cartoon contained minimal words.

In March 1946, I joined the *Hindustan Standard* as staff cartoonist and worked till August 15, 1946, with a break in June. But unfortunately I had to leave Calcutta due to ferocious communal riots there, which began from August 16, 1946, and continued for a long time.

RITU: What happened?

BIRESHWAR: In August 1946, an unparalleled communal riot broke out in Calcutta. Only by the grace of God and Marwari organizations did I manage to run away from Calcutta. I very narrowly escaped from Calcutta and returned to Banaras – my hometown. I approached the new manager of *Aj* for the job. He very gladly appointed me cartoonist of *Aj* and I resumed work. There was no problem.

These were riots between Hindus and Muslims close on the heels of the Partition into India and Pakistan. I asked Bireshwar to tell me about those days, but he avoided answering.

RITU: Why did you rejoin *Aj* and not any other newspaper?

BIRESHWAR: There was no other newspaper in the town better than *Aj*. Most of the staff was well known to me and I worked smoothly. I rejoined *Aj* because other papers were financially weak.

RITU: Around these years I saw that *Aj* published cartoons by S. Roble and Vasu. Did *Aj* have some arrangement with these cartoonists?

BIRESHWAR: During my absence caricatures drawn by S. Roble might have appeared in *Aj*. I do not know Roble. Cartoons of Vasu also might have appeared on a "courtesy basis."

RITU: I noticed that advertisements in *Aj* in the 1940s used cartoons and comic-strip style. Cartoonist Ahmed too had a long series of cartoon-based advertisements called "Wagon ka Vilap." Did you draw any of these cartoons?

BIRESHWAR: The advertisements in strip styles published in *Aj* in the early 1940s might have been published when I was a drawing teacher. I have no knowledge of those advertisements for I was dragged into cartoon work in 1943. I had not seen "Wagon ka Vilaap" by Ahmed or any other advertisements drawn by other cartoonists. I have no idea on this topic.

RITU: How did you join the *National Herald*?

BIRESHWAR: Vasu (Pillai) Sahib was a cartoonist of *Pioneer*; he had come to Banaras and told me that, if I wanted, I could join *Herald* since there was a vacancy. Vasu told me about the *Herald* editor Mr. Chalapati Rau's reputation and enthusiasm for cartoons. So I thought he would be good to learn with about cartooning. On July 1, 1947, I had an interview with Chalapati. I said, "I have heard your name and want to learn how to do cartoons from you." He agreed, and so I agreed to join the *Herald* and resigned from *Aj*. *Aj* did not accept my resignation, but I pleaded and they let me go. In 1947, I came to the *Herald*. I worked in the *Herald* from 1947–78. Chalapati Rau couldn't draw but he had very good ideas. Chalapati regarded me well and he taught me about ideas, how to make cartoons. I was there for thirty-one years and produced about six thousand cartoons. I used to make six cartoons a week and Sundays was off. My cartoons in the *Herald* were translated into Urdu in Quami Awaz as well as in Navjivan. In the *Herald* there was a financial crisis in 1978 and my work also ended then. The management of the *National Herald*, in an ambitious plan, started its Delhi edition in the 1970s, which could not compete with giant newspapers of Delhi – *Hindustan Times, Times of India, Statesman*, and so on – and ran into heavy financial losses. This loss was made up by the Lucknow edition, which finally collapsed. I had to resign to recover my dues like gratuity, provident fund, and so on. Without leaving the *Herald* I could not get my dues. The paper was closed but the management cleared my dues in a year in installments. After joining the *Herald*, I remained in Lucknow and built this house gradually.

In Bireshwar's cartoon strip I saw a character resembling David Low's Blimp, and asked him about the influence of British cartoonists.

BIRESHWAR: Thank you for sending photocopies of my own and my guruji's cartoons published in *Aj*. The Blimp-like character you see drawn in "Aj Ki Duniya" is of a well-fed British officer, a food specialist sent to India to help the mass of hungry people in famine in Bengal. Thousands died in the Bengal famine for want of food. Those were horrible days of British rule. Corruption, activities of black-marketeers, unemployment, dearness, and the hypocrisy and duplicity of politicians and their mischief were my subjects after independence. A cartoonist lives by attacking mischief, corruption, the double-standard of politicians. I drew cartoons exposing all these aspects which my readers appreciated. Defending the mischief of politicians would certainly not be liked by readers. I think copying the style of the West and following the works of cartoonists there could not have been successful for Indian cartoonists. The problems in India which cartoonists face here are quite different from Western countries. My cartoons went abroad too, in the *New York Times* and in Germany. There my cartoons were reproduced though I did not send them, they took them from the *Herald* as the newspaper used to be sent abroad.

Hindi cartoons

BIRESHWAR: While at the *Herald*, in between I used to contribute to *Shankar's Weekly* too. Shankar Sahib sometimes went abroad, so when he couldn't create cartoons for *Shankar's Weekly* he told Chalapati Rau to ask me to send cartoons. In his absence Kutty, Prakash Ghosh and I used to complete Shankar's work in *Shankar's Weekly*. In the annual numbers of the weekly, Shankar Sahib would ask me to make one page of Uttar Pradesh political cartoons. So in the annual numbers, my cartoons came in U. P. politics.

Cartoonists in the Hindi newspaper have to draw cartoons for Hindi mass readers who can understand easy ideas. Readers who know Hindi are different from readers of English newspapers. I don't think English cartoons are sophisticated. After leaving *Aj* I drew cartoons for the *Hindustan Standard* and the *National Herald* in a different way to appeal to English-speaking readers. Most ideas were Western, taken from English stories and history and based on literature. These were entirely different from work in Hindi newspaper. I think Hindi and English readers have different sensibility and notions of cartoons.

I do not think there were influential cartoonists in the Hindi press like Shankar and Ahmed who had established themselves in English newspapers. I had associations with Hindi cartoonists like Manoranjan Kanjilal and Shiksharthi, with no other language cartoonists. I have been a reserved type of man and did not mix with journalists and other politically minded people in the coffee house, where they all used to meet.

Those who make cartoons in English are better liked by readers. Cartoonists in English newspapers are highly paid, whereas cartoonists in Hindi newspapers are not given high salaries and the same importance. Hindi newspapers prefer freelancers, because freelancing cartoonists suit them economically and financially. In local Hindi papers today, the cartoon trend has declined and there are hardly any political cartoons. This is the newest trend, there is no political cartoon in Hindi papers. In the vernaculars there are many good cartoonists in Madras and in Kerala, but in Hindi that's not so. The trend is less political cartoon, more emphasis on sex, crime, and pocket cartoons with much writing. For example Virendra Kumar [a fictitious name][14] creates a small cartoon and writes four or five lines. Only on reading the lines is the humor discernible. In Hindi papers people don't pay attention to cartoons – they are only used for illustration.

Bireshwar's observation of the decline in Hindi cartooning was echoed by several others I would meet in the coming years. The distinction between English-language and Hindi cartoons resurfaced in the context of pocket cartoons, popularly associated with India's most celebrated cartoonist today, Laxman. Bireshwar expressed an interest in seeing his *Aj* cartoons and a copy of Doust's book on caricatures. I had seen the *Aj* cartoons and made copies from the microfilms in the Nehru Memorial Museum and Library and mailed them. However, I was unable to send the used copy of Doust's book, before Bireshwar's demise after celebrating his grandson's wedding in 2007.

Separate worlds and the relational self

It often surprised me that, despite being contemporaries, Kutty and Bireshwar did not much speak of each other. Their cartooning life had common threads in their migration to other cities, their experience in Calcutta and Lucknow, with the important English-language newspaper *National Herald*, and in their access to political elites such as Jawaharlal Nehru. Shankar and his journal, *Shankar's Weekly*, was a common platform for both cartoonists. In their mature years, residing in New Delhi, India's capital city, Kutty was at the heart of national–political and social activity. In Lucknow, the capital of India's politically significant state, Uttar Pradesh, Bireshwar shied away from the social hub – the coffee house where journalists met. This temperamental difference aside, their life stories are deeply entrenched in separate worlds that defy assumption of a culture of cartooning in India. Such life stories highlight subjectivities elusive to the concept of "culture" but were yet a part of "culture" (Crapanzano 1980).

Anthropological attention to the individual was also a motive for "writing against culture" (Abu-Lughod 1991). In its attention to individual and not "culture," the motivation of this return to the individual is strikingly in opposition to earlier personality studies as a window to culture by Du Bois (1944), for example, and the popular anthropological practice of biographies of "informants" as a residual product of the ethnographic project, what Roger Sanjek calls 'anthropology's hidden colonialism' (1993; giving a twist to Sanjek's observations, soon after our series of correspondences, Kutty authored his autobiography).[15] Bringing together my interactions with Kutty and Bireshwar as a pivotal intersection for telling their life stories and the story of cartooning's early years in India, I hope not to have effaced my presence or conveyed a "picture, frozen within" (Crapanzano 1980, pp. ix, 8–9). Kutty and Bireshwar, charting their own narrative paths, responded to my questions and sometimes refused to respond by not addressing them. In this way, their stories surfaced in relation to a story of cartooning in India, as well as to other people, notably their gurus and well-known cartoonists abroad, such as Low and Vicky, and their individual lives rooted in their social milieux. The difficulty in separating narrative lines and what makes a life story anthropology, ethnography, and autobiography has long been recognized though not settled.[16] My conversations and correspondence with Kutty and Bireshwar were complemented by their contemporaries, who all had an association with *Shankar's Weekly*: Samuel (New Delhi), Reboti Bhushan (Gurgaon), and Laxman (Mumbai and Pune). These relational memories evoking their past as cartoonists intertwined, making it possible to think of separate worlds and a relational self.

5 Virtual gurus and the Indian psyche: R. K. Laxman

Finding a guru: drawing Mickey Mouse with one's eyes closed

Kutty and Bireshwar had been fortunate to find a guru who was instrumental in their professional success. But they did not mentor anyone nor did they become a guru to any of the current cartoonists. Their attempts to train younger cartoonists were thwarted by what they perceived as misguided assumptions by youngsters that cartooning was a skill to be learned overnight. Cartoonist Vins (Vijay Narain Seth) called this indifference to free mentoring a trait of the Indian psyche: "You can call it an Indian psyche that if something is given free they will not make use of it. I offered to teach cartooning free, then after a few days the person stopped coming, making some excuse or the other." A graduate of the prestigious Jamshedji Jeejabhoy College of Art (J. J.) in Mumbai, Vins was disappointed about the attitude toward cartooning in India and the dominant British *Punch* and Disney–US models that restricted a broader awareness of cartooning: "Every summer the Indian Institute of Workers in Worli had cartoon classes. Suresh [Sawant, a prominent Mumbai-based cartoonist] and I would conduct the classes. But mostly kids would come. Their mothers would say, 'My child knows how to make Mickey Mouse with his eyes closed, so please teach him.'"[1]

But gurus could be virtual, as was Walt Disney for Reboti Bhushan, whom Shankar hailed as the "best animal illustrator in India." Cartoonists can learn by looking at other cartoons. But what does this observation entail? Three junior cartoonists, Ram, *Vinay, and *Kunal, gave me a glimpse of this process of cartoonists observing cartoons.[2] The cartoonist who captured their attention and that of every other cartoonist in India was R. K. Laxman, the most widely known cartoonist in India. Born in Mysore in 1924, his career as a professional cartoonist began in the 1940s. For more than five decades, Laxman's career was closely tied to the mainstream English-language newspaper the *Times of India*, where he was the senior staff cartoonist (see Figure 5.1). Among several awards Laxman

146

5.1 R. K. Laxman, the most widely known cartoonist in India, with his Magsaysay medal at his home in Pune, July 17, 2009. Photograph by the author.

received, two deserve special mention: the Government of India's second highest civilian award, the Padma Vibhushan, in 2005, and the Ramon Magsaysay Award for journalism in 1984.

No conversation about cartoons I had during these past years was complete without a comment on Laxman. Love, admiration, and hate – I saw all these emotions at the thought of Laxman. "Everyone wants cartoons to be like R. K. Laxman's" – this popular observation was either voiced in approval of Laxman's unique skill or it was left as a puzzle: "Why did every one want to be like Laxman?"

The guru of all: Eklavya and Dronacharya

Ram, a junior cartoonist new at the *Times of India*, multi-tasked for the paper in Mumbai; he was both illustrator and cartoonist. Such multi-tasking was increasingly the norm for cartoonists still establishing their reputation. Moved by his guru Laxman's impact on his career, Ram penned an essay describing Laxman's cartoons as a peephole to the sprawling Mumbai that he could not know on his own. The essay, which Ram shared with me when I asked him about his meeting with Laxman, vibrantly captures learning by seeing the guru's cartoons.

Sixteen years before, when I came to Mumbai, my first Mumbai darshan was through R. K. Laxman's cartoons. Places I have never seen, people of Mumbai whom I have never bothered to observe so closely, city roads, potholes and so on. The way he draws Sharad Pawar's outward shirt, black pant, his hand and anatomy says he is Pawar without drawing his face at all. Just a circle says it is Jayalalithaa Jayaram.[3] During my graduation I was assigned a job of freelance cartoonist. I felt like somebody put me in the middle of the ocean and told me to learn to swim; Laxman's cartoons came like a log and saved me. I used to observe his cartoons for minimum twenty minutes a day. I looked at his every brush stroke thoroughly and learned where a stroke is necessary and where it is not required in a cartoon. His study of anatomy, the way he drew the same place at a different angle and in a different composition and perspective makes his cartoon different each day. How to observe things at a different angle that people have never looked at, I learned from him. He is the Amitabh Bachchan of the cartoon industry (Interview, October 23, 2003; essay n.d.).

The film star Amitabh Bachchan has ruled Bollywood's silver screen and India's film industry for over four decades, setting the standard for popularity. Given the Mumbai-based Bollywood's looming presence, to be considered the Amitabh Bachchan of cartooning was a way of scaling Laxman's national reputation.

My relation with Mr. Laxman is like Dronacharya and Eklavya. I learned a lot about cartoons without seeing him even once. And when I got an appointment with him, which is a rare opportunity for anybody, Laxman simply said, "What is there to learn in cartoon?" Fortunately he didn't ask my right thumb the way Dronacharya asked Eklavya as *gurudakshina* (n.d.).

Calling himself Eklavya, and Laxman Dronacharya, Ram evoked a well-known episode in the epic *Mahabharata* concerning the guru and his secret *shishya* (pupil). Eklavya, a "lower-caste" boy, acquired excellence in archery by secretly watching Dronacharya tutoring the Pandav princes. In requiring that Eklavya sacrifice his right thumb as *gurudakshina* (a token of appreciation, not a fee), Dronacharya ensured that Eklavya would never be able to use the bow again. Gurus are selfless teachers; but they also choose their disciples, and can penalize Eklavyas. Of course, Ram would not have to worry about sacrificing his thumb. However, prominent cartoonists could block emerging careers, and Ram was fortunate in that he was allowed to work with the *Times of India*. Laxman was aware of his many imitators and rarely took imitation as a compliment.

Yuva Mahotsav and the Gulf War in a "light" way

In 2003, I found myself in the Sapru House field in New Delhi. It had been more than decade since I was last there. This is the designated venue for the annual youth camp and contest called Yuva Mahotsav.[4] In the late 1980s and 1990s, this contest provided an opportunity for art students and others from non-art vocational colleges to win recognition and awards, launching careers in cartooning. Jagjeet Rana and Shekhar Gurera, popular cartoonists in India today, launched their career through this youth festival. An aspiring cartoonist, poster designer, and painter, I too had participated, and won three awards many years before. These awards were prestigious, and winning here was no mean achievement, since most participants were training to be professional artists. Those days came back to me as I scanned the field and fiddled with my camera, slung around my shoulder. But the event looked different today. It had fewer participants and was indescribably listless.

The evening was cooling very slowly; I covered my head with my dupatta to shield it from the sun. This was not just another day; it was March 23, and the USA had just launched a preemptive attack on Iraq. "Are you a journalist?" asked one of the contestants, Vinay.

RITU: No, I am writing about Indian cartoons and came to see the event.
VINAY: You are not writing for a paper?
RITU: No. I am writing a book.
VINAY: Where are you from?
RITU: I study in the USA.
VINAY: You don't look like you have come from the USA. Even your accent is not American and you are speaking Hindi.
RITU: I was born here, I went to the USA recently. I don't think I will acquire an American accent at this age. But I can copy the American accent.

[*Laughter*]

Later I learned that Vinay was a freelance, part-time cartoonist. He picked up assignments with small, regional Hindi newspapers. I looked around the shaded booth, durries, and chairs. Slowly the booths began filling with contestants sitting on the durries. Paints, pencils, erasers, and newspaper clippings were spread all over. Vinay looked more mature in years than the other contestants settling in for the competition. I wondered why he was here, and took the conversation as an opportunity to learn about his perspective on cartoons. "Are you an art student?" I asked, to direct the conversation toward him. "I am not an art student but art is my god-gift. I was always interested in drawing. Then as I grew when I saw cartoons in the newspapers, I felt an urge and enthusiasm to do something new, to produce a cartoon." "So who is your favorite cartoonist?" To my surprise, Vinay linked "favorite" to "guru."

VINAY: My guru is R. K. Laxmanji, I have not seen him till date but in the future I want to see him and touch his feet [pay my respects] and receive his blessings. In his cartoon he had a logo man, you may have seen him – a "Common Man." I was most inspired by this logo man's comments and feelings. It was fun reading. The neatness (*haath ki safai*) in Lakshamnji's art and in his cartoons inspired me. After that, other cartoonists also came. Among them is Shekhar Gureraji, I am influenced a lot by his cartoons. His cartoons have a lot of neatness, you could also say, clarity of line.

RITU: Did you try meeting any cartoonists?

VINAY: I long to meet cartoonists. I want to learn a lot in cartooning. Even now I consider myself incomplete in cartooning. Like they say, there is no progress without a guru. Based on this I have desired to be a disciple of a cartoonist. I went to *Amarji. I had three or four meetings with Amarji and then at the nth moment he said, "I don't have that much time to teach you about cartooning and make you my student." I think he got scared, seeing my style, that I might go ahead of him. Perhaps that was what was going on his mind. This could be his feeling. My feeling is that I want to meet my inspirational guru, Laxmanji; I want to touch his feet. I also want to meet Shekhar Gureraji. Then there is Unny in the *Indian Express*, I want to meet him too. But the manner in which Amarji behaved, now I don't feel like meeting any cartoonist. I am disappointed. I feel that all these cartoonists of big newspapers, they don't want to have a disciple.

Vinay's reservation about Amarji's treatment reminded me of Laxman's early days as a job-seeking cartoonist in Mumbai. After a gentle review, an established cartoonist in a mainstream newspaper advised Laxman to try provincial newspapers before attempting those in the capital. "Provincial" implied regional and vernacular-language newspapers. The advice to Laxman was to develop his skills in lower-tier newspapers before attempting mainstream newspapers. Insightful Laxman remained confident in his skills, and discerned that the advice was a polite dismissal from a senior cartoonist fearing a young rival (Laxman 1998, p. 82). Such guarding of territory and the power of peer reviewers are, of course, not unique to Indian cartooning or to the profession of cartooning.

As I continued the conversation with Vinay, I was struck by his enduring belief in the *guru shishya* tradition:

RITU: If there are no gurus now, why should we have the *guru shishya parampara*?

VINAY: My perspective (*andaaz*) is that human beings have come on earth but haven't become immortal. If the *guru shishya* tradition will not continue then the arts will finish gradually. These days if we see Madhubani art, there's so much craze for it. But its standard is falling. I don't accept this.

Vinay's reference to Madhubani art took me by surprise.[5] Now sold widely in India and abroad, this art form practiced by women from north Bihar has an interesting historiography tied to the colonial aesthete W. G. Archer and subsequent interlocutors, including Pupul Jayakar, David Szanton, and Jyotindra Jain (Rekha 2010). These art critics and patrons resituated this "folk art" as "fine art," a process that was also facilitated by the transition to paper rather than mud walls as the surface for these works. This shift in the status from folk to fine meant that Madhubani art came to be associated with individual artists, such as the celebrity Ganga Devi, and their unique styles. It also meant that with the new market and global status, there was a proliferation of new practitioners and schools where Madhubani painting was taught. At the time I assumed that Vinay lamented the widespread popularity and practice of Madhubani painting, where ill-prepared youth staked quick claims to expertise in this genre of painting and sold their work in fairs and on the open market. In retrospect, Vinay's evocation of Madhubani art when reflecting on cartooning in India strikes a different chord. Now it seems he was emphasizing the dilution in cartooning because gurus were reluctant to share their art, compelling the next generation of cartoonists to be self-made, as he was.

VINAY: I would like the *guru shishya* tradition to continue and remain so in the future. If I become a cartoonist of any big newspaper, by the blessings of God and Sai [Baba], if any student or god-gifted person would come to me, I will certainly make him my disciple. Knowledge grows by sharing it.

RITU: Can I take a look at this caricature and cartoon?

VINAY: Yes, see. In today's competition I have made in caricature Sri Satya Sai Baba Puthuparthi [see Figure 5.2].

RITU: This is very nice. You like to keep your lines neat.

Vinay's belief in the *guru-shishya* tradition reflected his conviction about the role of the mentor for professional success, especially for the youth. Hearing him punctuate his comments with "the blessing of Sai" told me that Vinay was a devotee of Sai Baba, the subject of his caricature. Sai Baba is a spiritual guru to millions all over the world. For now, only Sai Baba was his guru, and that was not enough. That Vinay considered Sai Baba a subject for his submission at the Mahotsav was a way of seeking a blessing through his submission; gurus could be caricatured in reverence. A win in this competition would certainly boost Vinay's future. But that was not to be, and it was puzzling; his was by far the best caricature in that competition.

I looked around to get a sense of how other contestants conceptualized cartoons. I could see examples of Disney characters, as Vins had lamented. Several participants referenced published newspaper cartoons and other drawings from their sketch books. But I also saw that several cartoons were about the US attack on Iraq from a few hours previously. Although contestants were free to choose any topic, the immediacy of the attack was apparent in the cartoons and the idioms conveying the war. Kutty's remark about the role of the popular television serials *Mahabharata* and *Ramayana*

5.2 Sai Baba caricature for the Yuva Mahotsav cartoon competition, March 20, 2003, New Delhi. Photograph by the author.

generating a visual pool for cartoonists came to mind as I saw *Ravi's cartoon on George W. Bush disrobing Saddam Hussein, evoking a key episode from the epic *Mahabharata*. "Cartoons show the Gulf War in a light way," said Ravi. The juxtaposition of warring characters from the *Mahabharata* with those from the modern war created a gender reversal: Saddam Hussein was feminized – he was Draupadi being disrobed, and the attack was rape.[6]

Laxman's style

If Ram's and Vinay's's tributes reveal not just Laxman's magic but also his inaccessibility, then other cartoonists I met took the opposite point of view. "He makes the same car, same airplane, same policeman, and the same potholes in Mumbai. It is as if nothing has changed. I hate the guy," said Kunal, a college student and part-time cartoonist, sipping a tall glass of cold coffee in Café Mondegar in Colaba, Mumbai.[7] Kunal's refusal to imitate Laxman's style was often expressed as a refusal to follow conventions.

Laxman's cartoon style and humor had become a convention, and for dissenting cartoonists, their own individuality and creativity demanded a break from Laxman. But breaking away was not easy, for at this time in his career, Kunal faced consistent demands from his editor to draw like Laxman. I argued with him, "Kunal, Laxman is still very popular and you can't deny that." Not easily persuaded, Kunal joked, "He is the Lata Mangeshkar of cartooning." To convey Laxman's status, Ram, a fan, had evoked the popular actor Amitabh Bachchan; now Kunal, a critic, was evoking Lata Mangeshkar, the popular playback singer[8] of Bollywood films who, due to her long reign, was also known as the "evergreen singer." The press and gossip columns also constructed her persona, involving intense rivalry with her younger sister and thwarting careers of younger singers trying to establish a name for themselves. Metaphorically referring to Laxman as Lata Mangeshkar, Kunal was alluding to status, popularity, rivalries, and the jealous guarding of professional turf.

Kunal's dilemma of having to draw like Laxman against his stylistic preference was matched by dilemmas other junior cartoonists also expressed about Laxman: "Sometimes Laxman is pathetic . . . you can't figure out his Jayalalitha etc.. . .. But don't mean to say Laxman is not the best . . . he is . . . his drawing is the best." This acknowledgment of Laxman's draftsmanship was by and large unanimous. However, there were many such as Kunal whose acknowledgment was riddled with doubt. At the core of this acknowledgment and doubt was the challenge of representation. Simply put, did Laxman's cartoons represent accurately or was he a prisoner to his style?

My conversation with *Anuj Kumar, a young aspiring cartoonist in college whom I met in Mumbai, reflects the response to Laxman's influence and how his work has come to define cartooning in the popular mind:

Yes, there are a lot of stereotypes. When I was with *Midday*, I had to do cartoons more on education, careers, and entertainment, so there was really no room for controversy. But now with *Ontrack Suburbs*, I have to create a lot of political cartoons, which can sometimes go against what the editor may call "press ethics." Actually the cartoons may be plain sarcastic, but it will look to the editor as offensive. That is one thing I had made clear when I joined, I would draw what I feel. But then again, that never successfully happens all the time. Moreover, it is also the style of cartoons which is stereotyped by newspapers . . . Laxman's stuff is like a benchmark, which I hate. Those kinds of lines, those figures. I am more for exaggerations. Also the sick old idea of having large heads and little bodies, how often have I heard people telling me about that! For most people, that is cartooning, which is wrong, that is crass exaggeration. But luckily, I did not have to face so many of the above problems with my editor, but yeah, it's safe to say that there are stereotypes in the press about cartoons. (Interview, October 24, 2003)

*Ravi Prasad, a professional engineer and cartoonist whom I met at his factory in Mumbai, echoed the sentiment: "Everyone has aped Laxman.

Laxman has aped Low. Miranda has aped Searle. All are fixated on style, then how are we going to be different?"(interview, October 24, 2003). His frustration at the "fixation" for style, and one that belonged in the West, struck at the heart of how creativity was recognized. For Ravi Prasad, cartoons in India were not ours, for creativity cannot be aped.

Cartoonists differed in their assessment. Artist and sometime cartoonist Raobail (Prabhakar Rao), with whom I corresponded about cartooning, brought this dimension to my notice. Raobail's observation provides a key to revisit the tendency to see Low in Laxman: "It is said David Low inspired Laxman. But Laxman's cartoon characters are cent percent [100 percent] Indian – whether the character is of a villager or a city white collar, beggar, industrialist, politician, or policeman. That is perhaps the reason the public easily identifies with his work." Where Raobail saw public identification in Laxman's style, Kunal and Anuj Kumar complained of Laxman's inertia, which they found alienating. Anuj Kumar's comments reflect a critique Laxman had made of the "vintage" vernacular *Punch* cartoons several decades earlier:

First, I think he is stuck up in the 1950s. His characters still look oldish, as in not modern. If one looks at his old drawings and his new, it will be hard to differentiate between the two, years-wise! The cartoons by Laxman of say 1980s are still the same as the ones in the 2000s! It looks stagnated! Second, the man is too arrogant anyways. As I said, he was lucky enough to be at the right time at the right place, with the right knack![9]

In Mumbai another cartoonist shared the turf with Laxman: Bal Thackeray (1926–2012). As I set my sights on learning more about Laxman, it soon dawned on me that I could not overlook Thackeray.

A cocktail of Thackeray and Laxman

In Mumbai, Suresh Sawant gave me insight into Bal Thackeray's influential cartooning style and the Marathi-language magazine *Marmik* that was launched in 1960 and provided the platform for the establishment of a regional political party, the Shiv Sena. The former Shiv Sena chief and its founder, Bal Thackeray, had an early career as a newspaper cartoonist and belonged to the cohort that included Laxman, Kutty, and Bireshwar. Showing me his collection of magazines and Thackeray's cartoons, the well-known Mumbai-based cartoonist considered Thackeray a "great cartoonist" and an inspiration during his early years in the profession (see Figure 5.3).

I used to sit on the steps of Thackeray's house. He was very moody; if he wanted he would ignore you. There would be many people crowding inside. One day he

5.3 *Marmik* cover. June 29, 1986. Courtesy *Marmik*. The Shiv Sena activist was shown as a "Border Satyagrahi" who threatened rival Congress politician Hegde, who was chief minister of the neighboring state of Karnataka – "All who spill Maratha blood will have their graves dug."

The graves pictured are of Afzal Khan, the Shiv Sena's hero Shivaji's adversary, and of Morarji Desai, a leading politician who opposed the was in a good mood and asked me in and showed how he drew cartoons. I didn't mind bearing his whims because I regarded him as great cartoonist. In Thackeray's home there is a photo of [David] Low and he worshiped him.[10]

In recent years, *Marmik*'s circulation had declined and another paper, *Saamna*, had become the Shiv Sena party's mouthpiece. During my conversations with cartoonists in Mumbai and those associated with *Marmik*, Thackeray, revered as Balasaheb, was repeatedly held up as a model cartoonist. Vikas Sabnis, a freelance cartoonist for *Marmik* as well as *Loksatta*, a rival Marathi-language newspaper, explained:

I loved cartoons of Bal Thackeray and Shrikant Thackeray [Bal Thackeray's nephew, also a politician]. How they used the brush was glamorous. I decided to try – to draw like Bal Thackeray. I contacted *Marmik*. At that time the office was in his residence. I used to go to Shrikant Thackeray and show him my cartoons. He would suggest changes and they would get published. In 1985 Bal Thackeray and Shrikant Thackeray retired from cartooning. They wanted a new generation of cartoonists to take over. Since Raj Thackeray [Shrikant Thackeray's son] is in politics, they offered the job to me. Mr. Raj Thackeray does occasional cartoons and as far as cartooning is concerned, he is the heir of Bal Thackeray. My style is a cocktail of Thackeray and Laxman.[11]

Time and again, cartoonists spoke of vernacular cartoons' regional identity. Their style and identity was tied to language and regional politics. As a freelance cartoonist for rival papers, Sabnis comfortably navigated such identity politics.

Today *Loksatta* is pro-Congress, *Marmik* is anti-Congress, but as a cartoonist I have to satisfy both the parties, that is my professional tack. There is a vast difference between English and vernacular. When you draw vernacular, you have to think issues of Maharashtra – it happens automatically. As a cartoonist I get satisfaction from both types of newspapers.
    When you draw for *Marmik*, you don't draw anything too high or too difficult. You draw such that the common person can understand. I believe in very good drawing. Drawing should not be ugly. I learnt this from Bal Thackeray; he didn't compromise on any line. He is much better than Laxman. Because his cartoons are published in Marathi, English readers are not familiar with his work.

Caption for 5.3 (cont.)

demand for a Marathi state. In 1960, the state of Bombay was split into two – Gujarat and Maharashtra – to mark a linguistic division. Hegde is accused of "inhuman atrocities" and his crime was to declare Kannada the official language of disputed Marathi-dominated towns bordering Karnataka and Maharashtra. *Marmik*'s cartoons portrayed Muslims as butchers and their politics weaved a tough Maratha as butchers and their policies weaved a tough Maratha Hindu identity against Pakistan and Muslims. In the process they even appropriated Gandhi's ideology of satyagraha to validate their violence.

Sabnis's "professional tack," and his understanding of how the vernacular language cartoons "automatically" render themselves to regional issues, is difficult to explain; it can only be intuited by the cartoonist as ethnographer. Sawant's and Sabnis's appreciation of Thackeray was echoed in my conversation with the artist-cartoonist Subodh Kerkar in Goa, who was instrumental in setting up my meeting with Laxman. But Kerkar was among several cartoonists I met who did not agree with *Marmik*'s virulent brand of humor: "As a child in school, I loved *Marmik*. Bal Thackeray's drawing was very good. Confident and good lines though he hits below the belt. Bal Thackeray has bad humor" (November 6, 2003). The bad humor was apparent in Thackeray's uncharitable cartoons of Muslims. However, there was some debate about Thackeray's stylistic inspiration. I had by now gotten accustomed to the insistence on establishing style and lineage, imparting both art and history to cartoons.

"My style is like Balasaheb's. Just as Amitabh Bachchan follows Dilip Kumar, Dev Anand follows Gregory Peck, and Lata Mangeshkar follows Noorjehan, Balasaheb was influenced by Dinanath Dalal. This happens in any art." *Marmik* cartoonist Sanjay Mistry said this in a matter-of-fact manner, drawing caricatures on my notebook (see Figure 5.4).[12] Sanjay Mistry's notion of style was couched as as individually owned or unique but as shadowing earlier artists. Cartoonists were similar to film stars and singers who emulated their idols, taking over the spotlight with the next generation. "*Saamna* readers love Balasaheb; they are fans, just like Michael Jackson's."

Sanjay Mistry's reference to Michael Jackson reminded me of the pop star's concert in Mumbai in 1996, more than a decade previously. The anti-Western Balasaheb had welcomed Jackson to his home, fêted and praised him and his artistic talent as an example of good aspects of American culture. This was a strange break from Shiv Sena's West-bashing. The Shiv Sena had built a formidable reputation as a moral guardian of Indian culture, criticizing Valentine's Day celebrations, among a host of other Western practices. Even more puzzling was Sanjay Mistry's comparison of Thackeray with Jackson. I quickly understood, however, that the parallel was with their large fan following and charisma. Pinpointing the rationale was difficult, telling much about the ways in which the concept of culture is a cocktail that is evoked, tweaked, resilient, and articulated regionally.[13] If consistency could be expected in Shiv Sena's cultural proclamations, then cartooning along Low's style was either considered an exception like Michael Jackson or as unproblematically integral to a postcolonial culture. There were other paradoxes, too. What did it mean for Sawant to evoke Low and for Sanjay Mistry to claim Dalal as Thackeray's stylistic influence? With these unresolved questions I proceeded to take a closer look at the public reception of Laxman's cartoons.

5.4 Cartoonist Sanjay Mistry caricaturing the Congress president Sonia Gandhi on my notebook. July 28, 2009. Prakash Café, Mumbai. Photograph by the author.

Sindhoor tilak

"Even if it is in the corner of the front page, the creation of RKL is really a *sindhoor* [vermilion] *tilak* in the forehead of India." Recalling this comment in a blog on Laxman's cartoons, I imagined a map of India with a vermilion stroke on the top. A mark for auspicious happenings in everyday Hindu life, depending on the context, the *sindhoor tilak* can signify honor and blessings. When a pinch of *kum kum* powder is rubbed as a stroke on the forehead, it becomes a third eye. Indeed, Laxman's cartoons were a third eye that urged readers to look deeper into their everyday life. They also were a *sindhoor tilak* of another kind – postage stamps that travel the length and breadth of the country, and even abroad. On November 3, 1988, IndiaPost, the Government of India's postal service, issued a special golden stamp to commemorate the sesquicentennial year of the mainstream newspaper, the *Times of India*. The golden stamp prominently featured the newspaper's cartoonist Laxman's Common Man. This celebration of a mainstream newspaper through its cartoonist's popular character recognized the importance of Laxman and his cartoons, which have appeared in the *Times of India* since 1951. The stamp, a collector's item, is a cultural artifact; it is a synergetic commemoration of the history of the newspaper, cartooning, and the nation. Though such national attention to a cartoonist is exceptional, and shared by only one other cartoonist, Shankar, it provides a vantage point from which to acknowledge Laxman's unique place in contemporary India.[14]

This golden stamp's public juxtaposition of Laxman's character the "Common Man," or "logo man" as Vinay called it, and the *Times of India*, acknowledged their inseparability. Laxman's long uninterrupted connection with the *Times of India* is an unmatched feat. There are some who heap credit on Laxman for rescuing his newspaper from obscurity. News editor *Sushil Kar dismissed the *Times of India* as a "useless newspaper" that featured "who sleeps with whom" (interview, November 30, 2003, New Delhi). For him, people bought the newspaper "only for Laxman's cartoons. ... Once he stops drawing for them or (touch wood) he dies, no one will buy the *Times of India*." Cartoonist Unny emphasized Laxman's genius: "his genius is to tune in to the need... Bombay in those days was a destination; it was a desire. So even if readers were outside Bombay, that kind of mindset was everywhere *Times of India* reached and Laxman was appreciated" (interview, December 2, 2003, New Delhi).

On the other hand, several cartoonists told me about their unpleasant experiences with Laxman: "When I was a student in J. J. [College of Art]," said one, "I took my portfolio to Laxman in the *Times of India*; he threw my file and said 'you'll never be a cartoonist!'" Rivalries were intense, too: "Laxman will not let anyone come near his castle." A leading Hindi cartoonist and contemporary of Laxman explained this territoriality as the newspaper's marketing strategy rather than as Laxman's personal politics: "When I was on the *Navbharat Times* [the Hindi edition of the *Times of India*] people used to talk of my cartoons. No one noticed Laxman's cartoons. Laxman was made a brand of the *Times of India*, so there was an effort at marketing him, promoting him, and squashing me. So I quit."[15]

Crossing the Laxman *rekha* (boundary)

After hearing all the Laxman stories from juniors and seniors alike, I was worried about meeting him. Gradually those worries blew away; every effort to contact Laxman and set up an appointment failed. Then I met someone in Goa – where I had gone to meet the cartoonist Mario Miranda – Nagesh Sardesai, an art teacher and cartoonist, who had a huge collection of newspapers dating back to the 1960s. Sardesai recommended that I meet the artist Dr. Subodh Kerkar, "Goa's favorite cartoonist," who did not produce cartoons any more but had been popular during his student activist days. Kerkar was Laxman's fan. He had hosted Laxman at his home during an exhibition and sale of Laxman's sketches and drawings. By now I was getting comfortable with the unexpected directions and surprises my meetings with cartoonists took. This also meant that on several occasions I made quick decisions to travel to meet cartoonists.

When I reached Kerkar's studio, his secretary Carmine asked me to wait until he returned from an assignment that took him away that day. It was a long wait. As dusk set in, the mosquitoes gave me a difficult time, feasting on my toes and ankles. A mosquito repellant near my chair seemed to encourage the mosquitoes; they grew fiercer as the evening grew festive, Goa style. I had a train to Delhi to catch later that evening, and I was cutting it too close by waiting so long. Finally Kerkar reached his studio.

"Have you met Laxman?" The question half surprised me. Most conversations began with a question for me about someone I had already met. By now I had met a number of cartoonists in New Delhi, Mumbai, Kerala, Kolkata, and Goa, but Laxman eluded me. "It is very difficult to meet him. I have made endless futile attempts and now I have given up. He has written much and interviewed so many times, I will have to make do with that material." Kerkar was not persuaded. "You can't do this project without meeting Laxman, it is vital." "Can you arrange a meeting?" "Yes. When do you want to meet him?"

Back in Delhi, I sent Kerkar an email, and we spoke on the phone. When he said he would call back, I thought he might have forgotten our conversation. Then I got a call from him: "Laxman will see you on the twentieth." Immediately my local travel agent was at work for a *tatkal* ticket to Mumbai.[16]

The stories about Laxman haunted me. Would he throw me out of his flat if he did not like a question? Laxman has an enigmatic public persona. Several interviews note his soundproof exclusive office in the *Times of India* building, his black Ambassador car, and his disdain for questions that seek to investigate his creative process. Laxman's celebrity stature also opens his personal life to public review, but it comes as little surprise that, in his autobiography, Laxman does not wander into any personal realm that does not connect with his cartoons. His commercial success and corporate endorsements have done little to allay critics, who frown at his money-mindedness. So, it was with much trepidation that I met Laxman at his flat in Warden Road.

Drawing mass appeal: automatic or inescapable?

I hoped that Laxman, a keen observer of everyday life, would not sense my nervousness. "Why are you nervous?" he asked as I tried to settle in (Interview, December 20, 2003). "I have read all your interviews," I said. "A cartoonist is a political analyst and an artist," he insisted, gesturing toward his famous drawings of the crow and various scenes lining the living room of his Mumbai home. Indeed, along with his daily cartoons in the *Times of India*, Laxman has had several sketches published. His earliest brush with fame began with sketches for his famous brother R. K. Narayan's novels. He is known to be condescending to other cartoonists. "You see, I am an artist. Not everyone can do this," Laxman told me as his assistant wheeled him around the living room (he was recuperating from a stroke), showing me each of the wonderful sketches on the wall. "Count the number of crows in that tree and you will see there are thirty-five. Not everyone can do this." "See these awards." I was awestruck at the shiny pile of trophies on the floor, neatly lined up. His autobiography noted the "irony of the situation" that many years ago the J. J. College of Art refused to enroll him, but now invited him as their chief guest at the annual exhibition of students' paintings (Laxman 1998, p. 61).

"Cartooning is something that comes as a reaction. David Low is the only cartoonist I liked." Laxman's reference to Low was not unexpected. Both Shankar's and Laxman's style are often compared to Low's, though not all cartoonists acknowledge the resemblance, prompting questions about how style is recognized and articulated. Laxman situated himself in a time of cartooning when lines were free flowing and distant from *Punch*'s constraining academic style and the "mythological ideas" replete in India's vernacular *Punch*es (1998, p. 74). Laxman took pride in his drawing ability. "Anatomy and details support satirical details. Cartooning is an art, it requires skill of drawing." The numerous sketches and black-and-white crow paintings adorning the walls of his home announced to all visitors that he is an artist. But good drawing had other returns, too; "a drawing done well has mass appeal, even if people don't understand it, the drawing has appeal." For a cartoonist, then, drawing skill was essential, for unlike art that has an elitist clientele, the daily newspaper cartoon has to appeal to the many and in minutes, leaving them wanting more the next day. "I am not a member of any association; I don't like to mix my work with socializing. Although I don't mind others copying my cartoons and know editors show me as example for younger cartoonists, it is not the right thing to say to these younger cartoonists. Each must develop his or her own style."

This individualization of style asserted the cartoonist's identity and brought cartooning to the realm of art. It also announced that Laxman had his own style and that he did not see himself as mimicking Low by merely replacing British characters with Indian counterparts. Nevertheless, mimicry was a crucial step in the process of developing individual style. For Laxman, the history of Indian cartooning involved copying *Punch*, and later, Low. Such deliberate mimicry, sparked by the Indian cartoonists' need for "inspiration" and "guidance," produced individual style: "gradually they produced their own style and sense of humor" (Laxman 1998, p. 74). This transition from copying to individual style was not unique to Indian cartooning; it was, according to Laxman, inescapable worldwide, while also a boon for less talented practitioners (p. 75). The global phenomenon of copying triggered by the wide circulation of *Punch* and Low's cartoons provided the world with a model that was widely embraced. This perspective on mimicry brings forth an explanation for how styles travel and then lose their identity when talented practitioners make them their own. By Laxman's time, mimicry was not used as a subterfuge to circumvent proscription, like the claims of the *Agra Akhbar* editor in colonial India who questioned British objections to Urdu cartoons even though they mimicked the celebrated *Punch* (see Chapter 1). Mimicry was a rite of passage for becoming a cartoonist. Laxman's observation pointed me to look for both the inescapability of style and the blossoming of individual style rather than a cultural pattern that could be bracketed as Indian cartooning. Although in his autobiography Laxman records an early reprimand from his older brother for copying, there is little in Laxman's writings and interviews to suggest that mimicry was critical for the development of his own style.

There was another puzzle before me. Although on my first visit to his home Laxman emphasized his artistic ability, he saw artistic training as an impediment to cartooning. He pointed out that India's early cartoonists, producers of vintage cartoons in newspapers such as the *Hindi Punch*, were actually painters, not cartoonists – hence the paucity of caricature in their work (p. 73). Ironically, Anuj Kumar, the aspiring cartoonist that I met in Mumbai, pointed to lack of caricature in Laxman's style. This shifting terrain of what constitutes caricature marks the times in which it is defined while also seeing it as a critical aspect of cartooning.

"Cartoons soften the harshness of life. When people laugh it softens the blow. The goal is as far as possible to see the ridiculousness of it all. Have you read my autobiography?" Laxman asked me soon after we began talking. "Yes," I said. "You will find all the answers there," he responded, seeming to signal that he did not want any more questions from me. However, I asked him, "How are you doing now?" and sincerely thanked him for agreeing to meet me. "You are the first person to interview me after the stroke." But Laxman, though he did not mind my presence, clearly did not want to be interviewed. When I mentioned one of the popular cartoonists, quite characteristically he dismissed the name in disgust, "Chee. You call him a cartoonist?" In Laxman's world, no one else in India was worthy of being called a cartoonist. "The effort to provincialize cartoons is not necessary," Laxman insisted when I asked him about regional and provincial cartoons. "I don't believe in it. Cartooning is imported but now it has got ingrained in our society. You have to be literate to understand it. I don't see vernacular cartoons." It seems that, for Laxman, the notion of provincializing cartoons as a sign that they were indigenous is irrelevant because cartoons were now at home in India.

I came away from these conversations with mixed messages. Contrary to Laxman, other cartoonists conveyed an understanding that English signified an encompassing national humor that was translatable, whereas regional-language cartoons were local and resisted translation. Laxman's cartoons and Marathi cartoons emerged from the same region, Maharashtra, and at the same political time, but their sensibility was different even if, most of the time, their readers might be the same. The place of vernacular cartoons and the identities they took on would surface again in my fieldwork, especially when cartoonists discussed Hindi cartooning.

"Are you making cartoons at home?" I now asked him. "Yes, I fax them to the *Times of India*." Laxman did not make large editorial cartoons any more. Over the years, the editorial cartoon was being displaced by the smaller "pocket cartoons." Unlike the "big" cartoon, which typically spread over three columns of the newspaper, the pocket cartoon was smaller and occupied one column, usually at the edge of the front page. Laxman's pocket cartoon included a caption below the scene he caricatured. The stroke affected Laxman's drawing. The sparse lines and tentative breaks in between communicated to readers that Mr. Laxman was not well. His post-stroke cartoons showed how much he had become a part of the *Times of India* and the readers' newspaper ritual. If those drawings were far from perfect, contrary to Laxman's demand that they should be perfect, it did not seem to matter now. Even the trace of Laxman's long-running cartoons was comforting, in a strange way.

I visited the Laxman home again; the last time was in 2009, in Pune. After Laxman's health improved, he and his wife Kamala had moved to Pune, not far from Mumbai. Now, I would call and visit at a good time, and not have to resort to *taktal* tickets. As I was leaving, Mrs. Laxman said "Wait," and bustled into the kitchen. She returned with some *kum kum* (vermilion, also called *sindhoor*), put a crimson stroke on my forehead and, raising her hand over my head, blessed me. "Next time bring your daughter."

I had to leave early because the Indian president Pratibha Patil was visiting Pune that evening, and traffic would soon come to a halt. The Laxman household and their companion, Naidu, had all the information – they were well-connected. The former president and nuclear scientist Dr. A. P. J. Abdul Kalam and many other important people were Laxman's fans and friends – Laxman's "Common Man" mesmerized millions, but its creator was no ordinary man.

A trusted Indian and a distrustful democracy

Since the beginning of India's nationhood in 1947, cynicism has been the hallmark of Laxman's cartoons. Spanning the course of his long partnership with the *Times of India*, executing cartoons daily, Laxman's *oeuvre* easily comprised several thousand cartoons. These consisted broadly of two types – big editorial cartoons that appeared on the front page, and the smaller pocket cartoons. For several decades, both formats were daily fare for readers. These cartoons have been republished as pocket-book editions by Penguin and elegant coffee-table books of editorial cartoons. He frequently remarks about his cartoons: "I am continually surprised to note that most of them are timeless in their relevance to any given moment in our history" (Laxman 2000, p. xii). As a pathway to also know about other things, the repetitive cartoons of development's failure allow public knowledge of India's corruption to be presented as daily news.[17] Woven around a plot about democracy and development, Laxman structures his cartoon news through a plot about corruption and a set of characters. This news is visualized and circulates through the recurring figures of the Mantri (Minister), the Common Man, and the trope of flight symbolized by the aeroplane. Laxman's cartoon narrative runs counter to the official discourse of the modern nation and development. Therefore, his cartoons are counter-hegemonic. However, in India this parallel discourse is not proscribed; in fact, it is celebrated.

Due to their political and social context, long time span, and acuity, it is not surprising that Laxman's cartoons have also been assembled to narrate the history of the Indian nation. These cartoons offer a cynical and cyclical view of democracy at work, questioning the logic of the development model that marks India's political and social agenda. Laxman's cartoons show that, in India, democracy and development do not sit well together. Recently newspapers in India have been recognized as a significant "mechanism in public culture for the circulation of discourses of corruption" (Gupta 1995, p. 385). Indian newspaper cartoons, exemplified by Laxman's popular Common Man character and his disenchantment with India's politics and development, provide a visual route to track the discourse of corruption. Through scenes of home, administrative offices, laboratories, and villages, Laxman's cartoons portray the realm of everyday life in India. These ordinary scenes framing the perspective of the Common Man and his experience of the modern state cut the politicians down to size, portraying them as incapable of common sense. Laxman's newspaper cartoons are a striking contrast to the poetry and images in Tamil newspapers that result in the "aestheticization of the state" and attribute divinity to such politicians as Jayalalitha (Bate 2009). In Laxman's cartoons, the inept political mortals are fatal accidents of democracy.

Science fiction and political science

Laxman's timeless visual plot about democracy and development shows the impossibility of achieving the ideal of development: development as the central narrative of the nation's progress and growth is a never-ending project. In his cartoons, Laxman repeatedly holds the representatives of the modern nation – the democratically elected politician and the retinue of developmental specialists – accountable for the failure of progress for the masses (see Figure 5.5). Although the readers-as-public ritually witness the breakdown of the nation in Laxman's daily cartoons, they experience this failure in their daily life. In a cannibalistic twist, when

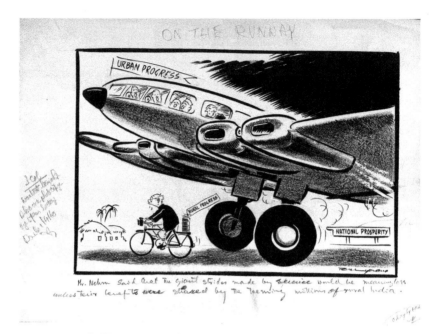

5.5 R. K. Laxman, "On the Runway." *Times of India*, April 1, 1960. Mumbai. Brush and ink artwork. Personal collection.

Under the drawing is written: "Mr. Nehru said that the giant strides made by science would be meaningless unless their benefits were shared by the teeming millions of rural India." The labels read, "URBAN PROGRESS, RURAL PROGRESS, NATIONAL PROSPERITY." The Common Man on the bicycle was the "teeming millions." On the left, a note indicates that the editor has approved the cartoon to be published as a big three-column cartoon. The right corner notes, "OK by editor."

looking at these cartoons, readers consume their own public reality: the pleasure of grim realities, the anticipation of daily cartoons that will meet expectations of picturing lopsided development and the official fêting of the state's public critics. However, with bureaucrats, politicians, and citizens, the scene shifts to new themes: airports, water supply, science and technology, and gender inequalities – all reconfigure the making of a unique democratic nation. These cartoons on the human condition echo Donna Haraway's persuasive observations about the narrative of science as "stories about stories" (1989, p. 4). Repetitive plots and characters familiarize a story about stories of the nation state and development. The cartoon history of the nation is not a story with a happy ending; in fact, it is a cyclical reproduction of the themes of lack of development, corruption, and a social (dis)order consisting of new haves and have-nots – those who have common sense and those who do not. Although Laxman's critics point to the repetition in his cartoons, readers seem to appreciate their daily dose of them. Despite or perhaps because of their ordinariness, the anticipatory aspect of Laxman's cartoons makes reading them a popular ritual among readers.

But why does the combination of democracy and development fail, and what narrative of the postcolonial state does it generate? In Laxman's cartoons, democracy fails because of a breakdown of the electoral process, which generates corrupt leaders. It is simultaneously also a failure of scientists, statisticians, and policy makers – all the experts designated to pave the path of development. Laxman's cartoons are a key register for the discourse of corruption. The discourse of corruption and lack of development parallel the corruption of common sense. Politicians and developmental experts gain power and expertise at the expense of common sense, mutually serving each other rather than the masses. The scale of Laxman's analysis of corruption and development is everyday life. The space and moments where citizens encounter these processes of the postcolonial state as they unfold are quite ordinary – the government office, the village, and the airport, to list just a few. In fact, the ordinariness of these places and the daily routine make the discourse of corruption and its intimate tie with development obvious.

To conclude that the Indian state is corrupt replays Orientalism's stereotype of incompetent natives. Is this another form of the "auto-orientalism" (Mazzarella 2003, p. 138) that now frames political understanding in India? In the past two decades, corruption has prominently surfaced as a lens for discerning developmental agendas and for evaluating the correlation between democracy and the well-being or happiness of citizens. Central to these multi-disciplinary investigations is to understand the modalities and reasons for corruption, particularly in democracies where the assumption of citizens' political agency and the power of the ballot is expected to keep politicians in check. Statistical indicators of corruption reveal comparative patterns that emerge only when corruption is strictly defined and applied uniformly in surveys, making it a plausible analysis but one without much force. Furthermore, shifting the blame to bribe-payers does not corroborate the knowledge that developing economies and poor countries are centers of corruption. For example, in their review of corruption studies, Andvig, Fjeltsad, Amundson, Sissener, and Søreide (2001) show that Transparency International's bribe-payer survey (1999) presented a "surprising result": "US-based enterprises had as high propensity to bribe abroad [as the German ones] despite the fact that its Foreign Corrupt Practices Act has been in operation for more than two decades, making it illegal for US enterprises to bribe abroad" (p. 30).

Shifting vantage points in statistics and surveys of corruption yield such surprises and anomalies, defying neat equations between an impoverished economy, democracy, and corruption.[18]

At the time of completing this book, two events unfolded in India that renewed the centrality of corruption discourses in a postcolonial democracy. In 2011 and 2012, octogenarian and social activist Anna Hazare came into the limelight as leader of an anti-corruption movement that spurred several thousand people in India to protest at the country's endemic corruption. Laxman's Common Man statue that stands aloft on a rock pedestal in Pune's Symbiosis College campus was garlanded to celebrate Hazare's fast as part of his protest.[19] The movement roused considerable support, and its goal to seek a strong Jan Lok Pal (Citizen's Ombudsman) Bill to curtail corruption in the government received a measure of success as it moved along the legislative passage in February 2013.

Around that time, in January 2013, sociologist Ashish Nandy was embroiled in controversy sparked by his comment in the Jaipur Literary Festival. Nandy was accused of claiming that the OBC (Other Backward Castes) and Scheduled Castes – social categories that constitutionally mark historically marginalized and Dalit (oppressed) communities – constituted the majority of India's corrupt. Nandy's protestation of the misinterpretation of his remarks as anti-Dalit was quickly broadcast in various interviews and statements. While reiterating his comment, Nandy clarified that his intention was to present corruption as a "social equalizer" in a country burdened by a history of inequities in which caste was a deep fault line, preventing members of the OBCs and Scheduled Castes from equally sharing resources.[20] To illustrate his argument, Nandy drew a parallel between such corruption and elite networking where favors such as providing positions in universities for each other's kin, by "putting in a word," barely receives notice, let alone a reprimand. Nandy's reframing of corruption as a welcome social and economic activity among the marginalized, in India's context, would not surprise anthropologists. Corruption, when approached more broadly as a compensatory social practice that articulates deeply entrenched histories and cultural understandings, brings to the fore knowledge of reciprocity and cultural expectations that can barely be comprehended through easy translations such as bribery and embezzlement (Sissener 2001). The coincidence of Hazare's and Nandy's divergent concern with corruption in India shows that corruption resonates in different ways among activists in India. Therefore, culture is not an adequate explanatory framework for (divisive) understandings about corruption. Instead, the discourses of corruption and anti-corruption can be seen as a cultural critique of access among elites and others. Laxman's cartoons are replete with such possibilities.

In 2003, when the popular Indian cricketer Sachin Tendulkar scored his twenty-ninth century, Fiat, a company Tendulkar endorses, gave him a Ferrari 360 Modeno as a gift. Upon request, the Indian government exempted Tendulkar from paying the hefty import duty on the car, which was valued at approximately $350,000. This exemption sparked a national debate around the propriety of the waiver. The issue was taken up by officials in the Delhi High Court, and Justice Vikramjit Sen, inspired by the Laxman pocket cartoon on this incident, was moved to issue a Public Interest Litigation against Tendulkar. In his judgment, Justice Sen cited Laxman's cartoon as an example that the "greatest truths were spoken in jest."[21] Laxman's cartoon, set in a modest low-income dwelling, a common domestic space in his pocket cartoons, shows an old man, possibly the grandfather, blessing a young boy so that on becoming a super player, the government might exempt all his income from endorsements of soft drinks, toilet soaps, and toothpaste from tax. The Common Man watches from the corner of the room. Justice Sen's public acknowledgment of the impact of Laxman's cartoon on his perception of this case of the government's special treatment and tax exemption reinscribes Laxman's cartoons as the perfect representation of India's social reality and the speech of truth.

Ethnography's contribution to studies of corruption has been its primary focus on observation and talk.[22] In recent years, scholars have asked for "more recently honed instruments for the analysis of daily life, representation, discourse, narrativity, and social poetics" (Zinn 2005, p. 231). Laxman's cartoons precisely fulfill this felt need through the intersection of the speech of vision and the vision of speech. Advocates of grounded ethnographic studies are candid about the difficulty of observing corruption – as it requires insider knowledge and experience to tap its occurrence. Laxman, then, has long been that insider who presents such ethnographic data through his cartoons' scenes and captions. Akhil Gupta (1995) has made a persuasive argument for an ethnography of the state that accounts both for the daily practices of local bureaucracies and the discourse of corruption. Gupta contends that discourses of corruption symbolically construct "the state," and to understand this process we must consider phenomena whose boundaries do not coincide with those of the nation state. Laxman's cartoons and the discourse of corruption they generate consistently identify the scene of corruption within the boundaries of the state. However, this discourse of corruption alludes to the source as lying in a skewed understanding of science and development, rendering both modern fictions. Thus, development as the agenda of the postcolonial state is problematic, as are the mediators of this agenda: the politicians, developmental experts, and the statisticians who magically demonstrate the nation's

5.6 Laxman's single-column pocket cartoon on the beauty of statistics. *Times of India.* n.d. Mumbai. Courtesy of R. K. Laxman.

"I have prepared this simple chart to show population increase, food scarcity, price spiral, sugar scarcity, growth of corruption, unemployment – all in one."

progress. Laxman's humor rests on this miscalculation and play of numbers, preempting Jean Baudrillard's caustic observation, "The beauty of statistics is never in their objectivity but in their involuntary humor" (Baudrillard and Maclean 1985, p. 581; see Figure 5.6).

Asking scholars to keep in mind two imporatant features in their ethnographic studies of democracy, Mukulika Bannerjee reminds us that "popular perceptions of democracy are expressed in both discursive and non-discursive ways" (2008, p. 64).[23] In Bannerjee's study, election times and years between elections yielded varying responses and silences to her questions about politics and people's opinions. Laxman's cartoons bring visual fluency to public perception about the state of democracy in India – they demand a rethinking of both democracy and development as models of progress. But while raising the paradoxes inherent in this model, Laxman does not offer an alternative. The solution remains ambiguous as democracy, lack of development, and corruption unfold before Gandhi's portrait, a fixture in bureaucratic offices and Laxman's cartoons. Political cartoons bring home the futility of the opposition between fact and fiction, situating caricature as the vantage point for realism, rather than its reverse. This exposé of India's postcolonial reality and the concomitant distrust in politicians is instrumental in Laxman's rank among the most trustworthy Indians. In a widely publicized 2010 *Reader's Digest* survey of the "100 most trusted Indians," Laxman ranked ninth.[24]

By way of comparison with another popular cultural figure who was politically influential, we can look at the life of the late MGR, the popular film star turned politician.[25] Sara Dickey has shown that among his fans, MGR was identified with his screen roles as an underdog who successfully took on the rich and powerful. Such association was buttressed by the issues MGR pursued when he became the chief minister. Legislation on "prohibition, subsidized housing, and food and clothing for children," Dickey points out, constituted "emotionally charged and easily identifiable issues" that mirrored his screen persona (1993, p. 169), and his support for them brought him enormous popularity.

Unlike MGR, Laxman is neither film star nor chief minister with any urgency for cultivating a clean or heroic image, but his cartoons portray identifiable issues and the public's emotion of distrust, which yield a public image of his own trustworthiness. This association between Laxman's cartoons and his public persona shows how the public makes extra-textual sense of representation: it disturbs any opposition between thought and feeling. The daily breakdown of political trust and its partial restoration as laughter, nostalgia, history, and revitalization suggest the multiple modalities with which the impossibility of development can be managed individually (Desjarlais 2003). The status Laxman commanded in a main-stream newspaper was incomparable, and the *Times of India* played a part in crafting his image, too. When I browsed through the *Times of India* archives for Laxman's writings and photographs, one caught my attention – it showed a nattily suited Laxman with a drink in one hand and a cigarette in the other. "No, don't take this photograph. This is not a good photo-graph." The librarian would not allow me to have a copy of this image for my book. I did not have the option to insist. And I understood that, where I perceived a smart photograph of Laxman enjoying an official social event, one I had not seen before, the librarian considered it inappropriate for my research.

It is tempting to see cartoonists as shamanic healers, eliciting emotion and magically transforming sickness into health, or at least restoring a modicum of hope. But Laxman dismisses such temptations: "Sense of humor does not give hope. It has nothing to do with it. Hope means what? Tomorrow everything will be all right? There would be a nuclear war? There would be Iraq, there would be Bush ... that kind of hope? Things are getting from bad to worse."[26] Laxman's articulation of his role as critic and analyst defines his approach to cartooning and the persona of the cartoonist. His contemporaries elaborated on other key dimensions of the purpose of cartoons. For Kutty, readers of Shankar's cartoons realized they prompted both thought and uproarious laughter: "Most of his cartoons provoked uproarious laughter, not just a smile or smirk. He gave courage to other aspiring artists to take the plunge and choose cartooning as a profession." For Kutty, the role of his own cartoons was to generate laughter. For Bireshwar, the purpose of cartoons was enlightenment. These different ways of conceptualizing the cartoon were visual modes (moods) of articulating a political critique. Criticize, think, laugh, and enlighten – they spell out the cartoonists' consciousness of their place in the realm of public discourse in a democracy. In introductory chapters to the published cartoon collections, Laxman clearly articulates his purpose and role: "The role of today's cartoonist is not unlike that of the court jester of yore. His business in a democracy is to exercise his right to criticize, ridicule, find fault with, and demolish the establishment and political leaders – through cartoons and caricatures" (Laxman 2000, p. v). This perspective on the cartoonist's business as a public critic of the government is shared by several newspaper editors. H. Y. Sharada Prasad, the eminent editor of the *Indian Express*, and later media adviser to India's former Prime Ministers Indira Gandhi and Rajiv Gandhi, observed, for example: "A cartoonist having a soft corner for a politician is like a mongoose which is carrying visiting cards from cobras" (Prasad 2004, p. 29).

It is a paradox that the targets of Laxman's cartoons – the politicians themselves – routinely celebrate his cartoons.[27] This paradox and pleasure sensed by readers was perhaps best articulated by the popular and former president of India, Dr. A. P. J. Abdul Kalam, when he inaugurated an exhibition of Laxman's cartoons in 2005:

I had occasion to go through his book *Brushing up the Years* which was presented to me, and savour the witticism and sagacity displayed by Shri R. K Laxman in his various cartoons so intelligently and thoughtfully ... Whether it was his cartoon in which he observed that living in India was not very different from living on the moon ... or the strange contradiction of potholes and cell phones governing the lives of the Indians ... Shri Laxman's cartoons all pack punch and power, carrying his unmistakable signature and displaying his immense capacity to observe, analyse, learn, and convey to his fellow beings what the lesser mortals apparently do not observe and discern. Life even for the Common Man becomes worth living with Shri Laxman's wit and wisdom in full cry. To laugh and make others laugh and to think and make others think is the unique gift of every cartoonist of repute. Shri Laxman excels himself in this.[28]

Elsewhere Abdul Kalam exhorted cartoonists to take up the cudgels true to their profession for the sake of memory, smiles, and "national growth": "Will you be remembered for bringing smiles with embedded thoughts on national growth?"[29]

By honoring Laxman with state awards, the democratic apparatus in India appropriates the discourse in Laxman's cartoons. Such hearty endorsements also materialize in relation to other cartoonists in India. National honors, commemorative postage stamps, appreciative prefaces to cartoon albums and books, and politicians enthusiastic for cartoon "originals" make the cartoon a "minor morality play" (Nandy 2002a, p. x). It is true that, when we turn to cartoonists such as Laxman's contemporary and Shankar's mentee O. V. Vijayan (1930–2005), whose "dark" style compels a sigh and nervous humor, there would be few, if any, awards and laudatory gushes. However, Laxman and Vijayan cannot be easily explained away as exemplifying the two faces of cartooning.[30] Laxman's enormous popularity and success compel another look at why his cartoons have garnered such favor with politicians of all stripes. Like Beriya Baba, the ascetic who criticizes the state but has politicians and Prime Ministers seeking his audience and being empowered by the Baba's curses (Cohen 1998, p. 281), Laxman is sought out by politicians; his caricatures are treasured and are a badge of pride. Laxman's stature and charisma are produced by his cartoons that serve as amulets to empower the state (Tambiah 1984). This official appropriation regenerates the discourses of corruption and emotional interpretations of cartoons to symbolically construct the postcolonial nation. Gender figures prominently in this symbolic repertoire. The signature character of cartoonists, the "Common Man," and the few women professional cartoonists disclose a subdued counterhistory of visuality.

6   Uncommon women and common men:
pocket cartoons and "situated knowledges"

Cartoonists I interviewed often referred to their peers and seniors as a way
to present a professional link. For example, when I met Sudhir Tailang,
then at the *Hindustan Times*, our conversation moved toward his mentor,
Abu (Abu Abraham). Kutty consistently returned to tidbits about his
guru, Shankar. Cartoonists also commented on their peers as a way to
distinguish their own ideological position and aesthetic preferences. Bitter
criticism surfaced. But that is not of import for this story. What struck me
was that in this referential world of a network, I consistently heard names
of men. It was a homosocial world into which women could not easily
meld.

I first came across women cartooning in the pages of the British news
compendium *Review of Reviews*. A brief world news item announced a
book of cartoons by the *Hindi Punch* editor, and proprietor's granddaugh-
ter, Minoo Bastavala. Soon I learned about other women cartoonists: the
late Maya Kamath (1951–2001, Figure 6.1), Manjula (Manjula
Padmanabhan), Mita Roy, Samita Rathore, and *Nalini Reddy. But
comic-strip artist, writer, illustrator and playwright Manjula does not
self-identify just as a cartoonist.[1]

During conversations, the names of cartoonists Kamath, Mita, Samita
Rathor, *Nalini Reddy, and Manjula surfaced only occasionally. One
reason for the scant references could be that Kamath had died early in
her life and Manjula, who became internationally famous as the winner of
the 1997 Onassis award for her play *Harvest*, drew a comic strip, not daily
political cartoons. However, this did not explain why Mita and Reddy –
both political cartoonists in Indian-language newspapers – were not more
widely acknowledged. In his study of Indian newspapers, Robin Jeffrey
recorded that in the the 1990s the "status of people connected with Indian-
language newspapers grew," and in daily newspapers "women and Dalits
were almost absent from the reporting and editing side of newspapers"
(2000, p. 139). "The way women are covered in local [newspaper] editions," editor and author Sevanti Ninan concludes, "is indicative of a
society in transition" (2007, p. 179). Although women are largely reported

6.1 Cartoonist Maya Kamath. n.d. Courtesy of the Indian Institute of Cartoonists.

in the press as victims, Ninan holds that there are "local stringers" who cover women's social and economic uplifting. Yet, "the point to remember about coverage of issues related to women in the local press is that the news force deployed is usually 100 per cent male" (Ninan 2007, p. 180). Media analyst and journalist Ammu Joseph recognizes the "spectacular success of a number of women in a wide range of high profile areas of journalism" considered "male terrains" in India. Yet, more often than not, women report not being given the chance to pursue what Joseph notes "is commonly, if erroneously, seen as hardcore, mainstream journalism" (2004, p. 136). Structurally, the demands of a journalistic career and its erratic schedule generate work and family conflicts. Furthermore, Joseph contends, the "night shifts" have particular cultural objections among traditional families in India, in addition to broader concerns of security (2004, p. 137). Given these cultural and structural constraints, it might seem that if there is a sphere in journalism where women might carve a niche, it would be cartooning. The flexibility of where to make the cartoon and its predetermined deadlines might appear as an attractive opportunity free from the obstacles Joseph outlines. But this is not the case.

The invisibility of women cartoonists in the talk about cartooning parallels the invisibility of female protagonists in pocket cartoons, where a woman appears chiefly as the wife of the Common Man. In their study of US cartoons of the 1995 Women's World Conference in Beijing, Gilmartin and Brunn assert that such visibility, even if it is not an outright negative portrayal but subordinates women, is an example of "symbolic annihilation" in the media (1998, p. 535). "Symbolic annihilation," a term introduced by George Gerbner to signal the absence of women's representation in the media (1972), was elaborated by Gaye Tuchman (1978) to include condemnation and trivialization as additional coordinates of representations of women in the media. Political cartoons' obliteration of women as central protagonists in the face of a history of prominent women politicians, such as Amrit Kaur, Sarojini Naidu, Vijaylakshmi Pandit, and Indira Gandhi, provides grist to ponder the link between reality and representation.

Why so few women cartoonists?

Mita was among cartoonists in whose life serendipity, rather than the guiding hand of a guru, transformed their future.[2] Mita's professional start is described at length by her editor in *Pioneer* at the time, Adarsh Varma. With a catastrophic flood in Lucknow in 1985, grim news began pouring in for readers. In the flurry of the photographer snapping pictures, Varma added: "A mile away from the *Pioneer* office in Lucknow's Vidhan Sabha Marg a girl in her late teens had other ideas. She went to the inundated colony and returned to draw a series of six cartoons." The cartoons mailed to the *Pioneer* editor reached Varma's desk and all six were published in the next day's newspaper. "Next morning, as the reporters were dispersing with their assignments after the morning conference, in walked this teenager. She introduced herself as Mita Roy."[3] Mita worked for the *Pioneer*, contributing cartoons in English, and she subsequently also contributed cartoons to the Hindi edition, *Swatantra Bharat*. Mita recalled her years in *Pioneer* and the public presumption about her age and gender: "Many times people expected me to be much older. And there are times when my name is read as a man's name" (Interview, December 7, 2003). At the time we met, Mita had moved from the *Pioneer* and was a staff cartoonist on the Hindi newspaper *Amar Ujala* in New Delhi. Several years ago, when relocating to New Delhi in a bid to seek a new cartoonist position, a family friend and fellow cartoonist advised Mita to abandon hopes of a career in the capital city. Undaunted by such cynicism, Mita established a succesful career, publishing both the editorial cartoon and the pocket cartoon in *Amar Ujala*. Almost ten years later, Mita is not a staff cartoonist with any newspaper. Unexpected family issues confronted her with limited choices and the responsibility of being a single parent. Mita overcame these constraints in her early career and achieved prominence; over the years she dedicated her time to raising her daughter and hopes to soon re-establish her career. Although the breakdown of social support and the family posed a challenge for Mita, her analysis of women cartoonists illuminated deeper confrontations.

I asked Mita why there were so few women cartoonists. She answered me with more questions: "When women get caught up in housework, where is the time to read newspapers? Where is the time for women who, with a family and at times joint families, are almost always in between chores, to think and be a political cartoonist?" Mita struck at an often-repeated description of their daily rituals that leading male cartoonists narrated to me that involved spending time reading newspapers. I recalled that Ninan (Ajit Ninan) of the *Times of India* liked to work early in the day and to be out of the house, "away from the domestic noise" (Interview, January 14, 2003). Rajendra Dhodapkar of *Hindustan Hindi* began his day reading newspapers and thinking in the afternoon (Interview, November 18, 2003). My question about the few women cartoonists was also one that several cartoonists asked me to explain when they acknowledged that few women were cartoonists. This reality, I suggested, was not an Indian issue, it was universal. Its universality also suggested that something more than the specific societal constraints in Indian society restricted women from cartooning. Gender returns to center stage in the possibilities it can hold for modern professions (such as newspaper cartooning), complicated by its entwinement with political humor. Gender also intervenes in field-work and the process of writing the story of newspaper cartooning.

When I met and corresponded with practicing cartoonists, our conversations did not build bonds of kinship, affection, and friendship. Unlike the world of *gupt* (secret and sexual) cartoons that Lawrence Cohen was privy to in Banaras (1995), my fieldwork did not involve sharing and seeing cartoons that circulate informally. But when I met Nalini Reddy and heard her story, it was as a friend, not as an anthropologist. Although we had not met previously, Reddy told me about her experience as a political cartoonist only from the standpoint of a friend. With friendship comes the confidence of secrecy. That alone provides reason enough for me to keep our matters of discussion confidential, so I did not experience the duality of stranger and friend that the anthropologist Hortense Powdermaker (1966) eloquently described in her biography of an anthropologist. I took Powdermaker's cue of not being dominated by one's own value system – which she regretted overlooking in her study of Hollywood. The value system I grappled with was that of anthropology, and the need to ask, "When does one stop recording?" And how does the ethical pact not to record escape its inscription in the anthropologist's memory? Although I realized that I could not compromise Reddy's trust by writing about her, our conversations continued, disrupting the "fieldwork" context of our interaction.

Fieldwork melded into friendship. Reddy's story intrigued me; her workplace incidents angered me. As I heard her tale in bits, the names she interspersed were already familiar to me. She told me of gossip floating about my meeting cartoonists, but she did not tell about its contents. With well-meaning friendly advice, Reddy cautioned me to be careful about some of the people I met, for they engaged in loose talk. Suddenly I felt the world shrink. Due to the troubles she encountered every day, Reddy was leaving her job as cartoonist and thinking of another vocation. She was hopeful that India's media boom would bring opportunities. I gave her advice that I too received in the frustrating early years of my career, "It will pass as you become senior. You should not let bullying bother you enough to leave what you like doing." But as months passed, I changed my position and supported Reddy in her plans for a new vocation. There was no point in suffering humiliation, even if it required sacrificing the distinction of being counted among the rare women political cartoonists in India. With her skills, Reddy could certainly gain a more fulfilling job. She had seen through the morass sooner than I could, although she still aspired to a life in cartooning. I was idealistic about women cartoonists making the leap to the next level of fame. I had visited Reddy's office twice and was disappointed at not meeting her there despite an appointment. In Reddy I saw someone achieve a goal I once had. But she was fascinated by my project: "You are really going deep into the subject. I admire you for that." Mita's and Reddy's experience does not speak for all women, however, and it would be premature to believe that all women were struggling and failing as cartoonists. Women cartoonists' successes, challenges, and failures demonstrate how gender is articulated through the politics of social expectations, sexuality, mentoring, feedback, and misinterpretation.

In a profession where women are yet to attain visibility, kinship of networks and mentoring are absolutely crucial. But forging such relationships can be misconstrued and elusive. Reddy did not have a network, but she had a mentor, who was long retired. Cartooning skills had secured Reddy a job in a well-rated small-size newspaper, but holding her position was proving difficult as she found herself mired in innuendos and criticism difficult to ignore. Her career had a good start, and that success lasted as long as she was perceived as a cartoonist. When a new management, ambitious of securing a national platform, turned things around, Reddy realized she was cast as a woman rather than a cartoonist. That was an ominous sign, accompanied by outright invitations for sexual favors. "I did not consent to these demands and they started punishing by asking me to make drawings for recipes, children's poems, and other articles. They turned me into an illustrator. They ruined my career. They ruined many other careers." When political cartoonists are directed by their editors to produce illustration rather than cartoons, it is a rebuff that dooms careers. Reddy's challenges were not tied only to the sexual hierarchy in her workplace and consequent demotion. "I saw a message on the phone. He referred to a political cartoon I made and asked, 'Is that what you really think?" and said it was a bad cartoon. But he did not leave his name." Such messages are part of the professional hazards of political cartooning; readers and politicians are quick to register displeasure or appreciation. However, the message on Reddy's phone was not from an offended reader or angry politician – it was a junior colleague at another newspaper. Reddy did not know it was a junior colleague; I understood who it was when the episode was recounted to me by this colleague to exemplify his "bold" assessment of the state of Indian cartooning.

Manjula's metaphor of cartooning as performance adds perspective to the acts of giving and receiving feedback:

If you think of the newspaper's pages as a stage then the cartoon – and the cartoonist – is a bit like a performer, alone on the stage. It's extremely important to get feedback. It's like getting (or *not* getting) applause at the end of a performance. Without feedback how do we understand whether or not our work is being appreciated or disliked or misunderstood? (Kamath 2005, p. 34)

During her early years as a cartoonist for the *Deccan Herald*, Kamath missed receiving feedback on her work (Kamath 2005, p. 34). Kamath worked from home, which gave her flexibility with managing her work and family. This arrangement shielded her from workplace politics, but it also foreclosed opportunities to talk with peer journalists and gain feedback. When feedback is presented by one's junior peers anonymously and questions "thinking," which was the case with the message for Reddy, it is troubling. Such comments in the name of anonymous "feedback" are a backlash. It shows the competitive lives of cartoonists, in which the hurdles to a career are not explained away by a patriarchal system alone. Peer rivalry and envy pose an additional layer of challenge – gender contentions that resonate with experiences in other professions and are not unique to cartooning.

To recognize artist and writer Manjula as a cartoonist would unnecessarily confine her identity: "I have been illustrator and cartoonist for a long time – ever since I left college. There is no conflict between drawing and writing. Just like you can open two different files on the same computer, my mind can work in two different formats, visual and verbal. I think most people can do this. They just don't realise it" (Padmanabhan 2004). Since her cartoon did not revolve around politics, it automatically made Manjula's work of marginal interest to newspapers. The character Suki, the frog, the python, and her quirky comments appealed to me. When I read about Manjula's life and work, I imagined *Suki* to have a biographical plot about everyday happenings: "Though she [Suki] started out as my alter-ego, she quickly established her own persona" (Padmanabhan 2005, n.p.). Suki even resembled Manjula, although perhaps that was my imagination. But when I look back, I realize the cartoon's quirkiness attracted a particular English-educated urban readership. So I was not surprised when the eminent Hindi cartoonist Kaak Sahib told me he could not understand Manjula's comic strip. Another cartoonist told me that the *Pioneer*, in which *Suki* appeared, occupied a niche in the market; it was not for the masses. This was the first I had heard of a cartoon's exclusivity. Manjula was aware of her cartoons not being understood – she made a couple of strips communicating her quandary to her readers.[4]

Time and again, scholars invested in recuperating women's contributions to history have observed their dismissal as true writers, artists, and scientists.[5] Seen from this vantage point, when cartoonists told me they did not understand Manjula's cartoons, I realized it was not adequate to situate their quandary in terms of Manjula's niche audience. *Ravi Prasad, the engineer-cartoonist I met in Mumbai, had a judgment on Manjula: "[She] is the Aubrey Beardsley art nouveau type. Her strip [*Suki*] was too conscious and biographical. She had an answer for everything – 'men will not appreciate this work' etcetera."[6] Although I did not admit it at the time, I am a fan of Manjula's *Suki* and the drawings she published for the feminist press, Kali. Ravi Prasad was a popular cartoonist, and I failed to understand why the biographical content or Manjula's certainties could be a critique. In hindsight, a feminist perspective might have troubled Prasad. R. K. Laxman's cartoons were no less biographical, but because he assumed the vantage point of the "common man" it was acceptable as neutral and therefore, uncertain.

In a chapter in the book commemorating Kamath's life, cartoonists Unny, Manjula, and others ponder the issue of gender, unanimously dismissing gender as a critical ingredient. Manjula returned to the issue, noting her surprise that Kamath's uniqueness went unnoticed: "There are a fair number of women strip cartoonists in the West these days, but of political cartoonists, I am not aware of even one" (Kamath 2005, p. 38). However, the marginal presence of women political cartoonists in India and elsewhere poses a question about the connection between gender, politics, and humor: Are women who satirize politics dangerous? Are women not prepared to laugh? One perspective is voiced by Manjula whose character Suki had a relatively short life in Mumbai's *Sunday Observer*, ending in 1986, four years after its first publication.[7] The strip revived for six years in 1992 and was published in New Delhi's *Pioneer*. For Manjula, "the problem isn't one of supply or of gender discrimination, but *demand*." That demand, according to Manjula, has to be made by "engaged and intelligent readers." Manjula places responsibility on the readers for the destiny of cartoonists in India: "Unless local strips are actively critiqued and appraised by their readers, local cartoonists will remain minor curiosities, never becoming the pop-sociologists that the best international strip cartoonists are" (Padmanabhan 2005, n.p.).

"Only boys scribble"

When I further engaged cartoonists to offer an explanation from their own experience, they either naturalized cartooning as a male activity or calculated that few men were cartoonists, so by default fewer women were in the profession. "Actually, there are few men in cartooning, too." Sanjay Mistry's comment suggested there was nothing peculiar in not having women cartoonists, since they reflected a trend even among men. But at the same time it evoked a gender lag: few men mean fewer or no women. Sipping South Indian filter coffee and eating *sambar vada* (lentil doughnut in a soup), I was meeting with Sanjay Mistry in Prakash Café near Dadar Railway Station (west) (see Figure 5.4). Mistry was associated with Shiv Sena's *Saamna*. "Why should that be?" I asked, taking another bite off my *sambar vada*. Turning my notebook around, briskly scribbling Sonia Gandhi's caricature on it, Sanjay Mistry elaborated, "even now there are fewer women cartoonists in India because as in Pakistan, there is no encouragement to women." "If women work, it is for money. In India we require character and marriage for women. Gents are not liberal and women do not have freedom" (Interview, July 28, 2009).

But men worked for money, too, I thought, and interpreted Sanjay Mistry's implication as being that women sought employment only out of necessity in the absence of earning males. His analysis also implied, to my surprise, that women's character continued to be adversely perceived if they were unmarried and employed. As for the general question of why there were so few women cartoonists, for cartoonist V. G. Narendra (Narendra), a disdain for laziness was the issue: "In the Indian context, cartooning has become a lazy person's activity. I mean for those who do it as a hobby, not the professionals. Women do not have time to do this kind of work. Only boys scribble" (Interview, July 23, 2009).

Women in pocket cartoons

The ambivalence about gender and cartooning seeped into the portrayals, too, as Mita explained about her character Bhaiyaji and her struggle to have her own Common Man rather than a Common Woman:

RITU: *You* made Bhaiyaji ("Older Brother") the backdrop [of your cartoons], washing dishes. How did your readers respond?
MITA: Bhaiyaji was very popular. I also did the editorial cartoon.

RITU: How do you get feedback that the cartoons are popular, did you receive many letters?

MITA: The circulation people told me that my cartoon was popular. The editor would tell me about those who wrote about my cartoon, sometimes they would give the letters. At the time I was quite young. Lucknow is a city with intellectuals and the literati. Some of them would tell my father, "Your daughter has made a very good cartoon." Then I did not understand these things and did not care. Later when I was with *Amar Ujala*, my husband once went to western UP [Uttar Pradesh] area, related to some work. There when people learned about me they showed him their albums of cuttings of my cartoons!

Bhaiyaji ("Older Brother") is the character Mita loves most of her three pocket cartoons characters, which also include Achuk and Sahiba. Bhaiyaji did not speak; his wife did all the speaking and thinking. Mita explained, "His wife is bold, both at home and outside. She commented on political issues. Unlike Sahiba, who I could not present everywhere because she was sophisticated (see Figure 6.3), Bhaiyaji's wife was everywhere. Perhaps I was projecting myself. I am a feminist."

Mita launched *Sahiba* at her editor's insistence that she replace her Common Man with a woman. "I was uncomfortable that he wanted me to do a woman." There was a particular type of woman the editor had in mind too: an IAS officer's wife. The IAS is the Indian Administrative Service – an elite bureaucratic force distributed throughout the country's various governmental divisions. The IAS denoted a position of social power and came with political clout, and its presumed identity is male, just as in the directive Mita got – an IAS officer's wife. Mita was not happy with the arrangement, because it meant that "the arena of the character got restricted." So although she proceeded with the concept, her character Sahiba was not an IAS officer's wife, she was a modern woman. Mita added a child to increase the scope and possibilities of the action in her pocket cartoon.

Kaak's *Jamadarin* (*c.* 1960) Manjula's *Suki* (1982, Figure 6.2), Kamath's *Gita* (1985), and Mita's pocket cartoon character *Sahiba* (1992, Figure 6.3) were the few cartoons and comic strips woven around female characters. Their cartoons were not my first experience with female characters. Decades ago, during my childhood, I used to read Pran's *Srimatiji* (1968). This comic strip was a regular page-wide feature in the Hindi women's journal, *Sarita*, which I am familiar with because my mother subscribed to the magazine. Srimatiji was a smart woman, and her problems and solutions caught my fancy and gripped my imagination, although she was certainly not the norm during my childhood. Comic artist Pran told me more about his character Srimatiji, in the comic strip of that name that I had read as a child: "When I started my career in comics there were senior cartoonists like Mario, Ahmed, Kutty, and Shankar,

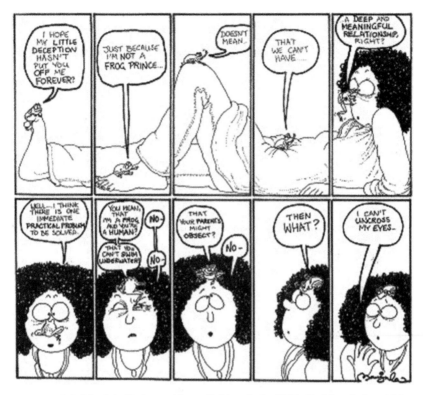

6.2 Manjula Padmanabhan, *Suki*. n.d. (*c.* 1990–5). Mumbai and New Delhi. Courtesy of Manjula Padmanabhan.

who were very talented and reputed. But they were all preparing political cartoons. No one was doing comics."[8] Pran was in a suit, sitting in his office, facing a room in which one could see a team of people working on a comic project. He was the proprietor of Diamond Comics, the largest-selling comic-book brand in India. A large framed painting of Nehru overlooked the office. It was Pran's painting, with Nehru's autograph. "So I thought, Why not create an Indian character and make comics on local subjects? I first started comic strips. In 1968 I made *Srimatiji* for *Sarita*. She is a middle-class housewife. The couple argued and cut jokes on [made jokes about] each other. They have two kids. I want to give entertainment but I also want to send some message. In *Srimatiji* several episodes are on sati, dowry, and tantrics." Messages on such topics are crucial, but they also gain acceptance as "women's issues" in women's magazines and for women readers rather than as political issues in contexts that address a broader readership.[9]

6.3 Mita Roy, "Sahiba; Elizabeth Taylor's Eighth Marriage," *Amar Ujala*. n.d. (*c.* 1995–2000). New Delhi. "Oh! The wretched woman has married for the eighth time and because of dowry I could not marry even once!!" Courtesy of Mita Roy.

The critique of dowry emerged from news about the Hollywood star's most recent marriage. Cartoonist Mita positioned herself as a feminist. Showing a senior woman reading news of Hollywood, cursing Taylor, and lamenting the loss of the opportunity to marry due to dowry demands, provided an unexpected moment for voicing a social vice. But it might also pose a question about the yearning for marriage due to its implications for women in India.

The cartoons featuring female characters embodied "situated knowledges" (Haraway 1988) about India's democratic society, as notably
comes through in Kaak's, Kamath's, and Mita's cartoons. Living in
modern times, these characters consistently sutured the politics of everyday life and they did so in distinct ways.

Kaak's outspoken and "sexy" *Jamadarin* was the socially peripheral
Dalit subject that spoke up and to the senior male character in Kaak's
cartoons; the *Jamadarin* with the broom, as the figure that cleaned up the
soiled environment, was also politically critical and clean. With this portrayal, it would be too quick to conclude that Kaak was a feminist. He did
not claim to be one and neither did he endorse any other "isms," hence his
refusal to contribute cartoons to the SAHMAT publication, *Punch Line*
(Upadhyay 1994).[10] Kaak's refusal was strikingly contradictory to his
peers, who banded together to critique the alarming rise of communalism
in the wake of what is known as the Babri Masji-Mandir issue that sparked
off organized Hindu violence against Muslims on December 6, 1992. At
the core of the violence was the claim to rescue and reclaim the Babri
Masjid – a sixteenth-century mosque in Ayodhya, in the state of Uttar
Pradesh, as a temple and birthplace of the Hindu god Ram. In this
remarkable moment of "interventionist cartooning" (Menon 1994,
n.p.), when cartoonists wielded their pens and pencils against Hindutva,
Kaak declined the invitation. When I asked Kaak why he did not join his
peers, the answer provided a context for situating his cartoon characters,
especially the *Jamadarin*. For Kaak, "communalism and other isms are a
perspective from some point."[11] Kaak clarified that it was not as if he did
not support women, but he cannot rally around "women" or magnify their
position as the suppressed subjects. For Kaak, the whole society was
suppressed, and although "there is no doubt women get suppressed,"
this also made them powerful and revengeful. Pointing to the epic
Mahabharata, Kaak concluded, "the whole Mahabharat was one of
revenge by Draupadi." This analysis of women's subjugated social
position as one that simultaneously embodied power complicates any
easy correlation between the representation of strong women protagonists
and a feminist intervention that proposes a gender analytics for revealing
social disparity. Mita's characters contrasted with and were a foil to Pran's
Srimatiji and to Laxman's Common Man. Mita made a clear distinction
between the two: "An important point was that Bhaiyaji's wife commented on political issues, unlike Srimatiji. Reading the newspaper was
important. It is most important for political cartoonists. Bhaiyaji's wife
read the newspaper and was able to articulate politics." Mita elaborated,
"Bhaiyaji's wife is vocal and gives her opinion. She is the stronger character. Bhaiyaji washes utensils in the background. She looks traditional,

wears a sari and reads the newspaper." She is the Common Woman, the counterpart of Laxman's Common Man.

The unCommon woman: the world of Maya

Remembering her in an interview with the *Asian Age* editor Nazreen Bhura, Kamath's daughter Deepa and son Nandan recalled that their mother took to cartooning after they had grown to be eight and ten years old.[12] "She kept no diary that I was aware of, she rarely gave interviews or wrote articles for newspapers and magazines, and the few times that she did give talks, they were largely spontaneous and unwritten. We couldn't even locate a real bio-data that belonged to her. This in spite of her being a recognized widely published cartoonist" (Kamath 2005, p. 1). "She was not a hard core career woman," wrote Bhura in an article on Kamath (Bhura 2002). Kamath initially "found it tough finding wholehearted acceptance in the male-dominated field of cartooning." Her cartoons were "distorted" and used as "fillers" but over time, Kamath's determination and position with the *Deccan Herald*, *Asian Age*, and several other newspapers gave her a national platform. Was she a feminist, Bhura asked Deepa. "She was a humanist who was sensitive to the environment around her. She was not a feminist in the traditional sense of the word" (Bhura 2002). For cartoonist-editor Govind Dixit, Kamath was *Asian Age*'s USP – Unique Selling Proposition: "Maya Kamath emerged suddenly and picked up very rapidly. She had a lot of energy and wit. Maya had a lot of following. After her passing, readers missed her."[13]

While the national edition of the *Times of India* was inseparable from the name of Laxman, its regional editions carried pocket cartoons by other cartoonists. Among them was Kamath, whose pocket cartoons were daily fare in the Bangalore edition. A recipient of the Karnataka Cartoonists Association's award, Kamath was among India's leading political cartoonists.

Her professional cartooning began in 1985 with the comic strip *Gita*. Over the years, Kamath expanded her portfolio to develop new vantage points for her witty takes on everyday life. Current affairs and politics attracted her, and she gradually carved a niche for herself working for various newspapers. Kamath's *oeuvre* consists of nearly 8,000 cartoons, and is now archived in Sparrow, a sound and picture archive for research on women. The short-lived and longer-lasting mix of comic strips and pocket cartoons are an indication of Kamath's determination to seek opportunities and carve a space in the world of cartooning. This world came to her through more stable appointments with the *Deccan Herald* and the *Asian Age*. In 1997, she began to enjoy a sense of belonging to

6.4 Maya Kamath, "Now, Now, You Can't Expect Me to Quarrel with Daddy." *Asian Age.* January 21, 1999. New Delhi. Courtesy of *Asian Age.*
Cartoonist-politician Bal Thackeray, leader of the Shiv Sena, is pictured with the Bharatiya Janata Party leader, former Prime Minister Atal Bihari Vajpayee. Kamath takes recourse to gender stereotypes – the tough father and soothing mother, to juxtapose familial and national politics and the injury to democracy.

the world of cartooning: "I am having a wonderful time with my cartoons. They're used every now and then on the front page, and on my part I am beginning to get the front-page-withdrawal-syndrome under control. Also I am doing some caricatures and things for the year-end special pages. I am finally beginning to feel I belong there" (Kamath 2005, p. 35).

To understand Kamath's unease and anxiety would be to acknowledge the hierarchy and turfs that marked social and political cartoons in India. As the pocket cartoon and Laxman's Common Man became widespread in the early years of postcolonial India, they embodied a developing hierarchy between social and political themes. In this division of creative labor, usually the senior cartoonist was delegated the big editorial political cartoon and the junior cartoonist worked on the social pocket cartoon. When, early in her career, Kamath drew the pocket cartoon for a regional edition of the *Times of India*, she was asked to keep within the boundary of the social because the political was the domain of the senior cartoonist, Laxman. The political scene outside the pocket cartoon was an invitation to political commentary. Kamath frequently engaged gender reversal and deities to reproduce these politics in a familial setting (see Figure 6.4).

Kamath's cartoons pry open the illusionary world of development through the perspective and voice of the common woman. To reduce the common woman to a housewife would be akin to reducing the Common Man to the husband – in the pocket cartoon, spousal identity,

6.5 Maya Kamath. *Deccan Herald*. February 16, 1993. Bangalore. "There
Will Be No More Water Supply, Madam. An ancient Ram temple has
been discovered below these water pipes." Courtesy of *Asian Age*.

Kamath's cartoons gave prominence to female characters, making
them equal participants in India's sociopolitical scene. This cartoon is
a fine example of the domestic, political, and religious confluence that
challenges the boundaries of public and private.

children, and pets constitute the family, connecting the nation and its
social life. This social drama can be read as politics with immediacy:
"There will be no more water supply, Madam. An ancient Ram temple
has been discovered below these water pipes" (see Figure 6.5).

The disruption of the water supply means that the daily rhythm of
domestic chores will come to a standstill. The controversial movement
for declaring the Babri Masjid a Ram temple took the ongoing debate to its
limit: how far would we dig for the past? And when will the present stop
succumbing to the past? This juxtaposition of the present and the past in a
scene about a basic necessity, water, transformed a political issue – the
preservation of old temples and mosques – into one that could be easily
resolved with common sense that did not lose sight of more pressing life
issues, such as water. Kamath's cartoons about Bangalore's chronic water
woes revealed that administrators were on a different wavelength: "Don't
worry about contamination madam. The sewage stays absolutely pure."[14]

With home and its vicinity as the space for politics in the social sphere,
the media in their various incarnations – television and newspaper – were
recurring props in Kamath's cartoons. A cartoon by Kamath was the point
of mediation, generating politics at home. This was the space, a normative
setup of family and friends, within which conversations occurred. The
home was not the place of dupes; here the media's complicity with powerful politics was easily unpeeled through common sense. If a way to rethink
the social is to see through its politics, then Kamath reinforced this connection by composing her pocket cartoon on two levels – visually narrating

two stories as one. The single column was creatively split in two, producing an implicit dialogue between social and political. In Kamath's cartoons the *maya* (illusion) of development was spirited away when home bumped against cutting-edge technology and bureaucracy: "Wish I could tell the wife about this telecom breakthrough. But our phone at home is dead," the scientist overseeing the launch of the INSAT satellite confides to his colleague. The Bangalore Development Authority (BDA) was reread as "Bungling, double-crossing, and apathy." Such revelations come from engagements within the family.

The state was visible in daily civic bungling and media management, as well as in gender inequalities dotting the social landscape. Time and again, Kamath returns to gender-discriminatory practices and casual moments that reveal the normalization of inequities. In these cartoons, sati, premature marriage, and female infanticide are reinscribed as contemporary issues, not matters of the past. "No, no! That's not my daughter" says a bespectacled man to his visitor who holds a newspaper with the headlines "rampant child marriage." "That's my daughter-in-law!"[15] The cognitive challenge surfaces when Kamath shows nation states' law-and-order vocabulary recognizing sati as murder, rather than an unfortunate vestige: A police officer assures two journalists at the site of a pyre, "Relax! It wasn't sati after all! It was just an innocent, harmless case of cold-blooded murder, that's all." Reordering sati as murder criminalizes the act, rendering it punishable. But in the process it wipes out the traces of the social and gendered aspect of the killing. In Kamath's cartoons the speaking subject for women's equality is not always the woman herself. Kamath's scene of a maternity ward with a sobbing woman consoled by her husband draws attention to women's socialization as inferior and subnormal beings: "Cheer up darling ... it's not such a terrible abnormality. After all, lots of people have babies that are female!"[16]

Gendered elites and subalterns

Kamath's cartoons reproduced the social gap between women activists and those in need of their intervention: "Now tell us frankly, which is your most crying need of the moment ... a comprehensive status report, or a demographic socio-cultural handbook?"[17] The aghast poor women can only look back. The crux of these cartoons was the ignorance of women activists, ignorance displayed by survey-driven social elites out of touch with reality. Other cartoonists depicted the absurdity of such positions, as well. Elites, particularly women with education and of the upper class, were frequently pictured in Shankar's cartoons, where lipstick on pouted lips signified class and gender (see Chapter 4). In Laxman's cartoons, such depictions were not a prominent feature but neither were they absent. In 1972, in a letter titled "Travesty of Facts" to the *Times of India* editor, Meenakshi Shane protested Laxman's portrayal of women activists as social elites. In that cartoon, Laxman depicted a plump activist running late to a meeting of housewives because she could not find parking. In her letter, Shane noted the travesty of facts:

We were pained to see the cartoon by Mr. R. K. Laxman caricaturing the serious demonstration organized by our committee to protest the misery of the common housewife (October 6/7 1972). More than a thousand women participated in this "dharna" [collective street protest] and sat in the scathing sun whole day. They belonged to various sections such as working women, housewives, prominent social and political workers etc. a majority of them consisted of women from the slums in Dharavi, Santa Cruz, Wadala, Matunga labour camp etc. The caricature in your paper gives the impression that the "dharna" was stage managed by some well-to-do socialites. It is not only a travesty of facts but also casts slur on our movement and its aims. If some well-placed women wish to join our movement, they are welcome. (*Times of India*, October 8, 1972)

At the time Laxman made this cartoon, in the 1970s, women owning and driving cars in India was a sign of elite status. Here driving a car signified class and skill that situated the woman activist distantly from the women she was leading. The comment about parking space would not be read in the same light today; it now signifies an urban ethos of a broad band of the middle class. Uniformed chauffeurs and plush car brands, however, would mark elite status.

But the manner in which gender is inscribed renders each cartoon unique. Laxman's use of lipstick and car, as well as the caricature of elite women activists – short hair, pouted lips, and obesity – were remarkably different from Kamath's cartoon of neat and poised women, with cool shades, debating between a report and survey as the panacea for women's poverty. In Kamath's cartoon, women become agents of the discourse of development. The range of participants and observers in Kamath's cartoons brings a variety of perspectives and women occupy a significant portion of the public space caricatured in these cartoons. When the arena of political action expands in multiple directions, it keeps the reader on the alert about political moments in the social space they occupy. Kamath's Common Woman reveals a tongue that is not always tied or safely tucked away in silence. The Common Woman's silent gulp and her tongue sticking out remind me of the Hindu goddess Kali, who is commonly pictured with her tongue sticking out. The cartoons reveal debilitating truths about the modern nation that the prose of news and specialists' jargon of all stripes refuse to acknowledge.

6.6 Life-size cast of Laxman's pocket cartoon character, the Common Man, on Mumbai's Worli seafront, July 27, 2009. Photograph by the author.

The Common Man and the epidemic of pocket cartoons

If you were to walk along Mumbai's Worli seafront, a *putla* (puppet), as the Meru cab driver who took me there called it, stands leaning on a rail and gazing at the Arabian Sea. This is a memorial to the Common Man – a life-size cast of Laxman's character (see Figure 6.6). About a hundred miles away, another life-size sculpture of Laxman's Common Man stands high on a pedestal. At Pune's Symbiosis Institute campus, against the backdrop of international flags, the Common Man is perched high up, looking out to aspiring MBAs and other students seeking a professional future by enrolling in this private institute. Inside, near the office, a framed recent caricature of the Common Man is displayed on the wall. Recently, when the activist Anna Hazare concluded his four-day fast against national corruption, supporters garlanded the Common Man sculpture on the Symbiosis campus. Such juxtaposition of privatization, street democracy, and the timeless Common Man captures the enigma of this gendered identity. Who is this Common Man? Why does he seem to appear in the small one-column format called the pocket cartoon?

The Common Man's story begins several decades ago; the story of his many avatars depends on who tells it. Although Laxman's Common Man was the longest running, at nearly six decades, there are many others. Every cartoonist I met reserved an opinion on the Common Man and the genre it spawned – the single-column pocket cartoon. In Indian newspapers of all hues and languages, the Common Man and the pocket cartoon blended to became a popular news format. Their unique character and pocket cartoon title marked the distinct style of each cartoonist, serving as the cartoonist's signature and the newspaper's brand identity.

Pocket cartoons sprouted a galaxy of Common Men. If each was sculpted and placed next to Laxman's Worli idol, it would make quite a sea of men: men only, please. We are common. The ubiquity of the Common Man also came to define cartoon stylistics in India. Kutty summarized the phenomenon in his correspondence with me:

Laxman is mainly responsible for the epidemic of pocket cartoons. Laxman's Common Man is a sort of peon. He looks like the fellow who gets pan [betel leaf and nut], cigarette or tea from outside for the people in the office. He is neither an observer nor a participant. Other cartoonists have followed his pattern. Everybody now copies Laxman's pocket cartoon with their own Common Man and gets away with the written matter under it. After Laxman's pocket cartoons became popular all newcomers started having a Common Man in their pocket cartoons as if it is a mandatory requirement. In most pocket cartoons the Common Man is redundant.

Laxman made the pocket cartoon political and the written matter also took over. What was printed under the cartoon became the important thing, rather than the visual. When it took this shape, the *Manorama* of Kerala went one step further. They commissioned a local artist to draw about two dozen drawings of the conventional size of a pocket cartoon. The drawings showed various familiar scenes. Every day they printed one of these with a suitable commentary based on the current news! It was a success for some time until the readers discovered the truth.

A medley of the many conversations I had with cartoonists, together with their published opinions, serves as a long conversation outlining a history, mediated by my questions and observations, and by questions journalists often asked the cartoonists:

KUTTY: John Bull used to appear in cartoons drawn by Indian cartoonists in those old periodicals. I cannot categorically say there was no stereotyped Common Man then. I can say only that I do not remember having seen one. The British cartoonists were our models. Britain had been traditionally depicted as a stocky man in a tailcoat, with a waistcoat made out of the British flag. He wore a top hat and boots. He was called John Bull. Britain was always represented by that figure. In England, Strube had a Common Man drifting in and out of his cartoons representing the average British in his bowler. Low had John Bull and Joan Bull to represent the British public. We in India continued that practice and adopted John Bull.

Shankar used to bring in a Common Man too into his cartoons occasionally, that is the turbaned chap you are talking about. To represent India, Shankar devised a farmer from north India. This man had a big turban, a dhoti [wraparound] coming up to his knee, and on special occasions a *baniyan* [undershirt] type of shirt. This was his depiction of a Common Man. Occasionally he used this figure of the Common Man. But this figure could not represent south India. It did not matter, since Shankar was drawing in a paper in Delhi. Shankar used to fill his cartoons with dozens of identifiable personalities in the older *Hindustan Times* days.

6.7 Kutty, "Smile Please." *Ananda Bazar Patrika.* August 3, 1965. Calcutta. Courtesy of *Ananda Bazar Patrika.* Pen and ink artwork for a four-column display or editorial cartoon. Photographer's sign: "Fourth ¼ target is 25 million tonnes of food grains." The Common Man is seated.

I remember once I counted thirty known faces in one of his cartoons. He insisted I too draw enough people inside the cartoon.

I too used to bring in a Common Man of the type of Shankar's. I copied Shankar and adopted his symbol of the Common Man and whenever I needed, drew him like Shankar's [see Figure 6.7]. When I wanted a Bengali or Kerala Common Man I drew one in the regional dress. I seldom needed the Common Man. I used to try to get away by filling up space by the Common Man and some such device. But Shankar dubbed it escapism and did not allow it. When I tried to bring in the Common Man into my cartoons unnecessarily, he [Shankar] used to kid me, saying I was trying to shirk work and taking the easy way out of filling space. "You are shirking work," was his reaction when I tried writing long passages inside the cartoon, too. True, I was lazy and wanted to avoid work. In my book *Laugh with Kutty* you will notice I have five or six or more known people in my cartoons. I took years to manage some sort of drawing ability. Shankar also had other characters, Bada Saab (Big Sir) and Memsaab (Madam).

Ahmed had his Chandu the *chowkidar* [guard] feature. Chandu represented the Common Man and sometimes did appear in his political cartoons as the witness of affairs. Chandu too was north Indian.

R. K. Laxman's Common Man is able to represent the whole of India. This Comman Man is a lower-middle-class chap and can fit in anywhere in India.

As I turned the yellow brittle pages of cartoonist Mita's copy of Ahmed's cartoons, Chandu's world came alive. He was not an ordinary *chowkidar;*

he traveled abroad. When abroad, thin Chandu's loincloth and bare torso gave way to a suit and tie; the bare feet had shoes, and at times he even opted for a long coat. The turban was in place at all times, as was his portly wife and companion – always in a sari. Chandu reminded me of Gandhi.

AHMED: I was desperately searching for a cartooning character ... an Indian version of Pop maybe. And then I saw this *chowkidar* at King George's Hospital, a funny ribald tough little man with a turban and a loin cloth. That was the model for Chandu. I had found my man (Interview 1974; see Shankar and Narula 1974, p. 89)

LAXMAN: The little man, who was with me all my life, hiding somewhere, not visible, came out. He has never said a word, others speak in the cartoons, he listens. But he is always there, in each frame, except once in three or four years, when I quietly drop him. Then I get angry letters from Guwahati [in Assam], from all the most unlikely places. (Interview 1985; see Contractor 1985, p. 10)

Laxman's Common Man has worn a plaid jacket and dhoti and does not have a turban. I remember in earlier versions his Common Man had a cap. The Common Man seems to have aged, too. When I saw Laxman's earlier artwork in the *Times of India* office, the Common Man seemed a middle-aged man. When I last saw his pocket cartoon, he had aged.

KUTTY: My cartoons were addressed to the Common Man. He was my audience, not a participant. All the participants in a particular scene I was recording were in my cartoon. He was not a participant in the drama unless I called him inside. Nowadays a cartoon means two figures or often one figure and lots of writing inside. Anyway I gradually realized I did not need a Common Man. Shankar encouraged me to bring more known people into the cartoons. Shankar did not need the Common Man because his cartoons were full of known figures participating in the action, and the reader was his Common Man. I followed the same system.

BIRESHWAR: I had drawn a *kisan* [farmer] representing him as a Common Man. He was slim, poor, wearing a loincloth, and barefoot. He had put on a typical turban and had a special moustache. India's major parts are villages, not cities or towns. Kisan generally lives in a village. So I took him as a Common Man.

KUTTY: You must remember India's economy was purely agricultural; the poor farmer fed the country. He bore the brunt of the taxation, too. The rich man had loopholes to evade tax; the poor farmer was exploited to the maximum. Shankar's Common Man was that man. Shankar used his Common Man occasionally when he was necessary in any particular situation. For example, on the day after the budget he used to appear having all these tax burdens heaped on his back or some such visual. I used to introduce him into my cartoons, too, on such occasions. Whenever new taxations came, or calls for sacrifices were made by our rulers, this man appeared in my cartoons. I abandoned that practice sometime in the late 1960s and then on rarely utilized him. I can speak only for myself.

RITU: Shankar's post-independence cartoons frequently included two donkeys, the socialites Bada Saab, and Memsaab. I remember there was an elephant and pig, too. Of course, these are elites and not common people.

SHANKAR: There is one whole class of people in India who succeed not because of ability but because of family. That is the baby elephant – playful, not really malicious or bad, but always being led into things by the man who loves dirt. And, *you* know, there is always that second group of people who are only at home in filth. They are the pig. (See Lyon 1952, p. 24)

RITU: In the Marathi cartoon weekly *Marmik*, I saw Bal Thackeray's cartoons had a Colonel Blimp-like character that reminded me of Low's cartoons.

KUTTY: Thackeray copied Low. So no wonder his Common Man was an Indian Blimp. Low very often drew himself in his political cartoons, too, to represent the Common Man, especially in crowd scenes. Low always appeared in his Colonel Blimp strip cartoons. Once Thackeray copied one such crowd and he drew Low too! He did not know it was Low!

Kevy's (Kerala Varma's) Common Man is also a rural farmer, like Bireshwar's *kisan*. In the 1960s and 1970s, he appeared on the covers of the magazines *Thought* and *Eastern Economist* (see Figure 6.8). Kevy's Common Man stands tall in front of politicians with incisive comments on policy and politics. In talking with politicians, he punctured their power with his shrewd remarks and questions. The turban, dhoti, and hut situated the Common Man within a rural and agricultural context. But Kevy's Common Man does not always laugh and outsmart the politician; he is at times shocked by political gimmicks.

When I visited the Indian Institute of Cartoonists (IIC) in 2009, I met cartoonist Narendra, whose cartoons and signature I recalled in *Shankar's Weekly*. Now he served as the director of this Institute. I asked him about the Common Man.

NARENDRA: In the Common Man, every day the reader sees his *pratirupa* [image/counterpart]. "I am there" – that is the direct role of the reader. He is viewing the situation; he does not speak. He is intelligent and has accumulated knowledge. Just like Laxman's Common Man. In our state, Karnataka, Ramamurthy created Mr. Citizen one day before Laxman's. Each newspaper wants its own Common Man.

The Common Man evoked my memory of Mr. Punch and the various vernacular versions in colonial India. Since political independence, in India the Common Man is closely tied to the pocket cartoon. Why is the Common Man and pocket cartoon popular among Indian cartoonists? I asked Bireshwar and Kutty.

BIRESHWAR: One Mr. Samuel of *Shankar's Weekly* started drawing pocket cartoons for the *Indian Express*. The heading was "Babuji." Babuji represented a middle-class clerk. Samuel tried and touched the problems of a clerk in wit and humor. Babuji became very popular [see Figure 6.9].

6.8 Kevy (Kerala Varma), "Gold Rush." *Eastern Economist*. November 3, 1978. New Delhi. "Government's gold policy has failed. Gold has passed into the hands of operators."

Kevy's grotesque style of caricature is exemplified in his portrayal of the Prime Minister Indira Gandhi. His favorite caricature showed Indira Gandhi as Charlie Chaplin. Kevy's Common Man was not a witness but took turns outwitting politicians and being crushed by their policies. The cartoon depicted Indira Gandhi's political maneuvers after her release from prison and the formation of Congress (I) to denote "Indira." Her ally Swaran Singh was in her bag; the play was on the word *swaran*, which means "gold."

KUTTY: Samuel was the first to introduce the pocket cartoon into an Indian newspaper. He is the father of the pocket cartoon in India. His creation Babuji was a commentary on Punjabi life. He did not need a Common Man, because all the characters in his cartoons were common men and women. His pocket cartoon was not political at all.

So, although Laxman's pocket cartoon is the longest-running, his contemporary Samuel introduced the first pocket cartoon, a single-column daily cartoon, which started the trend for this format in India and Pakistan.

The pocket cartoon and Babuji: "This is Delhi." No, "This is Lahore"

"Never a dull moment," I said, reading aloud the title of cartoonist Samuel's autobiography as he presented me with a signed copy. Samuel is an engaging

6.9 Samuel, "Babuji." Pen and ink artwork. n.d. New Delhi. Personal collection.

Babuji represented the lower middle-class clerk dwelling in the city and dealing with the pressures of a low income and inflation. Samuel did some research and lived with a clerk's family in New Delhi to develop his character Babuji and the pocket cartoon.

storyteller, and witty. I met him on several occasions and we often corresponded. Now recovering from cancer, he could only whisper. "How is your little one doing?" he would always ask. "She has grown quite a bit now, no more the toddler when I first visited you." "You need to do me a favor." "Yes," I said. "Before you leave, take this book to Mrs. Mankekar two houses down this road, and please tell her Mr. Mankekar came into my dream two days ago."

D. R. Mankekar, the famous editor of the *Times of India*, was instrumental in realizing the enduring significance of the pocket cartoon and the figure of Babuji, a "Common Man" or logo man, as *Vinay had put it at the Mahotsav (Chapter 5). Samuel, a contemporary of Kutty, Bireshwar, and Laxman, always addressed the late Mankekar with fondness and admiration. But he did not refer to him as his guru. In fact, Samuel did not mention any guru. It was striking that, although some of the cartoonists I met evoked a guru and displayed his portrait, Samuel, who did not mention a guru, was the only one to mention visits in his dreams. Dreaming of the guru can be a central experience of the *guru shishya* tradition. It can embody moments of intense practice and instruction of the guru.[18]

Samuel recounted how it all began. "It was with 'This is Delhi' that I started as a pocket cartoonist. Delhi had a lot of problems with the influx of refugees. My pocket cartoon started with traffic problems and day-to-day problems. This pocket cartoon was reproduced in Pakistan as 'This is Lahore' without crediting me." Could there be a copyright on day-to-day problems in the two new nations? Samuel and I had a hearty laugh over this "copyright infringement." India and Pakistan, for all their purported political differences, had the same issues to sort out, making it possible for Samuel's pocket cartoon to be popular in both countries.

RITU: How did Babuji begin?
SAMUEL: Babuji was based on the common secretarial clerk who was part and parcel of Delhi life during the 1950s. While there was a struggle to build up the circulation of Delhi newspapers, we thought of capturing the readership by exposing the day-to-day problems of the *babu* [clerk] class, and that got immediate response. I spent months to study the problems of the clerical community, and Babuji was the result.
RITU: What did you do for this study?
SAMUEL: Regarding my research on Babuji's lifestyle, you will be delighted to know that I lived with a secretarial clerk for six months and learned about their economics and their domestic problems before putting these in black and white. Dr. Mankekar, who was the resident editor of *Times of India* in Delhi, found it quite fascinating and asked me to start a feature on Babuji in order to widen the circulation, and it worked.

Babuji was not a silent character. He had his opinion on diverse subjects, and his brotherhood waited for the morning paper and quite a few of them sent in their comments. As it became popular, even the *New York Times* wrote a column on it. Laxman started his [pocket cartoon] "You Said It" column to fill the gap, as I left the *Times of India* to join the *Indian Express* where I worked for four years. The readers of *Times of India* and the *Nav Bharat Times* [the Hindi edition of the *Times of India*] pressured the management to get "Babuji" back, and that is why I was called back to the *Times of India*.

RITU: Before Babuji, you also had the strip in *Shankar's Weekly* called *Kalu and Meena*. Babuji is not your first character.

SAMUEL: Kalu and Meena are children of refugees from Lahore who couldn't afford expensive things. I am a refugee from Lahore, even after I joined the *Times of India* I used to make Babuji in chequered clothes. A lady wrote from London saying, Why can't I afford to buy him different clothes?

This was the third occasion Samuel referenced Lahore and refugees. Although Samuel did not say so, I could not but think of *Babuji* and the comic strip *Kalu and Meena* as his biography. The India–Pakistan Partition, usually seen as the displacement of Hindus, Muslims, and Sikhs, also involved Christians. The undetermined context of who belonged where during the Partition meant that choices about becoming citizens in India or Pakistan were made quickly and intuitively.[19] Even after reaching the places they thought they belonged, refugees had problems that Samuel broadcast through his cartoons and comic strip.

Babuji and *Kalu and Meena* did not necessarily reflect Samuel's day-to-day experience, but through "situated knowledge" of them he evoked the perspective of the displaced refugee in India's capital.

Tota Babu: the local Common Man

The daily experience of the Common Man in the pocket cartoon in mainstream newspapers such as the *Times of India* connected with everyday civic concerns of local readers, rendering it portable and translatable across cities and towns that were also serviced by local newspaper editions. Laxman's pocket cartoons would make sense not just in Mumbai but anywhere in India. Frequent power outages, sanitation problems, and corruption were common, ongoing worries that transcended political ideologies. But there were also subtle ways in which pocket cartoons made sense to India's regional publics. Caricaturing these issues required the portrayal of urban and rural distinctions. Talking about these regional variations brought to the fore the entanglement of language in Indian cartoons.

6.10 Jagjeet Rana. Three phases of making the pocket cartoon *Tota Babu*. *Dainik Jagran*. 2003. New Delhi. Courtesy of Jagjeet Rana. Hindi caption: "Air India has made a call for its officers to forgo a month's salary."

Tota Babu has morphed into the Air India logo, the Maharaja. In this cartoon he donned the Maharaja's dress but was impoverished, holding a begging bowl and sobbing. The government-run airline was facing financial stress at the time. The cartoon was sketched and all characters outlined with black ink. The text was handwritten. The coloring done by either hand or Photoshop. After scanning the cartoon, a digital photograph of an Air India aircraft was inserted to create a montage. Finally it was outlined with the series title and the cartoonist's name.

Jagjeet Rana, who makes the pocket cartoon *Tota Babu* (Parrot Babu) for India's largest-circulating newspaper, *Dainik Jagran* (see Figure 6.10), explained to me, "If you are in English newspapers, the [distribution] area becomes wide. That limits the discussion in the cartoon. With the Hindi cartoons and my pocket cartoon, *Tota Babu*, we are taking cartoons to the rural area. Earlier newspapers were not read far and wide. So in Hindi cartoons, we have to make it easy to understand – comprehensible." *Dainik Jagran* is among the world's most-read dailies, and *Tota Babu* appears in color on the front page. Babu, the Common Man character, has a Gandhi cap, which most Congress politicians wear, and carries a walking stick. The parrot is ubiquitous and a source of banter with the Babu.

"Until now the cartoon used to be *Hawabaazi*," continued Rana. "Our paper's policy is that it is for the man on the ground. Even now in our country, only the new generation, that is kids, has the sense for comprehending symbols. For example, in my cartoons I cannot use the dove or the peace sign [circle with two sloping and one vertical line]. Before, cartoons were like modern art, which some understood, some didn't.

Now even the neo-literates can understand. The newspaper sales come from the Common Man."[20] *Tota Babu*'s political focus brought issues of the world and of the nation into a single column. Rana's choice of language, shaped by his understanding of the reader's perceptions, made his cartoons usable for a broad Hindi-reading "man on the ground." He was not part of this rural public but with them, and through his visual vocabulary was performing the role of a translator. Laxman's Common Man and Rana's Tota Babu, even as they both wore the dhoti (garment worn by men by draping it between the legs and at the waist), were not interchangeable. With their decades of publication, Laxman's character and pocket cartoon had become a generic urban fable, and therefore translatable into several languages, including Hindi. English, the language of Laxman's cartoons and the paradox of urban life, was not a linguistic hurdle for transmission to any audience. Even when the play of Hindi could be translated, I wondered if Tota Babu would captivate a public reading English newspapers. Despite its publication in a leading Hindi newspaper that garnered a sizeable readership, Tota Babu did not attract much notice from peers in the English and Hindi press. Most likely it would be dismissed as local, but it is difficult to explain why, other than to feel its provincial humor and to situate it in the politics of taste that requires endorsement by the mainstream urban (and urbane) professionals. Remembering Bireshwar's assessment of Hindi cartooning and my own observations as I continued my conversations, I was curious about what the younger, emerging generation of cartoonists familiar with Hindi cartoons could tell me of its history and place in their professional world.

Desi cartoons

"I have heard of Kanjilal. I saw two cartoons of his in an old *Aj* file – it was desi humor," *Rahul, an upcoming English-newspaper cartoonist who also read Hindi newspapers, told me when I asked about Hindi cartoonists. That was the first time I heard the term desi to differentiate Hindi newspaper cartoons and their distinct sense of humor.[21] Referencing Kaak's cartoon characters – the old common man, the toothless Bhauji, the sister-in-law and the sweeperess – the journalist-editor Mrinal Pande elucidated on desi humor as emerging from a persona "behind which lurks a first-rate ability to spot all delusions of grandeur, hypocrisy and corruption, and expose their rotting roots (*Desi or Vilayati*) with merciless precision" ("Amazing Appeal" by Mrinal Pande. www. marketing-avenues.com/kaaktoons%20opinion01.htm). Vilayati meant foreign. For Pande, Kaak's desi humor drew on Indian traditions of the joking relationship between the younger brother-in-law and his sister-in-law (Devar-Bhabhi), as well as critiqued Western modernization claims of the English-speaking elites in India. Later I learned that desi could also be used to categorize Kutty's cartoons, an example that was far from my mind as I pondered the notion of desi humor and cartoons. Cartoonist Ranga (N. K. Ranganathan) held that a thorough knowledge of scriptures made Kutty's cartoons desi and "purely suited to Indian thinking" (Raghavan, 1994 p. 172). When browsing the net, I stumbled upon several references to desi cartoons, and found cartoons by Ashok Dongre, an engineer and cartoonist whom I met in Mumbai, included in this category.[22] Dongre's cartoons were in English and on Indian politics. Their humor rests in picturing scenes from the anomalies of life in India and sometimes through the play of Hindi words. Dongre's cartoon of the Congress Chairperson Sonia Gandhi holding up a mask showing the current Prime Minister Manmohan Singh's face and the caption "Manmohini" made me laugh. It is public knowledge that Sonia Gandhi holds the reins of the current government. The caption, "Manmohini," played on the Prime Minister's name and rendered it anew to mean the enchantress. Another desi cartoon site surprised me with an assortment of cartoonists, including Suresh Sawant, the Mumbai-based cartoonist.[23] "Desi" resonated outside India too. For a generation of teens raised in the USA, the term desi is widely used to signify a broad South Asian-American identity that includes Indian-Americans. Shalini Shankar explains that this recent term of usage among teens is embraced to elucidate a new inclusive identity of South Asians in the USA, who participate as "public consumers and producers of distinctive, widely circulating cultural and linguistic forms" (2008, p. 4). With these disparate references, the term desi generated more confusion rather than clarifying a category of cartoons. It signaled cartoons based on insider humor that was based on life in India and its cultural idioms. By that token this book is about desi cartoons.

"Hindi can have its own distinct cartoon"

When I asked the leading Hindi cartoonist of *Hindustan Hindi*, Rajendra Dhodapkar, to unravel the mystery of Hindi cartoons, he had much to say. As I took a seat near his busy desk, an eraser, a pencil, a simple felt-tip pen, and a sheet of paper were scattered around his drawing paper (see Figure 6.11). Known as Doctor Sahib, Dhodapkar is a physician; his cartooning tools were simple, the drawing sparse. But he may have thought about the cartoon all day, doubling as a writer and poet:

I feel that cartooning in Hindi was started by Kaak. His good time was in *Dinman* in the 1970s. When he worked on the newspaper *Jansatta*, he became a star

6.11 Cartoonist Rajendra Dhodapkar at his office in the *Hindustan Times* building, drawing and inking his cartoon. November 18, 2003. New Delhi. Photograph by the author.

overnight. Before Kaak, Kanjilal in *Aj* was very popular. Hindi newspapers did not take an anti-establishment stance, hence cartoonists did not flourish in the Hindi press. *Jansatta* was in the Express Groups tradition of anti-establishment. It was a desi paper.

Laxman is not strictly a political cartoonist, but in Hindi even that has not been there. There is no financial support for cartoonists. There are good cartoonists but no work. It is a bad time now but hopefully this is a transitional phase. The 1970s and 1980s were a good time for Hindi papers but liberalization ruined it. Liberalization of India's economy has brought with it less space for debate and opposition and more for conformity. Newspapers try for cartoons to be increasingly less political. But this will not last long. We have too many problems, and at some time cartoonists will have to stand up.

Our cartoon came from Britain. Laxman became a model because of his pocket cartoon. I have to acknowledge Kaak's *upkar* [favor] that *Hindi ka alag kartun ho sakta hai* [Hindi can have its own distinct cartoon]. It does not have to model Laxman. My cartoons have the influence of Vijayan and Puri. But the problem is that slightly educated readers don't understand abstraction. The Hindi elite is intellectual, not affluent as the English-speaking elite.

Humor is reference-related; it has a cultural reference. It is easy to make cartoons for the English-speaking audience because one knows their intellectual level. The Hindi audience is dispersed. Between the national papers such as *Jansatta* and *Hindustan Hindi*, there is a range of people. But the advantage in Hindi is that it is a *khuli zameen* [an open field], because nothing much is done in Hindi cartooning.

Every cartoonist has a few metaphors. For example, Laxman uses a punctured car. In a regional cartoon the readership is defined. In *Nai Duniya*, their cartoonist Devendra Sharma uses the local humor of Malwa. One doesn't have to universalize humor.[24]

In Dhodapkar's view, the fact that Hindi elites were intellectual rather than affluent provided a backdrop for understanding the bleak status of

Hindi cartoons. Sushil Kalra, a retired cartoonist of English and Hindi presses, added some history few knew:[25]

Hindi cartooning is quite recent. Before there were two or three people, who were perhaps not doing cartooning full time but their drawing had cartoon-effect. In the Hindi belt there were newspapers which had cartoon columns but they don't satisfy the definition of cartoons.[26] In India, it began with English cartoons. After the 1950s there was a revolution. Attached to this were Samuel, Puri, and Kanjilal. Ravinder had a popular column in the *Saptahik*. There are not many names in Hindi. When *Dharamyug* came, then Hindi cartoons *ziyada tour par phaele* [became widespread].

Saptahik and *Dharamyug* were Hindi magazines. I was surprised to learn from Kalra that *Shankar's Weekly* had a Hindi edition. "Ramesh Baxi was its editor. All our cartoons were published there; we got good space. Some were translated from the English edition of *Shankar's Weekly*. The Hindi edition closed a little earlier than the English, which closed with the Emergency (1975–7). The motive of the Hindi *Shankar's Weekly* was to capture Hindi readers in the north belt."

"How does one understand the different scales of newspapers that make them regional and national?" I asked Kalra.

The newspaper has a structure. Basically, national newspapers focus more on international news; the regional newspapers go for the national news. Regional papers feel national papers are models. The regional is filtered and presented as national. There is an opinion that regional issues are not real issues. It is the local news that national newspapers put on page 3 but regional papers show on page 1.

Despite this territorialization of cartoons and language, it may come as a surprise that the Common Man has been branded to convey a national ethos while simultaneously wooing regional metaphors. Air Deccan's campaign for popularizing air travel in India by using Laxman's Common Man tells that story.

Branding the Common Man

Why travel by train when you can fly? (Air Deccan advertisement, 2005)

In India, independence brought with it a new visual vocabulary with which to caricature the making of the nation: cricket, the villages, the slums, science, and air travel. Air travel, in particular, is a persistent theme framing the discourse of development in Laxman's cartoons. Laxman's cartoons have a recurring trope of the *mantri* (minister) traveling abroad. Political culture was best depicted at the airport. The airport, the scene of departure – the journalist jotting down the garlanded *mantri*'s quick soundbites, and the *mantri* in his traditional attire, coat and cap, with a retinue of bureaucrats in tow – these elements animated many of Laxman's cartoons on the politics of air travel.

These cartoons about the airplane were conceptualized at a time when flying was a political and elite luxury in India; it is now becoming commonplace through a fleet of economy airlines. Air Deccan, launched in 2003 by Captain Gopinath, a former air force pilot, was among the growing number of economy airline fleets of the twenty-first century. Air Deccan tickets could cost as little as 1 rupee to 500 rupees (roughly $10 US), an unbelievably enticing fare for air travel. Laxman's Common Man character was the brand ambassador for Air Deccan. This mascot marked a sharp contrast to the mascot of the Indian government airline, Air India: the royal Maharaja.

The introduction of flying as a mode of public transport means that a sizeable chunk of India's population has the novel experience of air travel. Along with the possibility of flying come anxieties and disappointments. For most travelers, Air Deccan is their first experience of air travel. Thus when overscheduling, bad weather, or glitches have led to flight cancellations, it could take an emotional turn. Newspapers have frequently carried stories of passengers' woes; a woman was reported to have threatened to kill herself after her Air Deccan flight from New Delhi to Kashmir was canceled due to bad weather.[27]

In 2009, I met with Captain Gopinath in Bangalore to learn about his airline's logo. A large cut-out of Laxman's Common Man leaned on the wall facing Gopinath's desk. Gopinath informed me that he was charmed by Laxman's cartoons and in particular a pocket cartoon about flying. One of the office staff handed me a copy of the cartoon. The cartoon depicted the discomfort of a well-heeled passenger with his co-passenger from the village, prompting the remark: "I am not really a snob, but if these airlines bring down the fares any further, I will start travelling by train or bus!" Although economy airlines broke social barriers to flying, they provided a new context for social capital to grimace at the unexpected proximity with rustic comport. Eager to establish that development had indeed taken place, and to demystify flying, Air Deccan subsidized prices, making it a feasible option for the common man (and woman) to fly. The tenacious Common Man was their logo as well as their customer, and Orchard, a subsidiary of the global advertising agency Leo Burnett, was given charge of developing the brand. Branding a stereotype with Laxman's cartoon character suggests an irreconcilable proposition. Yet Orchard's campaign did just that – it branded the common experience, suffusing it with ordinariness, emotion, and economy, persuading people to change their habits and fly.

"Laxman's Common Man is iconic. He does not look like the common man in India today, but he symbolizes the common man. We were looking for that symbol," explained Thomas Xavier, director of Orchard in their Bangalore office. "The story makes the difference. Advertising is making sure the difference is known to you. It is not a lie." The Common Man, then, was an "aesthetically designed truth."[28] This truth about the commonness of flying could not be advertised by casting Bollywood celebrities such as "Shahrukh Khan, a Hritihik or Akshay." The faith in Laxman's Common Man was founded on an intuitive understanding – "It was my gut feeling. I cannot rationalize my gut feeling," noted Xavier as we sipped coffee in his office. With the Common Man logo, the Air Deccan campaign was an Indian "blockbuster brand": "It is a unique thing. It explodes in the mind of a diverse set of consumers." Such brands had something for everyone, and the public becomes their advocate. Such magical impact could rarely be engineered. "The Air Deccan advertising was a little fuse that ignited the minds of the people – it lights the dynamite in public consciousness. You create something to lob it into the crowd. The groundswell of public support makes it big. Blockbuster brands are brands made by people," said Xavier. The Air Deccan business model was also considered a landmark for several reasons. It was a revolution because for the first time tickets were sold online and by phone. It was no-frill – they did not serve free drinks and food. The ticket stub had the Common Man on it. It was not on glossy paper. "In fact, we thought of the ticket as something that would most resemble a bus ticket." Xavier's evocation of the bus ticket and not a train ticket caught my attention. I realized the brand idea was to make air travel as ordinary as a bus ride, while accomplishing a distant journey that could only be otherwise possible on a train.

Branding the Common Man was also about striking at the exclusionary caste system. At 80.5 percent of the population, Hindus constitute the majority in India.[29] This majority is fragmented by the historically constituted caste system. Although the Indian state operates with a democratic setup, deep-seated orthodoxies continue to shape resource allocation and access. Such unequal access also marks the reality of various non-Hindu communities, including Muslims, Sikhs, Christians, and Buddhists. In a promotional video, Air Deccan built on this theme to show two interesting processes: in neo-liberal India, "lower-caste" individuals are succeeding, and Air Deccan made it possible for the earlier generation of "lower-caste" Indians to indulge in air travel – a practice perceived to be elitist and out of their reach (see https://www.youtube.com/watch?v=bEpXRFodZNA). These twin aspects of contemporary Indian experience portrayed in the video were based on a patriarchal model in which the son earns, aspires, succeeds, and respects his father by giving him a desirable experience – air travel: "Oh! This is a plane ticket!" exclaims the village mailman as he rips open the envelope to read aloud a letter he has for Hariram, who is evidently illiterate. Cycling away after conveying the good news, the ebullient mailman announces to all within earshot, "Hariram's son has sent a plane ticket!" The father's mind flashes back to his young son's school and the day when he showed his father a picture of a plane. The amused father could only smile indulgently at his son's fascination with flying. Soon the father, a carpenter, crafts a wooden plane for his son. In successive shots, the video zooms in on a village elder, who is informing Hariram that there are two types of luggage allowed on the airplane – checked-in and hand baggage. The elder, well clothed in a shawl and knowledgeable about air travel, signifies an upper-caste gentleman. He hands Hariram his own bag to use as hand baggage. Handing it over signifies breaking the taboo of touch related to caste hierarchies. Hariram checks in at the airport with the only luggage he has, a borrowed hand bag. The X-ray machine reveals barely any possessions and an outline of a wooden airplane. Hariram had saved the wooden toy – a prized possession, signaled by his tightly clutching the hand bag. The video lingers on to the X-ray monitor, morphing the outline into the Air Deccan airplane, and concludes, "For millions of Indians flying is not a dream."

However, despite the initial enthusiasm for Air Deccan, the Common Man was not profitable. Before Air Deccan sold its shares to the corporate group Kingfisher, its Common Man image became a bit of nostalgia that was replaced by a "Super Flier Program" to cater to its business travelers. The "business class," and not the targeted Common Man, proved to be the market for Air Deccan and, according to the Air Deccan spokesperson, Vijaya Menon, "it keeps swelling."[30] Barely six years after its founding, it provided a reasonably quick exit for the Common Man. Air Deccan's eclipse is a metaphorical disruption of the gendered Common Man, which subsumed all identity ties to gender, class, and caste. The effacement of these social distinctions could not withstand the market. Although, for many, this market and its accompanying capital herald the possibility of overcoming social inequality and inequity, in Air Deccan's case capital displaced the Common Man. Meanwhile Laxman's Common Man character too has gradually receded as the *Times of India* brand. "Laxman is not our brand" a senior executive elaborated, "In fact since our new Chairman took over, we insist on making our masthead our brand."[31] Compared to this adventure, the cartoon has made slow but steady encroachments in another space that has historically marked elite taste and aesthetic – the art gallery.

How to draw a rose

In 1988, Abu published a Penguin book of Indian cartoons, including
more than fifty of the "finest work" from "India's best cartoonists." Abu
carved a niche for himself as the first editorial cartoonist of the British
newspaper the *Observer* and joined an impressive list of immigrant cartoonists such as Low and Vicky, who were popular in the British press.
Browsing through this nifty book and familiar names, including cartoonists from the regional and language newspapers, I was surprised to see
Samuel's work missing from those pages. The root of the omission,
according to Samuel, was a long-standing spat over a comment on
Abu's drawing of a rose. A Lahore Art School graduate, Samuel spent
much of his retired time painting in his studio at his home. His watercolors
have a select foreign clientele (see Figures 7.1 and 7.2). Samuel's artistic
eye for detail landed him in a rough patch with Abu:

I consider it very wrong to engage a questionable character like Abu Abraham to
comment on the merits of the other cartoonists. Abu was junior to me when he
joined *Shankar's Weekly*, and Shankar and I had our reservations about his ability
in the field, as he spent more time with public relations than the study of his
subject. When he was sacked from the *Observer* and joined the *Indian Express* when
I left that job for the *Times of India*, we had some very serious differences about
executing a cartoon. He drew a pocket cartoon depicting a rose flower shedding
tears at President Zakir Hussain's death [May 3, 1969]. The rose flower he drew
had two simple leaves on its stem, and I telephoned to tell him that roses had
compound leaves. This irritated him so much that he was campaigning against me
all his life.

Similar sentiments of favoritism were expressed several years later when
Sudhir Dar, the "tasty Indian nut" well known for his wordless cartoons
and short stint as a *Mad* cartoonist, curated an exhibition celebrating
fifty years of India's independence in 1997, in London's Nehru House.
The exhibition was widely criticized by Indian cartoonists and provided
a context for setting the record straight: "The exclusion of 'masters' like
O. V. Vijayan, Kutty and Puri has led several Indian cartoonists to describe

7.1 Cartoonist Samuel in his studio. December 3, 2003. New Delhi. Photograph by the author.

Samuel was an art-school graduate and is credited with making the first pocket cartoon in India, which featured "Babuji."

the exhibition as a 'glaring scam,'" wrote one reviewer (Ghosh and Suri 1997). The alarm at who was exhibited and who wasn't gave occasion to articulate the "masters" of Indian cartooning, as well as trace the history of cartoonists that complemented India's fifty years of independence.

In the 1950s, Shankar, Kutty and Laxman sketched the trials of newborn independence, in the late 1960s the drawings of Puri, Abu, and Vijayan cast black humor on Indira's India and in the post-Emergency period the caricatures of Unny, Ravi Shankar, and Ajit Ninan drew a fine line between the tragic and the hilarious. Surely any exhibition calling itself the first ever of 50 years should have represented them. (Ghosh and Suri 1997)

These claims for a truer representation presumed the national significance and privilege of the big English-language newspaper cartoonists. Such a history of the style of cartooning and politics overlooked the "vernacular traditions of cartooning" – a sobering observation made by Puri in the midst of this chorus of complaints. The sponsor of this program, the Indian Council of Cultural Relations, was also in a difficult

7.2 Samuel, "Vendor and Housemaid with Baby Sharing a Light in the Park." Watercolor. n.d. New Delhi. Personal collection.
The thumb pin marks were testimony that this watercolor had been exhibited on several occasions. Samuel considered this an example that combined painting and cartooning. This park scene depicts the maid's social interaction and activities while on the job, taking the baby on a stroll – out of sight of her employers.

spot as it wondered "where to draw the line."[1] A similar editorial process is at the heart of historical narratives of Indian cartooning that center on Shankar or pivot around events. Framed around the landscape of "real, political interventionist cartooning" (Menon 1994, n.p.), events such the Emergency and the 1992–3 Babri Masjid Ram Mandir communal violence re-orient the cartoon narrative, such that 1993 can be celebrated as the "Year of the cartoonist," in which familiar mainstream cartoonists, such R. K. Laxman, Puri, Abu, Dar, Unny, among others, were pushed to vigorously protest.[2]

With these editorial possibilities in mind, perhaps in excluding Samuel from his book, Abu drew the line just as any selection would. But Samuel claimed their professional differences were sparked by disagreement over the execution of the rose cartoon.

Babuji, Abuji, Abu . . . I tinkered with these words to sense why the issue about compound leaves was important for Samuel and Abu, estranging them for decades and even now, after Abu's recent death. The crux of the matter is the place of art in cartoons. Cartooning in India is at the junction of political journalism and art. Kutty singled out his "visual cartoons" as his coming of age. These cartoons emphasized caricature and visual elements rather than the wordy caption. Bireshwar, Laxman, and Samuel, too, belonged to this camp. Abu and several others downplayed the visual and emphasized punch lines and witty captions. Samuel clarified, "There were two schools of cartoonists in India during my active days. Those like Laxman and me who would like a cartoon to be a perfect drawing to raise the standard of journalism, and those like Abu Abraham who were poor artists and took umbrage under the guise of shoddy drawing with high-brow captions." This balance between image and word animates much of the hierarchy between the drawing-oriented and the caption-oriented cartoonist. Not everyone agrees with this hierarchy, but it certainly marks the terrain of cartooning in India and brings attention to critical distinctions cartoonists made about their own practice and peers.

Cartooning in India, in historical and contemporary times, demonstrates a cultural space where style defies being pinned to a national identity, as well as other vernacular identities. It reveals a form of artistic agency that "arises from bodies of knowledge."[3] For example in a pioneering study of the Shiv Sena completed in the 1970s, sociologist Dipankar Gupta noted that the Shiv Sena's opposition to communism was related to the Left's ideological opposition to the freedom of expression in speech and art. Bal Thackeray, the Sena's founder and a well-known cartoonist in Maharashtra, considered himself primarily an artist (Gupta 1982, p. 136). Ironically, West Bengal, a bastion of the Left, has a rich tradition of wall cartoons. Thus both the political Right and Left have staked a claim on cartoon cultures. Three entwined issues were central to this complex negotiation of cartooning's place in India's visual culture: drawing, art, and India. These issues may be framed as questions: Is drawing important for cartooning? Is cartooning an art? Is there an "Indian" cartooning? The answers emerged in relation to cartoons' kinship with creative labor and its commercial ambitions. These contestations were pivotal for including and excluding specific cartoonists in a given collection, for deciding the place of cartoons in exhibitions and who to exhibit, and for settling ambiguity about the "Indian" in Indian cartooning.

The problematic of identity and cultural forms is not new, but it is persistent. Questioning the temptation to identify a national identity of global cultural forms such as newspaper cartoons is not simply to deny Indianness or counter it with smaller units of affiliations, asserting its multiplicity. That the "nation" continues to circulate as a stylistic referential among cartoonists and in public culture indicates the immense rhetorical force of national identity since colonial times. As we saw in Chapter 1, the early-twentieth-century cartoons in the *Review of Reviews* were organized along national lines, so that one could confidently remark on, for example, German cartoons, or French, and quickly surmise national attitudes. But nations, we know, are relatively recent and fluid configurations of land, language, and people – their boundaries in flux and their citizens mobile. The urge to seek the "nation" in cultural forms is a desire to locate both indigenousness and modernity at the core of creativity. To resist and complicate the idea of a "national" form is to be mindful of the discourse of creativity.

Nationalism, the historian of colonial Indian art Tapati Guha-Thakurta explained, "produced its special 'community' of artists, who saw themselves as different from all others before and around them, who also 'imagined' themselves as genuinely Indian by placing themselves on an imaginary line of continuity with a glorious past and a 'great art' tradition" (1992, pp. 9–10). In colonial India, the institutionalization of art and intellectual concern with its place in asserting a national identity provided a context for debate and claims on a modern Indian art.[4] The imaginary lines of continuity with a great tradition were available to Indian cartoonists – they looked to David Low, Vicky, Herbert Block, to *Punch*, *Mad* magazine, Henri Matisse, and Georges Braque, among others, to invent a possible tradition. Several cartoonists in India are art school graduates, but their professional identity brings them to the periphery of the art world. Their stakes in locating cartoons as art rest on the assurances of good draftsmanship and recognition of cartoons' relevance outside the traditional hold of politics – as journalism, although these artist-cartoonists are not alone in claiming a politically free space to measure a cartoon's scope and aesthetics.

Discussing the question of "indigenization" and the Victorian novel in India, Priya Joshi situates it in a process of "cultural translation and bricolage" (Joshi 2002, p. xix). Approaching the issue from a different cultural form such as newspaper cartoons invites other perspectives and gives voice to other cultural workers at the periphery of arts and letters.

Mysterious drawings

"Abu Abraham, the noted cartoonist, who I have been following for years makes a very welcome appearance in your magazine," wrote Ramnath Kelkar, a reader, in a letter to the editor of *India Today*. "I was very happy to see his cartoon in your regular feature *Cartoonscope*. But, frankly, I couldn't understand the cartoon of *sadhu* pointing to the Family Planning triangle and a woman with a baby standing nearby? I tried quite hard to figure it out, in every possible way but still . . . I would be grateful if Abu could send in an explanation for his mysterious drawing" (November 16–30, 1976).

7.3 Abu Abraham, "Cartoonscope," *India Today*. November 16–30, 1976. New Delhi. Courtesy of Abraham's daughters, Ayisha Abraham and Janaki Abraham.

A sadhu points to the Family Planning triangle. This cartoon puzzled a reader, who was also Abu's fan, prompting a letter to the editor.

Contrary to an often repeated charge by some of his peers that Abu filled his cartoons with writing, the *India Today* cartoon that escaped Kelkar was entirely visual (see Figure 7.3). Its sparse lines reminded me of an often-repeated observation that Abu was not attentive to anatomical details. Opinions about Abu were divided. The artist-cartoonist Gopi Gajwani presented me with a unique perspective on Abu's penchant for "making humor out of nothing":

Abu Abraham was excellent. Yes, some people have commented on his lack of drawing but it is very difficult to say what is good drawing – it is a broad subject. Abu once made this cartoon of a mother nightingale feeding a [musical] note to its young one – that was brilliant. I couldn't stop myself and asked Abu what he had eaten that day – I gushed so much Abu had to tell me to stop – so that is what I mean when I say making humor out of nothing – creating it. (Interview, April 30, 2004, New Delhi)

Along with his contemporary, Rajinder Puri, Abu discomforted Indian politicians with thorny cartoons while also participating in politics. For a six-year period beginning in 1972, Abu (whose full name was Attupuarthu Mathew Abraham) was a nominated member of the Rajya Sabha, the

Council of States.[5] Nominations to the Rajya Sabha are regularly made to prominent artists, social workers, musicians, poets, and academics. The lone cartoonist in the Rajya Sabha's list of 107 nominations, Abu fit the rationale of this national representation process: "the nation must also receive services of the most distinguished persons of the country who have earned distinction in their field of activity, many of whom may not like to face the rough and tumble of the election."[6] In India, Abu had an immense fan following and gave readers memorable characters such as the elephant and the crow in his cartoon strip *Salt and Pepper*.

Growing up in Delhi, I was familiar with his cartoons. He also authored several books of both published and unpublished cartoons. Abu was a contemporary of Kutty, Bireshwar, and Samuel. Like his peers, he cut his teeth on the national scene in *Shankar's Weekly*.[7] I frequently heard the epithet "cerebral cartoons" in relation to Abu's work, bracketing him with O. V. Vijayan, Rajinder Puri, and Unny. To point out a cartoon as cerebral was to emphasize its thought rather than its drawing. This distinction surfaced in almost every conversation, and led to discussions of the verbal and visual aspects of cartoons.

In 2002, Abu passed away on December 1; it was too late for me to make arrangements to visit Kerala, where he had lived.[8] His career was briefly outlined in an obituary in the *Independent* (London):

He was born Abraham Mathew in 1924 in Mavelikara in southern Kerala state, into a middle-class Syrian Christian household, and began drawing cartoons and caricatures even before formally starting school. After graduating locally in science, he joined *The Bombay Chronicle* in the western port city of Bombay as a reporter in the mid-1940s. Alongside, he freelanced as a cartoonist for the popular, ritzy *Blitz* weekly that frequently published bold pictures of scantily clad women and lurid political exposés. (Singh 2002)

To see an Indian cartoonist's obituary in the *Independent* and several main-stream contemporary British newspapers was not common. But Britain played a significant role in Abu's professional growth; it was the place where he was rechristened "Abu" to ward off public suspicion that he was Jewish and that his cartoons would have a concomitant slant (Singh 2002). Abu's stint in England began with the *Observer* in 1956. Ten years later, he joined the *Guardian*. "His style of drawing was astonishing and singular," wrote the journalist Michael McNay in another obituary. "It was utterly contemporary but as lithe as the decorative linearity of the 16th and 17th century Mughal courts of Akbar and Jehangir, hinting without excess at arabesque and curlicue, and as expressive as the hand movements of a classical Indian dancer." With such descriptions, I began to see Abu's cartoons through British eyes. This sparse style not only echoed for the British a classical and medieval past, but also it brought them to India in other immediate ways:

"Occasionally, when he illustrated features from the subcontinent his spare line almost evoked the smell of India" (McNay 2002).

Such a smell turned into a stink in 1975, and Abu stood out during this time, which is remembered as the Emergency, when Prime Minister Indira Gandhi invoked special powers to curtail corruption charges that threatened to void her recently re-elected government.

Cartoons like an oasis: escaping the censors' scissors

Barely four months before President Fakhruddin Ali Ahmed approved the Emergency in June 1975, the prominent newspaper the *Indian Express* had extolled the resilience and maturity of Indian democracy (Guha 2007, p. 492). Democracy, however, provided the tools to undo itself. During the turbulence that lasted until March 1977, measures to ensure the nation's law and order included imprisoning all who were accused of creating a public disturbance, namely, opposition politicians, journalists, and civil rights activists. Censorship of the media tightened the grip on cartoonists and all cultural workers – but that is only a part of the story. Listening to the personal narratives of people who lived through the Emergency, historical anthropologist Emma Tarlo has shown the calculated and misplaced program for India's development carried out at the time. Clearing slums – the dwellings of the poor – and encouraging techniques to enforce sterilization to curb large families, the Emergency affected everyone, but in different ways. The Emergency did not just produce victims; it turned victims into collaborators (Tarlo 2003, p. 179). With legal injunctions and state authority, the Emergency quickly replaced the colonial British years as the frightening reality of imperious attitudes that democracy should guard against.

"In the desert of conformist crap that newspapers are these days, Abu's cartoons are like an oasis," wrote L. K. Advani, the leader of the Bharatiya Janata Party and Hindutva (Hindu nationalist) politics (Advani 2002, p. 67). In prison for nineteen months, Advani maintained a diary, recording the news of the day and his daily activities. Published in 1978 as *A Prisoner's Scrap-Book*, this diary of Advani's imprisonment opened with Abu's cartoons. In these pages, Advani heaped praise on an Abu cartoon:

Anyway, I am sure the President is never going to forget Abu's cartoon on him today. It is brutal and irreverent, but well-deserved I must say. It is in today's *Indian Express*, and shows Fakhruddin signing the Press Ordinances in his bathtub, handing them over to a messenger who has intruded into the bathroom, and telling him: "If there are any more Ordinances just ask them to wait." (p. 77)

A few days later, Advani noted another appreciation for Abu's cartoon: "The *Sunday Standard* has another delightful piece from Abu. A caged parrot is shown prattling 'Work more, talk less; work more, talk less' ad nauseam. In a letter to Ghatate, I request him to convey to Abu our sincerest appreciation of his contributions – from his Barefoot Humor to his Bathtub Humor" (p. 77).

The president signed three ordinances related to the press: scrapping the Press Council, rescinding the press's immunity to defamation in relation to reporting parliamentary proceedings, and empowering the government to prosecute any newspaper found breaching the prohibition on objectionable matter (Advani 2002, p. 75). Abu's bathtub cartoon pinched because it questioned the urgency of getting these ordinances signed: President Fakhruddin was away on a diplomatic tour of West Asia and due to return in three days; rather than wait to obtain President Fakhruddin's signature, the Prime Minister expedited the paperwork, sending it abroad.

Advani relished Abu's daring humor, wit, and irreverence. He was among several politicians from the opposition who were serving long months of incarceration during the Emergency. Browsing through newspapers during his imprisonment, Advani experienced an extraordinary time to think about politics by way of cartoons. And Abu was the rare cartoonist whose cartoons were published at this time, though he also faced the censors' scissors on many occasions. Abu was reluctant to explain why and how his cartoons continued during the Emergency:

After my first few Emergency cartoons, beginning with the two 'speak-no-evil monkeys,' that appeared on June 28, two days after the Emergency was declared, pre-censorship was ordered. It was lifted after some weeks. It was again imposed a year later for another shorter period. For the rest of the time I had no official interference. I have not bothered to investigate why I was allowed to carry on freely. And I am not interested in finding out. (Abraham 1977, Foreword, n.p.)

Advani wrote in his diary,

The fact that Abu has always been a critic of the J. P. Movement makes his incisive cartoons against the establishment's Emergency antics all the more effective.[9] Today's *Sunday Standard* has a cartoon depicting the common man with a sleeping board of nails. At first glance, the cartoon does not register. But a second look reveals that the nails are numbered. The sleeping board carries exactly 20 *pointed* nails!" (Advani 2002, p. 59)

A "visual cartoon" that offered no textual context for the uninitiated, it attacked the adverse public impact of Indira Gandhi's twenty-point developmental program. Indira Gandhi first introduced her development plans as a ten-point program in 1967, when she was elected Prime

Minister. The next plan, the twenty-point program, came in 1975 with the Emergency and appended a four-point program initiated by her son and rising politician, the late Sanjay Gandhi. Although the various economic measures were exercised in the name of a socialist agenda to assist the poor, its outcome was for all to see: "it was not 'pro-poor' but, in a way, perpetuated the previous arrangement where the 'dominant proprietary classes' monopolized power" (Jaffrelot 2003, p. 139). Using the "bed of nails" trope popular among Indian cartoonists and a popular shorthand among British cartoonists for representing India, Abu's cartoon said much through its visual vocabulary. That it was published shows the sly ways in which visual cartoons eluded particular interpretations, escaping the censors' cut.

Abu's cartoons during the infamous Emergency years are celebrated as some of the few embers that continued to glow against the paradox of a dictatorship in a democracy, though some were, in fact, censored (see Figure 7.4). Published compilations of Abu's cartoons on the India–Pakistan war that led to the formation of Bangladesh, on the Emergency years, and on the Vietnam War were all visual comments on democracy in distress, at home and abroad. Abu's characters Salt the elephant and Pepper the crow from his self-syndicated strip *Salt and Pepper*, and the two Congress politicians together, created a universe of humor in Indian politics. Appreciation of Abu as a cartoonist with the Mughal style and his daring drawings contradicted Samuel's assessment that Abu did not meet the standard of cartoons with good drawing and a higher standard of journalism.

Beyond defining "good" drawing or holding it essential to cartooning, practitioners such as Kevy were firm about the distinction between art and cartooning while also conscious in their choices of employing "beautiful drawing" and the "grotesque." I met Kevy at his home in Shreepadmam Palace in Tripunithura, Kerala, and exchanged several letters with him. As with most cartoonists of his generation and later, I first saw his cartoons in *Shankar's Weekly*.

Kevy: cartoons in the days of instant idlis

In a rare tribute to his style and to his skill, Kevy's cartoons often appeared on the monocolored cover page of the magazines *Thought* and the *Eastern Economist*. The grotesque black lines would stand out against the lime green, pink, yellow, and sometimes white covers of these magazines. His merciless caricatures of the former Indian Prime Minister Indira Gandhi caught my attention. By 2003, when I met him in Tripunithura, Kevy had retired. He had built a reputation as a superb cartoonist and was in the

7.4 Abu Abraham, "Private View." July 18 and 21, 1975. New Delhi. Courtesy of Abu Abraham's daughters, Ayisha Abraham and Janaki Abraham. Drawn for *Sunday Standard*; stamps say "not passed by censor." Sign in first drawing: "Save(d) Democracy." Caption under second drawing: "I've decided that speech is silver."

Prime Minister Indira Gandhi declared an Emergency in 1975 that curbed the freedom of the press. Cartoons critical of the government were censored, and later Abu published his censored cartoons as a book.

Shankar's Weekly cohort, following a few years after Kutty. Kevy Varma belonged to the family of the renowned oil painter Raja Ravi Varma. Living now in Kerala, he was also an accomplished Kuchipudi exponent, a classical form of dance from the southern state of Andhra Pradesh.[10]

My uncle was the prince consort to the Maharani. He had a fantastic library and a beautiful collection of paintings. His guest house had a very good library, which had bound *Punch* volumes. I saw *Punch* in my high school days since my uncle read them. During my *Shankar Weekly* days there was a subscription to *Punch*.

7.5 Cartoonist Kevy at his home in Kerala, November 9, 2003.
Photograph by the author.

"When I took up my new signature, Kevy, I changed my cartooning
style from Low to Herblock. Then I gave up beautiful drawing and
turned to Thurber. I went in for bizarre and unconventional, giving up
beauty and proportions for grotesqueness. This is a process of growth."

We would buy *Mad* magazine on the footpath. *Mad* was a lovely magazine; it
was less conventional than British humor. We would also get magazines from
Eastern Europe and France, and from them I savored those free unconventional
grotesques in the style of Ronald Searle. I admire Mario Miranda. I saw him in the
Illustrated Weekly. He can draw grotesque plus beautiful drawings: he is an artist
cum cartoonist. Laxman is an artist but by today's standard he is not a cartoonist.
He does illustration and no American boy will recognize his work as a cartoon.

When I took up my new signature, Kevy, I changed my cartooning style from
Low to Herblock. Then I gave up beautiful drawing and turned to James Thurber.
I went in for bizarre and unconventional, giving up beauty and proportions for
grotesqueness. This is a process of growth [see Figure 7.5].

I regard a cartoon as a message. In that light, the merit of a cartoon depends on
how effectively the message is conveyed. When the message is efficiently conveyed,
drawing, composition, caricature, all will fall in place. Trivial or historic, in these
days of instant *idli*s [steamed rice cakes], a cartoon is in front of the reader for a
couple of minutes at the most. A message is transmitted at a certain wavelength. In
art criticism and appreciation, the findings can never be the same as in arithmetic
or algebra.

Kevy reversed Laxman's repositioning himself from cartoonist to artist as a
mark of contemporary times. By evoking the "American boy," Kevy's reap-
praisal once again returned the critical gaze to the West; it also distanced
cartoons from art – they were (political) messages, and nowadays, instant
messages. With Kevy, I saw that during the span of a career, style could
change and cartoonists were constantly engaging with a world of artists and
cartoonists. David Low and *Punch* gave way to *Mad* and a community of
cartoonists such as Searle, Thurber, and Eastern European and French

cartoons. This shift also marked a transition to the grotesque. Kevy was in good company with these new affiliations. Mario Miranda (1926–2011), whom Kevy admired, was also inspired by Searle's style. Vins in Mumbai, too, ruminated upon Eastern European traditions influencing his work and cartoons as a balancing act. And he perceived a "gap" in Indian cartoonists' knowledge of European cartoonists: "Leave the British cartoons such as *Punch* and the USA aside. No one would know the father of modern cartooning André François. European cartoons should be called contemporary cartoons. It is like art; you can hang it in your drawing room. There is a balance between idea and drawing."[11]

These assessments of cartoon, art, and balance further deepened my curiosity about the art of cartoons.

Creative labor

Delhi-based writer, artist, and cartoonist Manjula invoked another aspect of the labor of cartooning: "patience and doggedness are important qualities in a cartoonist. The willingness to repeat a number of mechanical actions, such as drawing the frame-lines, finishing the inking and erasing the pencil marks again and again, are exactly as important as having a sense of humor and being able to draw competently" (Kamath 2005, p. 28).

Cartoonist Mita Roy, too, echoed the sentiment that artistic labor and patience were integral to political cartooning. Mita's father trained her in cartooning, and to develop her skills he advised her to sketch for at least half an hour a day. When she was a cartoonist with the *Pioneer* and later on the Hindi-language *Amar Ujala*, a daily routine was necessary to produce topical and timely cartoons. Mita explained to me, "my daily routine was to read the newspapers and focus on the most important or second most important news of the day." For Mita, picking the important news sometimes posed a dilemma that was integral to her creative process. Turning to news as a context for creating cartoons did not diminish the creative labor involved: "Before caricaturing sad news and religion, it is necessary to consider public sentiment."

After selecting the news, Mita would develop that news into a cartoon – "draw it nicely with pencil and finally ink with a crow quill nib stuck in a holder." The nib was dipped in black waterproof ink. She preferred the crow quill nib because with it "cartoons looked neat." Even though there was the chance of messiness and ink leaks with the crow quill, it produced a desirable effect. Whitener could conceal any unnecessary blots. The other steps involved erasing pencil lines and marks. Later, for ease and efficiency Mita used a Rotring pen and scanned the cartoon for coloring and correction in Adobe Photoshop. Visual software facilitated coloring and inserting images from the cartoonist's archive: "if you need to draw a tree and have a scanned image then it is easy to fit it in a cartoon." Finally the cartoon was saved as a jpeg file. The digitization of cartoons is a feature of contemporary cartoons that complements the processes now involved with desktop publishing.

Printing acts

When I first met him, Jagjeet Rana of *Dainik Jagran* was in the process of digitizing his cartoons. Ranaji blended photographs with his drawing. Ranaji's cartoon montage incorporated digital photographs, visual software-generated background, and hand-drawn caricature. This gave *Tota Babu* the appearance of a collage in which varying scales of representation were juxtaposed. "I use photographs in places where I think I will have to use writing." To illustrate his point, Rana gave the example of a new entrant to Indian politics, Vasundhara Raje, who was not yet recognizable and therefore caricaturable. Even if he caricatured her, Rana would need to print her name to signal her identity. To overcome this dilemma and to avoid printing her name, Rana used Raje's photograph. The photograph enhanced the cartoon's visual component and reduced the written text. Although there was a convention of using newspaper headlines to anchor a cartoon and close the gap between news and cartoon, digital media has made it possible to integrate newspaper photographs and use a palette with ease.

When I spoke with Manjul, then a junior cartoonist with the *Economic Times*, a Times of India Group newspaper, he took a different point of view. "I don't like pasting from scanned images. If I make it too ready-made then there is no fun." Manjul showed me his cartoons prepared on the computer. He has a large computer screen, drawing tablet, stylus, and mouse, which along with software for visual graphics comprise a good part of his tool kit (see Figure 7.6). Manjul renders about twelve to fourteen drawings a day.

Politicians lampooned by Shankar and others of the senior generation frequently requested the "original." These gestures of appreciation were also part of the politicians' political performance. Digital cartoons and their disparate parts would make it difficult to ask for the original. "Is there an original?" I asked Manjul, as I saw the remixing that was crucial for efficiently producing so many daily cartoons and illustrations. He quickly proceeded to explain the artistic ramifications of digital cartoons. "This is not a painting. If you have to make five to seven things, then the idea should be to make it a printing act and easy for printing." Unlike the drawing sheets and several other smaller cartoons that cartoonists such

7.6 Manjul preparing a cartoon at the *Times of India* office, December 14, 2003. New Delhi. Photograph by the author.
   The digital tablet and computer are part of the cartoonist's tools and require a hand–eye coordination that fixed the gaze on the monitor and not the hand that wielded the pen.

as Shankar, Kutty, Bireshwar, Laxman, Samuel, and others of their time filed, the computer-generated cartoons left only digital traces and the composition-in-pieces. With the computer interface, digital files and directories became the repository.

Manjul's senior colleague from the *Times of India,* Ajit Ninan, showed me a catalogue of caricatures and drawings that could be adjusted to fit a quick cartoon when necessary. Cartoonists of Manjul's generation were socialized into digital media as part of becoming cartoonists. Digital techniques brought new production timelines and a focus on the cartoon in color. "I have done professional cartooning since the age of sixteen, from Kanpur," explained Manjul.

When I was in Lucknow, I saw a bound volume of *Punch* in the British Library. I got it photocopied. That is when I realized how serious cartooning is. When my friends were preparing for engineering, I joined a computer institute to learn programming. The first program I made was for a visual application. In Delhi there was a lot of use of computers.

In the early 1990s, New Delhi had become a growing hub for computer technicians and programmers. "My drawing was bad, even now it is not good. I don't know how I became a cartoonist. When one gets published, they enter a network of friends and interested people." If drawing was not key any more, then what was?" I wondered aloud. "Sensitivity," Manjul answered. "Cartoons show the mirror and puncture the ego; but one needs sensitivity for this. It can slowly poke you and irritate you. I do this because I can do this easily and I can't do anything else."

With these digital compositions and printing acts, cartoons took on a form that would seem alien to Shankar, Kutty, Bireshawar, and others of their generations. These publishing technologies brought with them a demand for "instant cartoons" and a profusion that was possible if a bank of images was already at hand.

Cartoons not for sale are art: a beautiful letter from Raobail

The cartoonist Raobail sent me the most beautiful letters from his home in Dharwar; his collages and scribbles made each letter a piece of art. Raobail converted scraps of newspapers and magazines into a colorful collage and inserted his drawings. When each of his letters reached me, I spent time admiring the envelope before carefully slitting it to read the letter, which was also profusely illustrated.

Raobail made a distinction between English-language and "language" (vernacular) cartoonists that hinted at the idea that regional cartooning in India is immune to Western influence. This interiorization of the regional made the vernacular a space of the non-West. It also pointed to the alignment of the English language with the West. This conceptualization of cartoon styles with language and place produces distinctions with which to organize India's complex cartooning scene. Such imperatives emerge again, as I show toward the end of this chapter, when outsiders seek the "Indian" in Indian cartooning.[12]

Dear Ms. Ritu Khanduri,

Wish you and your family, happy *new year*.

Often I wonder whether the "cartoonist" label fits me! From the beginning I entertained illusions of becoming a painter, attended painting classes for a year. Though I worked as a commercial artist,

I knew no one in ad agencies. Almost all of my friends were painters and I surrounded myself with books on painters like Matisse, Braque, Van Gogh, Lautrec, and Picasso. Ara [Krishnaji Howlaji Ara, 1913–85, who was a prominent artist and founding member of the Progressive Artists Group] was also a close friend, a still life he presented to me on his sixty-fifth birthday is right in front of me. Matisse, Braque and Ara are sources of inspiration for my still-life paintings today.

I produced illustrations for *Reader's Digest*, *Debonair*, *Times of India*, *Imprint*, *Blitz*, *Daily* and many Kannada magazines. I am an artist with *"some" talents* for cartooning. I have seen my friends Lokamanya and Suresh Sawant sitting in a crowded newspaper office, drawing political cartoons with so much ease, catching the likeness of politicians perfectly. When I had to do illustrations for articles (mind you, I was given full freedom by the editors), I found myself always struggling to get a picture to my satisfaction – that too under comfortable conditions in my room!

A painter paints whatever pleases him. He simply creates; any sale or trade comes later. Whenever I do something for myself, for self-satisfaction, I have been happy indeed. That is how I created "madding crowds and madding machines." I drew club caricatures in thousands. I turned ordinary postage stamps into mini-paintings, brought color on envelopes and letters. I was asked, "Why do you do these 'useless things'?" I told them, "Just for fun, nothing more than that."

A cartoonist is seen as a social critic by the general public. Once I saw in a language magazine a cartoon showing politicians running helter skelter at the sight of a cartoonist. That is high thinking indeed! One cannot believe that a cartoon can drill moral values into a corrupt politician or reform a slum lord. I think the humor element in a cartoon softens the punch, blunts the sting. A scamster may really appreciate a cartoon gag on corruption and laugh his head off!!

Perhaps you can pinpoint whose influence is reflected in my work. It was in the 1960s that a lady who bought a sketch saw Lautrec in my lines. An American who bought six oil paintings said that my cartoons are very much French. I have observed that most of the cartoonists contributing to English newspapers and magazines carry Western influence. But one doesn't see Western touch in [vernacular] language artists.

Every beginner says "I want to draw like Laxman." I have given many youngsters copies of Laxman's cartoons from my collection. Many times I come across someone who advises me to give up doing my type of "trash" and draw like Laxman! Mario is indebted to Ronald Searle and Suresh Sawant is inspired by Bal Thackeray. (December 29, 2004)

Raobail's observation about art as a creative process that preceded the potential for sale or trade made it an inspirational creation for the self. In this scheme of things crowded scenes of leisure and clubbability – club caricatures – could be transformed into subjects of caricature. Thus when newspaper cartoons are made not just for personal satisfaction but as topical comments under a strict timeline and professional requirement, they seem to fall outside the category of art.

"Beautiful pieces of art": an art critic's point of view

When I met art critic Prasanta Daw in Kolkata, it was an opportunity to meet an art critic who had written about an established artist's less noticed cartoons. Daw has written extensively on art and published a monograph on the cartoons of the nationally acclaimed artist Deviprasad Roy Chowdhury. Over tea, *sandesh* (a sweet), and a light breakfast at his home, sitting against a massive Deviprasad painting, Daw read out from his monograph and had more to say about the relationship between art, cartoon, and trade (see Figure 7.7):

After the demise of Deviprasad on 15th October, 1975, I made an attempt to write a book on his art and life. In the course of my search for the specimens of his boundless artistic aptitude, a few cartoons drawn by the artist were discovered ... I found them very interesting, because of their excellent ironies and sarcasms. These are masterpieces of satire, some of which provoke pure laughter. These ridicule human faults and follies. They have a value of their own, as they were not deliberately made to order, but emerged spontaneously in the wake of certain incidents of day to day life, the life which concerns everybody alike. (Daw 1978, n.p.)

Love for satire is one of the most distinguished traits of the character of Deviprasad ... He could make many hard and stiff matters understandable in a simple way through stories. This part of his life has been flashed in his cartoons of humors and caricatures ... There are many untold stories in the repository of all his arts and literatures which he has expressed boldly with feelings through satirical humors. Deep and versatile feelings of the life and the society have centered round these cartoons ... These sketches leave a deep impression in our conscious and sub conscious mind. As a real idealist he has exposed all the evils and lapses of society by the sharp strokes of a harsh brush ... The ironies and sarcasms of life as depicted by Deviprasad have been marked as cartoons, but as a matter of fact they are mere cartoons that have turned to be beautiful pieces of art.[13]

7.7 Art critic Prasanta Daw at his home in Kolkata reading his manuscript on Deviprasad's cartoons. February 22, 2003. Photograph by the author.

Listening to Daw's reading, just as I heard a barrier between cartoon and art collapse, I saw another built. For Daw, Deviprasad's "spontaneity" and the fact that his cartoons were not commissioned by any newspaper as a sold commodity made them art. In making this distinction, Daw was not endorsing all cartoons as art; only some.

Exhibiting cartoons

The larger question these assessments raise is the acceptance of what is understood as art. If Abu's cartoons prompted readers to think and some-times even puzzle, and divided his peers in the acknowledgment of its artistic elements, they provided one turf to debate the location of art in cartoons. Another arena for this debate among art critics was provided by cartoon exhibitions. During the course of my fieldwork and research, I noticed several cartoon exhibitions in art galleries. Their display (and sale) included original drawings and signed prints. Furthermore, for several decades now, inaugurating cartoon exhibitions has added to the repertoire of political performances expected of Indian presidents, elected officials, and other dignitaries. These different nodes of appreciation showed the complex ways readers, viewers, and practitioners absorbed cartoons. It is also helpful to remember that the specialized vocabulary of art criticism permits only the expert critic to formulate a review of the representation, be it a painting, a sketch, or a Madhubani painting. When readers also stake a claim as cartoons' interpreters equal to its appraisal in the art world, then the critic's authorized readings and convictions about art can crumble, as we see in the exchange below between art critic S. J. S., reviewing Laxman's exhibition, and the quick defense by a fan, Miss K. S. Konkan.

The specific process of looking

Although Laxman is fêted as a cartoonist, he is unequivocal about his status as an artist. His voluminous cartoons, drawing, sketches, and watercolors have garnered fans and collectors. Laxman's cartoon exhibitions began shortly after the *Times of India* expanded to publish a Delhi edition. These exhibitions, at the behest of the Times management, were meant to "boost the circulation of the paper in the capital" (Laxman 1998, p. 104). Laxman's cartoons have thus reached a broader public and claimed a position as art. Such a move from the newspaper into a gallery was debated and illuminates the unease with defining cartoons' form and purpose – do they provide an aesthetic experience, a political analysis, or a pretext for humor and laughter? The review by *Thought* magazine's art critic S.J.S. of Laxman's 1967 exhibition in Mumbai's prestigious Chemould Art Gallery offers a glimpse of what the viewer needs to experience when seeing a cartoon. At the time, exhibiting cartoons in an art gallery was a novelty and raised a question – is the cartoonist an artist?

The reaction to an exhibition of Laxman's cartoons, one assumes would be the aggregate of all the chuckles, the delight, the clarification of ideas which this brilliant cartoonist has afforded us over the years. In fact this is not so, for what makes a cartoon so effective is its timing and its appropriateness. Students of politics, I am sure could still recapture the fascination of past situations, but as this reviewer's interest in politics does not extend in depth, the weekly cartoons-in-retrospect fail to arouse much interest.

Which brings one to the doubt which has been hovering in one's mind. Does an exhibition of cartoons come within the purview of an art gallery? Laxman is a fine draughtsman, but there is a crucial difference between a cartoonist's drawings and those of an artist's. It lies in the specific process of looking. It is not important for the artist to record what he has seen, while the cartoonist must, even while giving it a personal interpretation.

The portraits of political leaders, which form part of this exhibition, however, retain a fresh appeal. They show Laxman's keen observation of physical detail, his unerring perception of human failing, especially the attitudes of trivial opportunism displayed by his subjects. These he exposes brilliantly, with plausible candor and with unfailing humor.

It is this last quality which has endeared Laxman to such a vast number of people (as is proved by the phenomenal attendance at this exhibition). Laxman is no cartoonist of despair. His satire is never destructive. However desperate the situation, he succeeds in conveying its vastly humorous aspects, leaving the viewer refreshed. In fact his perfectly timed highlighting of the frustrations we face in our everyday lives, has a wonderfully cathartic effect on most of us, and is a major factor in keeping us sane! (S. J. S. "Unfailing Humour," *Thought*, February 4, 1967, pp. 22–3)

Ascribing it to their "specific process of looking," S. J. S. insisted on a distinction between the artist and cartoonist. "To record what he has seen" and "personal interpretation" were the professional characteristics of the cartoonist. The artist, however, did not have to record what he has seen. This sharp boundary between cartoon and art contradicted the artistic merit of realistic drawing in cartoons, a notion Kutty, Bireshwar, Samuel, and Laxman held dear about their work: drawing life sketches was important training for the cartoon's art.

Laxman's medley of exhibited works included sketches, paintings, and cartoons, merging for S. J. S. two related but different vantage points of representation. For the art critic, Laxman's dual identity and presence in an art gallery – cartoonist and artist – forced a distinction between cartoon and art. If cartoons were art, then art history and codes for art criticism would need to be rewritten and codified.

Thought reader Konkan's passionate proclamation of the cartoonist as a rightful artist came at the heels of S. J. S.'s review in a letter to the editor:

Why does S.J.S. raise the question: Whether cartoons come within the purview of an art gallery? (*vide Thought*, February 4, 1967)

Cartoons are a work of art. Not every artist, not everyone who draws, is a cartoonist. It is a higher attainment than being just an artist. Discarding the proverbial ivory tower of the artist, the cartoonist stands in the open, and uses his art for communication of ideas. That he is a political commentator also cannot deprive him of his basic position as an artist. Artists there are many and political commentators by the dozen. But a combination of the two is rare: hence the importance of the cartoonist. Hence also his entry into an art gallery by right. (Konkan 1967)

The exhibition tacitly endorsed Laxman's work as art, or it might not have found space there. If the large attendance at the exhibition attested to Laxman's popularity, it also announced to critics that the public was willing to accept cartoons as art.

Couched in conventions of art criticism, the *Thought* reviewer struggled to strike a deeper interest in Laxman's cartoons, while the distinction between art and cartoon continued to bother him. This irresolvable puzzle requires a consideration of the idea that "to designate cultural products as art is itself a signifying practice, not a simple category of analysis" (Myers 2002, p. 7). Generating a genealogy of cartoon style, analyzing the creative impulse for making cartoons, addressing commodification, insisting on the creative labor of cartooning, and identifying an Indian style of cartooning – these were important aspects of the signifying practice, according cartoons the status of art and a history.

As director of the Indian Institute of Cartoonists (IIC) in Bangalore, Narendra pondered over the marketing and commodification of cartoons as an important pathway to their acceptance as art.

Creativity comes from paper

Narendra is driven by his passion to make a change in cartooning in India – to elevate it as art. Born the same year as *Shankar's Weekly*, he considered Shankar his guru. "Newspaper people have become business oriented. They safeguard their own business interest. That has definitely affected cartoons. I learned from Shankar that the cartoonist is always with the common man and anti-establishment."[14]

"Are political cartoons disappearing in India?" I asked. "A few days ago, a leading cartoonist's column ceased publication, and even the *Times of India* did not have any display cartoons. Those days seem in the past." "It may seem that cartooning is going away in India but it is not so," replied Narendra. "We want to give a platform to emerging cartoonists." To achieve this goal, Narendra and the new IIC have held retrospective exhibitions, lectures, and workshops, and sponsored the annual Maya Kamath Award for excellence in cartooning. Their establishment in Bangalore was impressive. Hearing Narendra's plans and vision, I believed the Institute would make a difference (see Figure 7.8). With humble beginnings in Narendra's home, the institute's enviable 5,000-square-foot space materialized through a donor, Ashok Kheny. "We have 65 members, including art lovers," said Narendra. For the inaugural Maya Kamath Award in 2009, Narendra received 68 entries in the political cartoon category. Several entries were emailed. The gallery format made me wonder how cartoons would fit in. Looking at Sandeep Adhwaryu's award-winning cartoon, I asked Narendra: "Are cartoons paintings?" (see Figure 7.9). "Cartoonists usually do their cartoons in a smaller size. When we put it on the walls in a gallery they need to be enlarged. We digitally print them to 18 by 12 inches. I want cartoons to be displayed and bought by the common man, just like photographs and paintings." With Kheny supporting all expenses, Narendra can channel

7.8 Cartoonist V. G. Narendra, Director of the Indian Institute of Cartoonists (IIC), at his office in Bangalore, July 25, 2009. Photograph by the author.

When I visited cartoonist Narendra's office in the Indian Institute of Cartoonists in Bangalore, in pride of place was R. K. Laxman's large autographed Ganesh caricature, hanging on the wall. The Hindu deity Ganesh is worshiped to mark an auspicious beginning to any project; he is also the god of wisdom. The new institute had the Ganesh caricature in prominent view: that it was Laxman's work also contributed to its aura. Shankar's framed photograph adjoins the Ganesh caricature. The institute seemed blessed indeed.

his energy to organizing. "I devote all my time to this institute and the development of this art. I should create this history. I will make it a flourishing art in India – that is my challenge." To generate such an environment, Narendra envisioned similar galleries in other parts of India.

Exhibitions come with catalogues, and art appreciation has a vocabulary; would that fit cartoons? Who would write about cartoon exhibitions? For Narendra, my questions were not an issue. Exhibitions would generate cartoon critics. The role of these critics would be to give suggestions and evaluate the message sent to people. Such criticism

7.9 Sandeep Adhwaryu, "Tale of Generational Change in Two Democracies." Photograph by the author.

Winner of the first Maya Kamath Award. 2009, Bangalore. "Obama Obama," "O Mama O Mama." Obama signified the change in the US democracy, while Rahul Gandhi holding the hand of his mother, the Congress president, to establish his political career as part of a political dynasty, marked the Indian democracy. The framed cartoon was purchased by a visitor to the exhibition. Cartoonist Narendra, the director of the IIC that sponsors the event and regularly hosts cartoon exhibitions, is hopeful that the display of cartoons as art will bode well for the profession.

would consider three aspects – conceiving of the idea, presenting the picture, and wit and humor. Cognizant of the linguistic diversity in Indian cartooning, the institute welcomes cartoons in all languages. In 2009, the awards went to English-, Kannada-, and Telugu-language cartoons. Digital cartoons posed issues about creativity. Narendra emphasized the material context of cartooning. "Creativity dies when we use the computer. But it helps to color. To develop the cartoon, the computer is necessary. However, for a cartoon to survive it needs to be on paper. Creativity comes from paper. This is what we teach in our workshops."

The workshops also emphasized that to learn cartooning was to observe, to copy, and then develop individual style. Copying cartoonists and seeing their work was a part of the process for acquiring the cartoonist's art, skill, and identity. Times had changed since the days when Narendra went to Delhi to learn and work with Shankar. Then he was amazed to see David Low's cartoon book, and realized that the leading practitioners during his youth, Laxman, Thackeray, and Shankar, all received inspiration from Low. Similar to the process Kutty underwent nearly twenty years earlier, Narendra showed his cartoons to Shankar and received suggestions and corrections. Shankar would send him along with a photographer to meet important leaders such as Atal Bihari Vajpayee and Indira Gandhi: "We would go to their office and take photos of front face, three-quarters on both sides, and exact profile." Despite the new digital tools, for Narendra creativity and artistic labor were integral to cartooning: "The cartoons should speak themselves. Writing should be supplementary."

Newspaper cartoons stress the conditions for art to reveal the language and prose of an Indian art. Beginning with the Samuel–Abu tiff about compound leaves, through the genealogy of styles, Laxman's Chemould Gallery exhibition in 1967, and the creative labor of making cartoons, to cartoons as printing acts, asking about the art in cartoons – these particular perspectives from the cartoonists and critics seem an overwhelming medley. This should not surprise us, because such seeming incongruity is not only about the in-between position of cartoons as art and journalism, it is also about the elusive concept of art and its originary moment – illustrated, for example, in the appropriation of the Madhubani folk form as Indian art. The discussion around cartoons' elements and their status as art shows that the originary moment for situating Indian cartooning is intractable if we seek to construct a genealogy and kinship.

Glancing at familiar feelings: the Indian cartoon

Casually glancing at cartoons during his India visit in 1982, *Telegraph* cartoonist Nicholas Garland began to notice what the British had left behind. In visiting and sketching India, Garland was following in the footsteps of a cartoonist he admired, Vicky. But he saw more. One of these things was political cartooning. He left with a thought about Indian cartooning: "The kind of points Laxman was making felt British. It felt familiar ...The cartoon characters wore Indian clothes but I don't know if India had idiosyncratic cartooning" (personal communication, May 23, 2011).

Does it? I found Garland's question difficult to answer. Instead, I returned to his book and the observation about Indian English. Noting the north Indian habit of punctuating conversation with *ahcha* (good, OK), Garland distinguished a verbal habit as a regional variation of India's north and south. But in a larger national frame of reference, Garland proposed that the Indian version of English was not quaint, but better appreciated as a foreign language. After all, he insisted in his journal, US English with its odd expressions does not receive any charges of improper English (Garland 1986, pp. 157–8). Extending this argument to claim distinct Indian cartoons as "foreign" rather than quaint versions of British cartoons would anticipate further questions, linking the plurality of Indian linguistic identity and the various forms of Indian English with style and form. Could there be a Hindi cartooning and Urdu cartooning? Maybe the rubric "language cartoons" is accommodating of vernacular pattern? Since India's linguistic uses can be mapped, would the desire to distinguish regional cartoon styles yield fruitful comparisons – a Maharashtra, Kerala, West Bengal, Goa, Uttar Pradesh, and Delhi style? How would such proposals accommodate translations and the movement of cartoonists across regions and various newspaper houses? More daunting would be to deliberate how else India's cartooning diversity could be articulated. A possible answer is to approach these questions through Abu's remark that cartoons are "a kind of folk art of our times" and Indian cartoons do not incorporate this folk dimension. Only in Mandoo's cartoons Abu saw the unique quality of "folk form being brought into cartooning" (Mandoo 1987, p. v). In this style, Abu did not see "artistry" and this lack precisely made it distinctive. The absence of folk form in Indian cartooning, Abu hints, might be attributed to the route cartoons took in reaching India, which made *Punch* and Low enticing models to emulate. However, Abu does not attempt to explain how Mandoo might have escaped the pressures of conforming to a Western model of cartooning, nor is it clear what constitutes the folk in Mandoo's cartoon.

When the Indonesian painter Abdul Djalil Pirous makes claims for an "Islamic art," anthropologist Kenneth George sees this discourse as "potentially equipping them [artists] with a way of talking back to and reclaiming authority from the West in a bid to change our globalized art circuits" (George 2010, p. 57). This is, George suggests, the productive agency of Indonesian artists. I heard such claims for Hindi cartoons in Kaak Sahib's work (see Chapter 6), when Kutty evoked prehistoric temple art in India, and when Raobail perceived no connection between Low and Laxman; it was a comment I also heard from other cartoonists in relation to Shankar's style. But these claims distancing Indian cartoonists from Low, from the

West, and from English were equally if not more voluminously countered by a perceived lineage to Low and others in the West. Not to claim Indianness, or to dismiss such terms of engagement that lead to appropriation and provincializing, is agency too. It is agency from a vantage point that denies difference and claims similarity. Similarity is a thread linking the colonial and the postcolonial, and is one of the discourses on cartooning in India that circulates among practitioners.[15]

Needless to say, the process of recognition and alienation is shaped by a world that is a hodgepodge of sights and sounds. This fusion of glimpse, place, time, and perception gives new ways for thinking about global forms such as newspaper cartoons and how to sense modern life. For many in India, the first glimpse of the famous Low's cartoons was in an Indian newspaper (see Figure 7.10). That earned Low a place in the cultural memory of Indian cartooning. This perspective allows one to entertain the idea of moving beyond the notion of appropriation and recontextualization, and accommodate lateral stories and a (con)fusion of traces. The "Indian" in cartooning should account both for Abu, Puri, and Dar catching the imagination and cartoonist jobs in England, and for the fusion of cartoons that marks the styles of cartoonists in India. It is in this dual movement that a possible "Indian" can emerge. The cartoonists Garland met and the cartoons he saw were from the English press. The people he met and spoke with were, I suppose, at minimum bilingual. But could cartoons in India parallel Indian English? There could be, as I suggested to Garland, in our phone conversation, a way of observing "Indian" in the pocket cartoons and the Common Woman/Man. But to see the increasing practice of this form, it is insightful to turn to the country's new cartoonists, who are early in their career and looking to mentors for ideas on how to succeed.

To see the new icons that shape cartooning in India is to ask an emerging cartoonist such as *Mahesh Gupta, a Fine Arts graduate from the Banaras Hindu University, about what he sees and records.[16] I met Gupta after his office hours in Nathu's Sweets. We talked about his career while chomping on a vegetarian *thali* (platter) of hot fried snacks – paneer tikka masala, samosa, and pakora.

Copying and making cartoons bazaroo

GUPTA: I see Binay's work in the *Business Standard*, Ninan's collection from the *Times of India*, and Jayachandran in *Outlook*. Ninan's and Jayachandran's thoughts are very good. Ninan's drawing is very good. In college [Banaras Hindu University, BHU] I saw Tailang's pocket cartoons "Here and Now" and Laxman's "You Said It." By then I developed a sense that there is

WATER JUMP

(Copyright For Eastern India)

7.10 David Low, "Water Jump." *Hindustan Standard.* January 26, 1945. Courtesy of *Ananda Bazar Patrika.* "Remember this is no time to slacken."

    The horse saddle denoted the British people. The river was labeled "Rhine." This cartoon was published about three months before the end of World War II in Europe. For several readers in India, Low's cartoons reached them through their republication in Indian newspapers.

cartooning and it has concepts. After completing my Fine Arts degree, I realized cartooning is also something.

    [The newspapers] *Dainik Jagran, Amar Ujala,* and *Aj* come to Bihar. In my childhood I even saw *Aryavarta.* Jagat Sharma's cartoons were published in *Aj.* When I met him the first time in Banaras, I thought, "Oh, is this the person whose work gets published? Is it his work that we see?" Jagat Sharma's father [Kanjilal] was also a cartoonist. People say the father's work was better.

    I am attracted to lines – their fluency; their strength. I am attracted to that. That is why I like Jayachandran's work. His pencil strokes are bold lines. They show that he has worked hard. After seeing his work one knows Jayachandran could paint. In Tailang's work there is simplicity. He makes cartoons with strong punches. The cartoon is a strong comment: it does not need drawing so much. In caricature that may not be the case. When the minister Rajesh Piolot died, Tailang made a simple line caricature. I immediately copied it. I used to copy and practice. I heard Tailang's interview a few times on the radio. He said on every face he sees animals; he used to study animals in his childhood. I interact with Manjul; he used to freelance with *Dainik Jagran*. Seeing him draw, I learned what the sequence of work should be, that lines should not break, there should be solidity of concepts and to differentiate between college work and professional work. Manjul's lines are simple and straight. I used to draw very fast from the printing point of view, so my lines were crooked. Many times Manjul would give me a concept. For example, when the government was selling companies, he told me to make a stall and show hotels being sold. In this way he told me how to make it *bazaroo* [commercial].

To be able to have a good style one should see good work. I have used Jayachandran's style. The way he draws the hands – protruding, slim, thick strokes in different directions. I have copied his work a lot. He gives the body a different color, for example, blue.

I am a member of Sanskar Bharti. It is an RSS [Rashtriya Swayam Sevak] cultural wing. All the artists come for this meeting for which I went to BHU. They guided me on how to get admitted to BHU etcetera. To enter the industry I need a first break, which I got on the basis of being a fresh graduate. But the subsequent breaks are all due to links.

Mahesh Gupta worked for a Hindi newspaper. Kanjilal, the Hindi cartoonist, and not Shankar or Low, was his historical vantage point. His deep connections with the RSS reminded me of the cultural and nationalist claims of Hindutva politics. But it would be hasty to conclude that all evocations of Hindi-language cartooning linked to right-wing Hindu ideology. During the course of the past decade, Kanjilal's name came up when speaking with Hindi cartoonists and was mentioned just twice by other cartoonists (both cartoonists, Priya Raj and Hemant Morparia, were based in Mumbai). Kanjilal was a contemporary of Bireshwar's guru, Kedarji (Chapter 5). Bireshwar's friend Ram Vilas, a resident of Allahabad, Uttar Pradesh, wrote to me about Kanjilal, whom he referred to as an artist:

Artist Kanjilal's name was Manoranjan Kanjilal. I am from Varanasi [Banaras]. Kanjilalji was also from Banaras. Earlier he used to paint, do wall paintings, banner paintings, film posters, commercial art, and book covers – he used to do all types of art work. At the time I was a student. My elder brother Harishankar was an artist and painter. That is how I got to know so much about Kanjilalji and am now able to tell you. Your question is very pleasant and interesting, the reason being that this question has taken me to the years of my childhood, adolescence, and youth – reaching that sweet memory, the past and the present which is today – in memory of that, a line has been drawn from that point and joined it to the (my) present. For this I am indebted (*sadhuvad*) to you.

Yes, as I was telling you, Kanjilalji was proficient in all types of [illustrative] work. In those days money, to be able to earn merely a single rupee was regarded highly. Victoria or King George's silver rupee was then prevalent, which would now be equivalent to 80 or 85 rupees. Therefore an artist had to do all sorts of work to fill his stomach. This was the helplessness of the artist – in those days.

You must have at some time seen a monkey's dance. The entertainer plays his drum and makes the monkey dance. An artist has to do all the dances in order to earn a living. And it is this compulsion that one day he has to acquire proficiency in all types of work. Kanjilalji was able to very skillfully handle all types of illustrative art. He did not only make cartoons. Kanjilalji was a Bengali. It so happened that Kanjilalji went to Calcutta. There, his inner art woke up. Calcutta was a big metropolis and there he worked a lot. And his workmanship blossomed. Then he returned to Varanasi. He became a success in the Varanasi art world. In those days along with cartoons he used to do all other work [art work] too. He was the incomparable cartoonist of *Aj*. He had a lot of fame in the world of art. He was very simple-hearted and kind. Whenever I used to go to him he would very affectionately encourage me. And he used to reminisce. I have also made a caricature of Kanjilalji and got his autograph on the picture. I have sent you the photocopy of that caricature.

He used to say that to become a successful cartoonist, life sketch whatever one can see with one's eyes in every walk of life – to portray that is important. From a sweeper to a state's leader – everyone in fact, even animals and birds – an artist has them in his paint brush. Only then can he be worthy of a multi-faceted artistic fame.

In Mahesh Gupta's palette and appreciation of bold, strong lines without breaks, I did not see British or American influence. The reference to the blue body evoked iconography familiar in comic books and visual art forms in India. In the awareness of *bazaroo*, the commercialization of cartoons was implicit in the nurturing of an aesthetic that tied the cartoonist to the newspaper – a commodity. The market resurfaced as a consolidator to discern the difference between cartoons and art; now it became central among stakeholders of "Indian" culture.

Part III

Global times

8   Crafty petitions and street humor

The curse of India

Kutty informed me that, in his early years as a young cartoonist in the 1940s for Nehru's newspaper, the *National Herald*, his cohort assumed an irreverent license to caricature. With independence, another "class of people" was center stage, deciding the parameters of humor and norms of newspaper cartoons:

In my time cartoons were a novelty. Actually very few newspapers were there. Most of them did not have cartoons. The few cartoonists were drawing only politicians. All those politicians were well-educated people. They were following everything the British did. They assimilated their values and so viewed cartoons as just humor only. That class of people did not mind if you accused them of anything, even heinous crimes. But if anybody hinted they had no sense of humor, they were furious. And so we lucked out.

Kutty's comment that he was a part of the generation that "lucked out" resonated with a widely held view that the colonial British had a sense of humor but the Indians did not. Good luck was necessary if cartoons were to thrive in India. He echoed his guru Shankar's sentiments: "the curse of India is its lack of humor."[1] For Kutty, this sensibility was also a result of education that attuned individuals to see cartoons as "just humor only." Kutty's nostalgic remarks about British colonial humor reminded me that, in the early twentieth century, British editors and critics repeatedly dismissed Indian vernacular *Punch* versions as inferior imitations, lacking the finesse and humor of the British *Punch*. Such celebration of British tolerance for "native" humor did not fit neatly with the practice of colonial surveillance of cartoons. Kutty's remark also moved me to wonder what transpired in postcolonial times to render humor obsolete. To grasp Kutty's lament about the present state of humor requires a deeper appreciation of how the cartoon and its humor is a special category of news in India. The reporting of news in India is ethically bound to uphold secular credentials by considering the religious, ethnic, and gender-based disparities within society. As news, cartoons were expected to uphold these ideals. But is

241

humor universal? This question is at the core of animated debates in the Press Council of India (PCI), a quasi-judicial body that monitors the Indian press and adjudicates petitions against the press. Media were integrated into postcolonial India's new bureaucracy in various ways, as part of the project of modern nation-building. Broadcasting, which was institutionalized as All India Radio in 1936, continued from colonial times.[2] The state-run Films Division was established in 1948, the Photo Division and Doordarshan (television) in 1959. Among these institutions, the PCI, founded in 1966, and the practice of cartooning, which increasingly became integral to print journalism and the institution of "propriety and taste," have been relatively unnoticed parts of the narrative of modern nation-building. The significance of the PCI rests in offering a forum for representation, for constituting interpretative communities and for taking a deeper look at how cartoons-as-news makes political sense in global times, which is coincident with the postcolonial. Anthropological contributions to the "textual content of news and the reception and circulation of news in everyday life" is not common (Bird 2010b, p. 3). This is definitely so in the case of newspaper cartoons, although recent ethnographies of Indian newspapers have shone light on the consumption of news as a mode for constructing "particular kinds of social and national subjects" (Peterson 2010, p. 172). Approaching the PCI petitions as integral to the ethnography of journalism "complicates narratives of journalistic crisis and redemption that pit an abstract system of 'capitalism' or a set of pernicious political interests against heroic media reformers" (Boyer and Hannerz 2006, p. 11).

Instituting a special category of news

Petitions against newspaper cartoons demonstrate the place of humor in modeling liberalism in postcolonial India. Open to public petitions against the press, the PCI is a forum for debate about media's social role. The PCI placed cartoons as a special category of news that demanded a more liberal reading from the public (i.e., newspaper readers) than prose did: "Cartoons and caricatures depicting good humor are to be placed in a special category of news that enjoy a more liberal attitude."[3] This specification echoed the influential journalist, editor, and writer Khushwant Singh's observation that "the role of the Indian cartoonists in forming public opinion cannot be exaggerated" (1971, p. 50). Cartoons compelled the PCI to signal shades of liberalism that could not be neatly encapsulated by the term "liberal" – it required more liberalism, testing imagination of what might be more than liberal. This guideline for the public also gestured to the cartoonists about how their visual journalism was different from the prose of news. The norm, guiding the press about the place of cartoons as journalism held that, as with all visual components of news, cartoons were expected to have "immediate impact" on people and were important to "highlight stories." Thus it was necessary that cartoons be "positive" and "avoid any negative implications." To exemplify how visuals could adhere to this norm, the PCI advised that photographs in stories about HIV and AIDS patients should "not breach the confidentiality or privacy of infected individuals and their families." Complementary examples for cartoons were not included, leaving the norm open to interpretation.

The Government of India instituted the First Press Commission in October 1952 to draw up an agenda for the role of government in the press of a free country and as part of its regulatory project.[4] The First Press Commission came across instances of "yellow journalism, scurrilous writing – often directed against communities or groups, sensationalism, bias in presentation of news and lack of responsibility in comment, indecency and vulgarity and personal attacks on individuals."[5] The commission pointed out that the "well-established" newspapers had, on the whole, maintained a high standard of journalism; they had avoided "cheap sensationalism and unwarranted intrusion into private lives." But the Commission remarked: "Whatever the law relating to the Press may be, there would still be a large quantum of objectionable journalism which, though not falling within the purview of the law, would still require to be checked." The Commission recommended the creation of two institutions: a Registrar of Newspapers for India (RNI) – a central government body intended to monitor the industry and collect statistics – and a Press Council to oversee ethics and hear complaints. Thus, following these recommendations, the PCI was constituted on July 4, 1966, as an autonomous, statutory, quasi-judicial body. The PCI was not constituted as a censorial body; instead it was a quasi-judicial forum where citizens could lodge complaints against the press and in the process uphold democratic principles and participate in the making of the modern nation state.

Justice J. R. Mudholkar, a judge of the Supreme Court at the time, was appointed the first chairman of the PCI. The objectives of the PCI included: (1) building a code of conduct for newspapers and journalists in accordance with high professional standards; (2) ensuring, on the part of newspapers and journalists, the maintenance of high standards of public taste and fostering a due sense of both the rights and responsibilities of citizenship; and (3) encouraging the growth of a sense of responsibility and public service among all those engaged in the profession of journalism. It is significant that the PCI formulated its principles in the context of a highly stratified newspaper readership based on linguistic and regional particulars. This readership and their access to governance was further compounded by a history of social disparity recognized in the post-independence years through the identification of minority communities. Despite official recognition of this diversity and disparity, the PCI has sustained a notion of a collective national public and press. The petitions disrupt this assumption, re-asserting difference as the mark of democracy.[6]

At the PCI

Madam ko chai dena ("Give madam tea"). Kishore, the office assistant, circled the inner rim of a cup, using his finger with a dash of water, to rub away stubborn tea stains. He poured hot sweet milky tea and brought it to Khema Nand's desk, where I was seated, browsing case files. Khema was a section officer, and all the PCI petitions passed his review. *Rituji kya Khanduriji aapke relation mein hain?* Khema was asking me whether I was related to Chief Minister B. C. Khanduri of the recently formed state of Uttarakhand, which was carved out of Uttar Pradesh. Hearing my last name, he and others in the office figured that I was from Uttarakhand, and assumed that I must be related to the chief minister. I was not. "Where are you from in Garhwal?" Khema's interest in my family's origins in Garhwal was not surprising; he belonged to the same area. By the time Khema had to move on to a meeting, we knew quite a bit about each other's families. Such introductions and exchange of familial backgrounds create comfort zones. In eliciting answers from me, this interaction shows that in the field, it is not always the researcher who asks questions.

Khema had already told me that all the archived files were "weeded out" when their department moved from their old office to the new building, Soochna Bhavan. Those files were in a godown (warehouse) and impossible to access. A few from recent years were on site, but none of them was on cartoons. Ram Palji, the record keeper, showed me the files and his catalogue. These files were periodically discarded after the cases closed. The record was not conducive to locating files easily, and the enormity of the exercise overwhelmed me. However, I went through some files to get a sense of the paperwork that was involved in registering a petition. After the petition was submitted, supplemented by appropriate newspaper cuttings as evidence, the PCI Law Officer marked up the copy and prepared a report on the merits of the complaint. This review was critical in determining if the case would move forward or be dismissed. If the petition was in Hindi or any regional language, then it would be translated into English, so that all council members could comprehend the matter.

My best bet lay in reading the edited reports of the PCI cases. Ms. Usha Rani, the librarian, helped me access the published reports. As I read through each case, searching for petitions against cartoons, sweat poured down my face. It was hot. Hot as an oven. Not too hot for chai. The power outage was unbearable, but I had to browse the reports. Ushaji was touched by my determination and did everything possible to help me out. She extricated some extra copies of the annual reports and loaned them to me, so I could work in comfort at home. In my next visits, the following years, the whirling coolers in the office had given way to sleek air conditioners. We triumphantly laughed back at those hot days that did not prevent us from gulping steamy chai. Kishore, the office assistant, removed the samosas I had brought from the hot case. "That was so nice of you." "Ushaji, Evergreen Sweets near my parents' home is well known for their samosas, so I thought all could have some with chai." I had already shared snacks with chai on earlier visits. It seemed to me that the staff probably took turns sponsoring appetizers from their canteen, and I wanted to reciprocate.

The reports showed that petitions encompassed a broad range of topics related to newspapers and magazines. Among these were complaints against administrators engaging in discriminatory practices in doling out government advertisements; defamatory writings and obscene prose and images; irresponsible reporting that had the potential to inflame communal violence between Hindus and Muslims; and the presentation of news that reinforced caste and gender biases. Cartoons fitted into some of these topical contexts. The name R. L. Kain leaped from these reports on several occasions. He was a frequent petitioner, and every one in the PCI knew him. I would come across his name again as I burrowed more deeply.

"We want more teeth"

The office of the chairman of the PCI, retired Justice G. N. Ray, was plush and expansive. He had a large executive desk. There was some interest among the staff that I was meeting the head of their organization. I had made earlier attempts, but Justice Ray was traveling abroad or busy. "You don't need to take your flask of water with you," Ushaji advised as I prepared to go to in. It would not be elegant or respectful to walk in with the flask slung across my shoulder. In the bureaucracy, hierarchy is respected. Gestures, accouterments, and comportment were part of performing respect. Although I kept it aside, I couldn't understand why my tidy flask seemed out of place.

Justice Ray described the composition and operation of the Press Council at some length:

Cartoon cases, when they come to the PCI, have been mostly about mythology and gods. The standard for obscenity depends on the social context and should not cross limits of decency – the question to ask is, "Are you seeing this with family members?" The lofty ideas before independence have given way to market forces. This has led to a trivialization of the serious nature of journalism. Most complaints are against the big newspapers. They have a heavy circulation and simultaneously publish editions from different cities.

The PCI was constituted about forty or forty-one years ago. It is a regulatory body; it has not been constituted as a penal forum. Unless there is the voice of the readers, it is difficult to regulate. The chairman, a retired chief justice of the Supreme Court of India, is nominated by a committee consisting of members of the Indian Parliament, namely, the chairman of the Rajya Sabha [Council of States], the Speaker of the Lok Sabha [House of the People] and an elected representative of the existing PCI. Thirteen working journalists serve the PCI. Of these, six are editors of newspapers and seven journalists. Six members either own or are concerned with the management of newspapers. One member should be a person who manages a news agency. Three members, each from the Sahitya Academy, Bar Council, and the University Grants Commission bring cultural, educational, and scientific knowledge to the council. Finally, three members from the Lok Sabha and two from the Rajya Sabha complete the composition. There are twenty-nine individuals in all.

The first step is to write to the newspaper editor. If that does not result in a satisfactory response, then the person could lodge a petition. The PCI translates petitions into languages other than English. However, if the complainant's case can be addressed at their doorstep, then it is more effective. When we travel to regional sessions, we are decreed state guests to facilitate our work. Any regulatory body must be insulated from the government. We can summon any one. We have asked the government for some more power and to amend the Act. Namely, if we censure a publication, then the government will not issue advertisements in it for three months. Also, if the adjudication is published in the newspaper, then people will understand that the newspaper's peers have reprimanded it. Finally, if the newspaper continues to err then we want the government to stop publication for two or three days. I am sure then that the PCI will have more teeth; beyond that we do not want more. We already have power – no one can ignore it.

The Indian experiment with PCI is doing well; it is a model for instituting a similar media body in Sri Lanka. The date sixteen November is annually celebrated as National Press Day in Delhi. I also travel abroad to present talks at seminars. Recently India was specially invited to a conference in Nairobi to present the PCI's experience to show how media bodies can be regulated (Interview, August 11, 2008).

My meeting lasted an hour; I was told it would be only a few minutes. The extended duration signaled to the staff that it was a good meeting.

The world of self-regulation and freedom

How does the PCI fit into the world of national press organizations? Press councils are, in general, considered the best media accountability systems – organizational structures for self-governance of the media. India is a founding member of the World Association of Press Councils (WAPC), and the PCI chairman, Justice Ray, is the current president.[7] When I last met Justice Ray, he was the vice president, a position now held by Kajubi Mukajanga of Tanzania. Its secretary general is Professor Chris Conybeare of the University of Hawaii. Regional conferences and an active website serve as forums for exchange and interaction.

Justice A. N. Grover, the PCI chair, proposed the idea for WAPC in 1983, at a conference to observe the International Communication Year. Dr. David Flint, a professor of law in Australia, drafted the charter that formalized the WAPC in 1992, in New Delhi.[8] The founding members included the press councils of Australia, India, Nepal, New Zealand, Sri Lanka, the United Kingdom, and Turkey. Justice P. B. Sawant of the PCI was the second chair to lead WAPC. However, it was almost a decade later that the WAPC was officially registered in Istanbul, Turkey, as a legal entity, in 2006. Key objectives of the WAPC include the establishment of a mechanism for "self-regulation" and sharing of information among various press councils, to promote the "freedom of expression and of responsibility in the international media."[9] The organization's constitution characterized freedom of expression "an inviolable human right." Furthermore, the emphasis was to disengage from governmental activities in order to secure organizational freedom. WAPC's membership has grown and now includes Kenya, Uganda, Zimbabwe, Malawi, Swaziland, and Zambia from Africa; Bangladesh and Azerbaijan from Asia, and the Honolulu Community Media Council from the United States; it also includes associate individual members. Australia, New Zealand, and the United Kingdom ceased to be members; the latter two joined the AIPCE – Alliance of Independent Press Councils of Europe.

Established in 1999, the AIPCE is a larger conglomeration of thirty-five press councils and media bodies. Its membership is not limited to European Union nations, but Sri Lanka and Thailand are the only Asian members and there are none from Africa. Turkey and Azerbaijan also retain membership in AIPCE. Its statement of aims emphasizes freedom of the press from government intervention. While privileging a nation's cultural context for measuring media regulation, it opposes the notion of a universal code of ethics. The alliance highlights the significance of "public feelings." These feelings were for the media to gauge, not the government.[10] At the surface level it may appear that the two organizations promote similar regulatory mechanisms and accountability systems but are organized regionally, with some exceptions – the WAPC being Asia- and Africa-oriented, while the AIPCE hosts a "loose network" of independent European press councils. Two key differences exist, however, in their conceptualization of media ethics and accountability. The WAPC insists on the freedom of expression as a universal human right; AICPE emphasizes a relative cultural perspective circumscribed within national cultures. The WAPC focuses on regulation and public participation in monitoring the press; AICPE upholds regulation, with an equal emphasis on safeguarding the freedom of the press.

Dual lineages and global contexts

In its manifesto, the PCI traced the logic of its existence to similar regulatory media bodies in Europe, Canada, Asia, Australia, and New Zealand. Some press councils, such as the one in New Zealand (in 1972) and in Australia (in 1976), were formed later, demonstrating that the concept was gaining ground all over the world. After citing the widespread recognition of the need for such bodies in the early twentieth century, the PCI manifesto elaborated on its nationalist and liberal lineage through Gandhi and Nehru, respectively. In this history of the PCI, Gandhi's notion of "self-regulation" was placed as foundational to all press councils:

The basic concept of self-regulation in which the Press Councils and similar media bodies the world over are founded, was articulated by Mahatma Gandhi, who was an eminent journalist in his own right, thus: "The sole aim of a journalist should be service. The newspaper press is a great power, but just as an unchained torrent of water submerges the whole countryside and devastates crops, even so an uncontrolled pen serves but to destroy. If the control is from without, it proves more poisonous than want of control. It can be profitable only when exercised from within."

Pandit Jawaharlal Nehru while defending Press freedom and warning of the danger its irresponsible exercise entails stressed: "If there is no responsibility and no obligation attached to it, freedom gradually withers away. This is true of a nation's freedom and it applies as much to the Press as to any other group, organisation or individual."[11]

The dual lineages of contemporary liberal democracies on the one hand, and of Gandhi and Nehru on the other, provided the logic, common sense, and therefore legitimacy for the self-regulatory mechanism of the PCI. "Control from within" and the notion of freedom with obligation nicely described the scheme for management of the press in contemporary India. Underlying this model of management was also the belief that the press was powerful and thus had the potential to be dangerous to the ideals of the democratic nation state. The twin principles of freedom with obligation and participation in nation-building through the responsible use of power became mutually constitutive of the philosophy of the modern state and the modern individual. Through this template, neither was the nation nor were its constituent organizations, groups, or individuals exempt from the exercise of this responsibility. This shared self-regulation bound the individual to the state, organizations, and to other individuals. Such mutual responsibility was also an assurance against the persistence of caste- and gender-based domination, which was expected to cease with the end of colonial rule in India in 1947.

The immersion of the individual self in state governance made regulation commonsensical, everyday, and consensual. Common sensibility as the logic for reprimanding certain acts of the press made such actions disciplinary, not censorial. This was an important distinction to maintain. The new democratic nation state was anxious not only to establish its credentials in the context of a perceived universal model of democratic politics but also to mark itself apart from the preceding colonial state that had ended barely two decades earlier. During my fieldwork, this charge of the PCI was encapsulated in a comment from the PCI chairman, Justice Ray, who reminded me that their goal was not censorship; instead, it was comparable to a parent mending the ways of a disobedient child. Yet in assuming the role of the guardian, the PCI was also replicating a familiar and familial colonial position in which subjects were infantilized and reformed.[12]

Furthermore, the PCI is also a space that structures the face-to-face interactions that constitute the debate over newspaper cartoons' meaning. Thus what is produced is "not only an analytical problem; it is also a participants' problem, to which there are creative, if often evanescent, solutions" (Irvine 1996, p. 136). The ambivalent judgments by the PCI that frustrate newspaper editors and activists alike point to an interesting dilemma: through its engagements, the PCI is an example of institutions that historian Dipesh Chakrabarty holds we need; that is, ones that do not replicate the cultural history of the European middle class, that work with cultural differences, and handle "the fuzzy logic with which identities are built" (1995, p. 3379).

In session

"This is trickery and calculated harm; it is a joke on the PCI" (July 25, 2008), surmised the complainant, Mr. Singh, a police officer of rank, who was seated at one end of a long seminar table. Mr. Singh had complained against defamatory articles against him published in a local newspaper, and today he would follow up on his written petition, and so would the newspaper. The PCI was in session (see Figure 8.1). All members of the council were seated at the table. Immediately behind the officials, I took my place among the PCI staff, who were witnessing, taking notes. The

8.1 Monthly meeting of the Press Council of India. July 25, 2008. New Delhi. Photograph by the author.

Here petitioners present their case to council members. This is a public session, and there are seats to accommodate visitors.

public could observe the proceedings seated in chairs at the end of the room, facing the council members. The center of activity was the chairman, Justice Ray, and the serving bureaucrat, the secretary Vibha Bhargav. Chai was passed around in white ceramic cups and saucers, for the members, the complainants, and the staff.

A visibly agitated Justice Ray exclaimed, "You are challenging the authority of the PCI." Both Mr. Singh and the chairman were responding to the absence of a response to the complaint from the erring newspaper. Although the newspaper had dispatched their information officer, he had nothing to report. "There is no intention to challenge your authority," the information officer calmly retorted. "You are taking it very lightly," scolded Justice Ray. Mr. Singh chimed in, advising the council: "Summon the director of the organization that issues the newspaper, you have the authority to do so." "Get all the details tomorrow and send it by email. This is your last chance," warned Justice Ray, as he deferred the unsuccessful proceedings connected with Mr. Singh's complaint. There was a short break before the next case could be taken up. I asked a council member to explain what was happening. "They are playing tricks," he said. By not responding to the complaint and sending a representative who could not convey any defense, the newspaper was frustrating and delaying the process. Mr. Singh had traveled to Delhi from a neighboring city and planned his leave from work to be at the PCI session. But it seemed futile, because there was no opposition to engage in a face-to-face debate.

The next complaint was from two senior citizens from Lucknow. They petitioned the PCI to take action against an offensive advertisement that appeared in leading newspapers such as the *Times of India*, *Hindustan Times*, and *Midday*, among others. The advertisement offering massage services, they argued, was a sly reference to prostitution: "In a veiled way this advertisement is soliciting something that cannot be done openly." As in the previous case, there was no representation from the defense, the *Times of India*, against whom the complaint was specifically made. "A philanthropy-conscious citizen has brought this activity to the attention of the government. We are powerless. But that does not mean others are powerless. We are thankful to you," said one of the petitioners, realizing that once again their efforts and travel would not yield results. "In your last meeting you said that you would call the heads of the newspapers. We pay for the travel from our pension, arrange for our stay in Delhi, visiting from Lucknow, and you say the newspaper heads from Delhi cannot come here?" As the disappointment gave way to disbelief and frustration with the PCI's powers, the chairman adjourned the case: "This type of advertisement is doing lots of mischief to society, particularly with the younger generation. This is the recommendation we can give the government. We are disposing the case by giving a recommendation." The two petitioners were requested to come again. "The defense has given a medical certificate [to justify his absence]. We have observed your trip was unnecessary. We will warn him that he should notify you in advance, unless of course there was a sudden accident or something like that."

After the two cases, the council members and staff gathered for a catered lunch of rice, naan (bread), *matar paneer* (peas and cottage cheese), *aaloo subzi* (potato), and dal (lentils). The council members sat together, some gathering around the chairman. I joined the staff at another end of the room, and reflected on the place of such proceedings in the practice of liberal democracy in India.

Defining liberalism in India

Indian democracy offers a context for recognizing that the trajectory of Western liberalism is not universal (Hansen 1999, p. 6). Liberalism's distinct form in India has been analyzed as a political position with a broad spectrum. Historian Ramchandra Guha identifies three founding features of liberalism in India (2001, p. 4664): first, a critical attitude toward the past and sometimes extreme hopefulness about the future; second, an implicit and somewhat unselfconscious patriotism; and third, close attention to the promotion of institutions of civil society and to the fostering of rule-bound procedures within them. Guha further proposes three categories of liberals: those who were unwavering in their commitment to democracy and human rights and would tilt to the West; those who were enchanted by the economic model of the Soviet Union; and finally, those "traditionalists" who thought family and community were not to be sacrificed in the march to modernity. Such distinctions remain fuzzy, and Guha contends that liberalism in India can be best understood as a sensibility.

Against this backdrop, cartoon talk about liberalism is important; it counters and appropriates a "Western language that speaks of civil society, bureaucracies, political desires and liberal forms." India's historical entanglement with the modern state led to an initial reliance on this Western political vocabulary, even though liberal politics takes on distinct forms in postcolonial societies (Kaviraj and Khilnani 2001, p. 5). The more "liberal attitude" that the PCI extended to cartoons, compared to prose, hinges on the question of whether or not cartoons are taken to be "direct speech," which is more protected than reportage or commentary.[13] The PCI's caveat that a "more liberal attitude" would be tolerated in the case of cartoons was consistently challenged and negotiated through the debates on the cartoons' meaning. Although the PCI does not define the liberal aesthetic, it treats it as an intuitive sensibility that is evoked and clarified through debates to settle petitions. Thus the significance of petitions against cartoons lies in providing moments that compel a clear articulation of liberalism both as an aesthetic and a political category. Otherwise, these fine distinctions in aesthetics and form remain intuitive, afloat, and in suspense. These oppositional liberal sensibilities also claim priority over each other by emphasizing their correspondence with post-independence India's constitutional agenda. The three major petitions I discuss below highlight the process through which cartoons as "direct speech" and "indirect speech" generate interpretative dilemmas that are debated in the meetings of the PCI. The deliberations over the cartoons' meanings are forms of reported speech that document reception.[14] Each petition fitted a distinct category of offence: "Principles and publications," "press and morality," and "communal, casteist, anti-national and religious writings." (Khema Nand conveyed to me in a note through another staff member that complaints against the press fell into the following categories: Defamation and Right to Privacy, Non-Publication of Complainant's

Reply and Non-Publication of Letters to Editor, Obscenity, Morality, and Indecency, Communal and Casteist, Advertisement Ethics, Plagiarism, Anti National Writings, Election Related, Professional Misconduct and Others. Complaints by the press were recorded in the following categories: Denial of Advertisements, Denial of Accreditation, Denial of other facilities, and Harassment by Police, Harassment by other Authorities, and Election Related and Internal Disputes, including assault on journalists and newspaper establishments and others.) Matthew Hull notes that the "material qualities of files enables kinds of reported discourse not possible in an oral channel" (2012, p. 147). At some level this is indeed true for the PCI files for they include newspaper cuttings, letters to the editor, the petition itself, the PCI's translation of petitions from one of the regional languages into English – the paper trail of a bureaucracy in action. But the back and forth between cartoons, petitions, and oral deliberation complicates the distinction between oral and written because it is intercepted by a sensory disposition to the humor anticipated by the visual representation in the cartoon.

'Humpty Tumpty' has a great fall

In 1990, the PCI was confronted with a case that involved two leading "national" dailies and "big-sized" newspapers, the *Times of India* and the *Hindustan Times*. The rivalry between the two newspapers can be gauged by their circulation figures. In 1993, the *Times of India*'s percentage of daily circulation for its English, Hindi, and Gujarati editions was 9.8 percent of the daily circulation of newspapers in India. The *Hindustan Times* and its English and Hindi editions accounted for 4.2 percent. The case emerged in the context of an ongoing circulation war between the two English editions of the dailies, each claiming to be the most widely read newspaper in the country. Due to the high-profile nature of the case, both newspapers presented their arguments through legal counsels. Categorized as a petition about "Principles and Publication," this case offers a unique opportunity to look closely at the discursive construction of humor and liberal taste. The arguments presented by legal counsels for both newspapers highlight the place of class and "cultural capital" in relation to both the enjoyment of good taste and the ability to comprehend subtle humor (Bourdieu 1984).

The complaint registered by the *Hindustan Times* was against a cartoon-based advertisement produced and published by the *Times of India*, which mocked the *Hindustan Times*'s claim regarding its circulation figures and ridiculed the failed attempt of the *Hindustan Times* to increase the number of pages of its daily issue. In its complaint, the

Hindustan Times claimed that the *Times of India*, in its issues of April 8 and 9, 1988, had published a cartoon bearing a caption in bold print: "Humpty Tumpty has a great fall" (see Figure 8.2). The cartoon exhibited an egg-shaped character falling from a high wall. Juxtaposed with the falling character was a graph to show the depth of Humpty Tumpty's great fall, having come down steeply from twenty pages to sixteen pages.[15] Asoke Sen, the counsel for the complainant *Hindustan Times*, contended before the Inquiry Committee of the PCI that publication of the cartoon-cum-advertisement in question was in violation of accepted standards of journalistic conduct and ethics, and contrary to good public taste, which the Press Council is required to uphold and improve. He further submitted that the impugned pictorial publication, captioned "Humpty Tumpty has a great fall," was circulated to ridicule the *Hindustan Times* and lower its image and credibility in the eyes of its constituents and the general public.

Dr. L. M. Singhvi, the counsel for the *Times of India*, contended that the advertisement was not intended to malign the complainant. The impugned advertisement was only a cartoon. He continued that such cartoons have their own language and vocabulary, and have to be taken in good humor. They do not furnish adequate cause for action by the PCI merely because the complainant is so sensitive as to find that the humor also hurts. To illustrate his point, Dr. Singhvi referred to a cartoon appearing in the magazine *India Today* and in certain other journals, calling the *Times of India* "the old lady of Boribunder." *Boribunder* can be translated as "the place where goods are harbored." *Bunder* means "port," and *bori* means "sack"). To that cartoon, submitted the counsel, the *Times of India* never took umbrage, but took it in its stride. While maintaining that newspapers have a right to humor, Dr. Singhvi urged that 'Humpty Tumpty' was a mythical character comparable to someone in a similar situation. He asserted that the publication in question depicted, in a humorous way, nothing but the truth: contrary to the promise held out by the complainant that the newspaper would regularly bring out twenty-page issues of the *Hindustan Times* beginning on April 1, 1988, he pointed out that the *Hindustan Times* had failed to publish issues comprising twenty print pages, not only on April 7 and 8, 1988, but also on fourteen more occasions thereafter. Dr. Singhvi stressed that even according to the complainant, the impugned advertisement had not, in fact, adversely affected its circulation, revenues, or reputation.

During my fieldwork, when I met cartoonist Sudhir Dar, the *Hindustan Times* cartoonist when this petition was filed, and asked him about this case, he half-jokingly pointed to his own face and head, and said Humpty Tumpty resembled him (Interview, December 26, 2003)!

8.2 *Times of India* advertisement, "Humpty Tumpty Has a Great Fall,"
April 9, 1988. New Delhi. Courtesy of the *Times of India*.

Humpty Tumpty, the purposeful play on HT (*Hindustan Times*), and
including the words "This is it!" which was the name of *Hindustan Times*
cartoonist Sudhir Dar's pocket cartoon, left no doubt about the object of
the humor during the circulation rivalry between the two big newspapers.
The *Hindustan Times*'s petition to the PCI generated a long discussion on
liberal humor.

After counsels for both newspapers had presented their arguments, the PCI's committee deconstructed the various elements of the image and made the following observations with regards to the cartoon-based advertisement:

Any reader of average intelligence, having knowledge of English, on seeing this cartoon, would at once be reminded of the egg-shaped nursery rhyme character who fell from a wall and broke into bits. In the common consciousness of readers, therefore, Humpty Dumpty symbolizes something which, once it is damaged can never be repaired, restored or made operative again. Not only this, in the impugned cartoon the first letter 'D' of Dumpty has been deliberately changed into 'T' so that the initials of Humpty Tumpty are the same as those of *Hindustan Times*, indubitably conveying to the readers that the egg shaped falling object shown in the cartoon is none other but *Hindustan Times*. The satirical comments accompanying the cartoon including the words, "*dust*," "urb" and "on" in descending order along the graph line, hammer home to the readers the message that the "claim" made by the *Hindustan Times* to publish regularly a 20-page issue from April 1, 1988 was false and in fact, as depicted in the cartoon, its credit was crashing to its doom. No person of ordinary prudence . . . would call this failure of the complainant to publish 20 pages for one or two days, a . . . default. Even if the respondents could discover a scintha [*sic* scintilla] of truth in the first and the second defaults committed by the complainant, even then also there was no justification to distort and exaggerate it in the ironical manner exhibited in the cartoon. Nor could it be said that these cartoon/news-advertisements were published in good faith and in good humor because they tend to ridicule and discredit the complainant, and had not been made with due care and caution. It is not correct, as has been contended by the respondent, that the cartoon in question is of a type of which no man of ordinary temper and tolerance should take umbrage (p. 97).

Dilip Padgaonkar, editor of the *Times of India*, admitted before the PCI that the cartoon in question had come before him for his approval and he had allowed its publication because he thought it generated good humor only. In the opinion of the committee, he erred in his understanding:

The question of propriety or otherwise of the cartoon for publication should have been considered by him from the standpoint of a reader of average prudence and sensibility, and not from that of a sophisticated person of ultra-liberal culture and high intellectual attainments. Had he applied such a yardstick, placing himself in the position of an average reader, he could have, acting with due caution, gone no further than holding that the advertisements in question were in the gray area bordering on the line between professional propriety and indecency, and between good humor and scurrility, and as such it would not be prudent to allow their publication.

. . . the impugned publications violated the norms of the conduct and ethics of journalism, and were contrary to good taste, even if, on the basis of facts admitted and proved, no charge of defamation in law had been made out (p. 99).

For the committee, this lapse was all the more regrettable in that it was committed by a reputable and prestigious organization, the *Times of India*, which was supposed to "set the tone, temper, and standards of journalism in India." In conclusion, the committee expressed displeasure at the conduct of the *Times of India* for publishing the impugned cartoon-based advertisements. The PCI determined its ruling through its intuitive understanding of the standpoint of the "average reader" and not of sophisticated ultra-liberal cultural and intellectual standpoint of which editor Padgaonkar was an example. According to the PCI, in the absence of such cultural capital not only was it difficult for the readers to relate accurately to the cartoon, but the ignorance of the newspaper editor about the lack of such capital among his readers made the editor of the *Times of India* irresponsible. The cartoon was in a gray area, and its public interpretation had to be assumed from the perspective of an average person. Since the aesthetic dimension of the cartoon was to be gauged from the perspective of an average reader, to determine this in advance was the responsibility of the editor, even though he himself was an ultra-liberal person.

The debate around this petition gave a glimpse into implicit notions of liberal conduct and its opposite. Liberal sensibility emerged in relation to the "ultra-liberal" and not in opposition to the illiberal. Paradoxically, the PCI's projection of an average reader as someone lacking in the "ultra-liberal" skills allowing one to understand specific types of humor tells us much about the thin ice upon which Indian liberalism skates. Although the PCI does not emphasize these distinctions in its other petitions, this measure of liberalism is a subtext when it evokes the constituency of a general public.

Tru – Lies

Dr. Kalpana Kannabiran, of Asmita, a resource center for women, in her complaint dated August 19, 1996, brought to the notice of the PCI a cartoon that appeared in a regular cartoon strip titled "Tru – Lies" in *Asian Age*.[16] The PCI report noted that according to this complaint, "Sachin [Tendulkar] on his becoming captain of the Indian Cricket team, while accepting congratulations from Azharuddin mockingly quips 'could he keep Sangeeta too?'"[17] Sangeeta [Bijlani] was at that time the fiancée of Azharuddin, outgoing captain of the team, and married him later. Moving beyond "impressions" in her petitions, Kannabiran establishes the link between image, representation, society, and politics in the cartoon to show how everyday spaces that tend to be ignored need scrutiny because they normalize discrimination. Gendered representations were a central theme of this petition, but it also spilled into the domain of class. In its ruling supporting Kannabiran, among the critiques the PCI offered was that the cartoon displayed "street humor" and "very cheap taste." In fact, for the PCI these aspects were conclusive evidence that there was no humor in the cartoon.

Kannabiran's protests regarding the cartoon and the futility of demanding an apology based on the humorous intentions of the cartoonist touched on several important issues. First, Kannabiran made a case for a serious consideration of representation in cartoons because of the potential of humor to "normalize discrimination." Rather than trivialize representation in cartoons, Kannabiran argued for a political interpretation of visual humor in the newspaper. Second, in making a case for interpreting the politics of cartoons, Kannabiran distanced herself from being considered censorial by highlighting a patriarchal reading of the cartoon that tends to normalize discrimination against women in the "popular consciousness." Third, Kannabiran rejected authorial intent as the basis for interpretation and contended that social and political context bears on the production of meaning. Finally, Kannabiran fortified her critique by recasting the newspaper cartoon spatially as a public space that should be out of bounds to private matters, including family, marriage, procreation, motherhood, child bearing, and education.

Kannabiran, a feminist sociologist, appeared in person before the council, while Kaushik Mitter, the resident editor, represented *Asian Age*, the newspaper in which the cartoon was published. According to Kannabiran, the cartoon was defamatory per se and conveyed the idea that women were an item of property to be owned by and exchanged between men. In her oral submissions, she stated that the cartoon was defamatory of not only Ms. Sangeeta but of all women. These types of cartoons lowered the image of women in the society.[18] The editor of the *Asian Age* in his written statement submitted that "the concerned cartoonist had no intention of hurting anybody's sensitivities. It was further pointed out that the cartoonist was merely mocking the farcical code of conduct established by the Board of Council for Cricket in India which stopped players from entertaining even their wives and mothers at their hotel during overseas tours." The resident editor of the respondent newspaper, reiterating what had been submitted in the written statement, added that "the cartoons were to be taken in a lighter vein and not seriously. The impugned cartoon was a humorous one."

The Press Council committee examined the cartoon and complaint, and came to the conclusion that the cartoon offended good public taste and did not serve any public interest; the mention of the name of Ms. Sangeeta in the cartoon was unwarranted:

The whole cartoon was defamatory not only of Azharuddin and Sangeeta but also of women in general. It was a slur on women and was most derogatory of womanhood. The cartoonist and the newspaper had displayed very cheap taste unbecoming of decent persons. They had indulged in street humor which deserved more condemnation because it found its place in a prestigious newspaper. By no stretch of the imagination could the impugned cartoon be termed as humorous. The explanation offered by the newspaper was completely unsatisfactory.

The committee therefore censured *Asian Age*. As a penalty, the newspaper had to carry the gist of the committee's adjudication and present a copy of the issue both to the committee and the complainant. Kannabiran filed a second complaint as a rejoinder to an unsatisfactory apology that had already been made by the editor of *Asian Age*. The objection to that apology was that it was not adequate to defend the issue by claiming or citing what the cartoonist intended.

When I contacted Kannabiran and Asmita's office, they located the file on this case, which provided more details. From the perspective of Asmita, the cartoonist's particular representation was against the norms of a democratic society; it generated an interpretation of women's subjectivity that was detrimental to women's rights and their citizenship. In her complaint, Kannabiran informed the Press Council of the context of the objectionable cartoon:

The cartoon which appeared in *Asian Age*, on 14 August 1996, depicts a conversation between two men, Sachin Tendulkar and Mohammed Azharuddin regarding the change in captaincy of the Indian Cricket Team. To briefly recapitulate the facts which are relevant in this case: (1) there was a fairly large public debate on the fairness or unfairness of this change of captaincy; (2) roughly coinciding with this change was a change in Azharuddin's personal life, when he divorced his wife and married Sangeeta Bijlani (who is mentioned in this cartoon); and (3) alongside this was a third factor i.e. the announcement by the Board of Cricket Control in India that wives and mothers cannot accompany cricketers during their overseas tours. These three factors are, as we can see quite clearly, simultaneous but unconnected. However what the cartoon depicts is Sachin saying to Azhar, "Azhar, now that I am captain, can I keep Sangeeta too?"

Kannabiran further noted:

In his written apology, the editor of the *Asian Age*, Mr. Shekhar Bhatia, has said that "the cartoonist was merely mocking the farcical code established by the Board of Control of Cricket in India which stopped players from entertaining even their wives and mothers at their hotels during overseas tours." However, the cartoon contains no explicit or implicit reference to this announcement by the Board. We would like to assert at the very outset that our objective in calling the *Asian Age* [to] account is not to be censorious, but to underscore the necessity of eliminating all forms of discrimination against women and other classes of people who have historically been denied fundamental rights.

Kannabiran also gathered together legal, human rights, and ethical perspectives to strengthen the case against the cartoon. First, she argued that it was a violation of legally stipulated norms; specifically, Article 51(A)(e) of the constitution, which enjoins on every citizen of India the duty "to renounce practices derogatory to the dignity of women." The complaint noted, "although it is not a legally enforceable provision, it should be read as a limitation on the Right of Freedom of Expression under Article 19(1), and therefore subject to appropriate action by the PCI." From a human rights perspective, Kannabiran held:

It is our contention that the depiction of the woman in the said cartoon objectifies and depicts her as a property that can be exchanged between men. The words "keep Sangeeta" carry an explicitly sexual connotation in this depiction: woman as a sexual object to "be kept" by men and thereby constitutes violence against women as defined by the UN ... Since cartoons are an important and powerful tool of public and political discourse, representations like these militate against notions of democratic rights and citizenship for women, by reinforcing patriarchal stereotypes of women as chattel to be exchanged between men. Media representations of this kind use "humour" to normalize discrimination against women in the popular consciousness.

Furthermore, on ethical grounds, the cartoon was defamatory per se under Section 499 of the Indian Penal Code:

While the persons thus defamed might or might not initiate defamation proceedings in the courts, the PCI is authorized to ensure high standards of public taste, the fostering of a sense of rights and responsibilities, and the building of a professional code of conduct in the Press by section 13 (2)(b), (c) and (d) of the Press Council Act of 1978, all which have been violated by the said cartoon.

This cartoon thus constituted an infringement on the Right of Citizens to Privacy:

With respect to Article 21, a citizen has a right to safeguard the privacy of his own, his family, marriage, procreation, motherhood, child bearing, and education among other matters. None can publish anything concerning the above matters without his [or her] consent ... if he does so, he would be violating the right to privacy of the person concerned and would be liable in an action for damages (*R. Rajagopal* v. *State of Tamil Nadu* 1995 SC (Supreme Court of India decision) 265). In this regard we contend that the infringement on the Right to Privacy in the present case is a matter of public concern because it took place in public space and therefore subject to appropriate action by the PCI.

The petition concluded that the central point was not about the cartoonist's intention but about the fact that the cartoon was a violation of the norms of public discourse:

Our key contention is that there has been a violation of the norms of public discourse. And that the cartoon in question involves a representation of women that militates against their rights and position as equal citizens in a democratic, egalitarian society, and further urge that appropriate action be taken to ensure the establishment of democratic norms in the media.

The PCI agreed with Kannabiran's protest and dismissed the cartoon as reflecting "cheap taste" and belonging to the category of "street humor." The resident editor was to ensure that an appropriate apology was published in *Asian Age* and a copy of the apology sent to Kannabiran. Thus the proceedings came to a close with a judgment that validated a humor aesthetic expected in a liberal democracy.

Kannabiran's petition, which was categorized as a case about "Press and Morality," illuminated two significant issues: a feminist perspective on media censorship and the liberalism debate in India in relation to gender inequities. In an insightful reading of protests against offensive representations, Shohini Ghosh questioned feminist politics that strived to censor words and images and argued for the distinction between sexually explicit images and sexism (2004, p. 449). Discounting image as a pretext for sexism, Ghosh compelled critics to attend to the broader sociohistorical context for framing sexism. Kannabiran's petition, which was not a call for censorship, draws attention to sexism in a cartoon about cricket. In this cartoon, Kannabiran's arguments suggest that it was not about a visual representation, but instead that gender was a central point of the humor and was expected to be "misrecognized" as peripheral. However, to emphasize the violations in the cartoon, Kannabiran evoked an oppositional class-based "street humor" that was in tune with PCI's logic for determining the degree of liberalism or even its absence. With this maneuver, the petition reinscribed for the average Indian citizen PCI's dictum for mainstream English newspapers that they be the model of responsible liberals. This relation between media image and liberal subjectivity slipped into another thorny aspect of the debate on liberalism – individual rights of women. The inequities in women's experience in India and the conflict between the state's fundamental right to equality and the community's right to religion make it problematic to claim a uniform civil code of rights based on gender (Parashar 1992; Sunder Rajan 2008). However, in the realm of media images such as the "Tru – Lies" cartoon, a strategic evocation of a gendered subject enables a reiteration of democratic ideals of equal citizenship that critiques women's objectification. This is significant because the print media at the time was predominantly a male domain and such gendered critiques were not just about representation but also about who was doing the representing.

"SC"

In 1994, a complaint was filed by R. L. Kain, general secretary of Dr. B. R. Ambedkar Vichar Manch, a Dalit activist organization in New Delhi, against the *Pioneer* daily for publishing the caste of B. Shankaranand, a Union minister, in a cartoon and news item page under the caption "Confident."[19] As with his previous petitions, this too was categorized as a case about "Communal, Casteist, Anti-national, and Religious Writings." Kain stated in his complaint that the caste of one of the Cabinet rank ministers in a cartoon about the current securities scam was deliberately mentioned as "SC" in the cartoon and "Scheduled Caste" in the associated news story, and that this hurt the sentiments of Scheduled Caste people. According to the complainant, the report deliberately identified the minister as belonging to a Scheduled Caste and added that he would be remain unscathed from the charges by using the fact of his being one of the very famous members of the Scheduled Castes in former Indian Prime Minister Narasimha Rao's team. In this complaint, Kain was arguing against the impression conveyed by the cartoon and article that due to his minority status of belonging to a "Scheduled Caste," the guilty minister Shri Shankaranand would be unfairly pardoned for any crime.

Ramindar Singh, senior editor of the *Pioneer*, responded that hardly a day passes when Indian publications do not refer to the caste of a public servant, or a minister in particular. He argued that caste is an important factor in India public life and it would be foolish to deny it. At the *Pioneer*, he said, they greatly dislike referring to the caste of a minister or a public servant but cannot ignore the facts of life as they exist today. In addition, the respondent noted that, incidentally, the points made in the item in the *Pioneer* about Shankaranand were also made in many other papers. Therefore there was no reason either to apologize or to regret the item.

When Kain and Singh came in person to the council, Kain added that he objected to the *Pioneer*'s statement justifying the mentioning of caste because, "That means that in spite of what is enjoined by the constitution of India and the guidelines issued by the Press Council of India, they will continue to refer to castes. In other words they want to perpetuate the caste system in India." In response, Singh stated, "Nothing derogatory was intended by us, there is no malafide intention. It is a part of daily life in India to refer to castes." After the hearing, the PCI asked the *Pioneer* to publish an apology and warned:

In a series of adjudications, the Press Council has consistently stressed that, in general, the identification of a person belonging to Scheduled Caste or depressed class, with reference to his caste, should be avoided, particularly when in the context, it conveys a sense or attributes a conduct or practice derogatory to that caste. ... The offence had been further aggravated by saying that Shri B. Shankaranand will get away. ... Further, the caricature of Shri Shanakaranand published by the paper carried a badge with 'SC' in bold letters, and Shri Shanakaranand indicating to the badge with the thumb of his left hand. This had further accentuated the gravity of the offence committed against journalistic ethic[s] and good taste.[20]

Vinod Mehta, the editor-in-chief of the *Pioneer*, protested against the decision of the Press Council. He wrote that the judgment of the council was so preposterous and absurd that he was afraid he could not publish it. He could not believe anyone working in the profession or having some experience in it would pass such a judgment. He offered to appear before the Press Council to represent his case. Mehta added that the council does not add to its dignity and authority by passing such a judgment. The council did not agree with the recommendation of the inquiry committee, which is allotted the task of assessing evidence and issuing recommendations to the council, that Mehta be allowed to appear before the council, and concluded that the stage for a personal hearing was already over.

The PCI's mandate that identifying individuals with caste was against ethical norms amplified the offence against "good taste" that harbored unsubstantiated charges of corruption against a minister of the minority community. Marking Dalits and women with excess visibility is central to the process of the postcolonial state's legal framework for redressing crimes (Rao 2005, p. 143).[21] In a parallel move, the PCI addressed unethical images as symbolic violence that, as petitioners argue, normalizes discrimination in the name of humor.

The PCI is a toothless body

R. L. Kain, in a white safari suit, welcomed me into his living room. A child romped through the room and his mother promptly plucked him away. When Mrs. Kain entered the living room, I greeted her, handing her a box of sweets – a customary gesture in India. "*Yeh kyun laye beta?*" ("Why did you bring this, child?"). "Aunty, this is something I am accustomed to and I wanted to bring something." "He keeps working all day and night," said Mrs. Kain, sitting down at the edge of a divan (settee). Kain looked a busy man with a mission. His cell phone rang several times. He was a community organizer and held various positions, leading Dalit causes in the Delhi area. An Ambedkar follower, Kain was critical of Gandhian politics and its brazen nationalization. "Look at this note. Why should it have Gandhi's face pictured on it?" I stared at the five-hundred rupee note. For Kain, the Indian nation had short-changed B. R. Ambedkar, the Columbia University law graduate, who is hailed as the architect of the Indian constitution. This was symptomatic of Hindu and elitist hegemonic politics. Kain's cause was to oppose the normalization of this Hindu privilege and that included countering offensive representations of Dalits and of the Buddha. It is worth noting here that the origins of the Buddha imagery have animated scholarship in Indian art history (Verma 2007). Kain's objections to the Buddha cartoon extend this debate about representation to the realm of caricature.

Paper trail

"I am not a Babu, who has all the paperwork filed all over my room and is able to take out particular files at any time" (Interviwe, June 17, 2008). Kain sieved through a mass of papers scattered on his computer desk. "I am not gaining anything personally. This work is for my entire community." "But you have an organization, Mr. Kain," I said in a tone that was part statement and question. The PCI reports said he was president of the Ambedkar Vichar Manch, but that might have changed in these past years, I quickly reminded myself. Swinging both his arms up, twisting his hands, Kain retorted, "Now let that be ... you know." I did not know and assumed Kain was alluding to the fact that, even though he was "President," it was an honorary role that did not come with much office infrastructure. Kain had been in the government service for several decades, from which he had retired. He was conversant with the process of pushing paper and composing petitions. This experience also attracted others, who came to Kain to represent their cases and help them file petitions.

As I moved on to ask about his petitions against cartoons, Kain wanted to tell me about Ambedkar and the Indian constitution. I could not concentrate on the details Kain spelled out from the facsimile copy of a voluminous document. A piece of news I had read just before leaving home wrenched my heart. A seven-year-old child was raped by the bus driver on her last school day, before the summer vacation. The news report, though brief, had enough details to dispel faith in life. That residential area where it occurred was near Kain's neighborhood. My mind was numb. I felt ashamed for pursuing a project on cartoons and political humor when there were graver issues to confront. I took leave of Kain, to return after a few days.

I could only return to this project at the thought of completing it to build a professional foundation that I hoped would empower me to engage publicly with the pain and disappointment of human actions, and their unsuspecting victims. I thought about Kannabiran's analysis of objectifying women in cultural texts such as the cartoon and its tendency to normalize such attitudes through humor. I recalled that the feminist media theorist Shohini Ghosh had written an incisive article on pornography that made a case for "a broader socio-historical context for framing sexism." Ghosh cited a case in which a child's rapist was acquitted on grounds that the offender had seen too many blue films. If claims of such power in images can defend a child's rapist, then within the Indian socio-historical context, feminists must consistently generate strategic and flexible critiques of visual culture.

Offending Buddhist sensibility

"In 1984 and 1989 when the Indira Gandhi and BJP governments conducted nuclear tests, they were conducted on Buddha *Jayanti* [birth anniversary of the Buddha]," said Kain at our next meeting. Thereafter, there arose a tradition of composing cartoons on nuclear tests with the caption "Buddha is smiling," or some version of it. Indeed, it was odd that a nuclear test, which did not leave much to imagine about mass violence, was twice organized on a day on which Buddhists celebrate his birth. Kain was angry about the disrespect and insensitivity shown to Lord Buddha, at the official level and by cartoonists of all stripes, including R. K. Laxman, who depicted the Buddha in a 1983 cartoon. Bireshwar, too, had used the Buddha to caricature politicians. "The International Buddhist Conference, in its meetings, held that no cartoon in any newspaper, magazine, or commemorative or regular stamp can be issued by any country on Lord Buddha, as the same is thrown on road after its use," continued Kain. "This decision forced us to keep surveillance on media and government. I being an expert in the matter scrutinize the derogatory material from the media."

Since Kain was a familiar figure in the PCI, it seemed their adjudicatory system was worthwhile for community activists: "They make a laughing stock over the heads of other religions. Most of the time impugned cartoons did not require their publication or public attention. Our members and sympathizers also keep us informed about the impugned cartoons. After scanning them, I register my complaint with Press Council of India and contest the cases regularly." But this criticism of "they" – newspapers, cartoonists, and editors – extended to the PCI, too: "They have made a joke of all these things. They don't care, even the PCI. They write a few lines and get rid of the case – solve it." That happened to Kain's complaint about the cartoon showing a weeping Buddha.

The weeping Buddha

"My first complaint was a cartoon in 1983, against the *Times of India*. To date I have filed twenty-eight complaints against different newspapers on different matters. We keep close watch over ridiculous, sacrilegious, and derogatory cartoons of Lord Buddha published by print or electronic media; usually fundamentalist journalists hurt the sentiments of minorities, that is, Buddhists." The *Hindustan Times*, too, had published a Buddha cartoon, but they were quick to issue an apology. On not receiving a similar response from the *Times of India*, however, Kain, who was at the time general secretary of the Delhi Scheduled Castes Welfare Association, took the case to the PCI. I had seen this complaint in the PCI report.

In the complaint dated October 8, 1983, Kain alleged that the *Times of India* had violated the accepted norms of journalistic ethics by publishing a highly objectionable cartoon of Lord Buddha, depicting him in a very pitiable condition that had hurt the religious sentiments of the Buddhists.[22] The editor, Girilal Jain, in his comments stated that the impugned cartoon was published to show the contrast between the teachings of the Lord Buddha and the action of his followers in Sri Lanka, and they had no intention to show any disrespect to Lord Buddha. The matter was considered by the Inquiry Committee at its meeting on July 5, 1984, and Kain and the editor Girilal Jain appeared before the committee.

Kain submitted that there was a convention in Europe not to show Lord Buddha even on stamps. He stated, however, that he had no objection to the publication of a photograph of Lord Buddha. He added that a similar cartoon was published in the *Hindustan Times*, and the newspaper had published an apology. Jain submitted that there was nothing wrong with the cartoon that had been published and that the condition in which Lord Buddha had been shown symbolized the state of affairs that existed in Sri Lanka on the Tamil question. After hearing the arguments of both the parties and examining the cartoon, the committee was of the opinion that Lord Buddha had not been shown as an object of ridicule and that the cartoon was not meant to show any disrespect to him. The council decided to reject the complaint.

Over a delicious lunch of spicy chana, puri, rice, and paneer, catered from his son's restaurant nearby, Kain recalled the incident and cartoon:

The *Times of India* published a cartoon on Lord Buddha in a weeping position and tears were on his cheeks. This is a very old case, and its record is not readily available with me except the judgment of the Press Council of India in its annual report. However, from memory lane I narrate the gist of the story. The *Times of India* had published a cartoon of a weeping Lord Buddha ... tears crawling down his cheeks, on its cover on the massacre of Tamil citizens in Sri Lanka. The caption carried out with the cartoon indicated: "Had the Lord Buddha been alive now He would have wept over the ghastly incident in a Buddhist country." I protested that no cartoon or commemorative stamp of Lord Buddha should be published as a goodwill gesture toward Him. Secondly, I protested that no Hindu god or goddess were shown weeping over the massacre, macabre killings, and burning of Scheduled Castes people in India by the Hindu fundamentalists in their day-to-day life in India. Why has the Lord Buddha been selected to be compared to the killings in Sri Lanka? The Press Council of India filed my complaint when the undersigned contested my complaint when one of the members of the Inquiry Committee compared it with a similar situation and said that, had Gandhi been alive now, he would have wept over the piquant situation of the Congress Party. I objected to that comparison of Gandhi with Lord Buddha as he [Gandhi] was just a politician not a religious head of any sect and we know his life and contribution in the field of religion.

The PCI's unfavorable judgment disappointed Kain: "the Press Council of India is a toothless body and is also not a free and fair institution. The Indian press is also biased and prejudiced towards Scheduled Castes, Tribes, and Minorities ... When you complain about a Buddha cartoon, they say 'it is not Buddha.'"

Kain's concern with Lord Buddha's caricatures and casual uses of his name, as well as his opposition to Gandhi, left him with many critics and too many battles. "The Gandhi people got irritated with me when I protested that Gandhi cannot be called Buddha [the Enlightened]. Gandhi is a social reformer and political figure, not the head of a religious sect, so there's no comparison." Gandhi and Buddha had merged earlier, too. I remember seeing popular prints from the 1940s that incorporated Gandhi and Buddha as avatars in the Hindu pantheon. The two names were uttered in the same breath many years ago during Gandhi's centenary celebration in 1968. Prime Minister Indira Gandhi proclaimed Gandhi the "greatest son of India since Buddha" (Durga Das 1969, p. 441).

Thinking about Kain's cases, I noticed that the PCI was tolerant of cartoons with images of gods; they dismissed complaints that took umbrage at religious portrayals.

This is not Ram: new darshans

In 1988, the PCI dismissed a complaint lodged by K. Ramasarma about a cartoon published on the front page of the Bangalore edition of the *Indian Express* dated June 15, 1988. Under the caption, "My lord, shall we call the IPKF too?" it portrayed Lord Rama as "a pigmy [*sic*] weak and ugly in stature," claimed Ramasarma, and it was satirical, demeaning, offensive to religious sentiments, politically motivated, and ridiculed religion (see Figure 8.3).[23]

In his written and oral submission, Arun Shourie, the editor of the *Indian Express*, clarified that a mere glance at the cartoon would show that it was not Lord Rama who was being portrayed but Arun Govil, a TV

8.3 Ravi Shankar. *Indian Express*. June 14, 1988. New Delhi. Courtesy of the *Indian Express*. "My lord, shall we call the IPKF too?"

The figure on the right is pictured as Hanuman, Rama's loyal aide, whose army of monkeys played a critical role in rescuing Sita from captivity in Sri Lanka. The stone on the right says "Allahabad," where film star Arun Govil (who portrayed Lord Rama in the popular TV serial) was campaigning as a Congress candidate. In the cartoon, as during Govil's election campaign, the real life and the screen roles merged. However, when such merger is shown in caricature, it can cause offense.

actor who was then campaigning in Allahabad. At the time, the popular and long-running TV serial *Ramayana* had captured the public imagination. The Bollywood film star Arun Govil had gained wide recognition for his role of Rama in this serial. This popularity catapulted him into being a favored candidate in the general elections for a constituency in Allahabad. The cartoon evoked the Sri Lanka link from the *Ramayana* – it was the island where Sita, Ram's wife, was held captive; the Indian Peace Keeping Force (IPKF) was instituted ostensibly to restore normalcy during Sri Lanka's ethnic conflict. The Inquiry Committee opined that no reader of ordinary prudence and sensibility could say that this cartoon was intended or calculated to ridicule Lord Rama or threaten the religious sentiments of any community. According to the committee, the cartoon depicted only good humor and did not offend public taste.

The *Indian Express* cartoonist Ravi Shankar had also caricatured Prime Minister Rajiv Gandhi, N. T. Ram Rao, as well as Arun Govil, as modern incarnations of Lord Rama. It would help to bear in mind that, in the context of postcolonial India, the boundaries of the secular and religious have blurred on many occasions, particularly when constructing public images. Film stars turned politicians have repeatedly drawn on their screen personae and portrayals of deities to claim authority and public goodwill when vying for election in India's representative democracy. The Buddha imagery, too, has long been an acceptable trope of Indian cartoons. In sharp contrast to the evocation of a civic good and public taste to contest moral, social, and gender inequities normalized in cartoons, representations of gods silenced the PCI – they dismissed such complaints. Kain's partial successes with the PCI points out that lodging a complaint in the name of the public is not adequate; for a complaint to be successful it has to be framed as a threat to liberal ideals. The theme of faith seemed to pose a challenge that required a different vocabulary and logic.

Sensory exclusion and inclusionary pretense

The refusal to laugh and the PCI's deliberations not only articulate competing notions of liberal aesthetics and politics, but also become grounds for managing a fragmented public sphere in India. Cartoons and their multiple publics produce cultural politics that confront Indian democracy and its promise of an equitable society. Furthermore, the PCI's and the petitioners' evocation of their constituency as newspaper "readers" opens up a space to frame the way we understand representative politics: the "idea of a public is a cultural form" (Warner 2002, p. 8).

Through the vocabulary the PCI offers for lodging petitions, the newspaper cartoon is transformed into talk that calibrates liberalism as "cheap," "average," or "ultra-liberal." These petitions about the meaning of cartoons and explications of "good taste" can serve as an interpretative framework for the connection between senses of humor, liberalism, and democratic politics. As registers of cartoon talk, the petitions and the PCI point to a public space where liberalism encompasses an "elite symbolic repertoire" (Hill 1999, p. 686). In this space, particular aesthetics in humor, even at the cost of evoking censure as "illiberal," symbolize liberal identity.[24] The newspaper cartoons deliberated in the PCI's precincts incite debate about liberalism and caste. They bring to the surface the cleavages in a modern democracy, the creative energy of minority activism, and the question: "Do we belong?" The cartoons' interpretative dilemmas situate this question against the backdrop of "inclusionary pretensions of liberal theory and the exclusionary effects of liberal practices" (Mehta 1999, p. 46). Deliberations over the cartoons' meaning demonstrate that newspaper cartoons are an arena in which the effects of these exclusionary politics are felt. They operate within a presumed context of liberalism, a political discourse that has its own peculiarity in India. Cartoon talk and the PCI's ambivalent stance on cartoons' meanings reinscribe the fuzzy liberalism that marks India's experience of democracy. It also leads to questioning the implications of representation as misrepresentation in relation to a historically stratified society. Is misrepresentation compounded when it caricatures a minority subject in postcolonial India?

Kannabiran and Kain protested at such representations on grounds that they perpetuated gender-based and caste-based discriminatory politics. The rulings against the *Asian Age* and the *Pioneer* evoked the norms of "good taste" that, within a democratic setup, meant sensitivity to discriminatory practices experienced by a broad spectrum of Indian citizens. Both petitions focused on images and not the cartoonists' intention. Within this framework, images, specifically newspaper cartoons, were not about representing reality, that is, existing social biases, but concerned their force in normalizing the presence of such reality. Furthermore, liberal politics were expressed in the nature of the image, not the individual reader. Although the petitions brought forth a debate on the parameters of India's liberal politics, such an approach to the social role of images is counterproductive to minority rights. By emphasizing the agency of the image rather than individuals, Kannabiran and Kain replicate an approach that holds media and not the individual responsible for uses of stereotypes and image.

This leads to the question: what is the relationship between liberalism and the prohibition of specific images that do not fit the framework of cultural rights? This question would be answered with passion, emotion, and politics in an unexpected global event – the Prophet Muhammad cartoon controversy, also referred to as the Danish cartoon controversy.

9   "All our gods and goddesses are cartoons"

On September 10, 2010, the German chancellor Angela Merkel awarded the M100 media award to Danish cartoonist Kurt Westergaard. This recognition, at a recently instituted forum for Europe's media practitioners, did not go unnoticed around the world: the *Times of India* promptly reported the event.[1] Westergaard was no ordinary cartoonist; in 2005, his Prophet Muhammad cartoons in the Danish newspaper *Jyllands Posten* inflamed passions, as well as debates about liberalism and cartoons. In years to come, the Danish controversy and Westergaard's 2010 endorsement will be a pivotal point in considering how cartoons became a litmus test for modernity and its others.

It would be a mistake to assume that violent protests immediately followed the cartoons' publication. The timeline reveals a developing series of events that began on September 17, 2005, with a Danish newspaper report about writer Kaare Bluitgen's futile search for an illustrator for a book on the Prophet Muhammad. To counter the perceived fear of reprisal from Muslims, *Jyllands Posten* invited cartoonists to submit illustration of the Prophet Muhammad based on their imagination, and published twelve cartoons. Following a protest outside the *Jyllands Posten* office by a crowd of 5,000 people, ambassadors of ten Islamic countries requested but were refused a meeting with the Danish Prime Minister Anders Fogh Rasmussen. Meanwhile, a Danish Muslim delegation to the Middle East embellished the set of cartoons, which along with various rumors thickened the plot with uncertainty. On January 30, 2006, *Jyllands Posten* issued an apology couched in the claim that the cartoons complied with their journalistic norms. Danish imams accepted the apology and were surprised at the growing momentum worldwide. The Danish government's reluctance to discuss an issue they viewed as an independent concern of the *Jyllands Posten*, propelled seventeen Arab countries meeting in Tunisia to issue a joint call to the Danish government to punish the editor, Flemming Rose. Simultaneously, the call to boycott Arla Dairy products, a major Danish exporter to the Middle East, and the republication of the cartoons in various European newspapers, brought new players onto the scene. On February 3, 2003, the International Association of Muslim Scholars called for observing "a day of anger." Protests were reported in Indonesia, India, and Pakistan, among other places.[2] The simultaneity of reactions and overreactions defy a neat timeline, proving the futility of tracking cause and effect.

The Indian cartoonist, journalist, and author Rajinder Puri has written that "two nations gained from the cartoon crisis. America gained because Islamic fury will draw Europe closer to America's world-view. Iran gained by becoming more firmly entrenched as a leader of radical Islam." Elaborating on this impact of the 2005 Danish cartoon controversy and the long-simmering animosity toward Islam that engulfed at least half the world, Puri asked, "So, why the hatred?"[3] Religion, claimed Puri. And returning to religion, "rediscovering" it, was also the solution to this tension. C. M. Naim, Professor Emeritus of South Asian Languages and Literature at the University of Chicago, called the controversy a "clash of fanaticisms." Mentioning editor Flemming Rose's refusal in 2003 to publish Christoffer Zieller's illustration of Jesus Christ to avoid offending Christians, Naim concluded: "Hypocrisy, rabble-rousing, and fanaticism is not always swarthy and hook-nosed, as often it comes fair-skinned and blonde too. As also in every other hue that mankind has."[4]

When the Danish cartoon controversy gripped the world, I was back in the United States after two years in India. I felt frustrated that a subject I had been tracking for almost ten years attained attention of global proportions while I was in Texas, without access to the cartoonists and activists with whom I would have chatted about the developing events. The controversy also invited a new perspective to my project – it was timely: "This is right up your alley and you could write a commentary in the newspaper," said friends. But I didn't. It was a bizarre moment for me. With little warning, the unexpected spotlight on cartoons, a subject that sometimes received a cool smile and polite nod, became hot. Over a quick smoke on an oppressive Texas summer afternoon, Asif, a visiting anthropologist, analyzed my hesitation to make a public comment: "The historian in you is stopping you from writing." There was no dearth of public conversation: remarkably, everyone assumed expertise to comment on cartoons. The controversy rendered everyone a critic, evaluating why cartoons and Islam, and even more broadly religion itself, matter in the modern world. But the story depended on who was telling it. Indeed, this is the power of cartoons. I took a deep breath of second-hand smoke to ponder Asif's remark.

I lamented my sense of isolation in Texas during these momentous times until, quite by chance, I met Ion. A member of a junior cartoonist collective based in Bangalore, with whom I conversed by email, informed me that a colleague of his was nearby! Ion, pen name of the skilled cartoonist of the *Daily Texan* – Austin's university campus newspaper – was from India. An insider to India's cartooning scene, he had turned to a career in science. I met Ion on a weekend, in his physics lab, and interviewed him on email and Google chat. "India has a bad reputation of zealously guarding 'religious freedom,'" he said.

We were the first to ban *The Satanic Verses* and even considered banning *The Da Vinci Code*. And lastly because some parties protested, Prime Minister Manmohan Singh had to formally protest against the Danish cartoons. The Danish cartoons had different reactions in different parts of the world. In the Middle East it erupted in violence, flag-burning in Pakistan, condemnation in India, and so on. In the Western world where the voice of moderate Muslims is strong, they treated the episode more maturely. (Interview on August 19, 2006)

Ion's comment gave me pause – I was struck by his swift equation of moderation and maturity. Indeed, the various forms of protest around the world served as a reminder that Islam in all its varieties was also grounded in places and national politics. How protests surfaced and were articulated told as much about Islamic perspectives as about the relationship between nations and their ideologies of freedom. No matter what one's vantage point, history shadowed the ongoing controversy. "We are all amateur historians with various degrees of awareness about our production. We also learn history from similar amateurs," noted Michel-Rolph Trouillot in a trenchant analysis of how and where we learn about the past (Trouillot 1995, p. 20). Ion recalled the "Rushdie Affair" – a global event when British author Salman Rushdie's book *The Satanic Verses* created a furor for satirizing the life of Muhammad, leading to the Iranian cleric Ayatollah Khomeini's fatwa (religious ruling issued by a mufti) for Rushdie's death. How far back is the past, and why do we feel the need for history to make sense of the present?

Blasphemy, condemnation, and emotional integration

The worldwide discussion of the Danish cartoons catapulted cartoons into a social text that made politics transparent. "Boycott Denmark products – Cadbury chocolate, 7UP drink, Lego toys, Hall chewing gum and any product with bar code number starting with 57."[5] This text message that circulated during those days created a mode of protest that was already familiar in India: Gandhi's call for boycotting foreign goods as part of his satyagraha politics. Text messaging became the "best way" to protest the cartoons. Although the recent public pro-democracy movement in Egypt put the spotlight on social networking and the mobilizing reach of Facebook, the Danish cartoon controversy set the stage for the political use of social networks. In the wake of the cartoon controversy, there was an added twist to this boycott and use of text messaging: technologies developed by the Western countries were to be used against them.[6] This combination of new media, boycotting Western commodities, and social networking also eschewed violence while charting a future for mobilizing protest, specifically when religion is the issue.

On behalf of the All India Muslim Majlis-e-Mushawarat (AIMMM), in February 2006 its president, Dr. Syed Shahbuddin, published a resolution regarding the Danish cartoons in the *Milli Gazette*: "On Blasphemy against the Holy Prophet (PBUH) in Europe."[7]

The Markazi Majlis-e-Mushawarat (MMM) [a division of the AIMMM] strongly condemns with deep indignation the publication of caricatures of the Holy Prophet (PBUH) by a Danish paper and its re-publication in several European papers and looks upon it as a despicable expression of Islamophobia which has been on the rise in the West particularly after 9/11 and as a provocative move, designed to humiliate the Muslims and to misrepresent Islam and to incite hatred and contempt against them among the people of the West who are for peace [and] have opposed war against Muslim States.

The MMM rejects the justification for this deliberate act of blasphemy in terms of Freedom of Press. All freedoms have limits and entail responsibility and sensitivity to the values and interests of the others.

The MMM considers that all European states in one form or the other practice double standards and Islamophobia has behind it the West's historic hostility to the world of Islam.

The MMM realizes that the West is not prepared to countenance the resistance of Muslim communities to cultural assimilation at the cost of their religious identity but the plurality of the world today demands mutual respect and tolerance and nationalism calls for national integration but not assimilation.

The MMM fully supports the right of the Muslim world to register its protest but is convinced that an excessive and violent response, which is against the tenets of Islam, only serves the agenda of those elements in the West which are writing a scenario for eventual collision between Islam and the West.

The MMM, therefore, urges Muslim communities all over the world, and particularly in India, to eschew violence and articulate their feelings peacefully and through the representatives of the Western Governments and mass media in their countries and their own governments.

The AIMMM was constituted after India's first post-Partition "communal bombshell" – a Hindu–Muslim in 1961 conflict sparked by rival bidi (Indian cigarette) producers in Madhya Pradesh. The conflict took on disturbing proportions after the discovery of a love affair between the son and daughter of the two rivals. Business rivalry, romantic liaison, and belonging to two different communities flared into violence along religious lines. Newspaper reports played no small role in inflaming passions as the story was reworked to imply that the Muslim boy had conspired to rape the Hindu girl. Such communal conflict in post-Partition secular India disillusioned many. Alarmed by the turn of events, Prime Minister Jawaharlal Nehru instituted the National Integration Council (NIC) to "promote emotional integration in the country" (Engineer 1992). The council was delegated to counter the evils of communalism, casteism, regionalism, linguism, and narrow-mindedness. After its formation, the council did not meet until 1968, leading to doubts about NIC's goals and objectives. The council ceased meeting in 1992, though it was reconstituted in 2005.[8] Disappointed with Nehru's limited intervention, in 1965 a group of concerned Muslims formed the AIMMM, a "consultative committee" of various Muslim groups and political parties.[9] Not a political party itself, the AIMMM set an agenda that included the defense of Muslim identity and dignity. As a body that engaged nationally and internationally, the AIMMM works within a framework of national interests that upholds democracy and secular principles. Thus it promotes "national unity and national integration, communal amity and social harmony as well as cooperation among Muslim organizations at all levels."

The Markazi Majlis-e-Mushawarat (MMM) is a key working division of the AIMMM. Its fields of activity include administration, banking management, commerce and industry, culture and fine arts, diplomacy, education, Islamic learning, journalism, language and literature, law, politics, medicine and other professions, science and technology, social welfare, and sports.[10] The MMM remains active, with branches at various organizational levels to include more cities and villages. For the MMM, the Danish cartoons made transparent a number of things about the West: Islamophobia, misrepresentation of Muslims, expectation of assimilation to Western norms, proffering the imaginary notion of an inevitable clash between the West and Islam. The MMM argued that the way Muslims reacted to the cartoons could either puncture or promote the conspiracy theory about Islamic militancy. Here was an occasion to script, show, and hold the Western world to their cherished ideals of rationality and freedom of speech.

If text messaging was a Western technology to be used against the West, then rational debate was the technique of persuasion that, along with mass media, could be called upon to mobilize against a skewed sense of freedom without responsibility. Taken to its logical conclusion, such mobilization was necessary to save the West from transgressing its own ideals.

In 2008, I finally had the opportunity to return to India. Among my first visits was to the weekly *Milli Gazette* editor, Dr. Khan, a graduate of Manchester University. I had already met Dr. Khan in 2003, when I saw the cartoons in his weekly. The newspaper was associated with the Mushawarat (MMM): the *Milli Gazette*'s topical cartoons consistently criticized the Hindu political parties, the Bharatiya Janata Party (BJP) and its ally the Vishwa Hindu Parishad (VHP), as well as the United States. I wanted to meet his cartoonist, Yusuf,[11] but this proved impossible. "From the very beginning we have done cartoons. Yusuf is not a real cartoonist," Dr. Khan had told me. From his comment I had assumed that Yusuf must either be an amateur or a part-time cartoonist, and so I did not insist on knowing more. This visit I wanted to know about Dr. Khan's response to the cartoon controversy. Dr. Khan was also the president of the MMM, having succeeded Syed Shahbuddin since my last trip. His reminder that there were other pressing issues for the Muslims in India humbled me, and I was embarrassed to be harping on the cartoon controversy almost two years prior. Apologetically, I asked if he could tell me about what happened at the time. Over a cup of tea, Dr. Khan graciously shared his thoughts.

"There are many ways to say things"

DR. KHAN: The joke is one way to say things. If you go to any office in Egypt, you will be asked, "Have you heard the latest Nukta?" The Nukta is a humorous way of saying things that can't be said straight way. Any cartoon has three types of readers: those who like it, those who don't, and those who think with it. The problem was not with the Danish cartoons per se; the problem was showing a bomb in someone's head and turban. This is an offense. What does it mean? It means, "This man is a terrorist." Branding someone a terrorist is an offense. It happens in the USA – evangelicals show every Muslim as a terrorist. And no action is taken against such portrayals. Denmark is part of the same ideological sphere. West means the USA but Europe and Canada are part of this West. Their philosophy, historical and religious experience is the same. West is West.

The West still suffers from the defeat in the crusades. Before medieval times and the crusades, the Europeans were not able to conquer this land. Most of the countries that were later colonized were Muslim. Even India was one with a substantial Muslim community. All these politics today has to do with the West's historical experience.

The Qur'an does not teach terrorism. Violence does not solve problems. In the Qur'an, Allah belongs to everyone but be careful with Mohammed. Muslims believe Prophet Mohammed was an example of everything that was good. From personal experience, no Muslim thinks he is going to take over Europe or the USA. We want to be left alone. First they colonized us; we got freedom somehow. We paid great sacrifices – two million were killed in Algeria. They want to keep us in slavery, not liberally. People in the Muslim world are against this. But there are some Muslim governments still under the USA. The problems in Egypt are because of Mubarak's pro-USA stance.

If the BJP or VHP come to power in India, the West accepts it as part of the democratic process. But not so in the case of Muslim countries. In Egypt, politicians are put in prison before elections – there is no real democracy. In a real democracy there are free elections. Even if the Devil wins, give him four or five years, after which he has to go and if he is good, he can stay. This kind of democracy is not allowed in Turkey, Egypt, and Palestine.

There is no central Muslim organization. The MMM does not organize protests – they are spontaneous. Sometimes the issue is raised during the Jumma service; sometimes it is raised by the imam, as in Kolkata and in Delhi. There were protests against the Danish cartoons in Mumbai, Srinagar, and Delhi. These were spontaneous local events based on newspaper reports. *Milli Gazette* also reproduced one of the cartoons, but we cut out the bomb. The context of the publication and comments affect the people. This rage is manufactured; it is not real.

Recently, regarding India's nuclear deal with the USA, the CPI (M) and Marxists said that the nuclear deal was anti-Muslim. I at once wrote to them – no one authorized them to speak for Muslims. But we are against the nuclear deal. Why didn't Mayawati of the BSP oppose the deal by saying it was anti-Dalit? Muslims are a free commodity for any political party to use.[12]

Dr. Khan's laying out a large map for popular perceptions of Muslims and his suggestion of multiple Muslim organizations, prompted me to seek out the leader of the Majlis-e-Ittehadul Muslimeen (MIM), Asaduddin Owaisi, who protested the cartoons. Through a common friend, who knew Owaisi as a "moderate" Muslim, I managed an interview.

Liberal imperialism

A Member of Parliament from Hyderabad, in the state of Andhra Pradesh, and a barrister-at-law of London's Lincoln's Inn, Asaduddin Owaisi represents a regional political party. He explained to me the offense of the Danish cartoons. In his official Ashoka Road residence in New Delhi, Owaisi recalled his organized protest in June 2006. The initial permission to hold the protest meeting inside a mosque was rescinded an hour before it was to begin. Nevertheless Owaisi continued and some violence ensued outside in which "a few scooters and shops were burnt." Owaisi continued:[13]

The cartoons were not an issue in India or for us because this happened in Denmark. If we make it an issue, then our followers will think we are making light of more important matters. There is a difference between sacrilege and critique. Critique is to differ but sacrilege is to ridicule. If you differ with me about the Prophet, that is fine. But you cannot ridicule the Prophet.

When I asked Owaisi what it meant to cast him as a "moderate" Muslim, he brushed aside the label: "What we have now is liberal imperialism. If I disagree with [French President] Sarkhozy's statement about the veil then

I am considered a fundamentalist. If I disagree with terrorism then I am considered liberal." The liberal imperialism Owaisi pointed to was a sign of the failure of democracy. It showed the state of Indian political affairs in which labelling MIM "communal" or a worthy coalition partner of centrist political ideology, such as the Congress Party, was a matter of strategic convenience. MIM had supported the fatwa against Salman Rushdie and Taslima Nasreen. In a departure from this stance, MIM did not support the politician Haji Yaqoob Quereshi's fatwa against the Danish cartoons that put the sum of 50 crores (approximately US$ 8 million) on the head of the cartoonist. Owaisi explained why:

> Not just anyone can proclaim a fatwa – it has to be a religious head, a Mufti. The person in Meerut [a city in the state of Uttar Pradesh], who issued the "fatwa" – that is not a fatwa. I do not agree with such crazy people. NDTV (a TV channel) organized a panel on the cartoon issue. There I said, "if you have 50 crores then give it to your Muslim brothers who have been killed in the violence. After the panel discussion he [Quereshi] told me, "*aapne to hava hi nikal di. Kachra kar diya*" ("You have punctured the issue. Trashed it").

Owaisi's refusal of Quereshi's fatwa rested on a politician's inappropriate usurping of clerical authority. The fatwa has an ethical and authoritative dimension; it is a "response to questions about how to live rightly" and a "primary means of exercising Islamic authority" (Agrama 2010, p. 2). Thus the fatwa is conveyed as part of everyday life and can be requested by followers to address moral and social dilemmas. In the Western context, the widespread reference to and public notice of the practice of fatwa is recent and is linked to controversies (Agrama 2010).[14] Fatwas issued in the wake of books by Salman Rushdie and Taslima Nasreen and the Danish cartoons have led to an increasing reference to and assumption of the fatwa as a death sentence and a cash award named on the offender's head. Since these controversies responded to "offending" individuals in different parts of the world (the UK, Bangladesh, and Denmark), they caught global attention and conveyed the idea of addressing an outraged pan-Islamic public. For Owaisi the global connection of Islamic politics is undeniable, but he does not view this is as a pan-Islamic identity. Quereshi's pronouncement signaled that the fatwa is conceptually misunderstood even among some South Asian politicians, who represent and uphold an Islamic identity: "The difference between the Hindu and Muslim in India is that the Muslim is affected by external politics – Iraq, Afghanistan, and Palestine. I do not consider this pan-Islamism. But this is what it is – we respond to both the external and the internal. The cartoon controversy has to be seen in the context of what is happening all around."

The traffic of the Danish cartoons created new lines of empathy and identification. In their play with representation and a presumed sense of humor, these cartoons signaled the extent of contemporary imperial power. Cartoons stirring alliances and empathy are not new. Palmira Brummett notes the impact of images of suffering Indians in the early-twentieth-century Ottoman Empire. Images of imperialism and the suffering of "fellow" Muslims in India generated a rhetoric of unity and resistance that transcended national and ethnic lines (Brummett 2000, p. 111). Furthermore, the image of India served to show "how complete and how extensive Britain's imperial conquest could be" (pp. 110–11). The Danish cartoons provide a recent context for situating these processes, politics, and feelings while demonstrating the geographical, political, and cultural arena where this mattered. Not restricted to national boundaries nor explained away as "pan-Islamic," the Danish cartoon politics are a form of cosmopolitanism that brings together politics and culture (Hannerz 2004). Owaisi asserted, "We all see cartoons." Indeed, the objections were not about an aversion to cartoons as a form of representation or the lack of interpretative skills. The cartoons of the *Milli Gazette* give a peek into these politics of seeing and caricaturing culture.

Muslim worlds

Milli Gazette's free online presence makes the weekly widely accessible. In the online forum for letters to the *MG* editor and Dr. Khan's reply to them, cartoons were frequently commented upon, demonstrating the imbrications of belief and seeing. One reader, Akbar Batcha, questioned the *MG* cartoonist's conflation of Arabs and the Muslim world (see Figure 9.1): "It is too harsh to have such cartoon in *Milli Gazette*! *Milli Gazette* forgets to note that Arabs are not the only Muslim world! It could have been better if the cartoonist wrote 'Arab World' instead of 'Muslim World.' Anyway, drawing the Kabah [*sic*] has made me [keen] to send my comments."[15] When Akbar Batcha saw the cartoon as depicting the "Arab world" not the "Muslim world," he was urging a distinction of geopolitics rather than of faith, which formulated Muslims into groups of various stripes, not a cohesive unit. Khan's response to Batcha's comment in the *Milli Gazette* insisted that the cartoon was the view of a "simple Muslim," opening the opportunity to teach readers such as Batcha how to interpret the cartoon from a simple political standpoint that did not engage the more complicated world of which the reader was aware.[16] This simplicity, according to Khan, was exaggerated because "a cartoon is an exaggeration of an existing fact and it tries to jolt people to think about a problem." This perspective may have simplified some aspect of the hues

9.1 Yusuf, "Muslim World." *Milli Gazette*. February 24, 2004. New Delhi. Courtesy of the *Milli Gazette*.

The "Muslim world" kneels before the United States, turning his back on the Kaaba in Mecca, Islam's most holy site.

of Muslim politics, but it achieved the purpose of the cartoon – to make the reader think.

Another reader, Hassan Golsafidi, proposed that the prostrating figure in the cartoon should be "Muslim governments" – not Muslims. But for Khan the cartoon showed the big picture: Muslim elites were subservient to the United States. He did not reflect on the drawing of the Kaaba, which triggered Batcha's letter, until yet another reader, Imran Ahmed from the United Kingdom, raised the issue:

I have found the last drawing of a man prostrating towards Bush and the holy Qibla behind him very very upsetting, being a Muslim I feel very bad on this subject as you are trying to portray us, I do not know when you are with us or trying to portray us as bad. I hope you understand my view as I am sure most of the Muslims would agree with me.

"No offence is intended to Islam or Kaaba," responded Khan. "It is an old cartoon which caricatures the current position of Muslim rulers who bow towards Uncle Sam instead of our Qibla. The recent Arab summit at Tunis has again highlighted this fact." The direction of posturing was important. Muslims pray by turning in the direction of Mecca, signified by the Qibla.

Although Khan published other reader comments, too, he did not respond to all. In different ways, the readers' thoughts about *MG* cartoons questioned whether it was possible to assume a single Muslim world and that all Muslims are the same:

First of all I congratulate you for this great achievement in bringing this magazine. I am a regular reader of *Milli Gazette*. But today when I got the mail from you people about the updated version and in that I was very surprised to see the cartoon which u made. It did hurt my feelings and beliefs. I am sure majority of your readers might have got angry seeing this cartoon. How can u make a cartoon of a muslim who is bowing before a kafir and facing his back towards Kabah-shareef. I know that Muslim leaders are afraid of Bush not of *Allah* nowadays which is disgusting but your cartoon indicates that all Muslims are of this type.

Corresponding from Dallas, Texas, Muneeruddin Mohammed thus raised the question as to whether Muslim leadership truly represented all Muslims. To see such a cartoon evokes thought and emotion: this thought hurt feelings and belief; it may stir anger. The message of another reader, M. Sahib, was explicit about the different Muslims, while agreeing that the cartoon was in "bad taste." "If Muslims would have bowed down to USA, there wouldn't be the current 'Crusade' against Muslims. Muslims have stood firm against U.S. aggression. Those who are bowing to USA are the tyrannical rulers of the mid-east, Pakistan and the new rulers of Afghanistan."

In its distinct way, the *Milli Gazette*'s weekly cartoons continue a tradition of graphic satire that addressed Muslim politics in India. The pioneering comic newspaper *Oudh Punch* and the Muslim League's *Dawn* in colonial India exemplify the rich history of cartoons in Urdu and among followers of Islam. Furthermore, the links among politics and communities based on their religious affiliation is integral to Indian cartooning. The *Hindu Punch* cartoons from the 1930s, for example, are replete with stereotypes of Hindus and Muslims, and frequently caricatured Hindu deities. The *Hindi Punch* also included several caricatures of Hindu deities.

Believing and seeing

The politics of representation and its heady mix with religion was a familiar experience for media observers in contemporary India, and for Dr. Khan. The layered appeal of religion as politics, and politics as religion, is a consistent theme in the *Milli Gazette*'s cartoons. Given this tone of their cartoons, I was curious if the *Milli Gazette* received protests from Hindu organizations. During an email exchange, Dr. Khan informed me about one objection: "Only very recently some Hindutvites [Hindutva Followers], usually based in the USA, raised a storm against a certain cartoon claiming

9.2 Yusuf, "Indian Democracy." *Milli Gazette*. February 24, 2004. New Delhi. Courtesy of the *Milli Gazette*.

The figures were labeled POTA (Prevention of Terrorism Act) and Human Rights and TADA (Terrorism and Disruptive Activities (Prevention) Act. This Act lapsed in 1995). The crucifixion of a Muslim merged Christian iconography with political subjugation in India and the universal discourse of human rights. The Parliament in the background denoted the democratic source of these legislations, hence, the paradox of Indian democracy, which did not treat citizens equally.

that the character with 'POTA' written on his back was a 'sadhu' and that therefore we are insulting Hindus. There was very weak resemblance (the person had a *choti* which has now been removed)."

The Prevention of Terrorism Act (POTA) is problematic legislation. It has been used since 2001 to detain and interrogate individuals to preempt terrorism on the basis of suspicion. The *choti* Dr. Khan referred to is the tuft of hair Hindu males retain from birth. Among religious leaders and priests, the tuft is more pronounced, so that when it is braided, it protrudes like a small ponytail. This *choti* has become graphic shorthand for depicting Hindus, particularly those with right-wing leanings. Although Khan did not send me the illustration at the time, I followed the *Milli Gazette* cartoons, and assumed it might be the one published in February 2004 (see Figure 9.2). The cartoon played with the image of the crucifixion. On the crosses were Muslim men, distinguishable by their knee-length lungis. Their crucifixion represented the violation of human rights and democracy. The arbitrary, preemptive, and tortuous nature of POTA trod a fine line between permissible acts for national security and the prohibitive infringement of human rights. The act was repealed in 2004. The *choti* would squarely place POTA as an act of Hindu violence. Erasing the *choti* rendered POTA as state legislation – democracy crucifying minorities.

9.3 Yusuf, "Republic Day." *Milli Gazette*. November 20, 2003. Courtesy of the *Milli Gazette*.

The breakdown of democracy in the name of religion was a recurring theme in *Milli Gazette* cartoons. The cartoons consistently questioned the distinction between "communalism" and "secularism" in India. Here Gandhi as the spokesperson for democracy was bruised and injured.

The *Milli Gazette* cartoons were pointed in their critique of right-wing Hindu politics. A close look at the cartoons presents a paradox: a tension between the Hindu right as a communal subject and the Muslim as a political subject. Along with the United States, the BJP and its Hindu political allies formed the crux of the cartoonist's visual commentary about democracy's breakdown. In the process, the Muslim political subject provides the true interpretation of democratic ideals. In a 2003 cartoon by Yusuf, a bruised and disabled Gandhi leads the train of floats in the Republic Day parade, featuring "communalism" and "secularism," each displaying the damage they have caused (see Figure 9.3). The "coffin scam" perched atop the communalism float refers to a notorious case of corruption that came to the fore in 2002, after the Kargil War erupted between India and Pakistan. Senior Indian Army officers manipulated the purchase of inferior aluminum coffins and body bags from a US vendor,

Victor Baiza. The controversy showed that war, and the death of a soldier, was an occasion for profit.

Portraying Hindus and Muslims is central to the visual vocabulary at play in Yusuf's cartoons. A "true history of communalism," the celebrated historian Shahid Amin writes, "sets out to unravel not just what happened between India's two, or three, or four communities, but also how these communities remember, understand, explain and recount pasts and presents to themselves" (2004, p. 93). Amin noted the persistence of nationalist billboards that reproduced stereotypes of the Muslim male through the beard and fez. Although such visual cues do not necessarily reflect social experience in India, they repeatedly conjure a public expectation for imagining the Muslim. The *Milli Gazette* cartoons, then, provide a forum for repeatedly mediating Hindu and Muslim stereotypes. The beard and the fez picture Muslim selves, while the Hindus are represented as sadhus, holding a trident, or with the *choti*. (The gendered identity is unproblematic.)

The discussion of offending cartoons in India is not limited to representations of Muslims. Dr. Khan's note reminded me of letters I had seen that criticized cartoons for infringing upon Hindu and Christian sensibilities. The *National Herald* cartoonist Bireshwar had filed such a letter in his personal archive; it was among the cartoons, drawings, paintings, and letters he showed me when I met him in Lucknow in 2003. The undated letter to the editor was from Mahavir Prasad, a *National Herald* reader in Lucknow. The complaint against a cartoon by Bireshwar that depicted Hanuman carrying Sanjivani Mountain through the air was not against picturing a deity but of misrepresenting him. Morphing the *Ramayana* episode into contemporary politics jarred Prasad's sense of his religious past and the political present:

The main cartoon appearing in the *Herald* of 2nd July '67 does not bring credit to the secular and catholic outlook professed by the *Herald*. Hanuman is a great national hero who believed in accomplishing a thing rather than boasting about it. We know that his bringing the Sanjivani mountain from the Himalayas to Lanka to save the lives of Ram and Lakshman was done by him silently at the behest of the chief Physician attached to the *Vanarsena*.

The analogy between this great episode in the Ramayana and the bombast made by a political party of today in the cartoon referred to above is not only inappropriate but indecorous as well. It is a pity that your editorial staff has either forgotten or ignored the fact that Hanuman or Mahavirji happens to be the National Hero of this country and a deity of special reverence to the citizens of Lucknow. It would be highly appreciated if such distasteful misrepresentation of our great heroes is not repeated in your esteemed newspaper.

I wondered why Bireshwar had retained Prasad's letter critical of his cartoon, bundled together with other letters that praised his cartoons.

When I tracked the cartoon in the archives, I saw that Bireshwar had caricatured a popular iconography of Hanuman. The reader's charge of misrepresentation left unstated what constituted representation. Could there be an acceptable cartoon of Hanuman? I had a partial response to this question when I visited cartoonist Narendra's office in the IIC in Bangalore. There R. K. Laxman's large autographed Ganesh caricature was hanging conspicuously on the wall. The Hindu deity Ganesh is worshiped to mark an auspicious beginning to any project. He is also the god of wisdom. It did not surprise me that the new institute had the Ganesh caricature in prominent view; that it was Laxman's work also contributed to its aura. Along with Shankar's adjoining portrait, the institute seemed blessed indeed (see Figure 7.8).

Christians have also taken offense at cartoons. In May 2004, the All India Catholic Union National vice-president, Dr. John Dayal, and Delhi archdiocese Media Commission's Father John Paul registered a complaint to *Hindustan Hindi*, the Hindi edition of *Hindustan Times*. The newspaper had published a computer-generated image of the Congress party president, the Italian-born Sonia Gandhi, as Mother Mary. The newly elected prime minister of India, whose candidacy Sonia Gandhi supported, was shown in her arms as infant Jesus.[17] As reported in the Indian edition of the online *Christian Today*, a global Christian news network, the complaint observed: "The Holy Mother has a special place in the hearts of every Catholic in the world. Together with the Child Jesus, the Icon of the Virgin Mary is revered and venerated across the globe, and especially by those seeking peace and healing." For protestors in Bihar and Jharkhand, the distortion of this visual and Christian sentiment signaled collusion with right-wing Hindutva politics. It was seen as part of the Hindutva propaganda against Sonia Gandhi as an Italian Catholic who would be controlling the Congress-led United Progressive Alliance government.[18]

For the British and for Muslims in colonial and postcolonial India, the matter of iconic representation had a history, which was being repeated. On August 18, 1925, the London *Star* published David Low's cartoon celebrating the famous British cricketer Jack Hobbs's 2,000th test cricket run. Cricket was a popular sport both in England and in India. Hobbs's feat would certainly have captivated fans in the empire. Cartoonist David Low celebrated the occasion with a cartoon titled "Relative Importance." As he recorded in his autobiography:

Jack Hobbs, the famous cricketer, had touched a high point of his career in equaling Grace's batting record. I celebrated the event in a cartoon entitled *relative importance* depicting Hobbs as one of a row of statues of mixed celebrities, in which his towering figure overshadowed Adam, Julius Caesar, Charlie Chaplin, Mahomet, Columbus and Lloyd George. It was a piece of mere facetiousness, meaning nothing, but since the public interest in Hobbs was strong the *Star* gave it an importance it did not deserve by printing it twice the usual size.

It brought a large number of letters, eulogizing and applauding, which surprised me, and an indignantly worded protest which surprised me even more from the Ahmadiyya Moslem Mission, which deeply resented Mahomet being represented as competing with Hobbs, even of his being represented at all. The editor expressed his regrets at the unintentional offence and regarded the whole thing as settled. But no. Two weeks later cables from India described a movement in Calcutta "exhorting Moslems to press for resolutions of protest against the Hobbs cartoon which shows a prophet among lesser celebrities. Meetings will be held in mosques."

An additional complication arose. Not only one prophet but two had been profaned because the Moslem reverence Adam also. Bitterness and fury were redoubled. To quote a Calcutta correspondent of the *Morning Post*: "The cartoon has committed a serious offence, which had it taken place in this country, would have led to bloodshed. What was obviously intended as a harmless joke had convulsed many Moslems to speechless rage ... An Urdu poster has been widely circulated throughout the city, calling upon Moslems to give unmistakable proof of their love of Islam by asking the Government of India to compel the British government to submit the editor of the newspaper in question to such an ear-twisting that it may be an object lesson to other newspapers. The posters have resulted in meetings, resolutions and prayers."

The British government was unresponsive, for we heard no more. It is not without a twinge of regret that I reflect upon the loss to history of a picturesque scene on Tower Hill, with plenty of troops, policeman and drums, on the occasion of my unfortunate editor having his ears twisted on my behalf. When I was talking with Mahatma Gandhi some years later, he deplored the dearth of cartoonists in his country and suggested that the well-known appreciation of satire possessed by Indians might make it a place for me to spend some time professionally. I refrained from comment. (Low 1957, pp. 122–4)

"The whole incident showed how easily a thoughtless cartoonist can get into trouble. I had never thought seriously about Mahomet. How foolish of me," commented Low (p. 124). Since his cartoons were reproduced in newspapers abroad, they reached a wide audience that included readers in colonial India. This wide circulation of Low's cartoons meant they were seen and interpreted by a variety of constituencies, many unanticipated by Low himself; however, this did not exempt him from accountability to those who were hurt by his cartoons. The response in India to Hobbs's celebratory cartoon took Low by surprise, and the vehement protest in Calcutta deeply affected him. When he met Gandhi in 1931, six years had lapsed since the provocative Hobbs cartoon. By then Low, who was fond of caricaturing Gandhi and was beginning to have a profound impact on a generation of Indian cartoonists such as Kutty, was beginnning to nurse doubts about India's sense of humor. But there were other doubts churning in Low's mind and heart. Some three-quarters of a century later, during the Danish cartoon protests, several news articles in India noted the precedent of Low's cartoon in the *Star* in 1925 but did not cite Low's reaction to the episode, namely, his deep regret. Low's acknowledgment of a lapse came with a final self-assessment that returns attention to the link between seeing and belief: "I was ashamed – not of drawing Mahomet in a cartoon, but drawing him in a silly cartoon."

What would have been a suitable cartoon worthy of Muhammad that could do Low proud? While Low berated himself over a careless cartoon, he missed recognition of the fact that the very act of caricature was offensive. If this wasn't already apparent to the British, it became so in 1966, when a British *Times* cartoon depicting the Prophet met with protests in the postcolonial nation states of India and Pakistan. The British government could not afford to be unresponsive this time.

Srinagar 1966: Common Market mountain and burning Wilson's effigy

On November 11, 1966, Muslim students in India and Pakistan burned an effigy of Prime Minister Harold Wilson. The protest was organized against the publication of a cartoon in the British newspaper, *The Times*, which depicted Wilson as the Prophet Muhammad. The Grand Mufti of Jammu and Kashmir, Mohammad Bashiruddin, warned the British government of grave consequences if such cartoons were repeated. "The cartoon depicted Wilson as Mohammed and President de Gaulle as a Common Market mountain, an allusion to the proverb 'If the mountain doesn't come to Mohammed, Mohammed must go to the mountain.'"[19] At the time of the cartoon's publication, Wilson was attempting to gain Britain a seat in the European Economic Community and its Common Market, which was instituted in Brussels in 1957. The French president, General Charles de Gaulle, had vetoed an earlier bid, and in preparation for another attempt in 1967, Wilson announced a visit to France. The proverb, which was the basis for the cartoon of those political times, is well entrenched in the English language. Despite its long history of use in England, when represented as a cartoon that could be published or circulated overseas, the proverbial use ignited opposition in the Indian subcontinent. In 1965, India and Pakistan had recently been bruised by the second war with each other since their independence. Protests against the cartoon took place in India, in Srinagar and in Pakistan, in Karachi and Dhaka (then called Dacca).[20] The British High Commission in Karachi issued an apology for the unintentional distress, and quickly pointed out that the impasse did not constitute a government matter. They offered an explanation that the Danish government, too, resorted to in the cartoon controversy forty years later: the concerned newspapers were independent entities and the government had no control over them. The press was free.

Hindu–Muslim riots and the Danish cartoons

In 2006, agitation over cartoons depicting Muhammad again became news headlines. On March 3, during demonstrations in Lucknow against the cartoons after Friday prayers, "Muslims forced shopkeepers to down their shutters. However, according to a Muslim source disturbances started when *Khatiks* [Hindu slaughterers] stoned Muslims protesting against Prophet's cartoons. Then firing started from both sides in which 4 persons were killed. Majority of those injured were Muslims. In retaliation Muslims stoned many vehicles and damaged them and set fire to effigies of Bush."[21] Although the Danish cartoons were the critical context for the episode, the twists and turns of the violence confound attempts at reducing the conflict to a difference in visual interpretation. Why did the Danish cartoons morph into a communal issue and a public critique of US President George Bush?

Dr. Ashgar Ali Engineer, the chairman of the Center for the Study of Society and Secularism in Mumbai, is among those who have consistently examined Hindu–Muslim relations in India. As part of his series of annual surveys tracking communal violence, in 2006 Engineer noted that although there were relatively few episodes that year, there were some riots involving Hindus and Muslims. This should not come as a surprise: communal riots are endemic to contemporary Indian politics. Some of the skirmishes Engineer listed touched on the Danish cartoons. There is much written on why Hindu–Muslim riots happen in India. On the basis of several decades of research in Aligarh and adjoining cities in north India, Paul Brass pinned his explanation on "institutionalization of the riot system": "a system that can be activated when the time is ripe and that involves the utilization of a coherent repertoire of routine actions" (Brass 2004, p. 4848). This would suggest that no matter what the issue, a "riot system" consisting of political interests is set in motion to produce communal violence in India. The Danish cartoons, then, would be reworked in the Indian context to become a communal issue – they would become a prism through which Hindu–Muslim relations would, once again, be refracted to reproduce violence and a history of violence.

The politics in the street were one dimension of how the cartoon controversy was visible in India; the other came in forums such as the AIMMM's *Milli Gazette*. Reports in this paper showed, to draw upon Brass's analysis, the West's institutionalization of the clash-of-civilizations system.

Why the double standards?

In the pages of the *Milli Gazette*, scholars and specialists commented widely on the cartoon controversy. Dr. Mozzamel Haque, a contributor to the publication, wrote:

The cartoon images published in the Danish national newspaper, the right-of-centre, *Jyllands-Posten*, on 30 September, 2005, depicting the Prophet Muhammad (peace be upon him) with a bomb on his turban with a lit fuse is insulting, provocative and deeply offensive to Muslims. According to the Hadith, the sayings of the prophet, all depictions of Muhammad (pbuh), however complimentary, are idolatrous. As such, the image of the Prophet (pbuh) cannot be depicted.[22]

Noting the failure of Denmark's Prime Minister to accept an opportunity for discussion with a contingent of ambassadors from eleven Muslim countries, Dr. Haque further observed, "On 20 December, 2005, twenty-two former Danish ambassadors sent an open letter to the Prime Minister criticizing his decision not to open a dialogue with the international representatives." Dr. Haque reported that established public scholars and luminaries in Britain whom he interviewed, such as Lord Patel, Zia Sardar, Dr. Tariq Ramadan, and Lord Nazir, among others, converged in their objection to the cartoons and the Danish government's response. They also unequivocally supported freedom with responsibility, the call for a common humanity, and perceived the republication of the cartoons in seven newspapers in Germany, Italy, France, Spain, Belgium, and the Netherlands a deliberate act to inflame passions. The concluding pieces of advice Dr. Haque offered also emerged from these interviews: First, non-Muslims should know that there was no benefit to reap by denigrating the Prophet Mohammed. Second, Muslim scholars should take the lead in articulating a peaceful protest.

In the *Milli Gazette* columns, the incisive comments on the intent and context of the cartoons did not necessarily overlap in their emphasis. There was considerable recognition by those opposing the cartoons that a violent response would only reproduce existing beliefs and stereotypes about Muslims.[23] This estimate about the damaging effect of violence and of street politics on Islam's public image compels a look at petition as politics in which passions are inscribed in words and rational text. This diversion of protest from the street to the theater of debate disempowers some, while empowering others. At the core of this difference sits the ability to speak to the West in rational Western terms, and to learn the Western language of argumentation and refutation.[24] Deliberation compelled the West to acknowledge the futility of insisting on freedom of speech without responsibility. The Vatican, the United States, and Britain, among others that constitute the West, distanced themselves from the cartoons. They may have feared reprisals caricaturing their own gods and other subjects dear to their political identity. When the Iranian president announced an exhibition of cartoons on the Holocaust, it was one way of forcing the West not only to acknowledge the limits of freedom to caricature but also to produce an argument that could contradict their reaction to the Danish cartoons. Though this proposed exhibition made many shrink from their call for freedom, thoughtful comments in *Milli Gazette* did not celebrate caricature of the Holocaust; to form effective resistance, mimicry should be strategic. The editor of *Oudh Akhbar* demonstrated this principle in the early twentieth-century *Punch* vernacular newspapers (see Chapter 1).[25]

There were several stories afloat about the Danish cartoon controversy. Each place on the world map could tell the story from its own perspective, centering it on their local history. In this reconstruction, conspiracy theories, history, memory, half-truths, facts, and gossip are fictive kin that converge to knit a web of tales. There were many offensive pasts to visit. Saba Mahmood points out that "descriptions of events deemed extremist or politically dangerous are often not only reductive of the events they purport to describe, but, more importantly, are premised on normative conceptions of the subject, law and language that need to be urgently rethought if one is to get beyond the current secular-religious impasse" (Mahmood 2009, p. 838). To grasp the complexity of the simultaneous responses to the cartoons across the globe, it became fashionable to chart the anatomy of the controversy through a timeline or a map. This technique of representing a world event was also a way of displaying the interconnectedness of the movement across the world. It was a world story in which happenings in every locale, if tracked, were a part of the big picture. An imagined Muslim world made it compelling to connect every protest to a logical and larger global plot. The conspiracy about the West generated another about Islam's vast brotherhood that became transparent through reactions to the Danish cartoons.

To reflect on the Danish cartoon controversy in India as a type of response – "condemnation," in Ion's words, and not violence – reproduces an imagined India that is moderate and skilled in the theater of debate. Readings of any social text, the anthropologist Talal Asad reminds us, "inevitably reproduce aspects of ourselves" (Asad 1990, p. 240). India's "bad reputation of zealously guarding 'religious freedom,'" to return to Ion's words from an interview, is a story about minding your own democracy and secularism. Secularism, as a constituent of India's modernity, is "one of the terms through which the conflicts of the world are enacted" (Jakobsen and Pellegrini 2008, p. 3).

In 1988, the celebrated author Salman Rushdie challenged Indian Prime Minister Rajiv Gandhi, to learn how a free society should behave. Rushdie proclaimed that Indian democracy was becoming a laughing stock. The occasion for this advice was India's decision to ban Rushdie's book *The Satanic Verses*, the first country to do so. He addressed the Prime Minister in an open letter:

On Wednesday 5th of October, the Indian Finance Ministry announced the banning of my novel, "The Satanic Verses," under Section 11 of the Indian Customs Act.

A further official statement was brought to my notice. This explained that "The Satanic Verses" had been banned as a pre-emptive measure. Certain passages had been identified as susceptible to distortion and misuse, presumably by unscrupulous religious fanatics and such. The banning order had been issued to prevent this misuse. Apparently, my book is not deemed blasphemous or objectionable in itself, but is being proscribed for, so to speak, its own good!

This really is astounding. It is as though, having identified an innocent person as a likely target for assault by muggers or rapists, you were to put that person in jail for protection. This is no way, Mr. Gandhi, for a free society to behave.

Clearly, your Government is feeling a little ashamed of itself and, sir, it has much to be ashamed about. It is not for nothing that just about every leading Indian newspaper and magazine has deplored the ban as, for example, "a Philistine decision" (the *Hindu*) or "thought control" (*Indian Express*).

The right to freedom of expression is at the foundation of any democratic society, and at present, all over the world, Indian democracy is becoming something of a laughing stock.[26]

When Rushdie's book was burned in Bradford, England, a place with a significant South Asian Muslim community, such symbolic acts transformed prose into more than a text attuned for reading; the book became a material accouterment and a display for politics. In fact, one did not even need to read the text. Protests and book burning compelled the debate to shift to contemporary politics and to the politics of writing. In hiding for nearly two decades, Rushdie and others, too, were drastically affected by the reaction to *The Satanic Verses*. Before Rushdie was "released" from the fatwa in 1998, Hitoshi Igarashi, an assistant professor, who translated the book, was found slain in his Tsukuba University campus in the northeast of Tokyo.[27]

As I ruminated about a similar letter from *Jyllands Posten* to current Prime Minister Manmohan Singh, I wondered if indeed, as Rushdie predicted, Indian democracy had become a laughing stock? The several interpretations of *The Satanic Verses* made it obvious that a text could be seen in more than one way. Rushdie's book remains banned in India to this day. Invited to participate in a literary festival in January 2012, in Jaipur, India, which featured leading authors and poets, Rushdie changed plans and declined to attend due to death threats, prompting his peers to read from *The Satanic Verses*. On learning that video footage of the readings was available, the Jaipur police swung into action, demanding the recorded video tapes.[28]

In India, religion and politics both hold measures of the modern and the democratic experience, and feelings of hurt open a space for contemplating secular and modern selves. To exhaust the complexity of this democratic experience by measuring it with a ban on a book or a cartoon and to reduce it to the presence or absence of freedom is a futile exercise. Ways of seeing and their politics are critical for the public reproduction of the self. For example, Diamond Comics, India's largest producer of comic books, was, at the time of writing this book, embroiled in controversy over including sketches of the Prophet in its seventy-eighth weekly Hindi issue of *Comic World*. The episode was widely discussed on the Internet by various Muslim organizations and publications such as Sunni News, Rabita Islamic News Agency, and the *Milli Gazette*.[29] A report against the publisher was registered in New Delhi's Jamia Nagar Police Station. The proprietor, Gulshan Rai, apologized for the mistake and copies of the issue were withdrawn from stands. Meanwhile, in a write-up about the issue, the Delhi-based Urdu newspaper the *Hindustan Express* "inadvertently" published the images in question from Diamond Comics. Sultan Shahin, editor of *New Age Islam*, is puzzled by the dual standard: "None of the *ulema* have, however, condemned this Muslim newspaper for publishing the Prophet's images, even if it did that as an example, for which they are after the Hindu publisher's blood. Several have said that had this happened in a Muslim-majority country the publisher would have been by now killed."[30] The *Hindustan Express* had company when it "inadvertently" published the images. In *Milli Gazette*, Ghitreef Shahbaz pondered the same issue: "The flip side of this story is that the Urdu daily *Hamara Samaj* also reproduced the above sketch in its issue of 25 April, then it came with a lame excuse next day, but there was no reaction from the community against this paper at all. The question is: Why this double standard?"[31]

When postcolonial states opt to ban cartoons, they foreclose the opportunity to engage in a debate about the cartoon's meaning. They truly mimic the colonial state in pulling down the shutters on a cartoon that confuses. Meaning-making is precluded; the presumption of a volatile riot plays no small part in this decision. But beyond the ban, politics concerning cartoons continue to happen in India. Cartoons are surreptitiously reproduced, debated, protested. The public excitement over the Danish cartoon case rendered everyone an expert. It led to what Kath Weston notes, in another context, as an occasion for "street theorizing" (1995, p. 348). Such subjectivity, the cartoon controversy showed, could barely be accommodated in neat identities of the secular and the modern. Rather than emphasizing only the plural ways of being Muslim, it was also necessary to question the urge to insist on Islam's universality.

To understand the experience of the secular and the modern is to acknowledge its strategic placement in the contemporary world. Cartoons become politicized because as social texts they "intervene in political confrontations already in place" (Asad 1990, p. 242). But their generative capacity rests not only in ruffling existing politics but also in remaking connections to the past in order to forge a possible future. Despite our beliefs and political allegiances, many of us in India have, Ashish Nandy accurately observes, "come to gods and goddesses through politics, mainly through the politics of knowledge and democratic participation" (Nandy 2002b, p. 154). That holds true for the United States and other places, too. Cartoonist Kaak's pithy comment when I met him several years ago, in 2003, has now gained new meaning for me: "All our gods and goddesses are cartoons."

Conclusions: timeless myths and timely knowledge

Cartoons in India have a long history, and they have attained a wide circulation through their publication in newspapers. Since 1854, with the publication of the vernacular comic newspapers *Hindi Punch, Oudh Punch,* and *Hindu Punch,* among several others, the political cartoon has become integral to India's newspaper culture and remains a source for everyday political commentary. Thousands of newspaper cartoons circulate every day in India, and many more have left their imprint since colonial times. This vast assortment of visual material addresses Indian newspaper readers with diverse linguistic and regional attachments. In the words of cartoonist Kutty, who was among my interlocutors when researching this book, the life of a cartoon is like that of a firefly, and its hurt should feel as sweet as the lingering pain from the scratches of a lover's sharp fingernails. This short life span and lingering sweet pain metaphorically convey the enduring significance of daily cartoons punctuating India's past and present.

Caricaturing Culture in India presents life stories of cartoonists, newspaper cartoons, public perception of cartoons, and debates about their meaning as news and as a form of art in order to shed light on the making of a modern profession, illuminate colonial and democratic politics, spotlight the role of cartoons in political mobilization, and explore the meaning visual media hold for the Indian public. In highlighting cartoons as a distinct category both of news and art, this multi-sited research demonstrates how and why a socially peripheral form becomes symbolically central to colonial and contemporary politics. Beginning with colonial times, cartoons have informed political knowledge, on the one hand, and have generated cartoon talk about the way people interpret visual media and experience politics, on the other.

The overarching goal of this book, to use newspaper cartoons as a way of exploring and understanding history and culture, can be situated in the overlap of anthropologies of media (specifically news) and modern politics. While much attention has been paid to using photography, cinema, journalism, and television to examine postcolonial cultures and politics, very little has been done in the way of looking at newspaper cartoons from this perspective. New media technologies have provided a context for scripting the relationship between images, reception, and cultural production. However, the long history of cartoons and their continuing significance in our own times also emphasize the need to attend to persistent technologies and their role in shaping modern politics. This book weaves together a historical anthropological narrative on several different levels. First, it provides a reading of Indian history from deep in the colonial period up to the present; second, it is a history of cartooning in India; next, it traces my journey as a historian and anthropologist to research cartoons and cartooning in India; fourth, it is a narrative of the experience of fieldwork among cartoonists in India (and some who are abroad); and finally, it is a presentation of and commentary on a number of cartoons from colonial and contemporary contexts.

Two earlier studies of India's comic tradition, on which this work builds, were driven by the presence of laughter. In his study of India's comic traditions, Lee Siegel, a professor of religion, was seized by Buddha's question: "How can anyone laugh, who knows of old age, disease and death?" (1987). Anthropologist Susan Seizer was moved by her own alienation from the laughter she saw unfold during theatrical performances of the special drama *Atipiti*, in the southern state of Tamil Nadu. As an outsider, Seizer's puzzle begins with her inability to share the audience's sense of humor (2005). The question before her is: "How does the Tamil audience watch *Atipiti*, and why do they find it funny?"

In an illuminating combination of Sanskrit texts and an ethnographic study, Lee Siegel presents two types of laughter according to Indian literary theorists: "laughter that arises from perceptions of ludicrous incongruities and improprieties, from laughter's own determinants [*atmastha*]," and the other laughter, which "has as its only determinant the laughter of others [*parastha*]."[1] These two types are comparable, according to Siegel, to the Western categories of humor and satire. Humor sees from a distance, while satire is vigilant (1987, pp. 50–1). India has a long tradition of humor. The cartoonists I met during my long research years, however, did not evoke any Indian humor traditions to explain either their preferences or cartoon history. Only Kutty asserted a precolonial history to Indian cartoons, while others connected them to British influences through *Punch*, David Low, and Vicky. These different trajectories emerged from contrasting interpretations of the cartoon form. Madhukar Upadhyay, who edited a book of cartoons against communalism (1994), traced Indian cartoons to mythology and not history:

There is a character in Sanskrit, called Ashtavakra. He is deformed from eight sides, he never talks anything right, does everything wrong; he is a comic character ... All these Gods – Goddesses are also a manifestation. If you look at Ganesh, there is nothing you cannot laugh at. He is neither a human being nor an animal ... Cartooning as history, cartooning as an art form in India may be new, but in tradition is very old.[2]

For younger cartoonists, the vanishing point of India's cartooning aesthetics and history was closer, and they named as models those currently prominent, such as R. K. Laxman, who was familiar to all newspaper readers, and Kanjilal, who was familiar to Hindi newspaper readers. Such constructions of history and memory about cartoons give one pause about declaring and defining an "Indian" cartoon tradition.

Complementing Siegel's observations, Seizer notes laughter's "conventionality and ubiquity," suggesting that the audience's critical eye allows it to judge "within a shared context of known styles" (2005, p. 268). The portability of cartoons, their reproduction and circulation beyond temporal, political, and linguistic boundaries accords them an expansive level of accessibility that is unmatched by any other cultural form. With this accessibility, however, cartoons also encounter confrontation by unexpected readers, who might not share their style of aesthetics and humor. The visual inscription of humor renders it flexible and a revocable palimpsest of politics. In 2012, the debate in the Indian Parliament against the publication in a school text book of Shankar's 1949 cartoon of the Dalit leader and architect of India's constitution, Dr. Ambedkar, is one notable moment when a cartoon became a point of convergence, simultaneously local and global, contemporary and historical.

Liberal subjects in a cartoonscape

Newspaper cartoons provoke laughter, forging a community of shared humor; but they also generate a counter-community that questions laughter and expresses hurt. Cartoons in India show that readers of the same time may well differ in their interpretations. These readings may reflect the readers' new identities as secular and liberal citizens in a changing social context. From the vantage point of India's cartoonscape, traversing colonial times, national times, and global times dispels notions of a collective public humor, and instead demonstrates a fragmented public. These fragments of humor sensibilities emerge from particular ideological positions that bring to the surface the everyday manifestation of social inequities. In the process, newspaper cartoons are treated not as illustrated news but as an interpretative space that invites the public and public intellectuals such as Mahatma Gandhi, feminist advocates, newspaper editors, and Dalit activists to assert the politics of humor. Letters to editors, debates in the Press Council of India (PCI), and controversy around the

Danish cartoons show that religion is not always a counterpoint to modernity, but can play a variety of tactical roles in India's political experience.

The history of newspaper cartoons in India offers a peek into the emergence of a visual and humor sensibility that is tied to modern identity. Focusing on the entwining of cartoons as news and art, this book theorizes modernity as a tactical and sensory experience interlinked with visuality, political agency, and the competing aesthetics of humor. As a form that caused the colonial state anxiety, for example, and that provoked colonial proprietors' concerns about the potential effect on women and children (Chapter 1), newspaper cartoons provide a context illuminating the politics of humor and the ambivalence that accompanies our own visuality. Since cartoons' meanings are not mediated by art critics, they invite claims to specialist knowledge, the performance of expertise through social and political experience. The cartoonists' daily lampooning of Indian society and politics thus evokes pleasure and pain – and critique.

When I browsed cartoon archives, I was struck by both the humor and the aesthetic dilemmas cartoons generated. This dissonance prompted me to consider the fragmented public that read the cartoon, defying explanation of a shared sensibility between cartoonist and audience. Indian colonial and postcolonial democratic contexts serve time and again as vantage points to analyze an empire of cartoons that has tested senses of humor, to discern the limits of political and expressive freedom. In our own times, complaints registered and adjudicated by the PCI show that humor's luck often ran out in India, because in the postcolonial context the refusal to laugh is part of a demand for modern rights within the framework of liberal politics. The story of newspaper cartoons in India thus deepens our understanding of why cartoons matter and how they can make some laugh and wound others.[3] Cartoons provoke emotions, and through them modernity is thus seen as not solely about material accouterments and pleasure. Modernity is also about sensory experiences in which feelings could hurt and laughter can alienate.

The history of newspaper cartooning in India reveals the liberal subject conceptualized in relation to a key register: a sense of humor. Although the claim for generativity can be made for any form of public text, the cartoon's absent discourse, its in-between form as journalism and art, and India's postcolonial political context make the cartoon a point of access to debate, subvert, and reinstate particular notions of liberalism. In *The Ritual Process*, Victor Turner offers the term "power of the weak" to discuss how "communitas emerges from its small enclaves into public space when structures begin to break down in periods of major socioeconomic change." Identifying such a period as this as "liminal," signaling the potential for transformation, he points out that during the metaphorically liminal process of revolution, peasants appropriate images and accord them new meanings. Turner calls this an effect of "insurgent nationalism," a concept that partially illuminates the distinct politics that cartoons generate (Turner 1978, pp. 288–9). According to Michael Warner, this process fosters a counter-public that can be seen as emergent communitas in public space. Warner frames a counter-public as a public that "maintains at some level, conscious or not, an awareness of its subordinate status. The cultural horizon against which it marks itself off is not just a general or wider public but a dominant one" (2002, p. 119). The debates in the PCI provide a glimmer of this cultural horizon and begin to mark a dominant liberal public that is not attuned to the "symbolic violence of humor."

India's postcolonial context suggests an alternate formulation to Benedict Anderson's observation that "cartoons created collective consciences by people without access to bureaucratized or other institutionalized forms of political control" (1978, p. 292). In postcolonial India, the tension between liberalism and a discourse of cultural rights has surfaced as a national debate on several occasions (Bhargava 1990). The outcry over Salman Rushdie's novel *The Satanic Verses*, for example, and the opposition to the Danish cartoons – these protests about texts, representations, and cultural rights were staged in the street.[4] Unlike these incidents, the petitions discussed in Chapter 8 materialize within the precincts of the PCI. In postcolonial India, public access to the PCI is key to understanding the interpretative processes through which cartoons connect liberal politics and visual aesthetics. This makes the PCI one site for locating the particular "effective histories" of modernity in different institutional sites (Chatterjee 2008, p. 324). In this institutional space, modernity is articulated through the question: who is a liberal subject in modern India? These debates are not transformative as far as policy or constitutional amendments are concerned; instead, they are about the scale and nature of power and resistance that is "in between" (Fox and Starn 1997).

As reflective and productive of a shared imagination in India, the newspaper cartoons do not neatly approximate Anderson's projection of an "imagined community" through print culture (1983). The deliberations in the PCI and the editorial pages of the newspapers map the restless tension between liberalism and cultural rights; and religion is a key register for cultural rights. The complaints, petitions, and protests against cartoons of religious figures have significant implications for rethinking existing scholarship on visuality and religious experience in India and elsewhere. In India's context, for example, the concept of *darsan*[5] (Eck 1998) illuminates the link between "divine seeing" and the aesthetics in the images of Hindu gods and goddesses. If caricature exaggerates, then how does the viewer of a caricature experience divine seeing, that is, recognize the presence of the deity and therefore experience hurt? For, in fact, caricature continues to lead to recognition. Given the long history of caricatures of Hindu gods and goddesses, why does a reader object to the caricature of the Hindu god Ram? How can we understand similar objections by minority readers in India to caricatures of the Buddha, the Prophet, and Jesus Christ? These questions generated by cartoon conflicts thus offer a prehistory and advance ongoing scholarly investigations of the commodification of religious images and the political impact of media in re-presenting religious figures.[6] These new darshans invite us to rethink visuality and religious experience.

Cartoons and complaints of offense generate searching queries about how to interpret the cartoon's unique visual form. The blurry boundary between offense and humor is at the heart of such cartoons. How we respond to a cartoon tells us and others who we are. But if we take measured steps, we will know our "categories" for situating others and the need in ourselves to accommodate several shades of modernity. The cartoon's interpretative dilemmas show the tactical and tactile ways in which we consistently caricature difference to claim a modern self. Accounting for these moments illuminates a new context for situating newspaper cartoons and picturing news; it also alerts us to the nebulous path these cartoons weave. The visual complexity of the cartoon perceived in its lines, caricature, and anchoring text takes on a political form when vocalized and discussed. Such graphic news provokes us to awaken a suppressed politics. On learning of the widespread struggle over the cartoons' meanings, readers might come away feeling less modern and less liberal. Bringing these generative moments to think about representation, senses of humor, and modernity signals what caricature and anthropology strive to achieve even as they are grounded in a particular historical and regional context: making the familiar unfamiliar and the unfamiliar familiar.

Creative confrontations

I have often been asked if I supported the PCI's mission, including their adjudication of complaints against newspaper cartoons. Editors and petitioners hold divergent views of the PCI, and there has been a decline in its authority among the Indian press. Editor Mehta's rejection of the PCI's decision and dismissing the ruling as "preposterous" marks this trend (Chapter 8). In recent years, other mainstream newspaper editors, like Mehta, have begun to scorn the PCI and ignore its summons. The power of the PCI is limited to issuing warnings and asking editors to publish an apology. But since it is constituted of members of the press for the purpose of press self-discipline, ignoring the rulings of the PCI strikes at the roots of the logic of self-regulation. This challenge to the PCI marks fractures within the Indian press. More importantly, it signals a new ethos for the press in India, in which the norms of good taste in cartoons and humor – sensitivity to gender and caste identity – are considered illogical and not grounds to test liberal politics. In contrast to this trend, I was amazed that the prominent *Times of India* editor Girilal Jain had visited the PCI to defend his newspaper's cartoon about the Indian Peace Keeping Force (Chapter 8). In pressing a face-to-face encounter to debate cartoons, the PCI in this case enabled a confrontation in which the hegemonic and counter-hegemonic politics of taste came into conflict and were managed through debate. Thwarting this process by ignoring the PCI's summons and strategically delaying the proceedings is a missed opportunity for public engagement and representation on the part of editors.

The PCI is a remarkable public space to debate how and why the press and aesthetic sensibilities such as humor and its peripheral visual component – the cartoon – are about Indian democracy. Although internally there is a push within the PCI to grow more teeth and encompass other media such as the Internet, the PCI's strength lies in its mandate to scold and not censor. These public confrontations depict the bureaucratization of protest and a critique of liberalism that is shaped by India's history and politics. Such bureaucratization reveals the creative ways in which the form and content of the cartoon are cast as "cheap" (street), "average" (liberal), and "ultra-liberal" (sophisticated)" to make sense of the aesthetic sensibility of humor, contemporary politics, and identity. The class dimensions of this aesthetic judgment are oblique and negotiable. While reasserting and reshaping the belief in PCI's yardstick of "good taste" and liberal politics, petitioners stake claims to cultural meaning and participate in the hegemonic processes of fostering an aesthetic sensibility. The liberal attitude that newspaper editors claim would appear to hold that speech in cartoons is not attributable to the author of the cartoon as agent but merely stands as the representation of a stereotyped social position with regard to the topic at hand. This position on humor, in turn, presupposes shared positions on the stereotype being represented. On the other hand, the arguments made by the Dalit petition writer against the *Pioneer* cartoon (see Chapter 8) point precisely to the limits of this presupposition. Confronted by such petitions, the PCI is compelled to deliberate the social role of cartoons, namely, does the newspaper cartoon represent a social reality? Is it factual, as all news should be, or does the visual component and humor remove it from the category of news? Does representation normalize historical inequities?

But cartoons bring a twist to this negotiation. The petitions about liberalism, gender, and Dalit politics are also about the unique interpretative demands the PCI places with regard to cartoons: cartoon aesthetics demand a more liberal attitude. Disclosing its expectations of a relatively liberal attitude to cartoons, the PCI offers insight into the problematic of liberalism – it is a sensibility that is relational to the text. Yet when this more liberal attitude bumps up against representations of caste that are not in tune with a framework of equal rights, then the PCI rewrites its prescription for ways of seeing cartoons and perceiving liberalism.

I have drawn upon these conclusions to respond to another question that is often asked – would I support the ban on the Danish cartoons and the Indian government's censorship of select newspaper cartoons in the NCERT Political Science textbook? My reply is that petitions and protests about newspaper cartoons emerge from specific ideological positions that open a window into deeply cherished convictions about modern and liberal selves as well as the free press. As a historian and anthropologist of visual culture, I hold that these engagements also tell us much about the power of images. Newspaper cartoons are incomparable public texts that evoke a rich interpretative vocabulary that no other image can match. Those demanding an explanation – an apology – for laughter when seeing cartoons that poke fun at religion, gender, and caste, as well as other forms of social identity, can be seen as resolute believers in liberal ideals. Those who opt to laugh and dismiss such protestations are hardly dismissive of liberal ideals; through laughter they acknowledge the contradictions inherent in liberalism. The cartoon row, now popularly know as the Ambedkar cartoon issue, was not merely about the place of cartoons in a democracy; it was about the use of images in the pedagogical context of a prescribed political science textbook. In South Asia, history textbooks are a delicate subject that raise important questions about the authority of historians as activists and the narrative that counts as history.[7] Specifically in India's context, textbooks are rich contexts for controversy that have until now raised concerns about their "saffronization" (glorifying of Hinduism as pan-Indian and reproducing Hindutva ideology) – this (re) writing of the history of India has stirred passions in both India and in the USA.[8] The decision by the NCERT textbook advisors to include select cartoons, the politicians' protest and demand for excising an "offensive" cartoon, and the ensuing debate among academics on the controversy published in a newspaper – itself becoming part of the emerging public narrative on cartoons – are all claims on adjudication of meaning. Such claims made on the basis of expert knowledge or on the merit of popular mandate by electoral representation, betrayed inattention to a central concern: how did the teachers and students use these cartoons? In a conversation with a NCERT official, I was reminded of this omission and we wondered what might have been if the issue was discussed in the classroom, with teachers and their students. As I visited the NCERT bookstore, to purchase a copy of the textbook, the storekeeper informed me that all old copies were recalled and new pages pasted in lieu of the censored cartoon pages. The cartoon controversy is known to all, and as one young student in my neighborhood in India told me with a puzzled look, "We loved these cartoons; they made the class such fun." "Some politicans thought the questions and exercises around the cartoons were leading students to an incorrect conclusion," I said. "We actually did not do all those exercise and questions about the cartoons, we just saw them while reading the chapter," said the student, "and anyway, we see cartoons in newspapers every day." In this remark I heard a student claim the ability to engage with cartoons. Indeed, this conversation should not be seen as epitomizing how the cartoons were used in all classrooms, but a vote from teachers and students and their voices would certainly inform experts and politicians alike.

Timeless myths or a dying language?

To look at newspaper cartoons is to explore a visual form that is not circumscribed by journalistic and artistic standards. To become a professional cartoonist does not require a particular degree, though several Indian cartoonists I met since 2002, when I began research for this book, have been art school graduates. Cartoonists in India are ethnographers, historians, and artists – they represent people and places. In employing characters and symbols to plot their narratives, they caricature culture and produce knowledge. The play of recognition and misrecognition is key to these crafts. The immersion of cartoonists Kutty in Bengali culture (Chapter 4) and Samuel in lower middle-class culture (Chapter 7) resonated with anthropological motivations to participate and observe. Approaching Laxman's and Maya Kamath's newspaper cartoons as ethnographic material connects grim representations and fictions of developmental narratives (Chapters 5 and 6). India's developmental paradox elicits both silence and observation. Furthermore, India has a growing newspaper readership, and newspapers in India are among the "most important mechanism in public culture for the circulation of discourses on corruption."[9] This observation is perhaps especially true for newspaper cartoons in India, which are positioned as a perspective of the Common Man or Woman on political happenings. This approach acknowledges the intellectual role of cartoonists, makes the cartoonists collaborators rather than "informants," and opens a dialogue about modes of representation.[10] As a form of incisive news, political cartoons effectively reveal the futility of the binary – anthropologists and informants.

When readers from another era view a political cartoon rendered decades earlier, the underlying humor is usually a difficult code to crack. Its topicality and timeliness render the cartoon ephemeral, transforming it quickly into a historical document and, if it still resonates, timely knowledge becomes timeless myth. The durability of myths lies in their ability to give form to deeply held convictions about the world. Cartoon myths tell much about the history of ethnographic forms of knowledge and the persistence of "epistemological anarchy" (Cohn 1980, pp. 220–1). This anarchy grows from ignorance of the constructed nature and temporality of knowledge. Cartoons' symbolic repertoire thrives from the confounding persistence of recognition that coexists with a consciousness of knowledge as a construction.

Far removed from a changing India, the newspapers of contemporary British cartoonists portray India as a tiger, the snake charmer, a bed of nails, and the rope leading up to nowhere. In these cartoons, India, it seems, has barely changed since *Punch* days. British cartoonist Nicholas Garland frequently uses the tiger with its stripes spelling out "India" (see Figure Conclusion). His long career and many India cartoons are a window to the changing landscape of British caricaturing India. Even with their persistent use of tiger stripes, for example, cartoonists such as Garland recognize the gap between representation and reality, and the past and the present: "India is modern," Garland says, "but it is easily recognized through the figure of the tiger."[11] The imagery acts as a bridge for the reader. For Western cartoonists, this recognition also brings a sense of loss. The old symbols have lost their communicative edge: "The symbolic language of cartoons has become less useful as the world is homogenized today. It is difficult to use these symbols because they look patronizing and people now don't think with those symbols," observed Garland.[12] For him, such a mismatch between old symbolic shorthand and new readers points to a different time, and also a language that is dying. Remembering John Tenniel's famous cartoon on the 1857 Indian Mutiny, Garland noted, "Nowadays even English people don't think about lions [as a symbol of Britain]" (see Figure I.1). This diminishing relevance and symbolic alienation is complemented by a growing similarity: "Chances are if you see an image of a powerful and successful Indian, he'll look like a European. He would look like us and we look like them." Why, then, are the India images – tiger, snake charmer, bed of nails – so durable for British cartoonists today?

Garland seemed to find my question amusing. "Right till I visited, British people tended to think of India as exotic – about its history, culture, and wildlife. In the last ten years, India has seemed like a modern nuclear-armed country. This may seem strange to you but it takes a while to percolate the popular mind." It takes a while to percolate the academic mind, too. To ask why cartoonists work with particular timeless symbols in order to make meaning of places and people is to question why anthropologists work with timeless concepts. Now it was my turn to be amused and embarrassed. Anthropologists defer to another bridging logic. They evoke the "ethnographic present," a concept to caution readers that the story they write about culture is temporal; it is in the past tense because culture changes with time, it is always to be understood with its history. Pointing to the complex relationship among stereotype, perception, and the popular mind, Garland's comment reminded me that the "gatekeeping" imagination, through a pool of concepts and images, is as much a part of his vocation as mine. The anthropologist Arjun Appadurai has drawn attention to the impact of this gatekeeping:

The fact is that the anthropology of complex civilizations does exist, but in a peculiar form. In this form, a few simple theoretical handles become metonyms and surrogates for the civilization or society as a whole: hierarchy in India, honor-and-shame in the circum-Mediterranean, filial piety in China are all examples of what one might call gatekeeping concepts in anthropological theory, concepts, that is, that seem to limit anthropological theorizing about the place in question, and that define the quintessential and dominant questions of interest in the region. (Appadurai 1986, p. 357)

An increasing sensitivity to these processes has also led to a "crisis in representation," which begs the question of whether forms of representation such as history, anthropology, and cartooning are dying (Said 1989, p. 205). The lingering force of cartoon's symbols to generate meaning about nations and people illuminates the processes that shape anthropological theorizing. Just as Garland used the tiger and elephant to represent India, "a foreign country that meant that country," so also the concept of hierarchy and the social units of caste and the village have long formulated anthropological knowledge about India. The symbolic repertoire notwithstanding, among anthropologists and cartoonists there is no longer an assumed expectation to produce an island of quaint natives. "Natives" are everywhere. There are local idioms and sensibilities, and beyond it are people conversant with the rest of the world. Turning to cartoonists, anthropologists and historians can take some assurance that caricature also plays a vital role in informing.

Conclusion: Nicholas Garland. "Puss, Puss, Puss." *Daily Telegraph*. 1997. London. Courtesy of the *Daily Telegraph*.

During the Queen's tour of India, a series of petty protocol disputes – such as the exclusion from the state banquet at the eleventh hour of every British diplomat except the High Commissioner – suggested that the bilateral mood remains sour. The situation is a source of considerable embarrassment for Robin Cook who has been accused in India, and at home, of mishandling British policy on Kashmir.[13]

In some of his cartoons, Garland continues a long tradition, dating back to *Punch*, of depicting India as a tiger with its stripes spelling "India." Usually, the "India" stripes are across the tiger's body.

Notes

1. This term is drawn from Goldstein 2003.
2. See Pillai 1937, Ahmed 1951, Varma 2005, Laxman 1967, Samuel 1971, Ramamurthy 1975, Miranda and Narayan 1980, Abraham 1988, Kaak 1989, Kalra 1993, Lahiri 1994, Upadhyay 1994, Ranga 2002, Vijayan 2002, and Kamath 2005, among several other titles.
3. http://rni.nic.in/.
4. http://articles.economictimes.indiatimes.com/2012–01–02/news/ 30587531_1_newspaper-circulation-rni-language. The Fifteenth Census of India in 2011 recorded a literacy of 74.04 percent. This figure does not translate as the number of newspaper readers because literacy is defined as the ability to read and write in any language for anyone above the age of seven. Thus literacy records rudimentary knowledge and not formal education. www.census2011.co.in/literacy.php.
5. http://gombricharchive.files.wordpress.com/2011/05/showdoc85.pdf.
6. A grandson, Arthur Conan Doyle, authored the mysteries of Sherlock Holmes.
7. Fredeman 1983 discusses the neglected images of Queen Victoria in *Punch*.
8. Occasionally, newspaper sources have been modified slightly to ensure grammatical consistency. This is especially the case with online sources that might not be currently available. Interview transcriptions have all been edited.
9. See *American Review of Reviews* 47 (January–June 1913): 351 for Carruther Gould's caricatures of Lord Morley, including one of him as a snake charmer. Some cartoonists use pen names not connected to their official names; others are publicly known only by either their first or last names. In this book the pen names are used, with the official name in parentheses on first mention. At selected places, to remind readers, I repeat the pen name and official name in parentheses.
10. In a fascinating article, Kirin Narayan (1993) traces this trope to the colonial administrator Jonathan Duncan's "An Account of Two Fakers with Their Portraits," which was published in *Asiatick Researches* (1798).
11. I discuss this in Khanduri 2009b.
12. *Svang* can be translated as farce and theater, too, but here the reference to mimicry and farce makes it an appropriate translation.
13. An asterisk before a name indicates that it a pseudonym.
14. Johannes Fabian offers the concept "schizogenic use of time" to reflect the ethnographic denial that anthropologists and the people they study share

"coevalness" (2001, p. 21). Commonalities of time and culture are glossed over in the creation of the "other" whom one seeks to understand and explain. My fieldwork experience here points to the inescapable charge of schizogenic time even for the cautious anthropologist – whether "native" or "real outsider." Kirin Narayan's term "halfies" offered a way of rethinking the presumed difference between the two. Narayan holds that each anthropologist is defined "in terms of shifting identifications amid a field of interpenetrating communities and power relations" (1989, p. 671). This would entail a consideration of the "quality of relations with the people we seek to represent" (p. 672). Thus anthropologist and subject of study both participate in the creation of the "other." Lila Abu-Lughod offered a trenchant critique of anthropologists' role in producing the "other" through the concept of culture: "Culture is the essential tool for making other. As a professional discourse that elaborates on the meaning of culture in order to account for, explain, and understand cultural difference, anthropology also helps construct, produce, and maintain it" (1991, p. 143). Despite this critique, it needs to be acknowledged that, quite aside from anthropological inquiry, people claim "culture" to describe their choices and lives. "Culture" is a freely used word in India to differentiate why people do the things they do.

15. The intersection of history and anthropology has been at the center of much academic debate. There have been several junctures of disciplinary overlap, including an acknowledgment of the ways in which the postcolonial societies are shaped by a public persistence of history.

16. Interview, December 3, 2003.

17. Manjula Padmanabhan, interview with M. N. Krishnaswamy, 2004.

18. Elizabeth Bird explains the fact that anthropological studies of journalism are overdue as the result of a shyness to engage practitioners whose goals anthropologist share, namely, "describing and understanding reality" (2010b, p. 4). There is also a risk because anthropologists have "not taken well to being studied by journalists" (p. 5).

19. Of these, only Jackson has a book-length ethnography on the subject (2013; this book was in production when Jackson's book was published). Lewinson builds on Ulf Hannerz's argument for regions in a city where "cultural process is somehow intensified" (Hannerz 1994, p. 182).

20. This is not to claim that newspaper photographs cannot be appropriated. Indeed, a simple change of caption recasts photographs.

21. Singh 1992, p. 2.

22. See Sarah Pink 2001 and Banks and Ruby 2011 for an overview of visual anthropology.

23. Mathur 2000, p. 89.

24. See *New York Times*, January 4, 1968, July 30, 1968, and February 11, 1967. An advertisement for the Lawrence Lariar and Ben Roth volume of the *Best Cartoons from Abroad: 1955* in the *New York Times* that promised cartoons at which "all America was laughing," included the popular Indian cartoon weekly, *Shankar's Weekly* in its list of sources. With its inclusion in this "hit parade of international humor," *Shankar's Weekly* continued a history of accessible English-language colonial cartoon publications, becoming the

acknowledged form of Indian cartoons and humor, and political assessment. See *New York Times*, October 8, 1961.

25. I haven't discussed Thanu's cartoons. Thanu (1921–2007) retired from cartooning in the 1970s and gained fame as the pioneer of correspondence education and his institution Brilliant Tutorials.

26. For Kutty see June 5, 1960; for Laxman September 11, 1960, October 7, 1986; for Thanu in the *Indian Express*, September 25, 1960, November 5, 1961; for Samuel May 20, 1962; for Sudhir Dar, April 27, 1974.

27. Recent examples include "Cartoon Pranaam [Salutations]: A Tribute to Cartoonist Kutty" at cartoonpranam.blogspot.com, which hosts a long list of cartoonists and their contact details. See also Cartoonist Pavan's Facebook page at https://www.facebook.com/Pawantoon and Devendra Sharma's web-page at www.cartoonistdevendra.com/devendra-sharma.php.

28. This lacuna was addressed by Elizabeth Edwards's pioneering attention to the role of photographs in the production of ethnographic knowledge and its impact on anthropology (1994).

29. On the anthropology of senses, see Stoller 1989, Ong 1991, Stoler and Strassler 2000 and Desjarlais 2003. On the anthropology of media, see Mitchell 2003 and Pink 2005.

30. This engagement with media can be traced to a longer history of anthropology's interest in symbols and art for understanding the context of non-verbal communication. See Boas 1955, Turner and Turner 1995, and Price and Price 1999.

31. De Certeau 1984 notes, "To a rationalized, expansionist and at the same time centralized, clamorous, and spectacular production corresponds *another* production called 'consumption.' The latter is devious, it is dispersed, but it insinuates itself everywhere, silently and almost invisibly, because it does not manifest itself through its own products, but rather through its *ways of using* the products imposed by a dominant economic order" (pp. xii–xiii).

32. Appadurai 1996, p. 90.

33. Joshi 2002, pp. 30–1.

34. Talcherkar 1902, p. 1.

35. Talcherkar 1902, p. 1.

36. Kindle Locations 290–1.

37. See Pinney and Peterson 2003 for an exciting collection of articles that present the "history of photography laterally" (2).

38. Here I differ from Jennifer Jackson's observation about literacy and cartoons in Madagascar (2008). In her insightful reading of verbal political rhetoric – *Kabary* and the counter-visual rhetoric of cartoons – Jackson writes, "Often, it is only through this gathering of voices reciting the news and reciting interpretations of it – tying the wisdom of yesterday and yesteryear's news interpretations with today's – that many are able to know the subject of news they otherwise cannot read" (2008, p. 17). I was unable to reference Jackson's recent ethnography as my book was already in production.

39. Downe's essay provides an excellent assessment of humor and the anthropological context.

40. Although mapping liberalism shows the "divergent trajectories of non-Western modernities" (Naregal 2001, p. 3), liberalism itself, as well as its role in the making of modern subjects in India, remains a subject of debate (Goswami 2004 and Robb 2007).

41. This requires a turn to strictures placed on speech, appropriation of other avenues of creativity, and an assessment of degrees of freedom. See Visweswaran 1994, p. 30.

42. Edwards points out that the rawness of photographs' histories are due to their being "unprocessed" and "painful." They are open to a multiplicity of meanings, and their "truth-telling" and "performance of histories" can be painful (pp. 5–6). In his remarkable study of Indian photographs, Christopher Pinney (1997) highlights the absence of narrative that makes definite meanings particularly elusive.

43. The gendered dimension of professional cartooning is not unique to India; it may not be incorrect to claim universality for this aspect of the vocation.

44. Butalia 1993.

45. Bhura 2002.

46. The NCF proposed five guiding principles for curriculum development: (1) connecting knowledge to life outside the school; (2) ensuring that learning shifts away from rote methods; (3) enriching the curriculum so that it goes beyond textbooks; (4) making examinations more flexible and integrating them with classroom life; and (5) nurturing an overriding identity informed by caring concerns within the democratic polity of the country. NCF Report.

47. www.thehindu.com/news/national/scholars-quit-textbook-body-as-government-bans-1949-cartoon/article3409271.ece.

48. In *Shankar's Weekly*, May 23, 1954.

49. *Hindu*, April 2, 2012, www.thehindu.com/news/national/cartoon-issue-was-first-raised-by-rpi/article3273838.ece.

50. Aarti Dhar 2012, "Govt. to Probe Role of NCERT Officials in Cartoon Row," in www.thehindu.com/news/national/government-to-probe-role-of-ncert-officials/article3418734.ece. *Hindu*, May 15, 2012.

51. This debate was published in the *Hindu* and triggered as a response to economist Prabhat Patnaik's article, "Parliament's Say Extends to the Classroom," in www.thehindu.com/opinion/lead/article3443080.ece. May 22, 2012. For Bhattacharya, see "A Disquieting Polemic Against Academic Autonomy," in www.thehindu.com/opinion/op-ed/article3466557.ece. May 29, 2012. For Bilgrami, see "Academic Autonomy Not a Separation from People" in www.thehindu.com/opinion/op-ed/academic-autonomy-not-a-separation-from-people/article3487174.ece?ref=relatedNews. June 4, 2012. Historians Janaki Nair and Shahid Amin were among those who commented on this issue.

52. www.utexas.edu/news/2012/03/28/daily_texan_cartoon/.

53. Later in the online conversation, I noticed that Laurence did answer his/her own question: "After checking my dictionary, the term "colored was adopted in the US by emancipated slaves as a term of racial pride after the end of the Civil war. This controversy serves as a springboard to discuss terminology, learn history, and remain socially sensitive."

54. Punch-inspired cartoon magazines emerged worldwide. However, the *Hindi Punch* is a relatively early publication when compared to publications in Asia, for example, the *Shanghai Punch* (1918) in China. See Hung 1994, p. 29.

I UPSTART PUNCHES: WHY IS IMPERTINENCE ALWAYS IN THE VERNACULAR?

1. Interview, November 17, 2003. Ghaziabad,
2. Within Lucknow, the *Oudh Punch* had rivals like the weekly *Sir Punch – Hind*, which in December 1877 had a circulation of 150 copies (*Selections from the Vernacular Newspapers* [hereafter abbreviated as *Selections*], April 7, 1878, p. 33). Two new comic papers that started publication in 1878 added to the competition: these were the *Akhbaron ka Qiblagah*, that is, the father/patron of newspapers, at Lahore; the other was a supplement to the *Akhbari Tamannai* of Lucknow. *Akhbari* had a circulation of 112 copies and was published by Puran Chand. The *Qiblagah* had not yet turned in a circulation figure and was published by Fateh-ud-Din. Both were Urdu weeklies. *Selections*, April 7, 1878, p. 651.
3. Cartoonist R. K. Laxman (b.1924) wrote a brief history of cartooning in India in which he points to the *Hindi Punch* cartoons as a vintage form. The British *Punch* (1841–2002) and the cartoonist David Low (1891–1963) were consistently evoked as significant models for cartooning in India.
4. There is a substantial body of anthropological literature that focuses on biography through the lens of history and memory. For a recent contribution to the diverse forms of narrating biography in India, in which anthropologists emphasized that the term "life story" better captured the nuances of remembering, see Arnold and Blackburn 2004. The distinction in life history and life story is discussed in Peacock and Holland 1993.
5. In his path-breaking analysis from a subaltern perspective, Amin 1995 positions the "event" to analyze nationalist amnesia. My focus here is less shaped by the framework of nationalism, though given the colonial context it is a subtext in analysis.
6. See, for example, Jeffords and Rabinovitz 1994 on the economic boost enjoyed by Ted Turner's Cable News Network (CNN) when they hiked their advertising rates in the face of an increasing number of subscribers.
7. Dickens 1862, p. 463 (July 26).
8. Dickens 1862, pp. 463–4.
9. Dickens 1862, p. 462.
10. Raven-Hill 1903, p. 434.
11. In a long article for the popular *Pall Mall* (1903), Sir Francis C. Burnand, *Punch* editor from 1880 to 1906, narrated the story of the magazine's precursors and competitors in Britain. Leading the pack was *Diogenese* (1853) with its "unblushing imitation" of *Punch* cartoons.
12. Bernard Partridge's Colonia was introduced to appeal to the Indian market: "We should endevour each week to introduce something into the paper which might interest our Colonial bretheren; and it was really with this idea in view

that we introduced at the end of the year a charming Cartoon by Bernard Partridge, in which Britannia is shown dancing with Colonia."

13. Khanduri 2009b.
14. Low 1942, p. 41.
15. "The Baboos Progress," in the *Indian Charivari*, August 3, 1877.
16. "Saheb Babu" in *Hindu Punch*, June 16, 1927.
17. Scholars have noted that prior to the emergence of newspapers in colonial India, that is, in the 1820s, there existed a vibrant system of communication (Minault 2005). Thus while print media can be seen in relation to an emerging public sphere, as a part of a network of political information it was preceded by other ways in which the colony was accessing and engaging with the British print media and articulating its politics (Bayly 1999).
18. Among studies that have looked at the relation of print culture and the public sphere in India are Jeffrey 2000, Dalmia 2001, Naregal 2001, and Orsini 2002. The authors draw on Habermas's concept of the public sphere but also point to the distinct character of the vernacular public sphere. For Orsini, Habermas's concept is attractive since it was the European and in particular the English public sphere that Hindi and other Indian intellectuals had in mind while evolving their own vision. Additionally, the difference between the Hindi and English public spheres establishes the specificity of the European (English) case. Orsini offers a model for a three-layered – public, private, and customary – sphere as demarcating the social experience of Hindi readers (Orsini 2002, pp. 9, 15). For Jeffrey, the third phase of Habermas's public sphere, massification, implies that readers had no agency. Jeffrey argues that, in the context of the print media revolution in India, this does not hold true (Jeffrey 2000, pp. 12–13).
19. For example, in its early years the Hindi periodical *Kavivachansudha* carried a column entitled "Punch ka Parpanch," the tangles of gossip-mongering Punch. The most usual form of the column consisted of a dialogue, prompted by the discussions of the day between Punch and one or two characters about town (Dalmia 2001, pp. 252–3). Vasudha Dalmia points out that the *Punch* skits are not part of the *Granthavali*, the collected works of (Bharatendu) Harishchandra, the editor of *Kavivachansudha*. This omission suggests an ambivalence regarding the position of satirical forms as an acceptable literary form. Colonial records show the satirical mode also posed questions about its validity as journalistic content and form.
20. *Selections*, 1879, p. 283.
21. The Hindi-speaking area extended from the princely states of Rajputana (present Rajasthan) in the west to Bihar in the east, and from Punjab and Garhwal in the north to the Central Provinces and Berar in the south. The North West Provinces of Agra and Oudh (later renamed the United Provinces of Agra and Oudh), and especially the cities of Allahabad and Banaras, were at the center of the "Hindi heartland." The English-educated, bilingual middle class of Calcutta had no real equivalent in north India, where local traditions of learning remained strong among educated families, both Muslim and Hindu. Over this wide geographical area, the public use of Hindi was unevenly distributed; see Orsini 2002, p. 2.

22. See *Selections*, 1910, p. 4. The weekly edition had a circulation of 400 copies. The *Kannauj Punch*, an Urdu weekly edited by Abdur Rahim Khan, had a circulation of 500 copies; the *Rafiq Punch*, an Urdu weekly from Moradabad edited by Mahmud ul-Hasan, had a circulation of 450 copies; and *Etawah Punch*, too, was a registered newspaper but circulation figures were not noted. The *Sar Punch* from Shahjahanpur, an Urdu daily published by Saiyid Zehur Ahmad, had a circulation of 400 copies in 1914. See *Selections*, 1914.

23. The Urdu newspapers of the region with higher circulation were *Sadiq-ul Akhbar* from Bhawalpur, which in December 1877 registered 699 copies, and *Oudh Akhbar* from Lucknow, which in January 1878 registered 700 copies. Of these registered copies, several were subscribed by various government offices (*Selections*, 1878, pp. 32, 318).

24. The surveillance of comic newspapers was as much about content as it was about individuals and their community affiliations. For example, Somalal Mangaldas Shah, the editor and proprietor of the *Gujarati Punch*, was identified as a "Hindu Mesri Bania" and "thirty-five years old." Such caste and professional details attest to the colonial state's consistent profiling of social and political agents, especially journalists. The *Gujarati Punch* was an Anglo-Gujarati weekly with a circulation of 3,400 copies and published in Ahmedabad. The newspaper contained tracts of local news, public topics, and was moderate in tone and locally influential. *Gup Shup* was a Gujarati comic journal published from Bombay with a circulation of 1,400 copies. It was owned and edited by Shavaksha Jehangir B. Marzban, "a Parsi aged twenty-five." The *Hindi Punch* was an Anglo-Gujarati comic weekly published from Bombay and had a circulation of 800 copies. Its proprietor and editor Burjorji Nowroji Apakhtyar was fifty-two years old. *Hindi Punch* was an organ of Sir Phirozshah Mehta and of the Congress moderates. It was also a municipal critic. In addition to these large-circulation papers, the *Rewari Punch* from Rewari, Gurgaon, was a comic supplement of *Sadiq-ul-Akhbar* with a circulation of 300 copies fortnightly. The proprietor was Saiyid Maqbul Husain Sadiq, the son of Saiyid Motbil Husain, a resident of Rewari. Formerly a *hakim* (doctor), he was at the time a petty contractor in Bakanir state, where his father was a "camel sawar." He was a man of "very ordinary education." The editor was Saiyid Safdar Husain of Husainpur Konal, Gurgaon. *Selections*, 1879, pp. 732–3, 913. Bania refers to the community also known as Marwaris, who historically engage in trade and commerce. Mesri was a Bania subcaste (Singh 1998).

25. 1994, p. 158.

26. *Bombay Gazette*, January 5, 1909.

27. The *Indian People*, January 7, 1909.

28. The *Indian People*, January 7, 1909.

29. The *Indian People*, January 7, 1909. Here the allusion to class is to the refined execution of the cartoon and the sense of humor, rather than as denoting the class or elite status of readers.

30. The *Oriental Review*, January 20, 1909.

31. The *Indian Social Reformer*, January 10, 1909.

32. *Times of India*, February 17, 1909.

33. The *Oriental Review*, January 20, 1909.

34. *Hindu*, January 1, 1909. From Opinions of the Press on the Ninth Publication from the *Hindi Punch*.
35. *Bombay Gazette*, January 5, 1909.
36. *Madras Mail*, January 2, 1909.
37. January 17, 1909.
38. p. 260. In 1878 the Vernacular Press Act was passed to provide the colonial government with the power to seize printing machinery, issue search warrants, and enter premises without going to court. The act was repealed in 1882.
39. This opened the space to question the source of modernity: was it derivative or indigenous?
40. This is in contrast to Davis and Starn (1989, p. 5), "local memories are sources for writing the local histories ignored by historians of dynastic monarchy and the nation state; the private sphere and the practices of everyday life define and conserve alternatives to the official memory of public historiography." Also see White 1978.
41. Ernst Gombrich noted that the goal of the caricaturist was similar to that of the artist: "The caricaturist ... does not seek the perfect form but the perfect deformity, thus penetrating through the mere outward appearance to the inner being in all its littleness or ugliness" (Gombrich and Kris 1938).
42. *Hindi Punch*, January 13, 1927.

2 GANDHI AND THE SATYAGRAHA OF CARTOONS: CULTIVATING A TASTE

1. Gandhi 1993, p. 288
2. Gandhi 1993, p. 107.
3. Ethnography's emphasis on social relationships, Emma Tarlo contends, has marginalized attention to clothes. This is particularly evident for India: "The birth of fieldwork therefore coincided with the marginalization of dress in Indian anthropology" (1996, p. 4). Explaining the gap in meaning between Indians and the British, who emphasized the functional aspects of headdress, Bernard Cohn, drawing upon Lawrence Babb's work, pointed out that the symbolic charge in turbans and Indian headdress was associated with the cosmographical importance of sight for Hindus (Cohn 1996, pp. 160–1). Gandhi's recollections complicate this sensibility.
4. Gandhi 1993, p. 153.
5. Gandhi 1993, p. 154.
6. August 11, 1920. "The Doctrine of the Sword" in Mukherjee 1993, p. 98.
7. *Indian Opinion* was probably the first newspaper dealing with India-related politics in which cartoons were reviewed. It offers a unique opportunity to see a reverse process at work, in which "natives" interpret British cartoons. This reversal was occasioned by Gandhi's premise that his readers needed to acquire the skills and cultural capital to comprehend the politics of cartoons.
8. Sociologist Marie Gillespie introduced the comparable term "TV talk" to denote the integrative function of TV news among Punjabi youth in London. This concept shifts attention away from the text of TV programs to how viewers interpret and integrate by talking about the programs (1995, p. 58).

9. Mesthrie 2003.
10. Mesthrie notes that an important aspect of this quest for equality with the British was the emphasis on difference from Africans. Despite this separatist attitude and politics, *Indian Opinion* featured African grievances and concerns (Mesthrie 1997, p. 110).
11. For example, in its November 18, 1914, issue *Indian Opinion* reproduced four *Hindi Punch* cartoons entitled "India's Great Loyalty." For references to cartoons, see Gandhi 1960–94, vol. VII, p. 273; vol. IX, pp. 24, 37, 79; vol. XI, pp. 278, 447; vol. LXXXI, p. 39. For *Punch*, see vol. XI, p. 447. The cartoons of the *Hindi Punch* were reproduced in publications outside colonial India – for example, the *Review of Reviews* – and noticed by various newspaper editors.
12. *Indian Opinion*, December 28, 1907. Translated from the Gujarati in Gandhi 1960–94, vol. VII, p. 455. The "equivalents" received in response to Gandhi's invitation were also discussed the following year. See Gandhi 1960–94, vol. VIII, pp. 131–2.
13. Gandhi's public scheme for developing sensitivity to cartoons made it an early example of participatory cultures – a key concept in digital media culture scholars today. Following De Certeau's notion of poaching, Henry Jenkins introduced the concept "participatory culture" to mark readers and fans who used texts to create their own meanings and uses, and also establish a network (Jenkins 1992, p. 23).
14. *Indian Opinion*, April 2, 1910. Translated from Gujarati in Gandhi 1960–94, vol. X, pp. 202–3.
15. Gandhi 1960–94, vol. VIII, pp. 11–12. Translated from Gujarati from *Indian Opinion*, December 14, 1907.
16. Gandhi 1960–94, vol. IX, pp. 23, 25. Translated from Gujarati from *Indian Opinion*, July 29, 1908.
17. *Indian Opinion*, December 28, 1907. Translated from Gujarati in Gandhi 1960–94, vol. VII, pp. 460–1.
18. For example, in its November 18, 1914, issue *Indian Opinion* reproduced four *Hindi Punch* cartoons entitled "India's Great Loyalty,"
19. The *Transvaal Leader*, August 21, 1908, in Gandhi 1960–94, vol. VIII, p. 467.
20. *Indian Opinion*, January 11, 1908. Translated from Gujarati in Gandhi 1960–94, vol. VIII, p. 28.
21. *Indian Opinion*, February 8, 1908. Translated from Gujarati in Gandhi 1960–94, vol. VIII, p. 75.
22. Schoonraad and Schoonraad 1989, pp. 217–19.
23. December 3, 1913.
24. December 9, 1931.
25. I assume the cartoons were also translated into other languages.
26. The phrase "hidden transcript" is from Scott 1990.
27. These representations of Gandhi merit more attention than I can accord here.
28. I have discussed this in Gairola 1995, and Khanduri 2001 and 2012b.
29. Compare with Hansen's concept of "ethnic closure" in his ethnographic study of theater performances and radio shows of South African Indians and their self-deprecating humor (2005, p. 304).
30. Low 1935, p. 84.

31. His cartoons provided a template for several emerging cartoonists in India, and a few, such as the Mumbai cartoonist Dinanath Dayal (1916–71), adopted the goat.

32. Low also mentions this meeting briefly in *Ye Madde Designer* (1935).

33. For example, see this note on Gandhi entitled, "Interview to the Bombay Chronicle": "The interview which was drifting to grave political problems was at this stage enlivened by the appearance of Mr. Andrew in khadi shirt and dhoti with a copy of the latest London *Punch* in his hand. 'You are now immortalized, Mahatmaji, if you are not already so,' humorously remarked Mr. Andrews with a broad smile." Gandhi 1960–94, vol. XXVII, p. 122; from the *Bombay Chronicle*, March 27, 1924.

34. Writing from Allahabad in 1931, Nehru informed Bapu – his form of addressing Gandhi – that he had begun a regular subscription to the British *Punch*: "There was a lovely cartoon in *Punch* the other day about the 'Elusive Mahatma' – I wonder if you saw it. I was so taken by it that I forthwith subscribed to *Punch* as well as other English newspapers to read what they say about you." Letter to Mahatma Gandhi, September 17, 1931 (Nehru 1972, vol. V, pp. 42–3).

35. July 28, 1931.

36. Autobiography (Nehru 2004, p. 32).

37. The "Snake Charmer" cartoon appeared in the *Rand Daily Mail* on June 25, 1908. The *Indian Opinion* reproduced it with Gandhi's interpretation: "The *Rand Daily Mail* of the 25th has published a cartoon about the movement which we reproduce in the English section. General Smuts is shown as a snake charmer and the Indian community as a cobra. The caption in English under the drawing explains that the snake charmer is playing hard on his flute to charm the cobra. But the cobra remains undeceived." *Indian Opinion*, July 11, 1908.

38. *Harijan*, June 22, 1940, from Gandhi 1960–94, vol. LXXII, pp. 187–9.

39. In his biographical sketch of the Rev. Joseph J. Doke, who once served as the acting editor of *Indian Opinion*, Gandhi mentions Doke's support for the Indian political cause. Gandhi adds: "He was an artist of no mean order. Some of his paintings are worth treasuring. His irrepressible humor can be traced in many cartoons he drew for a New Zealand paper." From *Indian Opinion*, August 28, 1913. Translated from Gujarati in Gandhi 1960–94, vol. XIII, pp. 263–4. Similar references emerge repeatedly. For example, in a letter dated August 30, 1941, to his companion, personal physician, and fellow Congress activist, Sushila Nayyar, Gandhi enclosed a set of cartoons that he thought she might enjoy. See Gandhi 1960–94, vol. LXXXI, p. 39.

3 "DEAR SHANKAR . . . YOUR RIDICULE SHOULD NEVER BITE"

1. February 22, 1932; Nehru 1972, vol. V, pp. 360–1. The jail superintendent's permission to mail the magazine directly seemed to surprise Nehru, for he makes special note of it in his diary.

2. Letters to Indira Gandhi, June 11, 1939, and July 29, 1944; Nehru 1972, vol, X, p. 636, and vol. XIII, pp. 452–453. While imprisoned in 1944, Nehru

received *Life, Time, Foreign Affairs, Pacific Affairs, Asia, Readers Digest, New Republic,* and *Amerasia.* These were most likely subscriptions, though other newspapers and periodicals also reached him without subscription. Letter to Indira Gandhi, July 1, 1944; Nehru 1972, vol. XIII, pp. 440–1.

3. Letter dated March 31, 1937, in Gandhi 1960–94, vol. LXXI, p. 91. Gandhi was a prolific letter writer, sending notes with thoughts and comments on politics, morality, sexuality, and marriage, among a host of topics. A quick look at Gandhi's *Collected Works* reveals the breadth and volume of his writings. Anyone could write to Gandhi for advice. Under such circumstances, Gandhi was best served by the postcard.

4. Letter to Amrit Kaur, Gandhi 1960–94, vol. LXXI, p. 193.

5. In 1925, Naidu became the first Indian woman president of the Indian National Congress and she was a strong presence in the nationalist movement.

6. For a discussion of education and modernity in a contemporary context, see Liechty 2003.

7. See *Shankar's Weekly,* July 5, 1953, August 22, 1954, and Sepember 9, 1956.

8. September 28, 1939. Posted from Wardha, Gujarat, this letter is in the personal collection of the Shankar family.

9. Interview given by M. A. Jinnah to Beverley Nichols, December 18, 1943. In *Jinnah Papers,* vol. X (Jinnah 1993), p. 120.

10. M. K. Gandhi to M. A. Jinnah, July 17, 1944; *Jinnah Papers,* vol. X (Jinnah 1993), p. 575.

11. Interview given by M. A. Jinnah to Beverley Nichols, December 18, 1943. In *Jinnah Papers,* vol. X (Jinnah 1993), p. 123.

12. Patel 1972, January 2, 1947; Sardar Patel Papers, vol. IV, p. 1.

13. Patel 1972, March 16, 1947; Sardar Patel Papers, vol. IV, p. 13.

14. Patel 1972, March 22, 1947; Sardar Patel Papers, vol. IV, p. 17.

15. For an insightful reading of cartoons during the Partition, see Kamra 2003. Kamra points to the incommensurability of caricature during the Partition violence. This, Kamra contends, led editors to publish photographs instead of cartoons (p. 88). My findings complement this reading, leading to the broader question about the limits of representation in different media.

16. "Durga Das's arrival and the hiring of a number of reporters initiated such a change of culture within the *Hindustan Times.* This was not entirely to the liking of the tight-knit staff that had seen the paper through the 1930s and the turbulent early 1940s. In 1946, when Ramkrishna Dalmia, who had recently bought the *Times of India* in Bombay, wanted to start a newspaper on the same lines in Delhi, and decided to steal some of the *Hindustan Times's* best journalists, a large number, including Shankar the cartoonist, Krupanidhi its joint editor, and assistant editors Chalapathi Rau and Shamlal, left the paper to join the newly established *Indian News Chronicle.* With their departure a distinct phase in the development of the *Hindustan Times* came to an end and another began" (Jha and Das 2000, p. 37).

17. Cartoons were important for Durga Das's vision of journalism. In 1969 he instituted the Durga Ratan Award for excellence in journalism, partially modeled on the American Pulitzer award. Including investigative writing and reporting, the award named after him and his wife was also meant for

"the most outstanding portrayal of an event which attracted nationwide attention through pictorial reproduction or through a cartoon" (www.infa. in). Cartoonists Sudhir Dar and R. K. Laxman are among its awardees. A few years later, in 1974, Durga Das compiled a hefty selection of international cartoons on Gandhi that was published by the Navjivan Trust. A couple of decades later, in 2003, the former Prime Minister Atal Bihari Vajpayee released a commemorative postage stamp honoring Durga Das. This may come across as a belated gesture. Years earlier, such honor had already been bestowed on two cartoonists: Shankar and Laxman.

18. Soon after Shankar resigned from the *Hindustan Times*, he sought alternative positions such as editing a new newspaper for the industrialist Dalmia. This concerned Nehru. Writing to the *National Herald* editor Chalapathi Rau, Nehru shared his concern: "It would be a pity if Shankar tied himself again with some capitalistic concern or with irresponsible people like those who run the Free Press of Bombay." Letter to Chalapathi Rau, August 25, 1946; Nehru 1972, vol. XV, p. 587.

19. Guest book comment by K. Tyagrajan.

20. Writing about contemporary Japan, anthropologist Marilyn Ivy brings attention to the place of "tourism, folklore studies, education, mass media – and through everyday moments of national-cultural interpellation and identification" for the production of nostalgia as an "ambivalent longing" (1995, p. 10): "Thus the consuming and consumable pleasures of nostalgia as an ambivalent longing to erase the temporal distance between subject and object of desire, shot through with not only the impossibility but also the ultimate unwillingness to reinstate what was lost."

21. Rathan Kumar's comment in the Trivandrum, Kerala, guest book, n.d.

22. The disappointment at the end of publication of *Shankar's Weekly* was a reflection of unease about India's democratic status. The politician L. K. Advani, who was imprisoned at the time, noted in his diary that it was "a sad day for Indian journalism." "The *Shankar's Weekly*, the only cartoon weekly in the country, has decided to wind up. If Shankar and his journal are to be fitted into an ideological camp, it will be the same camp to which Indira Gandhi claims to belong. But even he feels so suffocated in the present atmosphere that he has chosen to fold his journal" (August 31, 1975). Along with Shankar, Durga Das too had suffered reversals and ceased his weekly, *States* (Advani 2002, pp. 39–41).

23. Trivandrum, Kerala, guest book, Shankar's Exhibition.

24. Annual Report of the Registrar of Newspapers in India, July 1–December 31, 1956, p. 72.

25. Annual Report of the Registrar of Newspapers in India, 1964, Part I, p. 127.

26. Annual Report of the Registrar of Newspapers in India, 1965, Part I, pp. 94–5.

27. Annual Report of the Registrar of Newspapers in India, 1967, Part I, p. 114.

28. Annual Report of the Registrar of Newspapers in India, 1965, Part I, pp. 94–5. "Big," "medium," and "small" signified the daily circulation of the newspapers. In recent years, "big" means more than 75,000 copies, "medium" more than 25,000 copies, and "small" less than 25,000. Both English- and Indian-language newspapers are counted among the "big" newspapers.

4 BECOMING A CARTOONIST: MR. KUTTY AND BIRESHWARJI

1. Langness and Frank 1981. See Chapter 1, particularly p. 24.
2. Behar and Gordon 1995, p. 7. I have in mind here the recent importance accorded to ethnographies by Zora Neale Hurston, B. J. Fernea, and others, as well as Catherine Lutz's analysis of the split in theory and description in the 'Gender of Theory' essay in this volume.
3. The conviction regarding an ethnographic writing style that would redeem anthropology of hegemonic forces and its own hegemonic force has led to experiments in narrative style that privilege the biographical, essay, and stories. See Abu-Lughod 1993, Behar 1993, and Visweswaran 1994.
4. I am drawing upon Johannes Fabian's observation that field notes are historiography (2001, p. 149).
5. Mali carved a niche for himself as the pioneering caricaturist in Tamil journalism. With the unparalleled success of the Tamil humor magazine *Ananda Vikatan*, which started publication in 1933, Mali's stature grew and he is counted among the best in the region (Muthiah 2003).
6. Literal translation: teacher student tradition; learning through apprenticeship. The student had a lifelong bond with the teacher. In this tradition the teacher was instructor, mentor, and spiritual guide to the student.
7. Davies and Ottoway 1987, p. xi.
8. Davies and Ottaway 1987, pp. 38–9.
9. Davies and Ottoway 1987.
10. Literally, the word translates as "noble company," but it is used colloquially for regular gatherings in temples or at home involving singing and readings in praise of God.
11. Both these magazines were exceptional in featuring cartoons on the cover and inside by the cartoonist Kevy, who also sent his work to *Shankar's Weekly*.
12. February 3, 1945, p. 3. The book was *9 Drawings by Vicky*.
13. Davies and Ottoway 1987, p. 123.
14. Bireshwar was critiquing a prominent cartoonist, so I decided to use a fictitious name to protect identity.
15. Roger Sanjek (1993) analyzes the modes in which the "native" point of view as informants and academics finds a space in US academia.
16. For example see Wolcott (2004, pp. 97–100) for the history of terms to identify the relationship between anthropology, ethnography, and biography. Such terms included "life history," "life story," "autoethnography," and "ethnographic autobiography."

5 VIRTUAL GURUS AND THE INDIAN PSYCHE: R. K. LAXMAN

1. Interview, October 26, 2003, Mumbai.
2. An asterisk before a name indicates that it is a pseudonym.
3. Sharad Pawar is a prominent politician of Maharashtra, who has served as the chief minister and in 2013 was India's minister of agriculture. Jayalalithaa is a major politician of Tamil Nadu.
4. The Mahotsav offers an example of a temporary event, an ephemeral field. Krista E. Paulsen discusses "temporary events" either as a "condensation of

existing cultural norms" or as "spaces where new elements of culture are introduced" (2009, p. 510).

5. Madhubani painting is also called Maithil painting. See Neel Rekha 2010 for an excellent historiography of Madhubani art.

6. Alf Hiltebeitel provides an in-depth study of Draupadi in *The Cult of Draupadi* (1988, 1991).

7. Interview, October 24, 2003, Mumbai.

8. In Bollywood films, the actors and actresses "lip sync" the songs, which are sung by singers such as Lata Mangeshkar and pre-recorded off screen. These singers are called "playback singers."

9. Interview, October 24, 2003.

10. Interview, October 28, 2003, Mumbai.

11. Interview, December 16, 2003, Mumbai.

12. Interview, July 28, 2009. Mumbai.

13. Marathi journals have a rich tradition of social cartoons. But *Marmik* was different. Sarvade, an engineer, is a freelance cartoonist who produces social cartoons for Marathi journals and newspapers. *Marmik* was not his cup of tea. But Sarvade was of the opinion that *Marmik* played a role in the region's cartooning: "It did encourage cartoonists in a limited way. It was politically biased but Bal Thackeray did create enthusiasm and inspire younger cartoonists to take up cartooning. But those who were inspired by him started copying him and it became an in-house cartoon magazine of the Shiv Sena."

14. Following Laxman, two cartoonists received similar honors from the postal department. Shankar's characters Bada Saab and Memsaab, and he himself, were the subject of one of a pair of cartoons issued to commemorate his life in 1991. Ranga's cartoon of Gandhi morphed as India was issued as a stamp in 1997 to celebrate 50 years of Indian independence.

15. Interview, November 17, 2003.

16. *Tatkal* means immediate or prompt. *Tatkal* tickets for trains can be purchased at a higher price without advance reservation.

17. I am drawing on Jack Katz's analysis of what makes crime news (1987, pp. 50, 60).

18. Also see Zinn 2005, p. 231.

19. zeenews.india.com/news/maharashtra/common-man-garlanded-in-pune-to-celebrate-hazare-s-success_698831.html.

20. india.blogs.nytimes.com/2013/01/30/a-conversation-with-sociologist-ashis-nandy/.

21. http://articles.economictimes.indiatimes.com/2003–08–14/news/27522141_1_import-duty-exemption-ferrari.

22. See Sissener (2001).

23. The other feature, according to Bannerjee, is to utilize surveys (p. 65).

24. Dr. A. P. J. Abdul Kalam was the most trusted Indian, as concluded by this *Reader's Digest* online survey. The results were publicized in February 2010; www.siasat.com/english/news/kalam-most-trusted-indian.

25. M. G. Ramachandran (MGR) (1917–87) was a popular Tamil film actor, producer, and director, before he became chief minister of Tamil Nadu for three terms before his death.

26. www.naachgaana.com/2008/02/06/its-nice-to-have-double-standards-r-k-laxman/.

27. Though this is not unique to Laxman. Cartoonist Ranga, who was well known for making two cartoons and caricatures, giving one to the individual pictured and keeping an autographed one himself, was described by L. K. Advani as "a very affectionate and warm-hearted friend" (2002, n.p.).

28. President's address at the inauguration of an exhibition of selected works of Shri R. K. Laxman, Jaipur. November 17, 2005, pib.nic.in/release/rel_print_page1.asp?relid=13381.

29. www.abdulkalam.com/kalam/jsp/display_content_front.jsp?menuid=28&menu name=Speeches%20/%20Lectures&linkid=68&linkname=Recent&content= 1819&columnno=0&starts=0&menu_image=-. In the case of Dr. A. P. J. Abdul Kalam, the chips fall differently because he is considered to be above petty politics. In the *Reader's Digest* poll that ranked Laxman among the top ten trustworthy Indians, former president Dr. Abdul Kalam ranked first – a rare feat for a politician.

30. Ashish Nandy makes a distinction in cartooning by contrasting Laxman and Vijayan, and Vijayan and Puri, and Vijayan, Puri, and Abu. Nandy holds that, unlike the public felicitation Laxman received, Vijayan's target would "slink away" (2002a, p. ix).

6 UNCOMMON WOMEN AND COMMON MEN: POCKET CARTOONS AND "SITUATED KNOWLEDGES"

1. Cartoonist, writer, and researcher Trina Robbins (2001) documented a century of women cartoonists. Her reflections on the industry's exclusions echoed the career experiences of the women cartoonists in India whom I interviewed. Samita Rathore made comic strips and was not considered a political cartoonist. Although Manjula too made comic strips and not political cartoons, she was widely recognized.

2. Adarsh Varma (2003, pp. 113–15). Editor Adarsh Varma's chance meetings with Dhir (Dhirendra Kumar), Iqbal, and Mita Roy gave them unexpected breaks, leading to their promising careers as cartoonists.

3. Varma 2003, p. 115.

4. See Padmanabhan 2005, pp. 2–3.

5. There is a large scholarly corpus that deals with this observation and seeks to recuperate women's presence in and contribution to history. In the Indian context, Chakravarti (1998), Minault (1998), Burton (2003), and Forbes (2005) are important examples.

6. Interview, October 24, 2003. Mumbai.

7. At the time of this book's production, Suki was relaunched in Padmanbahan's blog.

8. Interview, December 13, 2003. New Delhi.

9. Though I heard that some men also read *Sarita*.

10. SAHMAT is the Safdar Hashmi Memorial Trust named after Safdar Hashmi, a theater activist killed by the Congress party goons in 1987 while performing a street play in Ghaziabad. The organization spearheads activism against communal politics.

11. Interview, December 7, 2003. Ghaziabad.
12. Bhura 2002.
13. Interview, November 19, 2003. New Delhi.
14. *Deccan Herald*, June 23, 1995.
15. *Times of India*, March 31, 1987.
16. *Times of India*, May 11, 1987.
17. *Times of India*, May 11, 1987.
18. Denise Nuttall writes of "table dreams" that she and other students experienced when training with Ustad Allah Rakha Khan and Ustad Zakir Hussain (2007, p. 344).
19. For an excellent analysis, see Zamindar 2007.
20. Interview, December 9, 2003. New Delhi.
21. Bireshwar, who switched from the Hindi *Aj* to the English *National Herald*, did not use the term, though he told me English readers have a different sensibility. Bireshwar had seen and learned from both media, through his guru and through his editor Chalapathi Rau, as well as through Shankar.
22. www.unp.me/f98/funny-desi-cartoon-from-india-realy-funny-69734/.
23. http://forum.santabanta.com/showthread.htm?230153-Desi-Cartoons-depicting-quot-Today-s-India-quot.
24. Interview November 18, 2003. New Delhi.
25. Interview December 3, 2003. New Delhi.
26. The Hindi belt is a reference to the region in India where Hindi is known. It extends from east to west, including Rajasthan, Madhya Pradesh, Uttarkhand, and Bihar. Urdu, Garhwali, Kumaoni, and several regional dialects make this a linguistically rich region.
27. *Deccan Herald*, December 24, 2006. Air Deccan archives.
28. Interview, July 22, 2009. Bangalore.
29. This figure is based on available data by religion from the 2001 census; www.censusindia.gov.in/Census_Data_2001/India_at_glance/religion.aspx.
30. Chauhan 2006, p. 6.
31. Interview, July 16, 2009. Mumbai.

7 ARTOONS AND OUR TOONS: THE PROSE OF AN INDIAN ART

1. Ghosh and Suri 1997. www.outlookindia.com/article.aspx?204333.
2. Pramila Sharma's *Curzon Nama* (1999) presents *Hindi Punch* cartoons to tell the true story of Curzon in India. This is among the earliest research on the vernacular *Punch* versions in India that uses cartoons as historical evidence.
3. Morphy and Perkins 2007, p. 17. Among other themes, the anthropology of art has analyzed the imposition of Western categories for denoting primitivism in non-Western contexts (Price 2001), art objects' social agency (Gell 1998), and the making of high art when non-Western objects enter Western museums and auction houses as "art" (Myers 2002). Presenting a road map for the anthropology of art, Alfred Gell critiqued attention to art's aesthetic interiority and proposed its social relations aspect. This would mark the specific contribution of anthropology – seen as a social science and not one of the humanities – to the study of art. I am not making this distinction here. However, biography, aesthetic

judgment, techniques, artistic labor, and the cartoons' social lives in the news-paper pages, the Press Council of India, the archives, art galleries, and in the field are all part of the story about stories of cartooning from various vantage points.

4. The Art School in Madras in 1850, the Government School of Arts in Calcutta in 1854, the J. J. School of Art in Bombay in 1851, and the Mayo School of Art in Lahore became the centers for academic art training. The Delhi College of Art was instituted much later, in 1942.

5. Rajya Sabha or the Council of States is the upper house of the Indian Parliament. It consists of 250 members, of which 12 nominated members are chosen by the President of India for their contributions in the fields of art, literature, science, and social service. Source http://rsdebate.nic.in/.

6. rajyasabha.nic.in/rsnew/practice_procedure/book2.asp.

7. Abu worked with a major newspaper, the *Bombay Chronicle*, before joining *Shankar's Weekly*.

8. A year later, when I was in Ernakulum, Kerala, to meet cartoonists from *Shankar's Weekly* such as Kevy, BJ (B. J. Varma), Yesudasan, and several others, Abu's wife Psyche invited me to a memorial gathering that I could not attend.

9. It is helpful to remember that with India's independence in 1947, a multi-party democracy ensured a place for politics of all stripes to thrive. Beneath this theoretical possibility of electoral choices was a strong public attraction for what came to be known as the Nehru Dynasty. The Italian-born Sonia Gandhi, the current leader of the Congress Party, is Rajiv Gandhi's widow; she took hold of the party's reins after his assassination, although she was never prime minister. Aided by her son Rahul Gandhi, Sonia Gandhi and her supporters continue to stoke populist desire for their dynastic presence. Despite the dynastic stronghold, brief periods of tumultuous coalition govern-ments and regional politics have challenged Congress's authority; the J.P. movement did so just before the Emergency.

    After a wavering relationship with Mahatma Gandhi and with the Congress, in 1934 Jayaprakash Narayan (1902–79), popularly known as J. P., carved out a separate dissident wing that leaned to the Left – the Congress Socialist Party. Later in his life, he returned to embrace Gandhian philosophy. In 1974, lending his vision to the student-led movement against corruption in Bihar, J.P. charted a formidable opposition to Indira Gandhi. "I have given all my life, after finishing education, to the country and asked for nothing in return. So I shall be content to die a prisoner under your regime," he declared (Dandavate and Narayan 2002, p. 222).

10. Interview, November 9, 2003.

11. Interview, October 27, 2003, Mumbai.

12. Insiders too claim "Indian cartooning." For example, in a lengthy article about Indian cartoons, G. N. S. Raghavan notes the "unmistakable Indianness of the character and situations" depicted in Indian cartoons (1994, p. 169).

13. Interview, February 22, 2003, Kolkata and reading from Daw 1978, p. xii.

14. Interview, July 23, 2009, Bangalore.

15. In the context of multiple discourses, I find useful the term "discourse net-work" developed by F. A. Kitler: "Discourse networks do not disclose

preexisting or hidden truths. Rather, they articulate certain phenomena as natural or unproblematic targets or instruments of certain practices. Thus visualization, inscription, and articulation, in their contingent facticity and exteriority, are the only irreducible givens of discourse network analysis." See Tapper 1999, p. 6.

16. An asterisk before a name indicates a pseudonym.

8 CRAFTY PETITIONS AND STREET HUMOR

1. In his study of laughter in India, Lee Siegel (1987, p. 466) notes this comment in his meeting with Shankar.
2. Broadcasting started in India in 1927. Purnima Mankekar shows that, in 1984, with a shift from didactic to entertainment programs, television sought to foster "a pan-Indian national culture" (1999, p. 5).
3. Press Council of India: Norms of Journalistic Conduct (2010, p. 15).
4. Robin Jeffrey (2000, p. 188) points to the irony that marks this First Press Commission: "It brought with it a cynical irony. One of the members of the Commission was C. P. Ramaswamy Aiyar (1879–1966), who as a Dewan of Travencore had shut down *Malayala Manorama* in 1938."
5. This and the other quotes in this paragraph are from the PCI's homepage, http://presscouncil.nic.in/HOME.HTM.
6. Arvind Rajagopal observes for television that the affirmation of the Indian public as a single entity was "never before granted so much attention as in the wake of the Ramayan broadcasts" (2001, p. 151). However, as "caste assertions broke the Hindu vote apart," it generated a "split public."
7. The WAPC is among several other similar coalitions such as the Alliance of Independent Press Councils of Europe.
8. Professor Flint has a website that seems under construction and is available at: /www.davidflint.com.au/.
9. www.wapconline.org/lang_eng/aboutWAPC.asp.
10. www.aipce.net/aboutAipce/.
11. See the PCI website, http://presscouncil.nic.in/HOME.HTM.
12. There is extensive literature that has established this colonial attitude. Nevertheless, the anxiety over the Press Council of India morphing into a censorial body resurfaces repeatedly and is articulated and rationalized in the manifesto as it promises to guard against this very eventuality.
13. Voloshinov 1986. Benedict Anderson uses "direct speech" to discuss cartoons as "symbolic speech," which is more elusive for scholarly analysis because of the ambiguous relationship between "form and content" (1978, p. 285).
14. I take this from Voloshinov to mean speech within speech and at the same time speech about speech (1986, p. 115).
15. PCI *Annual Report* 11, 1989–90, pp. 93–9. This is an abstract of the report.
16. Due to legal concerns permission to use this image was not granted.
17. PCI *Review*, 19 (1), 1998, pp. 246–7. This is an abstract of the report
18. PCI *Review*, 19 (1), 1998, p. 247.
19. PCI *Annual Report* 15 (1), 1994, pp. 118–19. This is an abstract of the report.
20. PCI *Annual Report* 15 (1), 1994, pp. 118–19.

21. Here I am building on a reading of the Protection of Atrocities against Scheduled Castes and Scheduled Tribes Act of 1989 (PoA Act), in which Anupama Rao addresses how crime is compounded when it targets a minority subject in postcolonial India (2005).
22. PCI *Annual Report* 6, 1984, p. 106.
23. PCI *Annual Report* 11, 1989–90, pp. 134–5.
24. Focusing on Mock Spanish, Hill contends that a "white public space" permits whites linguistic heterogeneity and explicit disorder (1999, p. 684).

9 "ALL OUR GODS AND GODDESSES ARE CARTOONS"

1. http://articles.timesofindia.indiatimes.com/2010-09-09/europe/28266755_1_muslim-leader-angela-merkel-cartoons.
2. www.outlookindia.com/article.aspx?230133-2.
3. Puri 2006, www.outlookindia.com/article.aspx?230428.
4. www.outlookindia.com/article.aspx?230131-web.
5. www.expressindia.com/news/fullstory.php?newsid=63267.
6. www.expressindia.com/news/fullstory.php?newsid=63267.
7. www.milligazette.com/IndMusStat/2006a/995-aimmm-11feb06-resolu.htm. PBUH stands for Peace Be Upon Him.
8. For a complete list of meetings and the reconstituted NIC, see http://mha.nic.in/pdfs/NICmaterial020707.pdf.
9. The organization has a website, www.mushawarat.com/index.asp. Also see Engineer 1992, p. 1782.
10. www.mushawarat.com/index.asp.
11. Yusuf's identity was not disclosed to me by the newspaper editor.
12. In India's multi-party democracy, the CPI (M) is the Communist Party of India (Marxist) and the BSP is the Bahujan Samaj Party, a leading advocate of the Dalits.
13. Interview, July 13, 2009. New Delhi.
14. However, as Agrama points out, fatwa has been a part of the English vocabulary since the seventeenth century.
15. www.milligazette.com/Archives/15112002/1511200237.htm.
16. "Many thanks for your feedback. A cartoon is an exaggeration of an existing fact and it tries to jolt people to think about a problem. It is a fact that Muslim rulers and elite are subservient to the U.S. and many of them will soon overtly or covertly support the aggression against Iraq just as they are keeping mum about the Israeli gangsterism against the hapless Palestinians. The cartoon was drawn in this background by a simple Muslim who is unaware of the complicated world scene."
17. http://in.christiantoday.com/articles/indian-christians-protest-against-newspaper-cartoon-on-madonna-and-baby-jesus/12.htm.
18. Also see http://webcache.googleusercontent.com/search?q=cache:tCQhleEsXMgJ:www.eni.ch/articles/display.html%3F04-0326+sonia+gandhi+jesus+cartoon&cd=1&hl=en&ct=clnk&gl=us&source=www.google.com.
19. "Indian Moslems Burn Effigy of Wilson to Assail Cartoon," *New York Times*, November 11, 1966, p. 22.

20. Bangladesh became an independent nation in 1971.

21. Engineer 2007.

22. *Milli Gazette* online February 10, 2006. www.milligazette.com/dailyupdate/2006/20060210-cartoons-comments.htm.

23. This became poignantly clear with the chain of events following New York's Twin Towers crashes six years later, when al-Qaeda and Osama bin Laden became the public face of Islam's extremist politics, and quick reference points.

24. Such rhetorical and linguistic skill does not diminish violence. The persistence of violence in human lives – the making of terrorists, militants, and patriotic soldiers – constructs "bad" and "good" violence. The two categories of violence overlap with the opposing notions of passionate and reasonable violence. I have discussed this elsewhere in the context of Bazar prints and revolutionary violence (Khanduri 2001 and 2013).

25. Facebook's "Draw a Mohammad Day" in 2010 reproduced a visual duel on the subject. Believers and non-believers could only caricature. How could they draw what they had not seen?

26. www.nytimes.com/1988/10/19/opinion/india-bans-a-book-for-its-own-good.html?scp=2&sq=India%20bans%20salman%20rushdie&st=cse.

27. www.nytimes.com/books/99/04/18/specials/rushdie-translator.html.

28. www.ndtv.com/article/india/police-demand-tapes-of-reading-from-rushdies-satanic-verses-some-authors-leave-litfest-169277.

29. For example of a Sunni media site, see http://sunninews.wordpress.com/about/ An Islamic perspective is presented in Rabita Islamic News Agency, www.rina.in/.

30. http://urdutahzeeb.net/articles/blog1.php?p=9381&more=1&c=1&tb=1&pb=1.

31. www.milligazette.com/news/1297-blasphemous-sketches-condemned.

CONCLUSIONS: TIMELESS MYTHS AND TIMELY KNOWLEDGE

1. For Indian artists, especially in theater, the performance of human emotion (*bhava*) is codified in the Sanskrit text *Natyashastra* (*c.* second century CE). The eight primary emotions include love, humor, anger, compassion, heroism, wonder, disgust, and fear (Seizer 2005).

2. Poorva Khan 2006, p. 49.

3. Such deliberations sparked by reaction and "overreaction" occur elsewhere, too. The pages of campus newspapers in the United States and, on a much bigger scale, the Danish cartoon controversy offer a peek into these visual tricks.

4. Other provocations for protest include granting Taslima Nasreen asylum in India following a ban on her book *Lajja* (1993) in Bangladesh and the furor over artist M. F. Hussain's painting of the Hindu deity Durga, nude, portrayed as the nation, Bharat Mata (Mother India). Although the gendered portrayal of the nation as mother is common in colonial iconography, Hussain's painting caught attention two years after it was auctioned as a "nude" portrayal of Durga.

5. The variant spelling (*darsan*) is due to the fact that Eck uses diacritical marks, which I have avoided. Further references are, therefore, spelt as "darshan."

6. Davis 1999, Rajagopal 2001, Lutgendorf 2007, Zavos 2008, and Khanduri 2012a.

7. For Pakistan see Jalal 1995.
8. See Padmanabhan 2006.
9. Although, as Akhil Gupta contends, corruption conceptualized as the failure of the government to implement its policies was not the only cause for dissatisfaction with "development" (1995, p. 90).
10. Grimshaw and Hart 1993, and Sanjek 1993; Grimshaw and Ravetz 2004; Boyer and Lomnitz 2005, and Eyal and Buccholz 2010. Liisa Malkki (1997, p. 94) urged a rethinking of the binary between anthropology and journalism to better appreciate the shifting anthropological terrain.
11. As well as depicting India as a tiger, sometimes Nicholas Garland caricatures the map. I was fascinated by his Indira Gandhi cartoons, and was glad to be able to speak with him on the phone, having read his book several years ago. Personal communication, May 23, 2011.
12. Personal communication, May 23, 2011.
13. www.cartoons.ac.uk/browse/cartoon_item/anytext=puss?artist=Nicholas%20 Garland&page=1.

Bibliography

Abraham, Abu. 1977. *The Games of Emergency: A Collection of Cartoons and Articles.* New Delhi: Vikas.

  1988. *The Penguin Book of Indian Cartoons: A Selection of the Finest Work from the Portfolios of over Fifty of India's Best Cartoonists.* New Delhi: Penguin.

Abu-Lughod, Lila. 1991. "Writing Against Culture." In *Recapturing Anthropology: Working in the Present,* ed. by Richard G. Fox, 137–62. Santa Fe, NM: School of American Research Press.

  1993. *Writing Women's Worlds: Bedouin Stories.* Berkeley: University of California Press.

  2004. *Dramas of Nationhood: The Politics of Television in Egypt.* University of Chicago Press.

Advani, Lal K. 2002 (1978). *Prisoner's Scrap Book.* New Delhi: Ocean Books.

Agrama, Hussein A. 2010. "Ethics, Tradition, Authority: Toward an Anthropology of the Fatwa." *American Ethnologist* 37 (1): 2–18.

Ahmed. 1951. *Ahmed's Political Pot-Pourri: A Collection of Cartoons and Strips.* New Delhi: Hindustan Times.

Alex, Gabriele. 2008. "A Sense of Belonging and Exclusion: 'Touchability' and 'Untouchability' in Tamil Nadu." *Ethnos* 73 (4): 523–43.

Alexander, Meena. 1985. "Sarojini Naidu: Romanticism and Resistance." *Economic and Political Weekly* 20 (43): 68–71.

Alford, Finnagan, and Richard Alford. 1981. "A Holo-Cultural Study of Humor." *Ethos* 9 (2): 149–64.

Alter, Joseph. 1992. *The Wrestler's Body: Identity and Ideology in North India.* Berkeley: University of California Press.

Amin, Shahid. 1995. *Event, Metaphor, Memory: Chauri Chaura 1922–1992.* New Delhi: Oxford University Press.

  2004. "On Representing the Musalman." In *Sarai Reader 4: Crisis/Media,* ed. by Sarai Media Lab, 92–6. New York: Autonomedia.

Anderson, Benedict. 1978. "Cartoons and Monuments: The Evolution of Political Communication under the New Order." In *Political Power and Communication in Indonesia,* ed. by Karl D. Jackson and Lucian W. Pye, 282–321. Berkeley: University of California Press.

  1983. *Imagined Communities: Reflections on the Origin and Spread of Nationalism.* London: Verso.

Andvig, Jens Chr, Odd-Helge Fjeltstad, Inge Amundson, Tone Sissener, and Tine Søreide. 2001. "Corruption: A Review of Contemporary Research," available at www.cmi.no/publications/2001/rep/r2001-7.pdf

Appadurai, Arjun. Ed. 1986. *The Social Life of Things: Commodities in Cultural Perspective.* Cambridge University Press.

1996. *Modernity at Large: Cultural Dimensions of Globalization*. Minneapolis: University of Minnesota Press.

Appelbaum, Stanley. 1981. *Great Drawings and Illustrations from Punch, 1841–1901: 192 Works by Leech, Keene, du Maurier, May and 21 Others*. New York: Courier Dover.

Apte, Mahadev L. 1985. *Humor and Laughter: An Anthropological Approach*. Ithaca, NY: Cornell University Press.

Arno, Andrew. 2009. *Alarming Reports: Communicating Conflict in the Daily News*. New York: Berghahn Books.

Arnold, David, and Stuart Blackburn. 2004. *Telling Lives in India: Biography, Autobiography, and Life History*. New Delhi: Permanent Black.

Asad, Talal. 1990. "Ethnography, Literature, and Politics: Some Readings and Uses of Salman Rushdie's *The Satanic Verses*." *Cultural Anthropology* 5 (3): 239–69.

2009. "Free Speech, Blasphemy, and Secular Criticism." In *Is Critique Secular? Blasphemy, Injury and Free Speech*, ed. by Talal Asad, Wendy Brown, Judith Butler, and Salsa Mahmood, 20–63. Berkeley: University of California Press.

Asaduddin, M. 2008. "Lost/Found in Translation: Qurratulain Hyder as Self-Translator," *Annual of Urdu Studies* 23: 234–49.

Axel, Brian K. 2002. *From the Margins: Historical Anthropology and Its Futures*. Durham: Duke University Press.

Babb, Lawrence. 1981. "Glancing: Visual Interactions in Hinduism." *Journal of Anthropological Research* 37: 387–401.

Babcock, Barbara. 1978. "Introduction." In *The Reversible World: Symbolic Inversion in Art and Society*, ed. by Barbara Babcock, 13–38. Ithaca, NY: Cornell University Press.

Bacon, Francis. 1884. *Bacon's Essays and Wisdom of the Ancients*. Boston: Little, Brown.

Bakhle, Janaki. 2005. *Two Men and Music: Nationalism and the Making of an Indian Classical Tradition*. New York: Oxford University Press.

Banks, Marcus, and Jay Ruby. Eds. 2011. *Made to Be Seen: Perspectives on the History of Visual Anthropology*. University of Chicago Press.

Bannerjee, Mukulika. 2008. "Democracy, Sacred and Everyday: An Ethnographic Case from India." In *Democracy: Anthropological Approaches*, ed. by Julia Paley, 63–96. Santa Fe: School for Advanced Research Press.

Barber, Karin. 2007. *The Anthropology of Texts, Persons and Publics*. Cambridge University Press.

Barthes, Roland. 1984. *Camera Lucida: Reflections on Photography*, trans. by Richard Howard. New York: Hill and Wang.

1999 (1977). *Image, Music, Text*. New York: Hill and Wang.

2000 (1974). *S/Z: An Essay*. New York: Hill and Wang.

Bate, Bernard. 2009. *Tamil Oratory and the Dravidian Aesthetic: Democratic Practice in South India*. New York: Columbia University Press.

Bateson, Gregory, and Margaret Mead. 1942. *Balinese Character: A Photographic Analysis*. New York: The New York Academy of Sciences.

Baudrillard, Jean, and Marie Maclean. 1985. "The Masses: The Implosion of the Social in the Media." *New Literary History* 16 (3): 577–89.

Bauman, Richard, and Charles L. Briggs. 1990. "Poetics and Performance as Critical Perspectives on Language and Social Life." *Annual Review of Anthropology* 19: 59–88.

Bausinger, Hermann. 1984. "Media, Technology and Daily Life," trans. by Liliane Jaddou and Jon Williams. *Media Culture Society* 6 (4): 343–51.

Bayly, Christopher A. 1999. *Empire and Information: Intelligence Gathering and Social Communication in India, 1780–1870.* Cambridge University Press.

Beeman, William O. 1999. "Humor." *Journal of Linguistic Anthropology* 9 (1–2): 103–6.

Beer, Gillian. 1990. "The Island and the Aeroplane: The Case of Virginia Woolf." In *Nation and Narration*, ed. by Homi Bhabha, 265–90. New York: Routledge.

Behar, Ruth. 1993. *Translated Woman: Crossing the Border with Esperanza's Story.* Boston: Beacon Press.

Behar, Ruth, and Deborah Gordon. Eds. 1995. *Women Writing Culture.* Berkeley: University of California Press.

Benedict, Ruth. 2005. *The Chrysanthemum and the Sword: Patterns of Japanese Culture.* Boston: Mariner Books.

Berman, Marshall. 1988. *All That Is Solid Melts into Air: The Experience of Modernity.* New York: Penguin.

Bhabha, Homi. 1984. "Of Mimicry and Man: The Ambivalence of Colonial Discourse." *October* 28: 25–133.

  1990. *Nation and Narration.* New York: Routledge.

Bhandari, Dharmendra. 2009. *R K Laxman – The Uncommon Man: Collection Of Works From 1948 to 2008.* Mumbai: Bhandari.

Bhargava, Rajeev. 1990. "The Right to Culture." *Social Scientist* 18 (10): 50–7.

Bhura, Nazreen. 2002. "Satire with a Democratic Touch." www.hclinfinet.com/2002/JAN/WEEK1/5/AOSCS2frame.jsp

Billig, Michael. 2001. "Humour and Hatred: The Racist Jokes of the Ku Klux Klan." *Discourse & Society* 12 (3): 267–89.

Bird, S. Elizabeth. Ed. 2010a. *The Anthropology of News and Journalism.* Bloomington, IN: Indiana University Press.

Bird, S. Elizabeth. 2010b. "Introduction: The Anthropology of News and Journalism: Why Now?" In *The Anthropology of News and Journalism*, ed. by Elizabeth Bird. Bloomington, IN: Indiana University Press.

Boas, Franz. 1955. *Primitive Art.* New York: Dover.

Boellstorff, Tom. 2004. "Zines and Zones of Desire: Mass-Mediated Love, National Romance, and Sexual Citizenship in Gay Indonesia." *The Journal of Asian Studies*, 63 (2): 367–402.

Boellstorff, Tom, and Johan Lindquist. 2004. "Bodies of Emotion: Rethinking Culture and Emotion through Southeast Asia." *Ethnos* 69 (4): 437–44.

Bourdieu, Pierre. 1984. *A Social Critique of the Judgement of Taste.* Cambridge, MA: Harvard University Press.

Boyer, Dominic, and Ulf Hannerz. 2006. "Introduction: Worlds of Journalism." *Ethnography* 7 (1): 5–17.

Boyer, Dominic, and Claudio Lomnitz. 2005. "Intellectuals and Nationalisms: Anthropological Engagements." *Annual Review of Anthropology* 34: 105–20.

Brass, Paul. 2004. "Development of an Institutionalised Riot System in Meerut City, 1961 to 1982." *Economic and Political Weekly* October 30: 4839–48.

Brown, Judith. 1994 (1989). *Gandhi: Prisoner of Hope.* New Haven and London: Yale University Press.

Brubaker, Rogers. 2009. "Ethnicity, Race, and Nationalism." *Annual Review of Sociology* 35: 21–42.

Brummett, Palmira. 2000. *Image and Imperialism in the Ottoman Revolutionary Press.* Albany, NY: State University of New York Press.

Bryant, Mark. Ed. 1991. *The Complete Colonel Blimp.* London: Bellew Publishing.

  2000. *Dictionary of Twentieth-Century British Cartoonists and Caricaturists.* London: Ashgate.

Bucholtz, Mary, and Kira Hall. 2005. "Identity and Interaction: A Sociocultural Linguistic Approach." *Discourse Studies* 9 (4–5): 585–614.

  2008. "Finding Identity: Theory and Data." *Multilingua: Journal of Cross-Cultural and Interlanguage Communication* 27 (1–2): 151–63.

Burke, Timothy. 1996. *Lifebuoy Men, Lux Women: Commodification, Consumption, and Cleanliness in Modern Zimbabwe.* Durham, NC: Duke University Press.

Burton, Antoinette. 1994. *Burdens of History: British Feminists, Indian Women, and Imperial Culture, 1865–1915.* Chapel Hill, NC: University of North Carolina Press.

  Ed. 1999. *Gender, Sexuality and Colonial Modernities.* New York: Routledge.

  2000. "Optical Illusion." *The Women's Review of Books* 17 (5): 21–2.

  2003. *Dwelling in the Archive: Women Writing House, Home and History in Late Colonial India.* New York: Oxford University Press.

Butalia, Urvashi. 1993. "Hidden Gags." *New Internationalist* 249. http://newint. org/features/1993/11/05/hidden/

Chakrabarty, Dipesh. 1993. "The Difference Deferral of (A) Colonial Modernity: Public Debates on Domesticity in British Bengal." *History Workshop Journal* 36 (1): 1–33.

  1995. "Modernity and Ethnicity in India: A History for the Present." *Economic and Political Weekly* 30 (52): 3373–80.

  2000. *Provincializing Europe: Postcolonial Thought and Difference.* Princeton University Press.

Chakravarti, Uma. 1998. *Rewriting History: the Life and Times of Pandita Ramabai.* New Delhi: Kali for Women.

Chandra, Shefali. 2012. *The Sexual Life of English: Languages of Caste and Desire in Colonial India.* Durham, NC: Duke University Press.

Chatterjee, Partha. 1986. *Nationalist Thought and the Colonial World: A Derivative Discourse?* New Delhi: Oxford University Press.

  1993. *The Nation and its Fragments: Colonial and Postcolonial Histories.* New Delhi: Oxford University Press.

  2002. *The Politics of the Governed: Reflections on Popular Politics in Most of the World.* New York: Columbia University Press.

  2008. "Critique of Popular Culture." *Public Culture* 20 (2): 321–44.

Chauhan, Chanchal P. 2006. "Budget is the New Business Class." *Hindustan Times* July 23: 6.

Clifford, James. 1986. "On Ethnographic Allegory." In *Writing Culture: The Poetics and Politics of Culture*, ed. by James Clifford and George E. Marcus, 98–121. Berkeley: University of California Press.

Cody, Francis. 2009. "Inscribing Subjects to Citizenship: Petitions, Literacy Activism, and the Performativity of Signature in Rural Tamil India." *Cultural Anthropology* 24 (3): 347–80.

Cohen, Lawrence. 1995. "Holi in Banaras and the Mahaland of Modernity." *GLQ: A Journal of Lesbian and Gay Studies* 2: 399–424.

   1998. *No Aging in India: Alzheimer's, the Bad Family, and Other Modern Things*. Berkeley: University of California Press.

Cohn, Bernard. 1980. "History and Anthropology: The State of Play." *Comparative Studies in History and Society* 22 (2): 198–221.

   1987. *An Anthropologist among the Historians and Other Essays*. New Delhi: Oxford University Press.

Collier, Malcolm and John Collier. 1996 (1986). *Visual Anthropology: Photography as a Research Method*. Albuquerque, NM: University of New Mexico Press.

   1996 (1987). *Colonialism and Its Forms of Knowledge: The British in India*. Princeton University Press.

Contractor, Behram. 1985. "The Humorous World of Laxman." *The Afternoon Dispatch* October 8: 10–11.

Cooper, Frederick, and Ann Stoler. 1997. *Tensions of Empire: Colonial Cultures in a Bourgeois World*. Berkeley: University of California Press.

Coote, Jeremy, and Anthony Shelton. Eds. 1992. *Anthropology, Art, and Aesthetics*. Oxford: Clarendon.

Copeman, Jacob and Aya Ikegame. Eds. 2012. *The Guru in South Asia*. New York: Routledge.

Coupe, A. William. 1967. "The German Cartoon and the Revolution of 1848." *Comparative Studies in Society and History* 9 (2): 79–95.

   1969. "Observations on a Theory of Political Caricature." *Comparative Studies in Society and History* 11 (1): 79–95.

Crapanzano, Vincent. 1980. *Tuhami: Portrait of a Moroccan*. University of Chicago Press.

   1984. "Life-History." *American Anthropologist* 86 (4): 953–60.

Dalmia, Vasudha. 2001. *The Nationalization of Hindu Traditions: Bharata Harischandra and Nineteenth-Century Banaras*. New Delhi: Oxford University Press.

Dandavate, Madhu, and Jay Prakash Narayan. 2002. *Jayprakash Narayan: Struggle with Values, A Centenary Volume*. New Delhi: Allied Publishers.

Das, Durga. 1969. *From Curzon to Nehru and After*. London: Collins.

Das, Veena. 1998. *Critical Events: An Anthropological Perspective on Contemporary India*. New Delhi: Oxford University Press.

Davies, Russell, and Liz Ottaway. 1987. *Vicky*. London: Secker and Warburg Ltd.

Davis, Natalie Zemon, and Randolph Starn. 1989. "Introduction." *Representations* 26 (Special Issue: Memory and Counter-Memory): 1–6.

Davis, Richard. 1999. *Lives of Indian Images*. Princeton University Press.

Daw, Prasanta. Ed. 1978. *Cartoons of Deviprasad*. Calcutta: Mahua Publishing Company.

De Certeau, Michel. 1984. *The Practice of Everyday Life*. Berkeley: University of California Press.

Demetriou, Olga. 2004. "The Turkish Oedipus: National Self and Stereotype in the Work of a 1960s Greek Cartoonist." *History and Anthropology* 15 (1): 69–89.

Desjarlais, Robert. 2003. *Sensory Biographies: Lives and Deaths among Nepal's Yolmo Buddhists*. Berkeley: University of California Press.

Dhar, Aarti. 2012. "Govt. to Probe Role of NCERT Officials in Cartoon Row." *Hindu* May 15. www.thehindu.com/news/national/government-to-probe-role-of-ncert-officials/article3418734.ece.

Dickens Charles. 1862. "Punch in India." *All Year Round* 7 (151–75): 462–9.

Dickey, Sara. 1993. *Cinema and the Urban Poor in South India*. New Delhi: Cambridge University Press.

2005. "Still One Man in a Thousand." In *Living Pictures: Perspectives on the Film Poster in India*, ed. by David Blamey and Robert E. D'Souza, 69–78. London: Open Editions.

Dirks, Nicholas. 2001. *Castes of Mind: Colonialism and the Making of Modern India*. Princeton University Press.

Douglas, Allen. 2002. *War, Memory, and the Politics of Humor: The Canard Enchaîné and World War I*. Berkeley: University of California Press.

Doust, Len. 1936 (1932). *A Manual on Caricature and Cartoon Drawing*. London: Frederick Warne and Co. Ltd.

Downe, Pamela, J. 1999. "Laughing When It Hurts: Humor and Violence in the Lives of Costa Rican Prostitutes." *Women's Studies International Forum* 22 (1): 63–78.

Du Bois, Cora. 1944. *The People of Alor: A Social-Psychological Study of the People of an East Indian Island*. Minneapolis: University of Minnesota Press.

1980. "Some Anthropological Hindsights." *Annual Review of Anthropology* 9: 1–14.

Du Gay, Paul, Stuart Hall, Linda Janes, and Hugh Mackay. 1997. *Doing Cultural Studies: The Story of the Sony Walkman*. New Delhi: Sage.

Dundes, Alan, and Thomas Hauschild. 1983. "Auschwitz Jokes." *Western Folklore* 42 (4): 249–60.

Dundes, Alan. 1987. *Cracking Jokes: Studies of Humour Cycles and Stereotypes*. Berkeley: Ten Speed Press.

Duus, P. 2001. "Presidential Address: Weapons of the Weak, Weapons of the Strong: The Development of the Japanese Political Cartoon." *The Journal of Asian Studies* 60 (4): 965–98.

Dwyer, Kevin. 1979. "The Dialogue of Ethnology." *Dialectical Anthropology* 4 (3): 205–24.

Eck, Diana L. 1998. *Darsan: Seeing the Divine Image in India*. New York: Columbia University Press.

Edwards. Elizabeth. 1994. "Visualizing History: Diamond Jenness's Photographs of D'Entrecasteaux Islands, Massim, 1911–1912 – A Case Study in Re-engagement." *Canberra Anthropology* 17 (2):1–26.

2001. *Raw Histories: Photographs, Anthropology and Museums*. London: Berg.

Engineer, A. Asghar. 1992. "Communal Conflict after 1950: A Perspective." *Economic and Political Weekly*. 27 (34): 1782–5.

2007. "Communal Violence in 2006." www.csss-isla.com/arch%2075.htm

Erlmann, Veit. 2004. *Hearing Cultures: Essays on Sound, Listening and Modernity*. New York: Berg.

Escobar, Arturo. 1995. *Encountering Development: The Making and Unmaking of the Third World*. Princeton University Press.

Eyal, Gil, and Larissa Buccholz. 2010. "From the Sociology of Intellectuals to the Sociology of Interventions." *Annual Review of Sociology* 36: 117–37.

Fabian, Johannes. 1983. *Time and the Other: How Anthropology Makes Its Object*. New York: Columbia University Press.

2001. *Anthropology with an Attitude: Critical Essays*. Stanford University Press.

Ferguson, Frances, N. 1982. "Personal Adaptation as Observed in Female Gurus in India: The Similar Dynamics of Culture Change and Cultural Continuity." *Anthropology of Humanism Quarterly* 7 (2–3): 21–8.

Fiske, John. 1987. *Television Culture*. London: Routledge.

Forbes, Geraldine. 2005. *Women in Colonial India*. New Delhi: Chronicle Books.

2007. "Small Acts of Rebellion: Women Tell Their Photographs." In *Behind the Veil: Resistance, Women, and the Everyday in Colonial South Asia*, ed. by Anindita Ghosh, 58–82. New Delhi: Permanent Black.

Fox, Richard, and Orin Starn. 1997. "Introduction." In *Between Resistance and Revolution: Cultural Politics and Social Protest*, ed. by Richard Fox and Orin Starn, 1–16. New Brunswick, NJ: Rutgers University Press.

Fredeman, W. E. 1983. "A Charivari for Queen Butterfly: 'Punch' on Queen Victoria." *Victorian Poetry* 25 (3–4): 47–73.

Gairola, Ritu. 1995. "The Politics of the Visual: The Nation and the Nationalist in Late Nineteenth and Early Twentieth Century Colonial India." Unpublished M.Phil. thesis, Jawaharlal Nehru University.

Gandhi, K. Mohandas.1974 (1960–94). *The Collected Works of Mahatma Gandhi*. Ahmedabad: Navjivan Press.

1993 (1957). *An Autobiography: The Story of My Experiments with Truth*. Boston: Beacon Press.

Ganti, Tejaswini. 2012. *Producing Bollywood: Inside the Contemporary Hindi Film Industry*. Durham, NC: Duke University Press.

Garland, Nicholas. 1986. *An Indian Journal*. Academy Chicago Publishers.

Gell, Alfred. 1998. *Art and Agency: An Anthropological Theory*. Oxford: Clarendon Press.

George, Kenneth. 2010. *Picturing Islam*. New York: Wiley-Blackwell.

Gerbner, George. 1972. "Violence in Television Drama: Trends and Symbolic Functions." In *Television and Social Behaviour*, Vol. I, *Media Content and Control*, ed. by Rubin A. Comstock and George E. Rubinstein, 28–187. Washington, DC: US Government Printing Office.

Geurts, Kathryn L. 2003. "On Rocks, Walks, and Talks in West Africa: Cultural Categories and an Anthropology of the Senses." *Ethos* 30 (3):178–98.

Ghosh, Anindita. 2008. *Power in Print: Popular Publishing and the Politics of Language and Culture in a Colonial Society*. New Delhi: Oxford University Press.

Ghosh, Sagarika and Sanjay Suri. 1997. "Sketchy Selections: An ICCR Exhibition Raises Fears of a Cartoon Mafia at Work." www.outlookindia.com/article.aspx?204333.

Ghosh, Shohini. 2004. "Censorship Myths and Imagined Harms." In *Sarai Reader 4: Crisis/Media*, ed. by Sarai Media Lab, 447–54. New York: Autonomedia.

Ghurye, G. S. 1978. *India Recreates Democracy*. Bombay: Popular Prakashan.

Gillespie, Marie. 1995. *Television, Ethnicity and Cultural Change*. London: Routledge.

Gilligan, Carol. 1993. *In a Different Voice: Psychological Theory and Women's Development*. Cambridge, MA: Harvard University Press.

   1995. "Hearing the Difference: Theorizing the Connection. *Hypatia* 10 (2): 120–7.

Gilmartin, Patricia and Stanley D. Brunn. 1998. "The Representation of Women in Political Cartoons of the 1995 World Conference on Women." *Women Studies International Forum* 21 (5): 535–49.

Ginsburg, Faye. 2002. "Screen Memories: Resignifying the Traditional in Indigenous Media." In *Media Worlds: Anthropology on New Terrain*, ed. by Faye Ginsburg, Lila Abu-Lughod and Brian Larkin, 39–57. Berkeley: University of California Press.

Ginsburg, Faye D., Lila Abu-Lughod, and Brian Larkin. Eds. 2002. *Media Worlds: Anthropology on New Terrain*. Berkeley: University of California Press.

Ginzburg, Carlo. 1992. "From Aby Warburg to E. H. Gombrich: A Problem of Method." In *Clues, Myths and Historical Method*. Trans. by John Tedeschi and Anne Tedeschi. Baltimore: Johns Hopkins University Press.

Glenn, Phillip J. 2003. *Laughter in Interaction*. New York: Cambridge University Press.

Gluckman, Max. 1954. *Rituals of Rebellion in South-East Africa*. Manchester University Press.

Goldstein, Donna. 2003. *Laughter Out of Place: Race, Class, Violence, and Sexuality in a Rio Shantytown*. Berkeley: University of California Press.

Gombrich, E. H. 1963. *Meditations on a Hobby Horse and Other Essays on the Theory of Art*. University of Chicago Press.

Gombrich, Ernst H. and Ernst Kris. 1938. "The Principles of Caricature." *British Journal of Medical Psychology* 17: 319–42.

Goswami, Manu. 2004. *Producing India: From Colonial Economy to National Space*. University of Chicago Press.

Graham, John. 1961. "Lavater's Physiognomy in England." *Journal of the History of Ideas* 22 (4):561–72.

Graham, Laura. 2011. "Quoting Mario Juruna: Lingusitic Imagery and the Transformation of Indigenous Voice in the Brazilian Print Press." *American Ethnologist* 38 (1): 163–82.

Grimshaw, Anna, and Keith Hart. 1993. *Anthropology and the Crisis of the Intellectuals*. Cambridge: Prickly Pear.

Grimshaw, Anna, and Amanda Ravetz. Eds. 2004. *Visualizing Anthropology: Experimenting with Image-Based Ethnography*. University of Chicago Press.

Guha, Ramchandra. 2001. "The Absent Liberal: An Essay on Politics and Intellectual Life." *Economic and Political Weekly* 36 (50): 4663–70.

2007. *India After Gandhi: The History of the World's Largest Democracy*. London: Macmillan.

Guha-Thakurta, Tapati. 1992. *The Making of a New "Indian" Art: Artists, Aesthetics and Nationalism in Bengal 1850–1920*. Cambridge University Press.

Gupta, Akhil. 1995. "Blurred Boundaries: The Discourse of Corruption, the Culture of Politics, and the Imagined State." *American Ethnologist* 22 (2): 375–402.

1998. *Postcolonial Developments: Agriculture in the Making of Modern India*. Durham, NC: Duke University Press.

Gupta, Dipankar. 1982. *Nativism in a Metropolis: The Shiv Sena in Bombay*. New Delhi: Manohar.

Hall, Stuart. 1997. *Representation: Cultural Representations and Signifying Practices*. London: Sage Publications and Open University.

Hancock, Mary. 1999. "Women and Home Science in British India." In *Gender, Sexuality and Colonial Modernities* ed. by Antoinette Burton, 148–60. New York: Routledge.

Hannerz, Ulf. 1994. "Sophiatown: The View from Afar." *Journal of South African Studies* 20 (2): 181–93.

1996. *Transnational Connections*. London: Routledge.

2004. *Foreign News: Exploring the World of Foreign Correspondents*. University of Chicago Press.

Hansen, Thomas, B. 1999. *The Saffron Wave: Democracy and Hindu Nationalism in Modern India*. Princeton University Press.

2005. "Melancholia of Freedom: Humour and Nostalgia among Indians in South Africa." *Modern Drama* 48 (2): 297–315.

Haraway, Donna. 1988. "Situated Knowledges: The Science Question in Feminism and the Privilege of Partial Perspective." *Feminist Studies* 14 (3): 575–99.

1989. "Introduction: The Persistence of Vision." In Haraway, *Primate Visions: Gender, Race, and Nature in the Worlds of Modern Science*. New York: Routledge.

1991. *Simians, Cyborgs, and Women: The Reinvention of Nature*. London: Routledge.

Harder, Hans and Barbara Mittler. Eds. 2013. *Asian Punches*. Berlin: Springer.

Harding, Sandra. 1986. *The Science Question in Feminism*. Ithaca, NY: Cornell University Press.

Hasan, Mushirul. 2007. *Wit and Humor in Colonial North India*. New Delhi: Niyogi Press.

Haugerud, Angelique. 2012. "Satire and Dissent in the Age of Billionaires." *Social Research* 79 (1): 145–68.

Heidegger, Martin. 1982. *The Question Concerning Technology and Other Essays*. New York: Harper Perennial.

Herzfeld, Michael. 1992. *The Social Production of Indifference: Exploring the Symbolic Roots of Western Bureaucracy*. University of Chicago Press.

1997. *Portrait of a Greek Imagination: An Ethnographic Biography of Andreas Nenedakis*. University of Chicago Press.

2004. *The Body Impolitic: Artisans and Artifice in the Global Hierarchy of Value*. University of Chicago Press.

2005. *Cultural Intimacy: Social Poetics in the Nation-State*. London: Routledge.

Hill, Jane. 1999. "Language, Race, and White Public Space." *American Anthropologist* 100 (3): 680–9.

Hiltebeitel, Alf. 1991 (1988). *The Cult of Draupadi: Mythologies from Gingee to Kuruksetra*. 2 vols. University of Chicago Press.

Hogan, Michael. 2001. "Cartoonists and Political Cynicism." *Drawing Board: An Australian Review of Public Affairs* 2: 27–50.

Holdridge, Christopher. 2010. "Laughing with Sam Sly: The Cultural Politics of Satire and Colonial British Identity in the Cape Colony, c. 1840–1850." *Kronos* 36 (1): 29–53.

Hsu, Pi-ching. 1998. "Feng Meng-lung's Treasury of Laughs: Humorous Satire on Seventeenth Century Chinese Culture and Society." *Journal of Asian Studies* 57 (4): 1042–67.

Hull, Matthew. 2012. *Government of Paper: The Materiality of Bureaucracy in Urban Pakistan*. Berkeley: University of California Press.

Hung, Chang-Tai. 1994. *War and Popular Culture: Resistance in Modern China, 1937–1945*. Berkeley: University of California Press.

Huyysen, Andreas. 1986. *After the Great Divide: Modernism, Mass Culture, Postmodernism*. Bloomington, IN: Indiana University Press.

Irvine, Judith. 1996. "Language and Community: Introduction." *Journal of Linguistic Anthropology* 6 (2): 123–5.

"Shadow Conversations: The Indeterminacy of Participant Roles." In *Natural Histories of Discourse*, ed. by Michael Silverstein and Greg Urban, 131–59. University of Chicago Press.

Ispahani, M. A. Hassan. 1967. *Qaid-e-Azam Jinnah as I Knew Him*. Karachi: Forward Publications.

Ivy, Marilyn. 1995. *Discourses of the Vanishing: Modernity, Phantasm, Japan*. University of Chicago Press.

Iyengar, A. S. 2001. *Role of Press and Indian Freedom Struggle: All through the Gandhian Era*. New Delhi: A. P. H. Publishing.

Jackson, Jennifer, L. 2008. "Building Publics, Shaping Public Opinion: Interanimating Registers in Malagasey Kabary Oratory and Political Cartooning." *Journal of Linguistic Anthropology* 18 (2): 214–35.

2013. *Political Oratory and Cartooning: An Ethnography of Democratic Process in Madagascar*. Malden, MA: Wiley-Blackwell.

Jaffrelot, Christophe. 2003. *India's Silent Revolution: The Rise of the Lower Castes in North India*. New York: Columbia University Press.

Jain, Kajri. 2007. *Gods in the Bazaar: The Economies of Indian Calendar Art*. Durham, NC: Duke University Press.

Jakobson Janet B., and Ann Pellegrini. 2008. *Secularisms*. Durham, NC: Duke University Press.

Jalal, Ayesha. 1995. "Conjuring Pakistan: History as Official Imagining." *International Journal of Middle East Studies* 27 (1): 73–89.

Jeffords, Susan, and Lauren Rabinovitz. 1994. *Seeing through the Media: The Persian Gulf War*. New Brunswick, NJ: Rutgers University Press.

Jeffrey, Craig. 2002. "Caste, Class, and Clientelism: A Political Economy of Everyday Corruption in Rural North India." *Economic Geography* 78 (1): 21–41.

Jeffrey, Robin. 2000. *India's Newspaper Revolution: Capitalism, Politics and the Indian Language Press*. New Delhi: Oxford University Press.

Jenkins, Henry. 1992. *Textual Poachers: Television Fans and Participatory Culture*. New York: Routledge.

Jha, Prem Shankar, and Arvind N. Das. Eds. 2000. *History in the Making: 75 Years of the Hindustan Times*. New Delhi: Hindustan Times.

Jinnah, Muhammad Ali. 1993. *Quaid-i-Azam Muhammad Ali Jinnah Papers*, ed. by Zawar Hussain Zaidi. Vol. X. Islamabad: Oxford University Press.

Jones, Kate. 2005. "Politicians and Political Cynicism More or Less?" *Australasian Parliamentary Review* 20 (2): 116–29.

Joseph, Ammu. 2004. "Working, Watching and Waiting: Women and Issues of Access, Employment and Decision-Making in the Media in India." In *Women and Media: International Perspectives*, ed. by Carolyn M. Byerly and Karen Ross, 132–56. London: Wiley-Blackwell.

Joshi, Priya. 2002. *In Another Country: Colonialism, Culture and the English Novel in India*. New York: Columbia University Press.

Joshi, Sanjay. 2001. *Fractured Modernity: Making of a Middle Class in Colonial North India*. New Delhi: Oxford University Press.

Kaak. 1989. *Nazariya*. New Delhi: Rupa and Co.

Kalra, Sushil. 1993. *This Dilli! A Collection of 101 Cartoons by Sushil Kalra*. New Delhi: Sushika Publishers.

Kamath, Maya. 2005. *The World of Maya: Cartoons of Maya Kamath*. Mumbai: Sparrow.

Kamra, Sukeshi. 2003. *Bearing Witness: Partition, Independence, End of the Raj*. New Delhi: Roli Books.

Katz, Jack. 1987. "What Makes 'Crime' News?" *Media, Culture and Society* 9: 47–75.

Kaul, Chandrika. 2003. *Reporting the Raj: The British Press and India, c. 1880–1922*. Manchester University Press.

Kaviraj, Sudipta and Sunil Khilnani. 2001. "Introduction." In *Civil Society: History and Possibilities*, ed. by Sudipta Kaviraj and Sunil Khilnani, 1–7. New Delhi: Cambridge University Press.

Keane, Webb. 2005. "Signs Are Not the Garb of Meaning: On the Social Analysis of Material Things." In *Materiality*, ed. by Daniel Miller, 182–205. Durham, NC: Duke University Press.

2009. "Freedom and Blasphemy: On Indonesian Press Bans and Danish Cartoons." *Public Culture* 21: 47–76.

Kedia, Baijnath. 1930. *Vyanga Chitravali*. Part 1 Calcutta: Hindi Pustak Agency.

Kennedy, John G., and Hussein M. Fahim. 1977. *Struggle for Change in a Nubian Community: An Individual in Society and History*. Palo Alto, CA: Mayfield Publishers.

Khan, Poorva. 2006. "Freedom of Expression of Cartoonists." http://papers.ssrn.com/sol3/papers.cfm?abstract_id=1101483

Khanduri, Ritu. 2001. "Sacrifice and Suffering: Imaging Nationalism." *Sagar: South Asia Graduate Research Journal* 7: 49–63.

2007. "Routes of Caricature: Cartooning and the Making of a Moral Aesthetic in Colonial and Postcolonial India." Unpublished Ph.D. dissertation, University of Texas at Austin.

2009a. "Liberal Perceptions." Paper Presented at the Fourth South Asia Popular Culture Conference. University of Manchester, UK. July 6–7.

2009b. "Vernacular Punches: Cartoons in Colonial India." *History and Anthropology* 4: 457–84.

2012a. "Does This Offend You? Hindu Visuality in the United States." In *Public Hinduisms*, ed. by John Zavos, Pralay Kanungo, Deepa Reddy, Maya Warrier, and Raymond Williams, 348–64. London and New Delhi: Sage.

2012b. "Some Things About Gandhi." *Contemporary South Asia* 22 (3): 303–25.

2013. "Terror Myths and Scenes of Violence: A Visual Essay." *South Asian Popular Culture* 11 (2): 181–91.

Klausen, Jytte. 2009. *The Cartoons That Shook the World*. New Haven: Yale University Press.

Kohli, Atul. Ed. 2002. *The Success of India's Democracy*. New Delhi: Cambridge University Press.

Konkan, K. S. 1967. "The Art of a Cartoonist," Letter to the Editor. *Thought* February 25: 8.

Kurzman, Charles, and Lynn Owens. 2002. "The Sociology of Intellectuals." *Annual Review of Sociology* 28: 63–90.

Lahiri, Chandi. 1994. *Since Freedom: A History in Cartoons, 1947–1993*. Calcutta: New Central Book Agency.

Langness, Lewis L. and Gelya Frank. 1981. *Lives: An Anthropological Approach to Biography*. Novato, CA: Chandler and Sharp.

Larkin, Brian. 2002. "The Materiality of Cinema Theaters in Northern Nigeria." In *Media Worlds: Anthropology on New Terrain*, ed. by Faye Ginsburg, Lila Abu-Lughod and Brian Larkin, 319–36. Berkeley: University of California Press.

Lavater, John Caspar. 1878. *Essays on Physiognomy*. Trans. by Thomas Holcroft. 15th edn. London: William Tegg and Co.

Laxman, R. K. 1967. *You Said It*, Vol. I, Bombay: India Book House.

1984. "Freedom to Cartoon, Freedom to Speak." *Daedalus* 118 (4): 68–91.

1998. *The Tunnel of Time: An Autobiography*. New Delhi: Penguin.

2000. *The Best of Laxman: The Common Man Meets the Mantri*. New Delhi: Penguin.

2008. *Brushing up the Years: A Cartoonist's History of India 1947 to The Present*. New Delhi: Penguin.

Layard, George S. 1907. *Shirley Brooks of Punch: His Life, Letters, and Diaries*. New York: Henry Holt.

Lemon, Mark. 1870. *Mr. Punch: His Origin and Career*. London: printed by Jas. Wade.

Lévi-Strauss, Claude. 1961. *Tristes tropiques*. Trans. by John Russell. New York: Criterion Books.

Levin, David M. 1993. *Modernity and the Hegemony of Vision*. Berkeley: University of California Press.

Lewinson, Anne. 2003. "Imagining the Metropolis, Globalizing the Nation: Dar Es Salaam and National Culture in Tanzanian Cartoons." *City and Society* 15 (1): 9–30.

Lewis, Colin A. 1990. "The South African Sugar Industry." *Geographical Journal* 156 (1): 70–8.

Liechty, Mark. 2003. *Suitably Modern: Making Middle-Class Culture in a New Consumer Society.* Princeton University Press.

Lincoln, Kenneth.1992. *Indi'n Humor: Bicultural Play in Native America.* New York: Oxford University Press.

Lonsdale, John. 1990. "Mau Maus of the Mind: Making Mau Mau and Remaking Kenya." *The Journal of African History* 31 (3): 393–421.

Low, David. 1935. *Ye Madde Designer.* London: The Studio.

  1942. *British Cartoonists, Caricaturists and Comic Artists.* London: William Collins of London.

  1957. *Autobiography.* New York: Simon and Schuster.

Lowe, Donald M. 1982. *The History of Bourgeois Perception.* University of Chicago Press.

Lutgendorf, Philip. 2007. *Hanuman's Tale: The Messages of a Divine Monkey.* New York: Oxford University Press.

Lutz, Catherine. 1995. "The Gender of Theory." In *Women Writing Culture*, ed. by Ruth Behar and Deborah Gordon, 249–66. Berkeley: University of California Press.

Lutz, Catherine, and Geoffrey. M. White. 1986. "The Anthropology of Emotions." *Annual Review of Anthropology*, 15: 405–36.

Lyon, Jean. 1952. "The Funniest Man in Asia." *United Nations World* 6: 23–6 and 43.

MacKenzie, J. M. M. 1986. *Propaganda and Empire: Manipulation of British Public Opinion, 1880–1960.* Manchester University Press.

McLean, Thomas. n.d. *A Key to the Political Sketches of H.B., nos. 1 to 600: Arranged as Published, up to 21st May, 1832, Parts 1–4.* London: Thomas McLean.

McNay, Michael. 2002. "Abu Abraham: A Principled Political Cartoonist in Both Britain and India who 'Walked Tall While Others Crawled.'" www.guardian.co.uk/news/2002/dec/07/guardianobituaries.india

Mahmood, Saba. 2009. "Religious Reason and Secular Affect: An Incommensurable Divide." In *Is Critique Secular? Blasphemy, Injury and Free Speech*, ed. by Talal Asad, Wendy Brown, Judith Butler, and Salsa Mahmood, 64–100. Berkeley: University of California Press.

Mahood, Marguerite.1973. *The Loaded Line: Australian Political Caricature 1788 – 1901.* Melbourne University Press.

Malkki, Liisa. 1997. "News and Culture: Transitory Phenomena and the Fieldwork Tradition." In *Anthropological Locations: Boundaries and Grounds for a Field Science*, ed. by Akhil Gupta and James Ferguson, 86–101. Berkeley: University of California Press.

Malleson, George B. Ed. 1890. *Kaye's and Malleson's History of the Indian Mutiny of 1857–8.* Vols. 1–6. London: W. H. Allen.

Mandhana, Niharika. 2013. "A Conversation With: Sociologist Ashish Nandy." http://india.blogs.nytimes.com/2013/01/30/a-conversation-with-sociologist-ashis-nandy/

Mandoo. 1987. *Cartoons for Peace*. New Delhi: Allied Publishers.

Mankekar, Purnima. 1999. *Screening Culture, Viewing Politics: An Ethnography of Television, Womanhood, and Nation in Postcolonial India*. Durham: Duke University Press.

Manning, Paul. 2007. "Rose-Colored Glasses: Color Revolutions and Cartoon Chaos in Postsocialist Georgia." *Cultural Anthropology* 22 (2): 171–213.

Marcus, George E., and Fred Myers. Eds. 1995. *The Traffic in Culture: Refiguring Art and Anthropology*. Berkeley: University of California Press.

Mathur, Saloni. 2000. "History and Anthropology in South Asia: Rethinking the Archive." *Annual Review of Anthropology* 29: 89–106.

Maurice, Arthur Bartlett, and Frederick Taber Cooper. 1904. *The History of the Nineteenth Century in Caricature*. New York: Dodd, Mead.

Mazzarella, William. 2003. *Shoveling Smoke: Advertising and Globalization in Contemporary India*. Durham, NC: Duke University Press.

Mehta, Uday. 1999. *Liberalism and Empire: A Study in Nineteenth-Century British Liberal Thought*. University of Chicago Press.

Menon, Sadanand. 1994. "Cartoonists Against Communalism." In *Punch Line*, ed. by Madhukar Upadhyay, n.p. New Delhi: SAHMAT.

Mesthrie, Uma. 1997. "From Advocacy to Mobilization: Indian Opinion, 1903–1914." In *South Africa's Alternative Press: Voices of Protest and Resistance, 1880–1960*, ed. by Lee Switzer, 99–126. New York: Cambridge University Press.

   2003. "The Significance of *Indian Opinion*. Address to Conference on the Alternate Media to Commemorate the Founding of the *Indian Opinion*." www.sahistory.org.za/pages/artsmediaculture/pages/newspapers/indian-opinion.htm

Minault, Gail. 1998. *Secluded Scholars: Women's Education and Muslim Social Reform in Colonial India*, New Delhi: Oxford University Press.

   2005. "From Akhbar to News: The Development of the Urdu Press in Early 19th Century Delhi." In *A Wilderness of Possibilities: Urdu Studies in Transnational Perspective*, ed. by Kathryn Hansen and David Lelyveld, 101–21. New Delhi: Oxford University Press.

Miranda, Mario, and Rajan Narayan. 1980. *Elections Indian Style*. New Delhi: Jaico.

Mirzoeff, Nicholas. 2006. "On Visuality." *Journal of Visual Culture* 5 (1): 53–79.

Mishra, Shiv Narayan. n. d. (*c.* 1929). *Svang Chitravali: Caricature Album*. Cawnpore: Prakash Pustakalya.

Mitchell, Lisa. 2008. *Language, Emotion, and Politics in South India: The Making of a Mother Tongue*. Bloomington, IN: Indiana University Press.

Mitchell, W. J. T. 2003. "The Obscure Object of Visual Culture: A Response to Meike Bal." *Journal of Visual Culture* 2 (2): 249–52.

   2005. "There Are No Visual Media." *Journal of Visual Culture* 4 (2): 257–66.

Mitter, Partha. 1992 (1977). *Much Maligned Monsters: A History of European Reactions to Indian Art*. University of Chicago Press.

1994. *Art and Nationalism in Colonial India 1850–1922: Occidental Orientations.* Cambridge University Press.

Morphy, Howard, and Morgan Perkins. 2007. *The Anthropology of Art: A Reader.* Malden, MA: Blackwell.

Mukherjee, Rudrangshu. 1993. *The Penguin Gandhi Reader.* New Delhi: Penguin.

Muthiah, S. 2003. "The House of Happy Humor." www.hindu.com/mp/2003/10/08/stories/2003100800400300.htm

Myer, Birgit, and Annelais Moors. 2006. *Religion, Media and the Public Sphere.* Bloomington, IN: Indiana University Press.

Myers, Fred, R. 2002. *Painting Culture: The Making of an Aboriginal High Art.* Durham, NC: Duke University Press.

Nader, Laura. 1999 (1969). "Up the Anthropologist – Perspectives Gained from 'Studying Up.'" In *Reinventing Anthropology,* ed. by Dell Hymes, 284–311. New York: Pantheon.

Nandy, Ashish. 1995. "History's Forgotten Doubles." *History and Theory* 34 (2): 44–66.

2002a. "Laughter in a Mortuary: A Foreword." In O. V. Vijayan, *A Cartoonist Remembers,* vii–xii. New Delhi: Rupa & Co.

2002b. *Time Warps: Silent and Evasive Pasts in Indian Politics and Religion.* New Delhi: Permanent Black.

Narayan, Kirin. 1989. *Storytellers, Saints, and Scoundrels: Folk Narrative in Hindu Religious Teaching.* Philadelphia: University of Pennsylvania Press.

1993. "Refractions of the Field at Home: American Representations of Hindu Holy Men in the 19th and 20th Centuries." *Cultural Anthropology* 8 (4): 476–509.

Naregal, Veena. 2001. *Language Politics, Elites, and the Public Sphere: Western India Under Colonialism.* New Delhi: Permanent Black.

National Council of Educational Research and Training. 2005. *National Curriculum Framework Report.* New Delhi: National Council of Educational Research and Training.

National Council of Educational Research and Training. 2006. *Democratic Politics – 1: Text Book in Political Science for Class IX.* New Delhi: National Council of Educational Research and Training.

Nehru, Jawaharlal. 1972–80. *Selected Works of Jawaharlal Nehru,* ed. by Sarvapalli Gopal. Series 1, 15 vols. New Delhi: Orient Longman.

2004 (1936). *An Autobiography.* New Delhi: Penguin.

Ninan, Sevanti. 2007. *Headlines from the Heartland: Reinventing the Hindi Public Sphere.* New Delhi: Sage.

Nuttall, Denise. 2007. "A Pathway to Knowledge: Embodiment, Experience and Dreaming as a Basis for Understanding the Other." In *Extraordinary Anthropology: Transformations in the Field,* ed. by Jean-Guy Goulet and Bruce G. Miller, 323–51. Lincoln, NE: University of Nebraska Press.

Ong, Walter. 1991. "The Shifting Sensorium." In *The Varieties of Sensory Exerience: A Sourcebook in the Anthropology of the Senses,* ed. by David Howes, 25–30. University of Toronto Press.

Orsini, Francesca. 2002. *The Hindi Public Sphere 1920–1924: Language and Literature in the Age of Nationalism.* New Delhi: Oxford University Press.

Ortner, Sherry B. 2003. *New Jersey Dreaming: Capital, Culture, and the Class of '58*. Durham, NC: Duke University Press.

O'Shea, Janet. 2007. *At Home in the World: Bharat Natyam on the Global Stage*. Middletown, CT: Wesleyan University Press.

Padmanabhan, Manjula. 2003. *Life Lines*. Originally accessed on the newspaper *Pioneer*'s website, June 6, 2003; now unavailable.

2004. Interview with Murali N. Krishnaswamy. "There's More to the Mouse." www.hindu.com/mp/2004/01/27/stories/2004012700470100.htm

2005. *Double Talk*. New Delhi: Penguin.

Padmanabhan, Sudarsan. 2006. "Debate on Indian History: Revising Textbooks in California." *Economic and Political Weekly* 41 (18): 1761–3.

Paley, Julia. 2008. "Introduction." In *Democracy: Anthropological Approaches*, ed. by Julia Paley. Santa Fe, NM: School for Advanced Research Press.

Parashar, Archana. 1992. *Women and Family Law Reform in India: Uniform Civil Code and Gender Equality*. New Delhi: Sage.

Patel, Vallabhai. 1972. *Sardar Patel's Correspondence, 1945–50*, ed. by Durga Das. Vol. IV. Ahmedabad: Navjivan Publishing House.

Paulsen, Krista E. 2009. "Ethnography of the Ephemeral: Studying Temporary Scenes through Individual and Collective Approaches." *Social Identities* 15 (4): 509–24.

Peacock, James, and Dorothy Holland. 1993. "The Narrated Self: Life Stories in Process." *Ethos* 21 (4): 367–83.

Pedelty, Mark. 1995. *War Stories: The Culture of Foreign Correspondents*. New York: Routledge.

Peterson, Indira V., and Devesh Soneji. 2008. *Performing Pasts: Reinventing the Arts in Modern South India*. New Delhi: Oxford University Press.

Peterson, Mark Allen. 2010. "Getting the News in New Delhi." In *The Anthropology of News and Journalism: Global Perspectives*, ed. by Elizabeth Bird, 168–81. Bloomington, IN: Indiana University Press.

Pillai, Shankar. 1937. *101 Cartoons from the Hindustan Times*. New Delhi: Hindustan Times Press.

2002 (1983). *Don't Spare Me Shankar*. New Delhi: Children's Book Trust.

Pink, Sarah. 2001. *Doing Visual Ethnography*. Thousand Oaks, CA.: Sage.

2005. *The Future of Visual Anthropology: Engaging the Senses*. London: Routledge.

Pinney, Christopher. 1997. *Camera Indica: The Social Life of Indian Photographs*. University of Chicago Press.

2003. "Notes from the Surface of the Image: Photography, Postcolonialism, and Vernacular Modernism." In *Photography's Other Histories*, ed. by Christopher Pinney and Nicolas Peterson, 202–20. Durham, NC: Duke University Press.

Pinney, Christopher, and Nicolas Peterson. Eds. 2003. *Photography's Other Histories*. Durham, NC: Duke University Press.

Pollock, Sheldon. 1995. "Literary History, Indian History, World History." *Social Scientist* 23 (10–12): 112–39.

Poole, Deborah. 2003. "Figueroa Aznar and the Cusco Indigenistas: Photography and Modernism in Early-20th Century Peru." In *Photography's Other*

Histories, ed. by Christopher Pinney and Nicolas Peterson, 173–201. Durham, NC: Duke University Press.

Powdermaker, Hortense. 1966. *Stranger and Friend: The Way of an Anthropologist*. New York: Norton.

Prasad, Sharada, H. Y. 2004. *The Book I Won't be Writing and Other Essays*. New Delhi: Orient Longman.

Price, Sally. 2001 (1989). *Primitive Art in Civilized Places*. University of Chicago Press.

Price, Sally, and Richard Price. 1999. *Maroon Arts: Cultural Vitality in the African Diaspora*. Boston: Beacon.

Puri, Rajinder. 1971. *A Crisis of Conscience*. New Delhi: Orient Paperbacks.

    2006. "Bull's Eye." www.outlookindia.com/article.aspx?230428.

Radcliffe-Brown, A. R. 1940. "On Joking Relationships." *Africa: Journal of the International African Institute* 13 (3): 195–210.

Radin, Paul. 1999 (1926). *Crashing Thunder: The Autobiography of an American Indian*. Ann Arbor: University of Michigan Press.

Raghavan, G. N. S. 1994. *The Press in India (A New History)*. New Delhi: Gyan Publishing House.

Rajagopal, Arvind. 2001. *Politics after Television: Hindu Nationalism and the Reshaping of the Public in India*. New York: Cambridge University Press.

Ramamurthy, B. V. 1975. *Mr. Citizen*. Bangalore: Bangalore Print and Publishing Co.

Ranga [Ranganathan, N. K.]. 2002. *77 Steps: Atalji by Ranga*. New Delhi: Ocean Books.

Rao, Anupama. 2005. "Death of a Kotwal." In *Muslims, Dalits, and the Fabrications of History*, ed. by Shail Mayaram, M. S. S. Pandian and Ajay Skaria, 99–139. New Delhi: Permanent Black and Ravi Dayal Publisher.

Rappaport, Erika. 2008. "Imperial Possessions, Cultural Histories, and the Material Turn. Response." *Victorian Studies* 50 (2): 289–96.

Raven-Hill, Leonard. 1903. "To India with a Sketch-Book: Some Travelling Notes of an Artist at the Durbar." *Nash's Pall Mall* 29: 433–48.

Reddy, Gayatri. 2010. *With Respect to Sex: Negotiating Hijra Identity in South India*. University of Chicago Press.

Reddy, Sheshalatha. 2010. "The Cosmopolitan Nationalism of Sarojini Naidu, Nightingale of India." *Victorian Literature and Culture* 38 (2): 571–89.

Refaie, Elisabeth El. 2009. "Multiple Literacies: How Readers Interpret Cartoons." *Visual Communication* 8 (2): 181–205.

Rekha, Neel. 2010. "From Folk Art to Fine Art: Changing Paradigms in the Historiography of Maithil Painting." *Journal of Art Historiography* 2: 1–20.

Robb, Peter. 2007. *Liberalism, Modernity, and the Nation*. New York: Oxford University Press.

Robbins, Trina. 2001. *The Great Women Cartoonists*. New York: Watson-Guptill Publications.

Rofel, Lisa. 1999. *Other Modernities: Gendered Yearnings in China after Socialism*. Berkeley: University of California Press.

Roy, Rakhi, and Jaysinhji Jhala. 1992. "An Examination of the Potential for Visual Anthropology in the Indian Social Context." In *Visual Anthropology and India* ed. by K. Suresh Singh, 16–30. Calcutta: Anthropological Survey of India.

Rosaldo, Michelle Z. 1984. "Toward An Anthropology of Self and Feeling." In *Culture Theory: Essays on Mind, Self, and Emotion*, ed. by Richard A. Shweder and Robert A. LeVine, 137–57. New York: Cambridge University Press.

Ruby, Jay. 2000. *Picturing Culture: Explorations of Film and Anthropology.* University of Chicago Press.

S. J. S. 1967. "Unfailing Humour." *Thought* February 4: 22–3.

Sadiq, Mohammad. 1995 (1964). *A History of Urdu Literature.* New Delhi: Oxford University Press.

Sahay, Keshari N. 1993. *Visual Anthropology in India and its Development.* New Delhi: Gyan Publishing House.

    1998. *An Anthropological Study of Cartoons in India.* New Delhi: Commonwealth Publishers.

Said, Edward. 1989. "Representing the Colonized: Anthropology's Interlocutors." *Critical Inquiry* 15 (2): 205–25.

Samuel, Thomas. 1971. *Babuji: 100 Selected Cartoons.* New Delhi: Hind Pocket Books.

Sangari, Kumkum, and Sudesh Vaid. Eds. 1989. *Recasting Women: Essays in Indian Colonial History.* New Brunswick, NJ: Rutgers University Press.

Sanjek, Roger. 1993. "Anthropology's Hidden Colonialism: Assistants and Their Ethnographers." *Anthropology Today* 19 (2): 13–18.

Scalmer, Sean. 2011. *Gandhi in the West: The Mahatma and the Rise of Radical Protest.* Cambridge University Press.

Schoonraad, Murray, and Elzabe Schoonraad. 1989. *Companion to South African Cartoonists.* Johannesburg: Ad. Donker.

Schwarcz, Lilia M. 2013. "The Banan Emperor: D. Pedro II in Brazilian Caricatures." *American Ethnologist* 40: 301–23.

Scott, James. 1985. *Weapons of the Weak: Everyday Forms of Peasant Resistance.* New Haven: Yale University Press.

    1990. *Domination and the Arts of Resistance: Hidden Transcripts.* New Haven: Yale University Press.

Seizer, Susan. 2005. *Stigmas of the Tamil Stage: An Ethnography of Special Drama Artists in South India.* Durham, NC: Duke University Press.

Shankar, Alka. 1984. *Shankar.* New Delhi: Children's Book Trust.

Shankar, Shalini. 2008. *Desi Land: Teen Culture, Class, and Success in Silicon Valley.* Durham, NC: Duke University Press.

Shankar, Vijay N., and Yash P. Narula. 1974. "Cartoonists of India." *Imprint* 14 (April): 87–105.

Sharma, Pramila. 1999. *Curzon Nama: Autocrat Curzon Unconquerable India.* Trans. by Anjula Bedi. New Delhi: Eeshwar.

Shostak, Marjorie. 2001 (1981). *Nisa: The Life and Words of a !Kung Woman.* Cambridge, MA: Harvard University Press.

Siegel, Lee. 1987. *Laughing Matters: The Comic Tradition in India.* University of Chicago Press.

Singh, Khushwant. 1971. "Popular Journalism and Public Opinion." In *Freedom of the Press in India*, ed. by Abdul Gafoor Noorani, 50. Bombay: Nachiketa Press.

Singh, K. Suresh. Ed. 1992. *Visual Anthropology and India: Proceedings of a Seminar*. Calcutta: Anthropological Survey of India.

    1998. *People of India: National Series*. Vol. V. *India's Commmunities*. New York: Oxford University Press.

Singh, Kuldip. 2002. "Obituary: Abu Abraham; Unsparing Cartoonist Re-Named by David Astor." www.independent.co.uk/news/obituaries/abu-abraham-609963. html

Sinha, Mrinalini. 1995. *Colonial Masculinity: The 'Manly Englishman' and the 'Effeminate Bengali' in the Late Nineteenth Century*. Manchester University Press.

    2000. "Refashioning Mother India: Feminism and Nationalism in Late-Colonial India." *Feminist Studies* 26 (3): 623–44.

    2007. *Specters of Mother India: The Global Restructuring of an Empire*. Kindle edition. Durham, NC: Duke University Press.

Sissener, Tone, K. 2001. *Anthropological Perspectives on Corruption*. Working Papers, 5. Bergen: Chr. Michelsen Institute.

Smith, James H. 1998. "Njama's Supper: The Consumption and Use of Literary Potency by Mau Mau Insurgents in Colonial Kenya." *Comparative Studies in Society and History* 40 (3): 524–48.

Spielmann, M. H. 1895. *The History of Punch*. London: Cassell.

Spitulnik. Debra. 1993. "Anthropology and Mass Media." *Annual Review of Anthropology* 22: 293–315.

Sreenivasan, T. P. 2008. *Words, Words, Words: Adventure in Diplomacy*. New Delhi: Pearson.

Srinivas, Smriti. 2008. *In the Presence of Sai Baba: Body, City, and Memory in a Global Religious Movement*. Leiden: Brill.

Ståhlberg, Per. 2002. *Lucknow Daily: How a Hindi Newspaper Constructs Society*. Stockholm: Stockholm Studies in Anthropology.

Stark, Ulrike. 2003. "Politics, Public Issues and the Promotion of Urdu Literature: Avadh Akhbar, the First Urdu Daily in Northern India." *Annual of Urdu Studies* 18: 66–94.

Stoler, Ann. 1995. *Race and the Education of Desire: Foucault's History of Sexuality and the Colonial Order of Things*. Durham, NC: Duke University Press.

Stoler, Ann, and Karen Strassler. 2000. "Castings for the Colonial: Memory Work in 'New Order' Java." *Comparative Studies in Society and History* 42 (1): 4–48.

Stoller, Paul. 1989. *The Taste of Ethnographic Things*. Philadelphia: University of Pennsylvania Press.

Sturken, Marita. 1997. *Tangled Memories*. Berkeley: University of California Press.

Sunder Rajan, Rajeshwari. 2008. "Women Between Community and State." In *Secularisms*, ed. by Janet R. Jakobsen and Ann Pellegrini. Durham, NC: Duke University Press.

Switzer, Les. Ed. 1997. *South Africa's Alternative Press: Voice of Protest and Resistance, 1880s–1960s*. Cambridge University Press.

Talcherkar, Harishchandra. 1902. *Lord Curzon in Indian Caricature*. Bombay: Babaji Sakharam & Co.

Tambiah, Stanley. 1984. *The Buddhist Saints of the Forest and the Cult of Amulets: A Study in Charisma, Hagiography, Sectarianism, and Millennial Buddhism.* Cambridge University Press.

Tapper, Melbourne. 1999. *In the Blood: Sickle Cell Anemia and the Politics of Race.* Philadelphia: University of Pennsylvania Press.

Tarlo, Emma. 1996. *Clothing Matters: Dress and Identity in India.* University of Chicago Press.

2003. *Unsettling Memories: Narratives of the Emergency in Delhi.* Berkeley: University of California Press.

Tembekhar, Chittaranjan. 2011. "Love for Anna not just Skin Deep." http://articles.timesofindia.indiatimes.com/2011-08-24/mumbai/29921701_1_anna-hazare-tattoos-supporters.

Terdiman, Richard. 1985. *Discourses/Counterdiscourses: The Theory and Practice of Symbolic Resistance in Nineteenth Century France.* Ithaca, NY: Cornell University Press.

Thomas, Nicholas. 1991. *Entangled Objects: Exchange, Material Culture, and Colonialism in the Pacific.* Cambridge, MA: Harvard University Press.

Trouillot, Michel-Rolph. 1995. *Silencing the Past: Power and the Production of History.* Boston: Beacon.

Tuchman, Gaye. 1978. "Introduction: The Symbolic Annihilation of Women by the Mass Media." In *Hearth and Home: Images of Women in Mass Media,* ed. by Gaye Tuchman, Arlene Kaplan Daniels and James Benit, 3–38. New York: Oxford University Press.

Turner, Victor. 1978. "Comments and Conclusions." In *The Reversible World: Symbolic Inversion in Art and Society,* ed. by Barbara Babcock, 276–96. Ithaca, NY: Cornell University Press.

Turner, Victor, and Edith Turner. 1995 (1978). *Image and Pilgrimage in Christian Culture.* New York: Columbia University Press.

Unny, E. P. 2006. "The Indian Cartoon." In *Indian Media Delusion and Reality: Essays in Honor of Prem Bhatia,* ed. by Asha Rani Mathur, 276–84. New Delhi: Rupa & Co.

Upadhyay, Madhukar. 1994. *Punch Line.* New Delhi: SAHMAT.

van der Veer, Peter. 2002. "Religion in South Asia." *Annual Review of Anthropology* 31: 173–87.

Varma, Adarsh, K. 2003. *121/2 Management Mantras of Journalism.* New Delhi: Kanishka Publishers.

Varma, Kerala. 2005 (1960). *Crazy Cartoons.* Kochi: Cartoonads.

Venkatachalapathy, A. R. 2006. "Caricaturing the Political: A Brief History of the Cartoon in Tamil Journalism." In *In Those Days There Was No Coffee: Writings in Cultural History,* ed. by A. R. Venkatachalapathy, 42–58. New Delhi: Yoda Press.

Verma, Archana. 2007. *Cultural and Visual Flux at Early Bagh in Central India.* Oxford: Archeopress.

Vijayan, O. V. 2002. *A Cartoonist Remembers.* New Delhi: Rupa & Co.

Viswanathan, Gauri. 1995. "The Beginnings of English Literary Study in British India." In *The Postcolonial Studies Reader,* ed. by Bill Ashcroft, Gareth Griffiths, and Helen Tiffin, 376–80. New York: Routledge.

Visweswaran, Kamala. 1994. *Fictions of Feminist Ethnography*. Minneapolis: University of Minnesota Press.

    1996. "Small Speeches, Subaltern Gender Nationalist Ideology and Its Historiography." In *Subaltern Studies: Writings on South Asian History and Society*, vol. IX, ed. by Shahid Amin and Dipesh Chakrabarty, 83–125. New Delhi: Oxford University Press.

Voloshinov, N. Valentin. 1986 (1929). *Marxism and the Philosophy of Language*. Trans. by L. Matejka and I. R. Titulnik. Cambridge, MA: Harvard University Press.

Wade, Peter. Ed. 1998. *In Anthropology, The Image Can Never Have the Final Say*. Manchester: Group for Debates in Anthropological Theory.

Warner, Michael. 2002. *Publics and Counterpublics*. Cambridge: Zone Books.

Wechsler, Judith. 1982. *A Human Comedy: Physiognomy and Caricature in 19th Century Paris*. University of Chicago Press.

Weidman, Amanda. 2006. *Singing the Classical, Voicing the Modern: The Postcolonial Politics of Music in South India*. Durham, NC: Duke University Press.

Weston, Kath. 1995. "Theory, Theory, Who's Got the Theory: Or Why I Am Tired of That Tired Debate." *GLQ: A Journal of Lesbian and Gay Studies* 2 (4): 347–9.

White, Hayden. 1978. *Tropics of Discourse*. Baltimore: Johns Hopkins University Press.

    1988. "Historiography and Historiophoty." *American Historical Review* 93 (5): 1193–9.

Winegar, Jessica. 2008. *Creative Reckonings: The Politics of Art and Culture in Contemporary Egypt*. Palo Alto, CA: Stanford University Press.

Wolcott, Henry, F. 2004. "The Ethnographic Autobiography." *Auto/Biography* 12: 93–106.

Zavos, John. 2008. "Stamp it Out! Disciplining the Image of Hinduism in a Multicultural Milieu." *Contemporary South Asia* 16 (3): 323–38.

Zamindar, Vazira F. Y. 2007. *The Long Partition and the Making of Modern South Asia: Refugees, Boundaries, Histories*. New York: Columbia University Press.

Zinn, Dorothy Louise. 2005. "Afterword: Anthropology and Corruption: the State of the Art." In *Corruption: Anthropological Perspectives*, ed. by Dieter Haller and Cris Shore, 229–42. London and Ann Arbor, MI: Pluto Press.

Index